Discorrelated Images

Discorrelated Images

SHANE DENSON

Duke University Press Durham and London 2020

Designed by Drew Sisk
Typeset in Portrait Text by Westchester Publishing Services

Library of Congress Cataloging-in-Publication Data
Names: Denson, Shane, [date] author.
Title: Discorrelated images / Shane Denson.
Description: Durham : Duke University Press, 2020. | Includes bibliographical references and index.
Identifiers: LCCN 2019058965 (print)
LCCN 2019058966 (ebook)
ISBN 9781478009856 (hardcover)
ISBN 9781478010913 (paperback)
ISBN 9781478012412 (ebook)
Subjects: LCSH: Digital images. | Digital cinematography. | Motion pictures—Production and direction—Technological innovations. | Motion picture industry—Technological innovations. | Motion picture audiences. | Visual perception.
Classification: LCC TR860.D46 2020 (print) | LCC TR860 (ebook) | DDC 777—dc23
LC record available at https://lccn.loc.gov/2019058965
LC ebook record available at https://lccn.loc.gov/2019058966

Cover art: Karin Denson, *Glitchesarelikewildanimals! No. 1*, 2015. Acrylic on canvas. Courtesy of the artist.

For Amy:
you have taught me
more than anyone else about
how to make sense
of discorrelation

CONTENTS

ACKNOWLEDGMENTS

This book has profited from the support and encouragement of countless people. My colleagues at the Leibniz Universität Hannover, at Duke University, and most recently at Stanford University listened to me talk about the ideas elaborated here and read various bits and pieces of text that would eventually come together as *Discorrelated Images*. I am especially grateful for the detailed feedback that I received on two occasions at the Faculty Salon of the Stanford Department of Art and Art History, and for the opportunity to present this work to colleagues and graduate students at the Digital Aesthetics Workshop at the Stanford Humanities Center. Special thanks go to my colleagues for creating such a supportive environment at Stanford, particularly Scott Bukatman, Pavle Levi, Jean Ma, Karla Oeler, Usha Iyer, Alexander Nemerov, Jody Maxmin, Marci Kwon, Srdan Keca, Adam Tobin, Paul DeMarinis, Richard Meyer, Camille Utterback, Emanuele Lugli, Rose Salseda, Gail Wight, Nancy Troy, Fabio Barry, Jonathan Calm, Terry Berlier, Enrique Chagoya, Jan Krawitz, Jamie Meltzer, Bissera Pentcheva, Richard Vinograd, Xiaoze Xie, Beth Kessler, Henry Lowood, and Fred Turner. Directly or indirectly, all of you helped me find the strength to complete this project. Thanks also to former colleagues and mentors Mark B. N. Hansen, Ruth Mayer, and Peter Hutcheson, for whose continuing support I am forever grateful, and whose example encourages me to pay it forward to the next generation of students. I am gratified to have had the opportunity to work with and learn from some amazing graduate students, including Hank Gerba, Ankita Deb, Ron Reichman, Amber Harper, Jeff Nagy, Doug Eacho, Annika Butler-Wall, Natalie Deam, Daniel Cohen, Helen Krüger, Juan Pablo Melo, Frank Mondelli, Michael Metzger, Daniel Hernandez, Corey Anderson Dansereau, and Andrea Capra—you all inspire me; thank you.

I have benefited from opportunities to present this work at a variety of conferences, including the Society for Cinema and Media Studies; the Society for Literature, Science, and the Arts; the American Comparative Literature Association; the Association for the Study of the Arts of the Present; the Modern Language Association; the German Association for American Studies; the Electronic Literature Organization; the Spiral Film and Philosophy conference in Toronto; the Media Fields conference at UC Santa Barbara; and several of the excellent conferences organized by Richard Grusin under the auspices of the Center for 21st Century Studies at the University of Wisconsin–Milwaukee. Thank you to all the copanelists and audience members who engaged with this work and thus contributed to making the present book better. Thank you also to the many people who have invited me to speak on topics of post-cinema and discorrelated images at various venues around the world: Lisa Åkervall, Chris Tedjasukmana, and Gertrud Koch for inviting me to speak at the Post-cinematic Perspectives event in Berlin; Reinhold Görling, Marie-Luise Angerer, and Hanjo Berressem for the invitation to speak in their Ecologies of Practice series in Cologne; Jo Ann Carson and Peter Hutcheson for the opportunity to speak at Texas State University; Natalie Roxburgh and Marcel Hartwig at the University of Siegen; Bruce Isaacs at the University of Sydney; Russell Smith at the Australian National University; Caetlin Benson-Allott at Georgetown University; Ina Habermann and Michelle Witen at the University of Basel; Morgane Ghilardi and Hannah Schoch at the University of Zurich; Kevin B. Lee at the Merz Akademie in Stuttgart; Ruth Mayer and the American Studies Colloquium at the Leibniz Universität Hannover; Kathleen Loock and Frank Kelleter at the Freie Universität Berlin; Steven Shaviro for having me Skype in at Wayne State University; Julia Leyda for figuring out a way for me to spend a week at the Norwegian University of Science and Technology in Trondheim; Ahmet Gürata at the University of Agder in Kristiansand; Brian Price at the University of Toronto; Katerina Krtilova, Dieter Mersch, and the Media-Philosophical Working Group at the Zürcher Hochschule der Künste; Radhika Natarajan at the Sprache, Migration, Vielfalt series in Hannover; Zenaida Osorio at the Universidad Nacional de Colombia in Bogotá, where my family and I spent a nonstop, event-filled week; Giselle

Gubernikoff and Edson Luiz de Oliveira at the Universidade de São Paulo; and Florian Hoof and everybody at the Institute for Advanced Study on Media Cultures of Computer Simulation and the Center for Digital Cultures at the Leuphana University of Lüneburg, where I completed this manuscript during a generous research fellowship in the summer of 2019.

I would also like to acknowledge my debt to the peer reviewers who offered their incredibly helpful and insightful comments on this work: two anonymous readers and a certain "Reviewer #3," who turned out to be the incomparable Vivian Sobchack. I am beyond grateful for the work that you all put into helping me make this the best book it could be. Thank you also to the editors and reviewers at *Journal of Cinema and Media Studies*, where an earlier version of the first half of chapter 5 appeared (I am grateful for the permission to publish an expanded version of Shane Denson, "The Horror of Discorrelation: Mediating Unease in Post-cinematic Screens and Networks," *JCMS: Journal of Cinema and Media Studies* 59, no. 4 [2020]). Thanks also to the editors and reviewers at *Media Fields Journal*, where earlier versions of ideas developed in chapter 4 and chapter 6 first appeared (as, respectively: "Edge Detection," *Media Fields*, no. 14 [2019], and "Post-cinema after Extinction," *Media Fields*, no. 13 [2018]). An earlier, shorter version of chapter 1 first appeared as "Crazy Cameras, Discorrelated Images, and the Post-perceptual Mediation of Post-cinematic Affect," in *Post-cinema: Theorizing 21st-Century Film*, ed. Shane Denson and Julia Leyda (Falmer, UK: REFRAME Books, 2016). Portions of chapter 6 also appeared as "Pre-sponsive Gestures," in *ETC Media* 110 (2017): 40–45. My thanks also to Grégory Chatonsky for permission to reproduce images of his incredible post-cinematic artworks.

My especial thanks go to Elizabeth Ault, my editor at Duke University Press, to editorial associate Kate Herman, and to project editor Lisl Hampton. It has been a true pleasure to work with you all, and I am extremely grateful for the effort, enthusiasm, and attention that you and everyone at the press have devoted to this project. Thanks also to Paula Durbin-Westby for her expert work on the index.

Finally, my deepest gratitude and love go to my family. Thank you, Karin, for supporting me like no one else could, certainly more than I deserve. You have several times picked up and moved around the globe with me, each time turning our new environment into a home. Every single day, I find myself again in awe of your energy, creativity, and care. And Amy: this book is for you. You've taught me some of the central lessons that inspire this book, though I can hardly hope to have communicated them in a way that will do justice to the unspoken, possibly unspeakable truths you've revealed.

INTRODUCTION

Discorrelation and Post-cinema

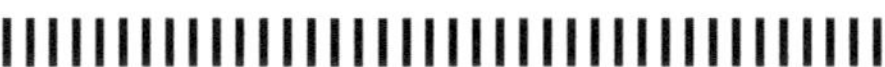

Discorrelated Images explores the transitional space-time between cinema and post-cinema. More precisely, it probes the transformational temporal and spatial articulations of contemporary moving images and our perceptual, actional, and affective interfaces with them as they migrate from conventional forms of cinema and enter the computational systems that now encompass virtually every aspect of audiovisual mediation. While the generation, composition, distribution, and playback of images increasingly become a matter of algorithms, software, networks, and codecs, our sensory ratios (as Marshall McLuhan called them) are being reordered, our perceptual faculties are being reformed in accordance with the new speeds and scales of imaging processes. In a post-cinematic media regime, that is, both the subjects and the objects of perception are radically transformed. Older relations—such as that between a human subject and a photographically fixed object—are dissolving, and new relations are being forged in the microtemporal intervals of algorithmic processing. With the new objects of computational images emerge new subjectivities, new affects, and uncertain potentials for perception and action.

At the heart of these transformations lie the generative dynamics of high-speed (often "real-time") feedback and feed-forward processes, which introduce (and modulate) new contingencies at the heart of post-cinematic mediation. We glimpse such processes in digital glitches, for example, which derail perception and inject the microtemporal misfirings of the computer into our subjective awareness. The underlying contingencies, however, are beyond the purview of subjective perception; the algorithms and hardware operations responsible for the glitch are fundamentally "discorrelated" from phenomenological processes of noetic intentionality. Moreover, the glitch reveals a more general instability attaching to computationally mediated images, which are highly volatile and always in danger of dissolution. Processed on the fly in an interval that is inaccessible to human perception, the images that populate our world are themselves discorrelated from human subjectivity—no longer tuned to the frequencies of human sensory access and thus no longer essentially bound to *appear* at all.[1] Nevertheless, various forms and manifestations of contemporary audiovisual media mediate to us these processes, providing sensory complements to subperceptual events, helping us in a sense to negotiate the transition to a truly posthuman, post-perceptual media regime.[2] These mediations and negotiations are the focus of the present book.

Discorrelated Images engages, in other words, with the transactions between human and machinic agencies as they together broker the ongoing transition from cinematic to post-cinematic media. Framed as such, the project must answer to a number of objections at the outset. Isn't the "death of cinema" a tired cliché? And isn't the very notion of post-cinema therefore superfluous? The machinery of cinema has changed, to be sure, but the cinema thrives even in a computerized world. Indeed, there is no hard break, no bright line between cinema and post-cinema; the vision of post-cinema advocated here is predicated not on cinema's "end" but rather on its envelopment within the larger space of an environment that has been thoroughly transformed by the operation of computational processing. There are real continuities between the experience of going to the cinema in the age of celluloid and that of watching movies stored and screened by way of digital apparatuses; we still consume moving images, and these moving images still mediate stories and other recognizably perceptual contents. But in focusing on these continuities, we risk overlooking the volatility or contingency of this correlation of subject and object, which in the age of computational processing teeters precariously atop microtemporal processes that are radically different in speed and scale from human perception. The perceptual correlation, in other words, pertains to a level of phenomenal experience that is abstracted from, and systematically blind to, the underlying discorrelation.

And yet, this book argues, the underlying discorrelation transforms our experience in important and far-reaching ways. Some of these effects are more readily apparent, like the sensation of being "blown away" by the ostentatious display of new visual effects, or simply taking (perhaps slightly annoyed) notice of formal changes introduced through nonlinear editing and digital color grading. Other experiential effects are far less obvious—for example, the subtle confusion between diegetic and extradiegetic spaces introduced through a digitally simulated lens flare, which at once simulates the physics of an analog camera (that asks merely to be looked *through* in order that we may perceive the simulated reality beyond) while also embracing the goal of ostentatious display (begging to be looked *at* for its stunning simulation of reality, right down to the interplay of light and a nonexistent lens). Phenomena of this sort refuse easy resolution; in oscillating between invisibility and display—or between the subjective and objective poles of experience—the virtual camera defies traditional phenomenological analysis. The computer-generated imagery (CGI) lens flare points, therefore, to the discorrelation of perceptual objects from viewing subjects and thus to the need to locate the experiential impact of contemporary images at a deeper level of affective materiality and embodiment.

Digital glitches, lens flares, and other such figures serve as concise emblems of discorrelation, and I read the films and videos that employ them as parables, fables, and allegories of the experiential transformations that ensue as a result of our encounters with the underlying processes of computation and its altogether nonhuman affectivities.[3] Across six chapters, this book explores a number of emblems and figures of discorrelation in order to understand the ways that contemporary moving images mediate our transition into a world of media not cut to human measure. The three chapters of part I develop the theoretical foundations of discorrelation as a theory of contemporary moving-image media and the experiential parameters of life that they inform. Chapter 1 sets out from what I am calling post-cinema's "crazy cameras," the irrationality of which is announced in their unsettling of subject/object (i.e., viewer/image) relations. Chapter 2 looks more closely at the images themselves, focusing especially on their material agencies and the forces that they harness across the divide between technical substrates and aesthetic forms. Next, chapter 3 builds on this foundation to rethink the notion of "screen time"—a figure that focuses our attention on the intersections between the generative temporality of computationally processed moving images and the time of human experience, thus culminating the argument for the transformative power of post-cinematic media.

Part II comprises three chapters that explore various aspects and implications of discorrelation, connecting post-cinematic technologies, techniques, and images to their modulation of affects in a range of (generic) forms. Chapter 4 probes the self-reflexive fascination evoked by acts of algorithmic "animation" in science-fiction films about artificial (computational, robotic, and holographic) beings. Chapter 5 looks at the displaced fear of new media, or of discorrelation itself, at the root of recent horror films that foreground glitches and other artifacts of digital imaging (and similar dynamics at the root of the real-world horrors of terrorist propaganda and mediations of drone warfare). Finally, chapter 6 turns to the threat of extinction, the ultimate scene of discorrelation, in post-cinematic productions about the end of the world. In all these forms, what is at stake is not only a statement of the fact of discorrelation but a proposition regarding how we might learn to live with or "make sense" of a transformation taking place beneath the threshold of sensory perception. First, in the remainder of this introduction, I will briefly introduce the concept and the stakes of discorrelation.

Correlation/Discorrelation

Something strange happens in the opening minutes of the first episode of ABC's hit television series *Lost*. "Pilot (Part 1)," which was directed by J. J. Abrams and originally broadcast on September 22, 2004, opens with an extreme close-up of a human eye, initially shut, as it twitches briefly before opening wide. The large dark spot of a dilated pupil shrinks rapidly, and the growing iris widens into a reflective surface speckled with light and shadows. There is a slight strain in the muscles around the eye, as the still-unidentified man struggles, we surmise, to comprehend what he is seeing. Indeed, such a shot, which holds the image of the man's eye for a full five seconds or so, is not designed simply to make us *infer* that a man is trying to understand what he is seeing; rather, the shot of the straining eye mirrors and exacerbates our own attempts to comprehend, and it makes us want to *see for ourselves* whatever the object of the man's vision might be. After several seconds, the camera relents and lets us see; it cuts to a lush, dense canopy of leafy bamboo crowns swaying in the breeze. This image answers the previous shot in several ways. First, it literally reflects the image we saw projected onto the man's iris, thus establishing a clear physical relation between the eye and the treetops; the former is below, the latter is above. Beyond just clarifying the relative positionality of the two images in space, however, the sequence of shots is clearly also establishing a *perceptual* relation between them. *Here* is an eye; *this* is what it sees.

The second shot is thus attached to the first in a precise and obvious way, and in this moment we as viewers are drawn into a relation of complicity: we

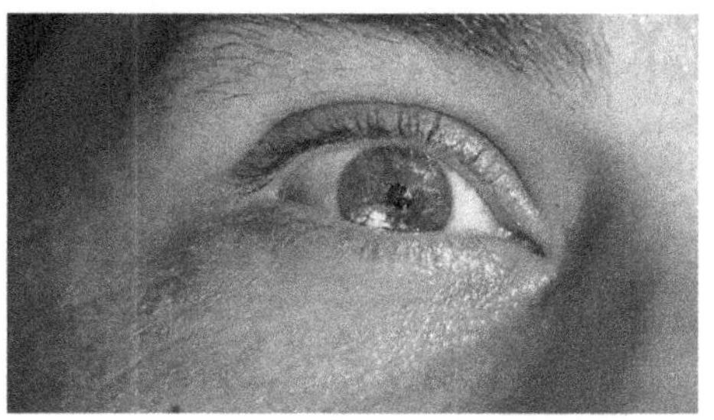
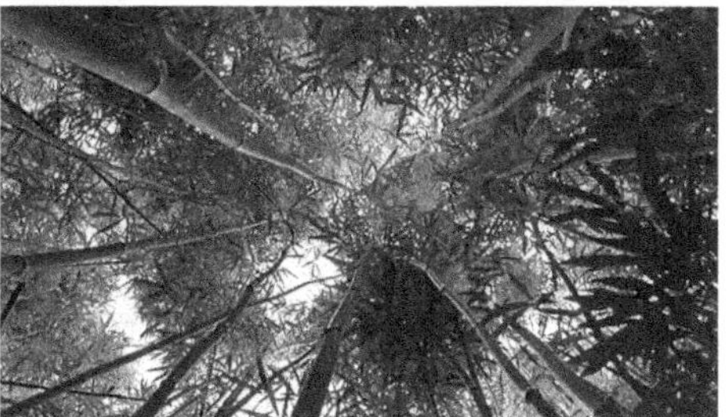

Figures Intro.1 and Intro.2. Opening shots from *Lost*, season 1, episode 1 (2004).

instantaneously come to share this man's vision, and in so doing we begin to assist in the construction of a coherent diegetic space within which the spatial and perceptual relations articulated in these two shots make sense. The second shot's heavenward-pointed camera holds its view for a good five or six seconds, giving us time to close the loop, to complete the circuit between our perception and the vision of an on-screen character, and hence to carry out the man's silent struggle to comprehend, to perceive. If, during this time, there is any doubt that this view of the treetops is a subjective POV shot, it is put to rest in the following shot, which frames a man's head and shoulders diagonally across the screen before pulling back and slowly rotating in a clockwise direction to reveal the full length of the man's body; clothed in suit and tie, the man is lying on the dark earth, seemingly paralyzed, surrounded by bamboo stalks and partially obscured by the speckled shadows they cast. The man, whom we will later come to know as Jack Shephard, a medical doctor and soon-to-be leader of a group of survivors whose plane has just crashed on a desert island, is still unknown to us; at this point, he has no biography—but he does have a body. And that body serves, initially, as the only point of reference to anchor our perception of the diegetic world, which seems as unfamiliar to this man as it is to us. The camera is "correlated" with the man's embodied senses, and it serves to "correlate" ours with his.

The basic mechanism by which the camera functions as such an instrument of correlation was famously theorized, in the 1970s, under the heading of "suture"—a somewhat contentious but nonetheless enlightening psychoanalytical concept designed to explain our imaginative investment in filmic narratives as a basically ideological relation. In his classic text on the subject, "The Tutor-Code of Classical Cinema," Daniel Dayan argues that suture is an "enunciation system" that "speaks the codes on which the fiction depends,"

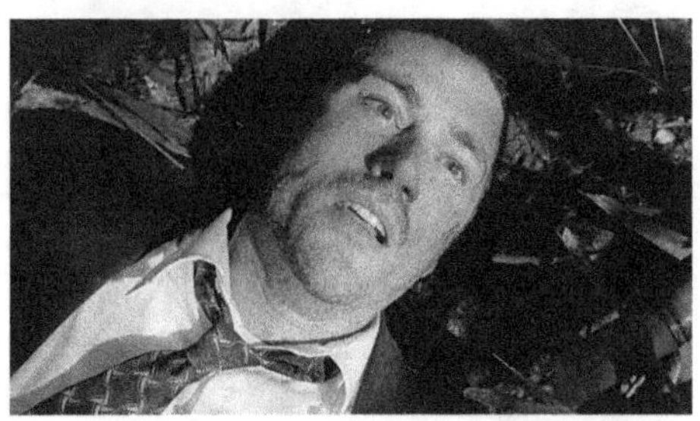
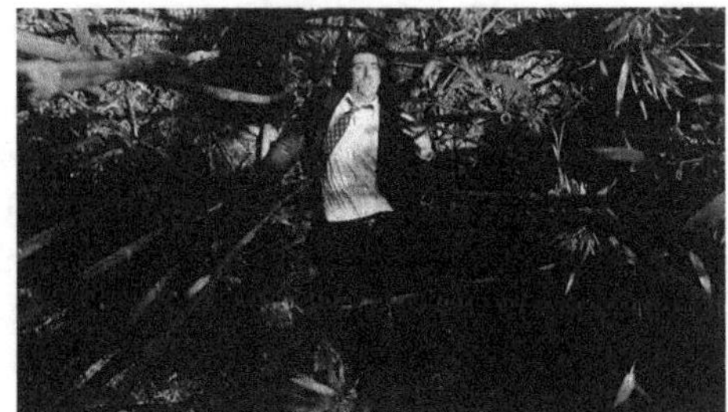

Figures Intro.3 and Intro.4. The body as perceptual anchor.

a system of shot-to-shot relations that depends crucially on transparency or an *invisible* and unquestioned operation by which the viewer is positioned with respect to the diegetic world.[4] For Dayan and others writing in the psychoanalytical-Marxist vein of so-called apparatus theory, the invisibility at question here is related to the workings of the Lacanian "imaginary," according to which the integrity of one's body and hence of a self or subject is guaranteed only through an act of misrecognition and according to which our contingent position in social space is "naturalized" or made to seem inevitable. "Being at the very center of what we perceive as our self, this [imaginary] function is invisible and unquestioned," and it serves to situate us in linguistic and other representational or discursive systems;[5] the naturalization of these relational positions is the very heart of ideology. In cinema, for Dayan, the invisibility of suture, as a function of our imaginary involvement and positioning with respect to the diegesis, is concretely embodied in the "invisible style" of classical Hollywood film, which is based in continuity editing practices such as the 180-degree rule (establishing an axis of action that the camera must not cross, lest the viewer lose spatial orientation) and the 30-degree rule (according to which subsequent shots must involve at least a 30-degree rotation of the camera around this axis, lest the illusion of diegetic space be destroyed, its constructed nature revealed by a jarring jump cut). When these rules are respected, according to this thinking, the spectator imaginatively closes the gaps between shots, perceiving through them a unified, coherent space; in the process, the subjectivity of the spectator is itself "sutured" into the narrative space of the film.

At the core of suture, that is, we find a syntactical system of shot-to-shot relations that serves to correlate spectatorial vision and cinematographic images. Putting aside its ideological component for the moment, the notion of suture is rooted in the unobtrusive transparency of shot/reverse-shot configurations, the question-and-answer relations that I have been describing, in *Lost*'s cold open, between a subjective (or quasi-subjective) perspective and an objective image to which it imaginatively (and conventionally) corresponds. We see an eye, we see the trees, we see a body with shadows on the ground, and we understand the spatial and perceptual relations established by the sequence of shots. We understand, moreover, because *we are perceptually involved* in their execution. And this involvement, as Dayan following Jean-Pierre Oudart emphasizes, is both a spatial and a temporal process; more precisely, the articulation of the diegetic world's spatial integrity depends on the imaginative integrity of the spectator over time, which serves to unite subsequent shots in a temporal process of relation and revision: the first shot initiates an anticipatory relation (what will the next shot reveal as the object of vision?), while the effect of subsequent shots is to retroactively stabilize earlier shots' meaning and the spatial/perceptual relations among them (decisively attributing a subjective shot to the character's vision and clarifying positionality through a shared perception).

In the pilot episode of *Lost*, this process of perceptual correlation is continued in the following shots: after we see the man's body from above, the camera cuts to a shot of his head, still pinned to the ground and thus framed horizontally, as he turns to look just to the side of the camera's lens. The following shot, from a camera situated close to the ground, hovers slightly to show blades of grass and the base of bamboo stalks; the framing suggests another subjective shot, and this is confirmed when the camera cuts back to a slightly longer shot of the man's still-prostrate body, as he gasps for breath and strains his eyes toward the camera. Yet another subjective shot follows, this time revealing a yellow Labrador retriever as it approaches and looks into the camera, which is aligned with both the man's point of view and our own. There follows another close-up of the man's face, with eyes wide and mouth open, and then another brief subjective shot as the dog starts toward the camera. A longer shot shows the dog rushing toward, then leaping over, the man's head, before it turns and runs off out of the frame. All this conforms to the perceptual conventions of classical cinema, where edits are closed or sutured in such a way as to ensure the integrity of the diegetic space, the closure of which depends crucially on the alignment of perspectives and our perceptual involvement.

But this is where things start to get strange. In a series of shots, the man struggles to rise to his feet, clearly in pain. He supports himself against the bamboo stalks and removes a small, airplane-size bottle of vodka from his pocket. Abruptly, the man begins racing through the thickets in a blur of shadows, stalks, and leaves. He exits the frame as the camera lingers on a shoe hanging inexplicably from the knotty trunk of a thin tree. We then rejoin the man as he emerges from the forest and looks in bewilderment at the scene before him. Without cutting, the camera moves close to his face as he turns his head to the right to survey what is now revealed to us as an empty beach with whitecapped waves crashing in the blue-green waters beyond. The camera pans to the left, revealing to us the full expanse of the beach. There can be no doubt, following the careful training we have received in the syntax of suture over the past two minutes of screen time, that the camera is mediating to us the man's view as he scans the horizon. While not a literal POV shot (because there was no cut from the objective view of his face to this concentrated pan across the beach), we are clearly aligned with the man's vision; here, as before, the camera serves as an instrument of correlation. But as the camera completes its semicircular arc to the left, the apparent subject of vision, the as yet unknown man, reappears abruptly and unexpectedly in the frame as its object. A subtle shock: the subject faces itself, sees its own seeing body, thus dissolving the integrity of self—both the man's and our own. The correlation of vision is broken.

Something similar happens in Alfonso Cuarón's *Gravity* (2013). The film opens with a carefully orchestrated thirteen-minute sequence shot, in which we see several astronauts completing a space walk outside their shuttle, floating impressively in the massive expanse of outer space while orbiting around a looming Earth. About eight minutes into this spectacular scene, one of the astronauts, portrayed by George Clooney, looks up at Earth in wonder; we see the globe reflected in his helmet before the camera turns to follow his gaze across the expanse, rotating to the right in order to mediate to us his vision of the planet, its oceans and continents, and the interplay of light and dark as night and day roll across the celestial body that fills the entirety of the screen. As the camera pans across this sublime (digital) image, the astronaut's vision is correlated with ours, and spatial relations are established by means of the subjective perspective. But just as in *Lost*, this apparent correlation is shattered when, at the conclusion of the camera's slow and lingering rightward pan, the apparent subject of vision appears again as its object; the camera ends up focusing once more on the astronaut's helmet, the reflective surface of which doubles the object of vision (the planet) while also conflating it with its subject (the looking astronaut, as well as the spectator who shared his vision).

I dwell on these shots because they offer an entry point for thinking about what I am calling the "discorrelated images" that characterize the shift from a cinematic to a post-cinematic media regime. Such shots subtly dismantle the

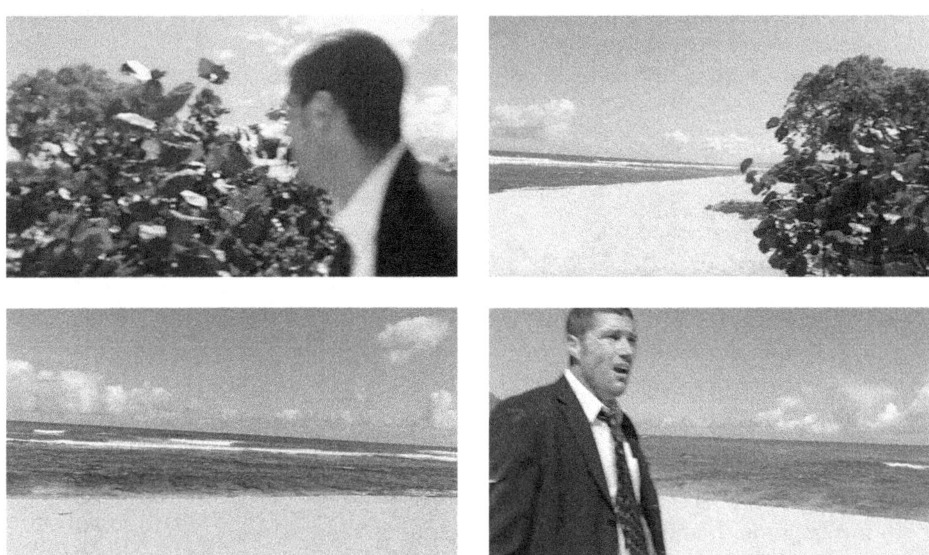

Figures Intro.5–Intro.8. The subject turns to face itself.

rational orderings of time and space that served, conventionally, to correlate spectatorial subjectivity with cinematic images. It will be objected, however, that such "false" point-of-view shots are nothing new; writing in 1975, Edward Branigan, in a short piece titled "Formal Permutations of the Point-of-View Shot," describes a number of ways in which the spatial coordinates established by POV shots, and therefore also the relation of the spectator to the diegesis, can be subverted, disrupted, or destabilized—including a "deviant POV" shot from Carl Theodor Dreyer's *Vampyr* (1932) that strongly resembles those of *Lost* and *Gravity*: "We see David Gray outside an Inn looking in a door toward camera; he glances up (shot A). We cut to a shot of the roof, then pan and tilt down to discover Gray walking along a wall *back (?)* toward the door and looking in the door again (shot B). Thus it is not clear what has been happening while we have been looking at the roof."[6]

Of course, subversion of this type works only if there is a conventional or normative baseline in place, against which the deviation can be registered as an affront to our expectations. If suture names that baseline according to which classical cinema correlated spectators perceptually with the spatio-temporal construct of the diegesis, then these false point-of-view shots make common cause with avant-garde practices designed to subvert the ideological underpinnings of the Hollywood system. Clearly, though, these more recent

Figures Intro.9–Intro.11. Discorrelated POV in *Gravity* (Alfonso Cuarón, 2013).

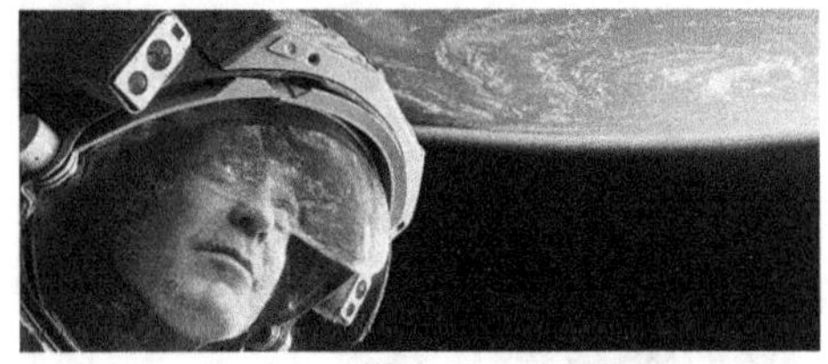

productions, one a popular television series and the other a blockbuster movie, are far from the avant-garde. Yet both of these scenes thematize perception as much as they instrumentalize it. The free-floating camera, like free indirect discourse, makes perception into an object (or quasi-object), disrupting the subjectively perceptual correlation of suture. These are subtle but significant affronts to conventional moving-image forms, focusing our attention on visual mediation itself and questioning the correlation of eyes, visors, and cameras with the objects of vision—the mediated images—that present themselves to us in a post-cinematic landscape.

Such questionings and confusions of subjective and objective views are widespread today across moving-image media, from TV, to theatrically released movies, to interactive digital media. Another example is provided by the videogame *Metroid Prime* (2002), which opens with a cutscene (a noninteractive sequence sometimes referred to as a "cinematic") in which we see asteroids hurtling toward an orangeish planet and blazing in its glowing blue atmosphere; a large spacecraft hovers off-planet, apparently rendered inoperative by the rock storm. A smaller craft arrives on the scene, from which a heavily armed and armored figure emerges. This is our first look at the game's main protagonist—and player avatar—Samus. The virtual camera makes several passes at the figure from various distances: first a medium shot rotating to the right to reveal the colossal *Gestalt*, then a leftward-arcing long shot that shows a vaguely sublime *Rückenfigur* facing the alien planet and emerging from behind a blinding (simulated) lens flare, before cutting to a close-up that fetishistically traces the figure's armored physique—starting at the crotch and working its way up a sleek, heaving abdomen, across the powerful exoskeletal chest, oversized shoulders, and toward the head with its reflective green visor. Cutting back to a long shot of the figure atop its spaceship, we see the armored body make a powerful leap high into the air, somersaulting rapidly and landing close to the virtual camera, which has to back up in order to fully frame the kneeling figure. The camera then circles twice around the figure, displaying this body of uncertain gender and species from all angles, as it rises to its

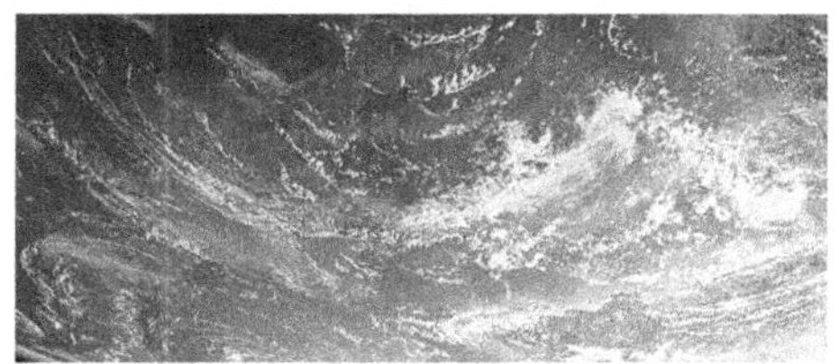
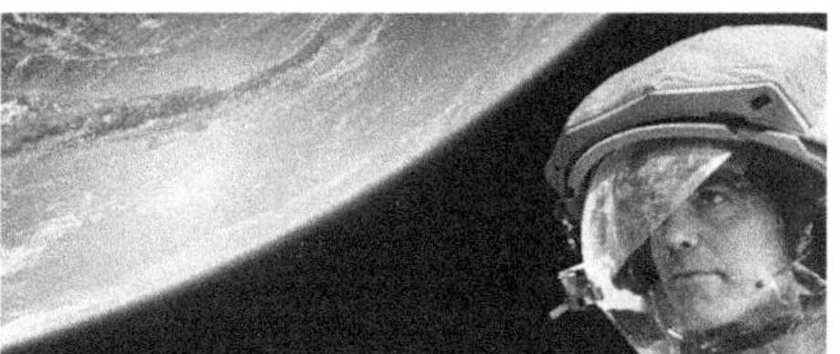

feet and begins to survey the scene. Having reached the figure's backside once more, the camera retreats briefly to reveal a wider view and then swiftly zooms in toward the head, penetrating into the figure through the back of the helmet, and merging our perspective with that of the figure's digitally enhanced heads-up display.[7]

Video scan lines briefly appear and then fade as we assume the figure's subjective point of view. Framed by numerical readouts and control components, and with a laser cannon attached to the right hand accompanying every shift of perspective in the lower-right corner of the image, the viewer/player watches as the anonymous figure turns its head to inspect the objects in its environment. A magnifying window emerges at the center of the screen and locks onto an object, and forensic visualizations appear peripherally, while the readout above indicates, "Scanning." Information is flashed onto the screen, a new object is scanned, and the figure tries out its weapon as the heads-up display indicates: "Press and hold L to lock onto targets." The game is instructing the player in the use of its images, which are no longer "cinematic" but radically operational and subject to real-time recalculation. There follows a brief cut back to an external view of the armor-suited avatar, which we see manipulating its visor as our screen flashes momentarily as if our own digital visor had been switched into a different mode. The figure looks off-screen to its right (our left), and the camera pans over to discover the object of its vision. The ensuing perspective, which frames an image from a vantage point that is clearly outside the armored body, is then in fact revealed, enigmatically, as a subjective shot: we are back inside the helmet, and the heads-up display is instructing us to press the direction-pad or the "A" button on our controller "to return to the Combat Visor." From this point on, we are in control of the figure, which is to say that we are actively responsible for the images that appear on our screen. And the screen, which doubles for the heads-up display and therefore vacillates between diegetic and extradiegetic spaces (that of space-traveler Samus's extraterrestrial journeys and that of my earthly living room), continues to mediate a radically ambiguous, discorrelated vision.

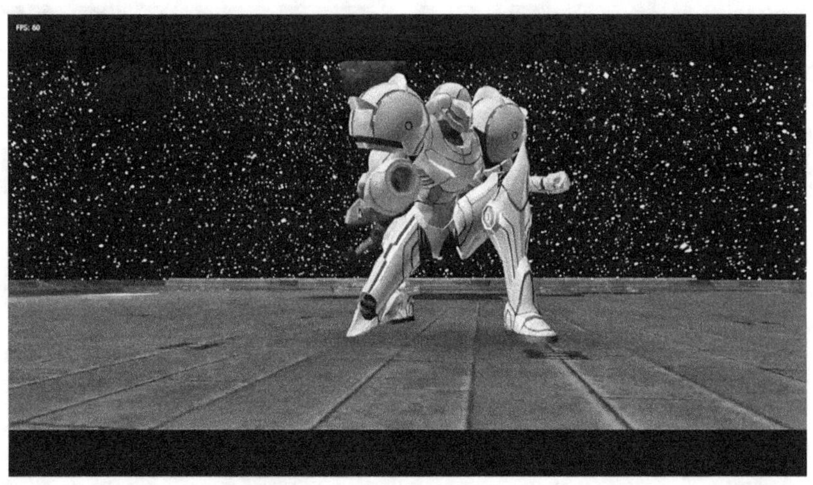

Figure Intro.12. Protagonist/player avatar Samus in *Metroid Prime* (2002).

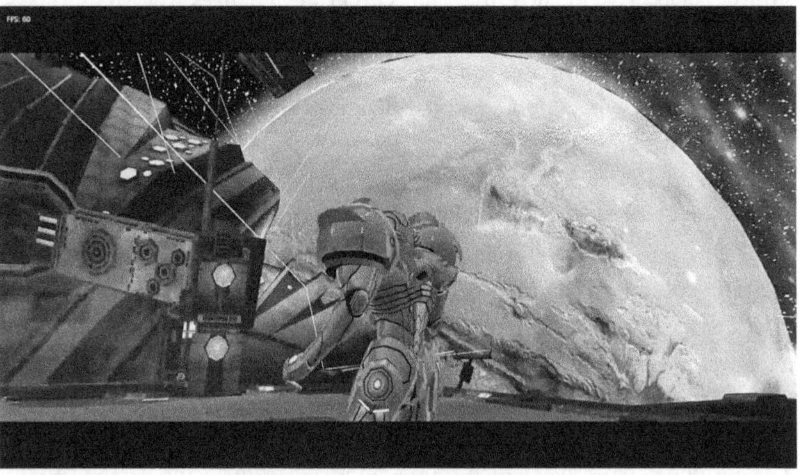

Figure Intro.13. Cosmic *Rückenfigur* in *Metroid Prime* (2002).

Clearly, videogames—especially first-person shooters like *Metroid Prime*—have a different relation to subjective POV shots than film and television do. But what we see here is another example of just how pervasive and relatively commonplace these acts of discorrelation have become. No longer particularly spectacular or exceptional, false point-of-view and similar violations of continuity and suture are now appearing all over the place. This would

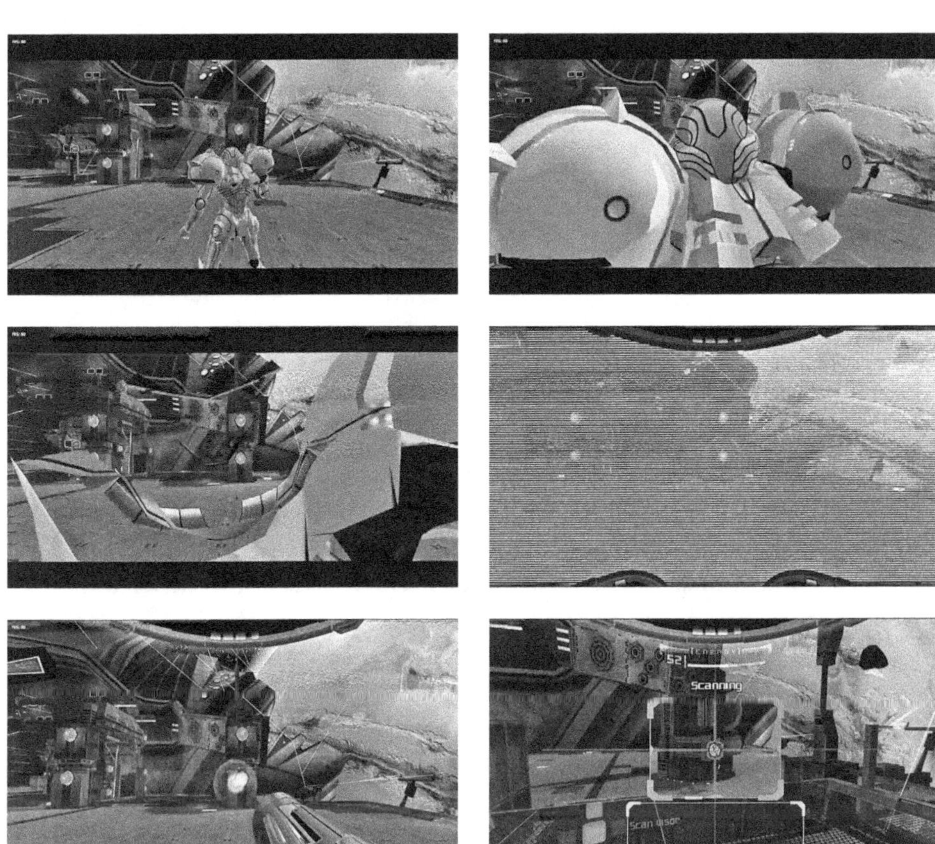

Figures Intro.14–Intro.19. Entering the helmet and assuming the avatar's POV.

suggest, of course, that they may not be of much use against the ideological power of the apparatus to position its spectators in narrative or social space. Indeed, these images stand in relation to a very different apparatus and may, as in the case of *Metroid Prime*, serve not to undermine the subject of the imaginary but, arguably, to bolster it by making the viewing/playing subject into the bearer of a more versatile masterful gaze that can *both* fetishize the objectified body *and* inhabit that body as an instrument of subjective vision and action. So while the violation of continuity may point generally to a shift away from the correlative bond known classically as "suture," it can tell us little else about the broader function and significance of discorrelated images. Indeed, to define the parameters of discorrelation in terms of classical continuity can only be a preliminary measure, one that alerts us to

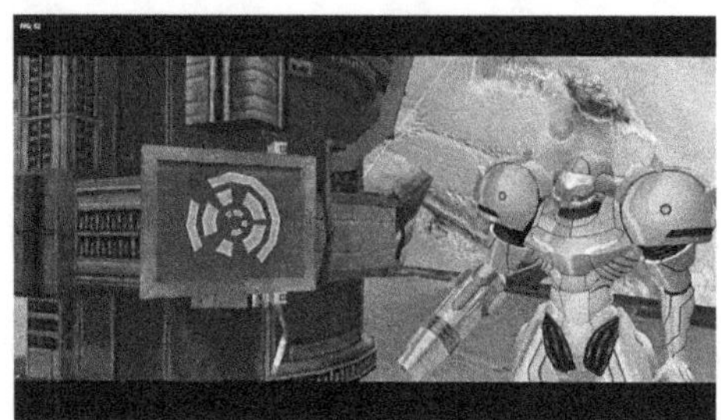
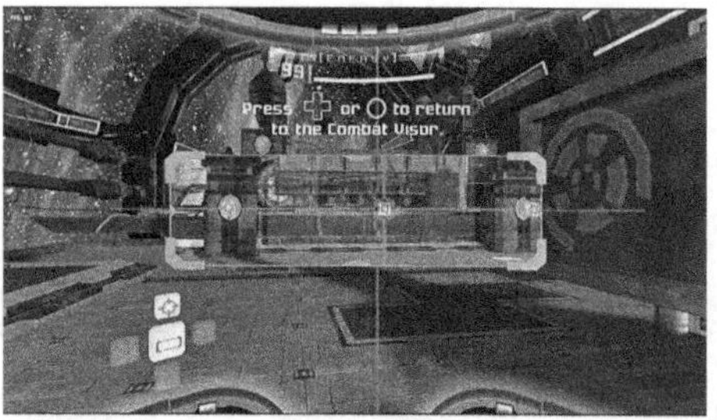

Figures Intro.20 and Intro.21. Confusion of objective and subjective perspectives.

moments, such as the false point-of-view shots in *Lost*, *Gravity*, and *Metroid Prime*, that offer a first glimpse of something deeper—something that must be sought in the relations between images' visible aesthetic forms, their underlying medial substrates, and the uncertain place of the viewer with respect to them.

Discussions of post-cinema that emphasize the visual "chaos" of editing practices in contemporary filmmaking, for example the rambunctious action of a Michael Bay, are not therefore wrong;[8] but if they stop here without inquiring about the visible image's relation to computational infrastructures and their transformations of spatial and temporal experience, then they remain at a superficial level of inquiry that can hardly shed light on more fundamental changes taking place. These changes, I am suggesting, are indexed but not defined or exhausted by continuity violations such as the false point-of-view shot, which has become more pervasive with the rise of digital imaging technologies.[9] A videogame like *Metroid Prime* is of course unthinkable apart from these technologies, upon which its interactivity depends; in this medium, the false point-of-view foregrounds the viewer/player's active role in constituting the image-object, which is no longer fixed in advance of viewing but generated on the fly at the time of playing. A noninteractive movie like *Gravity* seems less generative and volatile, in this respect, but its false point-of-view shots also gesture toward a changed relation between viewers and images that are composited with the help of greenscreen, motion capture, and extensive CGI; in this context, the ecstatic relation that the viewing subject comes to occupy, when the seeing body sees itself quite literally beside itself, both underscores the spectacle-nature of the visible image and foregrounds the viewing body's material-perceptual imbrication and reliance on the digital processes employed in the execution of that spectacle. And the false point-of-view in the pilot episode of *Lost*, while perhaps motivated narratively by the trauma of a plane crash or a dissociative disorder resulting from either natural or supernatural causes, cannot be divorced from the processes of digital video compression and transmission—either as the show was originally broadcast in 1080i widescreen format to be received by still-new digital TVs, or as it was later repackaged on DVD or streamed via YouTube or Netflix. When Jack Shephard runs through the bamboo forest, what might have been an analog blur of foliage and shadows is now more likely to render on-screen as a blocky mass of pixels and discrete digital artifacts, and when he surveys the beach only to discover himself looking, perhaps we too catch a glimpse of ourselves looking at an image that has been discorrelated from our perceptual subjectivity by these underlying digital processes.

In pointing to the role of computational infrastructures and relating them not only to the image forms they support but also triangulating them with the spatial and temporal forms of spectatorial experience that they enable or modulate, I aim as well to shift the conversation away from well-worn discussions of indexicality and its supposed demise in the digital era.[10] To understand discorrelation, we must move beyond these debates, which circle around a basically privative conception of image/substrate relations. I ask instead about the robustly generative, transformative relations between contemporary material platforms and aesthetic forms—including both concrete image forms and, more broadly, the forms of experience (*aesthesis*) that are possible for embodied subjects today. Situated at the border between film studies and digital media theory, this book aims to remedy various scholarly compartmentalizations—for example, the relative lack of communication between fields like media archaeology, which tends to focus on material substrates and infrastructures at the expense of their experiential implications (sometimes even going so far as to dismiss the phenomenological side of things as mere "eyewash"),[11] and film studies, which tends to focus on aesthetic forms to the detriment of a rigorous engagement with underlying technical processes.[12] Thinking beyond questions of indexicality and continuity, and coming to terms with the transition to a post-cinematic media regime defined by the discorrelation of images from human perception, requires that we take seriously both the phenomenological and the infrastructural vectors of this radical change.

Finally, and most importantly, it is not enough simply to establish a dialogue between the perceptual and the technical correlates of contemporary media, for the impact of discorrelation is precisely a transformation of both; experience and its infrastructure are related to one another in a mutually determinative, or transductive, relation, according to which shifts must be regarded holistically. It is imperative, therefore, that we approach the question of discorrelation neither as a purely aesthetic (e.g., formal or stylistic) nor as a reductively technological matter, but as a robustly philosophical problem. At stake in the question of discorrelation is not just a reshaping of cinema, or the development of new technical imaging processes, but a transformation of subjectivity itself. To treat discorrelation as a philosophical problem requires that we first understand correlation in a similarly philosophical fashion; concepts like suture point to relatively local or restricted mechanisms of correlation, whereby subjectivity is aligned with its objects in classical cinema, but the question that is broached in this model of the apparatus is one of more global import: it concerns the role of media more generally as the originary correlators of experience.[13]

Discorrelated Images therefore does not just concern the transformation of moving-image cultures and their implied spectatorial constructs; rather, it takes aim at rethinking the impact of contemporary media changes on what Edmund Husserl calls "the fundamental correlation between noesis and noema," or the bond between perceptual consciousness and its intentional objects.[14] This low-level phenomenological notion of correlation has been the target of attacks, recently, from proponents of "speculative realism" and "object-oriented ontology," who see Western philosophy more generally, and at least from Kant onward, as constrained by "correlationism," which seems to leave little room for thinking reality beyond its subjective determinations.[15] But while I find these interventions useful, heuristically, for decoupling subjectivity from its objects and thinking about the contingency of experience within a larger environment, my goal in thinking discorrelation is not to treat post-cinematic media and images as completely independent of the experiencing subject; rather, the point of emphasizing the discorrelation of contemporary images from perception—or the transformation of post-cinematic images into something that is not exhausted by their appearance as noematic objects—is precisely to understand the determinative or modulating agency of contemporary media on the "fundamental correlation" itself.

As I shall argue in part I, this agency is a broadly ecological one, as it pertains holistically to the correlation of subjects and objects and exerts its transformative force on them at a level of medial materiality that is both presubjective and preobjective. At stake, crucially, is a reorganization of temporality and its mediation. Apparatus theorists like Dayan emphasized the way that cinematic suture depended on an interplay between anticipations (what will the next shot reveal?) and revisions of past experience (retroactive stabilizations of meaning in the light of subsequent shots), whereby the diegesis and the viewing subject alike derived their spatiotemporal continuity and integrity from the operation of the imaginary. But post-cinematic media operationalize a much lower-level microtemporal domain, categorically outside the window of conscious perception, whereby the more basic operations of retention and protention in what Husserl calls the "phenomenology of internal time-consciousness" are themselves subject to revision.[16] And the role of embodiment is crucial to conceiving these impacts. Whereas cinematic subjectivity was theorized in terms of the correlative force of eyeline matches and similar perceptual alignments, the discorrelative force of post-cinematic images appeals to more basic embodied sensibilities as the site of microtemporal impacts that are divorced from integral subjectivity and perception altogether. Media, in this mode, become imbricated with the prepersonal "flesh" of the world, as Maurice Merleau-Ponty conceived it.[17] Discorrelated images therefore exert a properly affective force, acting on and reshaping our senses prior to the synthesis of perception. As a result, they also give rise, as I go on to explore in part II, to forms that—despite or because of their post-perceptual nature—can help us to "make sense" of our new situation in a world of discorrelated images.

Part I

THEORIZING DISCORRELATION

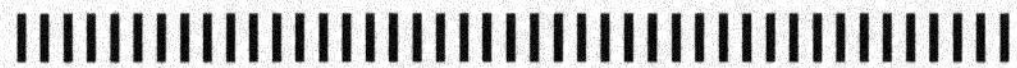

Crazy Cameras

With the shift to a digital and more broadly post-cinematic media environment, moving images have undergone what I term their *discorrelation* from human embodied subjectivities and (phenomenological, narrative, and visual) perspectives. Clearly, we still look at—and we still perceive—images that in many ways resemble those of a properly cinematic age; yet many of these images are mediated in ways that subtly (or, more to the point: imperceptibly) undermine the distance of perspective, that is, the spatial or quasi-spatial distance and relation between phenomenological subjects and the objects of their perception. At the center of these transformations is a set of strangely volatile mediators: post-cinema's screens and cameras, above all, which serve not as mere "intermediaries" that would relay images neutrally between relatively fixed subjects and objects but which act instead as transformative, transductive "mediators" of the subject-object relation itself. In other words, digital and post-cinematic media technologies do not just produce a new type of image; they establish entirely new configurations and parameters of perception and agency, placing spectators in an unprecedented relation to images and the infrastructure of their mediation.

The distinction between "intermediaries" and "mediators," on which I stake my claim for this transformation, derives from Bruno Latour, who writes in *We Have Never*

Been Modern: "An intermediary—although recognized as necessary—simply transports, transfers, transmits energy from one of the poles of the Constitution [i.e., the system by which modernity is said to separate all entities into either cultural or natural, subject or object, obscuring the role of hybrid quasi-objects]. It is void in itself and can only be less faithful or more or less opaque. *A mediator, however, is an original event and creates what it translates as well as the entities between which it plays the mediating role*."[1] Mediators thus instantiate "transductive" relations in Gilbert Simondon's sense of the term, that is, relations in which the related terms do not precede or exist outside of those relations: "Following the same path as the dialectic, transduction conserves and integrates the opposed aspects. Unlike the dialectic, transduction does not presuppose the existence of a previous time period to act as a framework in which the genesis unfolds, time itself being the solution and dimension of the discovered systematic: *time comes from the preindividual just like the other dimensions that determine individuation*."[2]

In other words, post-cinematic cameras and screens, the mediators of contemporary images, are in no sense neutral conveyors of preexisting contents to preexisting individuals; rather, these computational agencies are not only active in the real-time generation of images (more about this below) but also in the production of an *irreducible relation* between these new images and the novel sensory ratios or faculties that distinguish the viewing subjects to whom they are addressed. And, as in Simondon's description of transduction, the emergence of this new relation occurs in a space-time that is outside the phenomenological window of individual perception—in this case, in the microtemporal window of "real-time" computation. Images, that is, have become (in Wolfgang Ernst's term) "time-critical" processes rather than merely temporal objects: they are involved in, and dependent on, fine-tuned temporal events taking place in intervals fundamentally inaccessible to human perception.[3] This is one basic meaning of the discorrelation of images: their temporality is no longer tuned to that of their human receivers. This temporal determination is accompanied by the quasi-spatial dimension of discorrelation introduced above: subjects and objects are no longer aligned with one another, they no longer line up or fall in line according to relations of "perspective" or intentionality. The terms *tuning* and *alignment* describe temporal and spatial dimensions and arrangements of images with respect to human observers; *discorrelation* names deformations and failures in both dimensions. But discorrelation, as I aim to show, has a less privative flip side in the transductive production of new material and sensory relations at the microtemporal level—which amounts, in effect, to the very production of new spatial and temporal dimensions of experience: spatially, the separation of subject and object is complicated by presubjective and preobjective operations that pertain to the formation of images, while temporally, a new window of microtemporal processing is opened and brought to bear through these images on the possible subjects that can take shape in a post-cinematic world (as Simondon says: "*Time comes from the preindividual just like the other dimensions that determine individuation*").

The transformations at stake here pertain to a level of being that is therefore not only temporally but also *logically prior* to perception, as it concerns the establishment of a new material basis upon which images are produced and made available to perception. More generally, what is at stake here is a transformation at the level of what I have elsewhere termed the "anthropotechnical interface": "a realm of diffuse materiality . . . , the relational substrate which underlies the socially, psychically, and otherwise subjectively or discursively organized relations that humans maintain with technologies."[4] More elaborately, the anthropotechnical interface can be described as

> a material pivot in a realm of historical change that both exceeds and grounds our perceptual, conceptual, and linguistic faculties to register change or write history. Accordingly, embodiment—conceived as distinct from and ontologically prior to the discourses and social subjectivities founded upon it—is historically variable, and it varies in response to technological change; the affective body itself is decomposed and reconstituted when inserted into novel technological circumstances. Seen thus, embodiment (and, *a fortiori*, subjectivity) is not separable from these circumstances but is born (and re-born) from out of them; technological and human embodiment are co-constitutive, for the former redefines the shape of the latter as it opens new means of contact with the world as environment, while, on the other hand, the technological environment is meaningless or ineffectual without a body thus "environed" and affected. We are approaching here a theory of transitionality as the monstrous (re)birth of the anthropotechnical body in its movement *between* a given material environment and another.[5]

My concern with the transition from cinema to post-cinema is therefore quite different from the usual concerns of film studies and media history; it is a concern with a transitional reconfiguration of affective embodiment itself.

Seen in this light, and in accordance specifically with the notion that the critical transformation is one that is logically prior to perception, the phenomenological and post-phenomenological analysis that I undertake here of post-cinematic images and their mediating cameras points to a break with human perceptibility as such and to the rise of a fundamentally post-perceptual media regime.[6] Thus, in an age of computational image production and networked distribution channels, media "contents" and our "perspectives" on them are rendered ancillary to algorithmic functions and become enmeshed in an expanded, indiscriminately articulated plenum of images that exceed capture in the form of photographic or perceptual "objects."[7] That is, post-cinematic images are thoroughly *processual* in nature, from their digital inception and delivery to their real-time processing in computational playback apparatuses; furthermore, and more importantly, this basic processuality explodes the image's ontological status as a discrete packaged unit, and it insinuates itself—as I will argue in the following pages—into our own microtemporal processing of perceptual information, thereby unsettling the relative fixity of the perceiving human subject. Post-cinema's cameras thus mediate a radically nonhuman ontology of the image, where these images' discorrelation from human perceptibility signals an expansion of the field of material affect: beyond the visual or even the perceptual, the images of post-cinematic media operate and impinge on us at what might be called a "metabolic" level—thus implying a broadly ecological or environmental conception of the transition from cinematic to post-cinematic media.

In the following, I will unfold my argument for this perspective with respect to three concepts that help us to understand the transition to a post-cinematic media environment; I will discuss post-cinema's *crazy cameras*, its *discorrelated images*, and a fundamentally *post-perceptual mediation* as three interlinked parts or facets of the medial ontology of post-cinema. I will connect my observations to some of the formal, empirical, and phenomenological developments surrounding contemporary image production and reception, but my ultimate interest lies in a more basic determination of affect and its mediation today. Following Henri Bergson, affect pertains to a domain of material and "spiritual" existence constituted precisely in a gap between empirically determinate actions and reactions; with some modification, we can say that it fills the gap between the production and reception of images—which, today, means the microtemporal interval of "real-time" computational image processing. Affect subsists, furthermore, below the threshold of conscious experience and the intentionalities of phenomenological subjects (including the producers and viewers of media images). Bergson defines affect as "that part or aspect of the inside of our bodies which mix with the image of external bodies."[8] Referring to the Bergsonian image of the body as a "center of indetermination," affect therefore describes an intermixture of inside and outside, and an intensity experienced in a state of "suspension," outside linear time and the empirical determinateness of forward-oriented action—thus pertaining to both the spatial and the temporal dimensions of contemporary images described above.[9]

I contend that the infrastructure of life in our properly post-cinematic era has been subject to radical transformations at this level of "molecular" space-time or prepersonal affect.[10] Following critics like Steven Shaviro and other theorists of post-cinema, I suggest that something of the nature and the stakes of these changes can be glimpsed in our contemporary moving-image media, including by means of formal transformations of images and their production, editing, and distribution—which changes are themselves not infrequently taken up by post-cinematic productions in self-reflexive allegorizations of the new media environment and its novel situations of image-viewing. Ultimately, however, these media ask us to go beyond the level of allegory and to rethink the material and experiential forms and functions of the camera, the image, and the mediation of life itself.

Crazy Cameras and Spatial Paradoxes

My argument begins with an analysis of what I am calling the "crazy cameras" of post-cinematic media, following comments made by Therese Grisham in a roundtable discussion with myself and Julia Leyda on the topic of "Post-cinematic Affect: Post-continuity, the Irrational Camera, Thoughts on 3D."[11] Seeking to account for the changed "function of cameras . . . in the post-cinematic episteme,"[12] Grisham notes that whereas "in classical and post-classical cinema, the camera is subjective, objective, or functions to align us with a subjectivity which may lie outside the film," there would seem to be "something altogether different" in recent movies.[13]

> For instance, it is established that in [Neill Blomkamp's science-fiction film *District 9* (2009)], a digital camera has shot footage broadcast as news reportage. A similar camera "appears" intermittently in the film as a "character." In the scenes in which it appears, it is patently impossible in the diegesis for anyone to be there to shoot the footage. Yet, we see that camera by means of blood splattered on it, or we become aware of watching the action through a hand-held camera that intrudes suddenly without any rationale either diegetically or aesthetically. Similarly, but differently as well, in *Melancholia* [Lars von Trier, 2011], we suddenly begin to view the action through a "crazy" hand-held camera, at once something other than just an intrusive exercise in belated Dogme 95 aesthetics and more than any character's POV, whether we take this latter as literal or metaphorical.[14]

Grisham touches here, I contend, on a significant change in the mediation of images by way of post-cinematic cameras—a change that renders them strangely opaque to rational analysis. But what is it, precisely, that makes these cameras "crazy" or irrational? My answer, in short, is that post-cinematic cameras—by which I mean a range of imaging apparatuses, both physical and virtual—seem not to know their place with respect to the separation of diegetic and nondiegetic planes of reality; these cameras therefore fail to situate viewers in a consistently and coherently designated spectating-position. More generally, they deviate from the perceptual norms established by human embodiment—the baseline physics engine, if you will, at the root of classical continuity principles, which in order to integrate or suture psychical subjectivities into diegetic/narrative constructs had to respect above all the spatial parameters of embodied orientation and locomotion (even if they did so in an abstract, normalizing form distinct from the real diversity of concrete body instantiations). Breaking with these norms results in the discorrelation of post-cinematic images from human perception, where discorrelation is regarded here, to begin with, from a spatial or quasi-spatial angle, that is, in terms of spectating *positions* and perceptual *relations*.

With the idea of discorrelation, I aim to describe an event that first announces itself negatively, as a phenomenological disconnect between viewing subjects and the object-images they view. In her now-classic phenomenological account of film experience, *The Address of the Eye*, Vivian Sobchack theorized a correlation—or structural homology—between spectators' embodied perceptual capacities and those of film's own apparatic "body," which engages viewers in a dialogical exploration of perceptual exchange; cinematic expression or communication, accordingly, was seen to be predicated on an analogical basis according to which the subject- and object-positions of film and viewer are essentially reversible and dialectically transposable. But, according to Sobchack, this basic perceptual correlation is endangered by new—or "postcinematic"—media (as she already referred to them in 1992), which disrupt the commutative interchanges of perspective on which filmic experience depends for its meaningfulness.[15]

With the tools Sobchack borrows from philosopher of technology Don Ihde, we can make a first approach to the "crazy" quality of post-cinematic cameras and the discorrelation of their images. As will become clear, this sort of phenomenological analysis reveals irrationality, in the sense I am using it, to be nothing other than the spatial—that is, situational, relational, and ultimately phenomenological—manifestation of discorrelation, which is essentially a break with human-centered phenomenology itself. The analysis

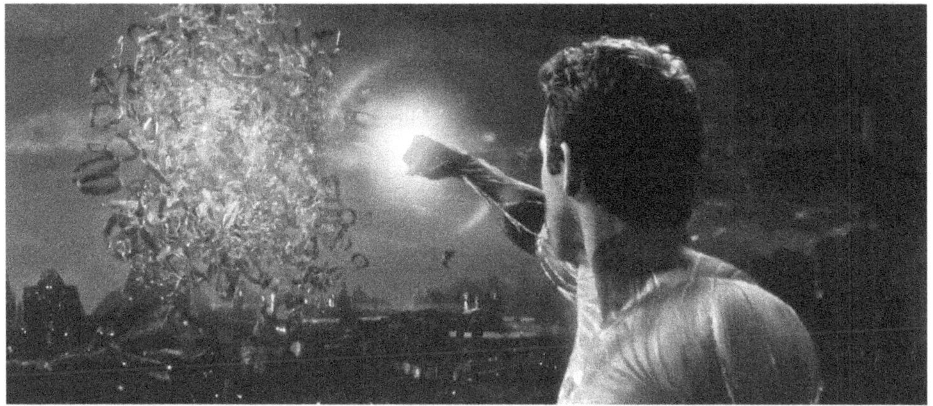

Figure 1.1. CGI-generated lens flares underscore (but exceed) diegetic realities in *Green Lantern* (Martin Campbell, 2011).

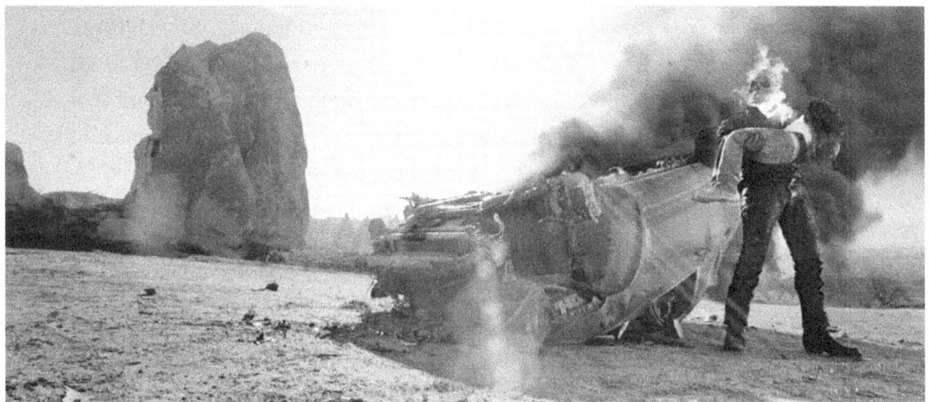

Figure 1.2. Directors Mark Neveldine and Brian Taylor use CGI lens flares to push the limits of 3D in *Ghost Rider: Spirit of Vengeance* (2011).

will therefore have to be supplemented by other theoretical means in order to discover its temporal dimensions and to overcome the anthropocentric (or subject-centric) limitations of our initial approach. Proceeding in this manner nevertheless has clear methodological advantages, for it is precisely through spatial/phenomenological paradoxes (or "irrationalities") that we, as subjects, are made aware of discorrelation in the first place.

Take the example of the digitally simulated lens flare, featured ostentatiously in superhero films like *Green Lantern* (Martin Campbell, 2011) or the *Ghost Rider* sequel directed by Mark Neveldine and Brian Taylor (2011), who brag that their extensive use of it breaks all the rules of "what you can and can't do" in 3D (see figures 1.1 and 1.2).[16] Responding to an interviewer's suggestion that *Ghost Rider: Spirit of Vengeance* "looks a lot more conventionally edited than your usual hyperkinetic style," Neveldine states, "There's a lot of places in the movie where, if we have a trademark style, I think you'll see it. Certainly the action is really fast-paced, we move the camera a lot, we broke every rule that supposedly was written about 3D and what you can and can't do."[17] The interviewer follows up later in the same discussion: "One of the supposed rules of 3D is that a shot has to be held a certain length in order to be perceived in 3D. Is that one of the rules you guys broke in *Ghost Rider*, and/or would break in a 3D *Crank* sequel?"[18] The interviewer's questions speak to a common concern in many discussions of post-cinema, especially when they are focused on recent action movies—namely, issues of formal editing practices, violations of continuity and the "invisible style" perfected in classical Hollywood cinema, and the acceleration of average shot lengths in recent productions. These are the primary variables in debates over the emergence of post-cinema as a formal break with a more conventional (or classical) form of cinema, as can be observed in disagreements between critics like David Bordwell, whose identification of "intensified continuity" recognizes acceleration but denies the occurrence of such a break, and Matthias Stork, who sees contemporary "chaos cinema" as radically incommensurate with Hollywood's established conventions for mediating action in a spatially coherent and comprehensible manner.[19]

Neveldine and Taylor show themselves largely uninterested in the parameters of such debates, however, and their responses subtly shift the ground of discussion. Neveldine replies to the interviewer: "Yeah, we didn't find any of the so-called rules of 3D were actually real rules. Through a process of testing and trying out different things and finding workarounds, we pretty much found we could shoot exactly the kind of thing we like to shoot, and it works great for 3D. We haven't had any complaints of people getting headaches from 3D, or puking. We expect to get that on *Crank 3*, but not because of the 3D."[20] Brian Taylor adds, proudly: "Yeah, but we have more lens flares in our movie than most 2D movies have, so we're happy with it."[21] Many reviewers were less enthusiastic, though; they complained about the overuse of lens flares, which were seen as generally gratuitous and sometimes nonsensical, and as the only thing that occasionally floats in 3D space in front of a basically flat surface picture. Generally, this use of lens flares fits with what I am theorizing as the irrationality of the post-cinematic camera and its disruption of a stable spectating-position. This disruption can be traced to the fact that Neveldine and Taylor's lens flares are positively insistent on the materiality of the camera, while being used to foreground the supposedly gritty (because "against the rules") potential of 3D *as* 3D; in other words, the technical infrastructure of 3D is foregrounded rather than rendered invisible or natural, all the more so as the lens flares occupy a different plane than the rest of the images. This self-consciously excessive use of three-dimensionality points to deeper disruptions of spatial relations that are deserving of more careful analysis.

Apart from the stylistically questionable matter of these images' excess, that is, a phenomenological analysis reveals significant paradoxes at the heart of the CGI lens flare—paradoxes that take us beyond matters of the formal composition of recent movies and that shed light on the irrationality of post-cinematic cameras and imaging processes more generally. On the one hand, a computer-generated lens flare encourages what Ihde calls an "embodiment relation" to the virtual camera: by simulating the material interplay of a lens and a light source, the lens flare emphasizes the plastic reality of "pro-filmic" CGI objects; the virtual camera, which enables our view of these objects, is to this extent itself grafted onto the subjective pole of the intentional relation, "embodied" or "incorporated" in a sort of phenomenological symbiosis that channels perception toward the objects of our visual attention. Ihde symbolizes embodiment relations thus:

(I—technology) → world

The arrow here indicates what Husserl designates the basic noetic relation, whereby a perceiving subject takes up an intentional relation toward some object or aspect of the world. In an embodiment relation, the subject and the mediating technology are bracketed together on the left-hand side of the arrow to indicate their cooperation in establishing the relation. The mediating technology, in such cases, becomes more or less transparent in the intentional act. Classical examples include Heidegger's famous hammer from *Being and Time*, Merleau-Ponty's only slightly less famous blind-man's cane from *Phenomenology of Perception*, or conventional optical technologies such as microscopes and telescopes. In such cases, we act and perceive *through* the instrument, which "withdraws" from our active awareness. To the extent that the CGI lens flare focuses attention on the virtual camera's simulated objects, the virtual camera is itself transparent in precisely this manner; it is fused with the subjectivity of the viewer, whose perspective on the (simulated) pro-filmic world is inseparable from the camera.[22]

On the other hand, however, the lens flare draws attention to itself and highlights the images' artificiality by emulating—and indeed foregrounding the emulation of—the material presence of a (nondiegetic) camera. To this extent, the camera is rendered quasi-objective, and it instantiates what Ihde calls a "hermeneutic relation": we look *at* the camera rather than just *through* it, and we interpret it *as a sign or token of* verisimilitude or "realisticness."[23] In contrast to the embodiment relation, Ihde symbolizes the hermeneutic relation thus:

I → (technology—world)

Here the mediating technology loses its transparency and becomes an object of interpretation, though still not the ultimate terminus of noetic intentionality, which aims *through* the mediating apparatus toward an object in the world. Thus, whereas an optical telescope tends to instantiate an embodiment relation as it disappears from view, a radio telescope instantiates a hermeneutic relation as a technology that has to be actively interrogated in order to learn about the heavens.[24] The CGI lens flare serves to place the camera in a similar position, as we are expected to marvel at, or at least take notice of, the lens flare as the guarantor of the virtual camera's conformity with the material laws of physics. The technical execution of transparence and realism is thereby foregrounded, and to that extent it both enables *and* disturbs said transparence. The paradox here, which consists of the realism-constituting *and* realism-problematizing undecidability of the virtual camera's relation to the diegesis—where the "reality" of this realism is conceived as thoroughly mediated, the product of a simulated physical camera rather than defined as the hallmark of embodied perceptual immediacy—points to a more basic problem: namely, to a disruption of the spatial-phenomenological relations between the viewer and the camera and thus to a transformation of mediation itself in the post-cinematic era.[25]

That is, the undecidable place of the mediating apparatus, the camera's apparently simultaneous occupation of both subjective and objective positions within the noetic relation that it enables between viewers and the film, is symptomatic of a more general destabilization of phenomenological subject- and object-positions in relation to the expanded affective realm of post-cinematic mediation. Computational, ergodic, and processual in nature, media in this mode operate on a level that is categorically beyond the purview of perception, perspective, or intentionality.[26] This is because, as I suggested earlier, these media are not mere "intermediaries" but "mediators" in a strong, transductive sense. To take stock of the post-cinematic camera's role as a mediator of images in this sense requires that we take a different sort of analytical approach. Conventional phenomenological analysis of the sort I have so far undertaken—an analysis that emphasizes the variability of technologically mediated intentional relations but assumes the basic integrity and existence of subjects, objects, and mediating apparatuses that are to be arrayed in some quasi-spatial arrangement—can therefore provide only a negative determination "from the outside," so to speak: it can help us to identify moments of dysfunction or disconnection, which announce themselves through the spatialized kinds of paradoxes we have seen here, but it can offer no positive characterization of the "molecular" changes occasioning them—changes occurring above all at the microtemporal level of computational imaging processes, to which an essentially spatial, diagrammatic analysis of subject-object relations must remain blind. Conceived as strongly transductive relations, the mediating roles of post-cinematic cameras defy attempts to situate them statically between the relata of subjects and objects, as those relata themselves are, by hypothesis, dynamically generated in relation to the mediator. If Simondon's claim that "*time comes from the preindividual just like the other dimensions that determine individuation*" applies to the individuation of viewing subjects and image-objects in relation to the microtemporality of computational processes, then any sort of analysis that proceeds from the preexistence of the phenomenological subject will only be able to register such dynamisms and generative individuations as the failure of spatial coherence or diagrammatic integrity. Hence the widespread fixation on the loss of indexicality as an indicator of digital images' categorical (and, in the estimation of many critics, lamentable) difference from cinema's photographic ontology.

The failure of material relation emphasized in such analyses reveals as much about the static, spatialized parameters of analysis as it does about the historical and technological changes occasioning the failure. My point is not that such analyses are *wrong* to identify the breakdown of indexicality, but that this breakdown marks only one aspect of the broader transformations in human-technological relations inaugurated in the transition to a post-cinematic media regime. More to the point, CGI and digital cameras do not just sever the ties of indexicality that characterized analog cinematography (an empirical or epistemological-phenomenological claim); they also render images themselves fundamentally processual—at once inextricably bound up in computational processes and simultaneously initiating a volatile feedback loop between these and the spectator. Such post-cinematic images, which fail to "settle" or coalesce into a fixed and distant position, thus displace the film-as-object-of-perception and uproot the spectator-as-perceiving-subject—in effect, enveloping both in an epistemologically indeterminate but materially quite real and concrete field of affective relation. Mediation, I suggest, can no longer be situated neatly *between* the poles of subject and object, as it swells with processual affectivity to engulf both.

Compare, in this connection, film critic Jim Emerson's statement in response to the debates over so-called "chaos cinema":[27]

> It seems to me that these movies are attempting a kind of shortcut to the viewer's autonomic nervous system, providing direct stimulus to generate excitement rather than simulate any comprehensible experience. In that sense, they're more like drugs that (ostensibly) trigger the release of adrenaline or dopamine while bypassing the middleman, that part of the brain that interprets real or imagined situations and *then* generates appropriate emotional/physiological responses to them. The reason they don't work for many of us is because, in reality, they give us nothing to respond *to*—just a blur of incomprehensible images and sounds, without spatial context or allowing for emotional investment.[28]

Now, I would like to distance myself from what appears to be a blanket dismissal of such stimulation, but I quote Emerson's statement here because I think it correctly and neatly identifies the link between a direct affective appeal and the essentially post-phenomenological dissolution of perceptual objects and bypassing of perception itself. If we take it seriously, though, this link marks the crux of a transformation in the ontology of media, the point of passage from cinematic to post-cinematic media. Whereas the former operate on the "molar" scale of perceptual intentionality (thus lending themselves to spatial/diagrammatic analysis), the latter operate on the "molecular" scale of subperceptual and prepersonal embodiment (Simondon's dynamic "preindividual" temporality as modulated by computational microtemporality) and thereby acquire the potential to transform the material basis of subjectivity and perception in a way that cannot be accounted for in traditional phenomenological terms.[29] But how *do* we account for this transformative power of post-cinematic media, short of simply reducing it (as it seems Emerson does) to a narrowly positivistic conception of physiological impact? To answer this question, it will be helpful to turn to Maurizio Lazzarato's reflections on the affective dimension of video and to Mark Hansen's expansions of these ideas with respect to computational and what he calls "atmospheric" media.

Mediating Affective Temporalities

According to Lazzarato, the video camera captures time itself, the splitting of time at every instant, hence opening the gap between perception and action where affect (in Bergson's metaphysics) resides.[30] Because it no longer merely traces objects mechanically and fixes them as discrete photographic entities but instead generates its images directly out of the flux of subperceptual matter, which it processes on the fly in the space of a microtemporal duration, the video camera marks a revolutionary transformation in the technical organization of time. The video camera, writes Lazzarato, "modulates the flows of electromagnetic waves. Video images are contractions and dilations, 'vibrations and tremors' of light, rather than 'tracings,' reproductions of reality. The video camera's take is a crystallization of time-matter."[31] Photographic (and cinematographic) apparatuses "trace" reality in a manner that lends itself to spatial analysis, while the vibratory nature of video cameras indicates their activation of a microtemporality that by virtue of its dynamism collapses the distance between the instrument and the object-world. The mediating technology itself becomes an active locus of molecular change: a Bergsonian body qua "center of indetermination," a gap of affectivity between passive receptivity and its passage into action. The camera thus imitates the process by which our own prepersonal bodies synthesize the passage from molecular to molar (from preindividual temporality to the space-time of subjects and objects), replicating the very process by which signal patterns are selected from the flux and made to coalesce into determinate images that can be incorporated into an emergent subjectivity.

This dilation of affect, which characterizes not only video but also (and especially) computational processes like the rendering of digital images—which is always done on the fly, in the space of what Wolfgang Ernst calls the time-critical processes of computation—marks the basic condition of the post-cinematic camera. It is this dynamic microtime of processing that disrupts spatial diagrams with an affective intermixture of inside and outside; affective processing constitutes the positive underside of that which presents itself externally as a negative, discorrelating incommensurability with respect to molar perception. As Hansen argues in his "Ubiquitous Sensation," the microtemporal scale at which computational media operate enables them to modulate the temporal and affective flows of life and to affect us directly at the level of our prepersonal embodiment—at a level that must remain invisible for any subject-oriented analysis, which by definition starts not from the process of individuation but from its product. The categorically invisible operation of computation "impacts sensory experience *unconsciously, imperceptibly—in short, at a level beneath the threshold of attention and awareness*. It impacts sensory experience, that is, by impacting the sensing brain microtemporally, at the level of the autonomous subprocesses or microconsciousnesses that . . . compose the infrastructure of seamless and integrated macroconscious [or molar] experience."[32] In this respect, properly post-cinematic cameras, which include video and digital imaging devices of all sorts, have a direct line to our innermost processes of becoming-in-time, and they are therefore capable of informing not only the individual subject but also the political life of the collective by flowing into the "general intellect" at the heart of immaterial or affective labor—or, in another analytical register, by transforming the practico-inert infrastructure of the shared world.[33] According to Lazzarato, "By retaining and accumulating duration, machines to crystallize time may help to develop or to neutralize the 'force to feel' and the 'force to act'; they may contribute to our 'becoming active' or to our being held in passivity."[34] This political dimension, in short, is contingent on the post-cinematic camera's ability to dilate and transform the preindividual space of molecular affect, and hence to reconstitute the anthropotechnical interface itself.

The *Paranormal Activity* franchise of "found-footage" horror films makes these cosmological claims more concrete and palpable through a series of experiments with various modes and dimensions of post-perceptual, affective mediation.[35] Each installment of the franchise uses a different camera or set of camera types to capture the unfolding events; the cameras themselves exist within the diegesis, and their mediation therefore comprises an essential part of the horror. After using handheld video cameras in the series' first installment (figure 1.3) and closed-circuit home surveillance cameras in *Paranormal Activity 2* (figure 1.4), and following a flashback by way of old VHS tapes in part 3 (figure 1.5), *Paranormal Activity 4* intensifies its predecessors' estrangement of the camera from cinematic and ultimately human perceptual norms by implementing computational imaging processes for its strategic manipulations of spectatorial affect (figure 1.6). A spinoff, *Paranormal Activity: The Marked Ones*, distinguishes itself through the use of GoPro cameras, while the final installment, *Paranormal Activity: The Ghost Dimension*, uses a more fantastic setup—it is the only film in the series that employs a completely fictional camera device, a modified video camera that can actually see the spirit dimension that is invisible to human eyes and that mediates such phenomena to spectators in bouts of CGI-heavy 3D footage. I will return, in chapter 5, to several of these cameras and the movies that employ them in a broader consideration of discorrelation in the horror genre. For now, however, my interest is in the role of computational imaging, as exemplified in the franchise's fourth installment.

In particular, *Paranormal Activity 4* uses laptop- and smartphone-based video chat and the Xbox's Kinect motion control system to mediate between diegetic and spectatorial shocks and to regulate the corporeal rhythms and intensities of suspenseful contraction and release that define the temporal/affective quality of the movie. Especially the Kinect technology, itself a crazy

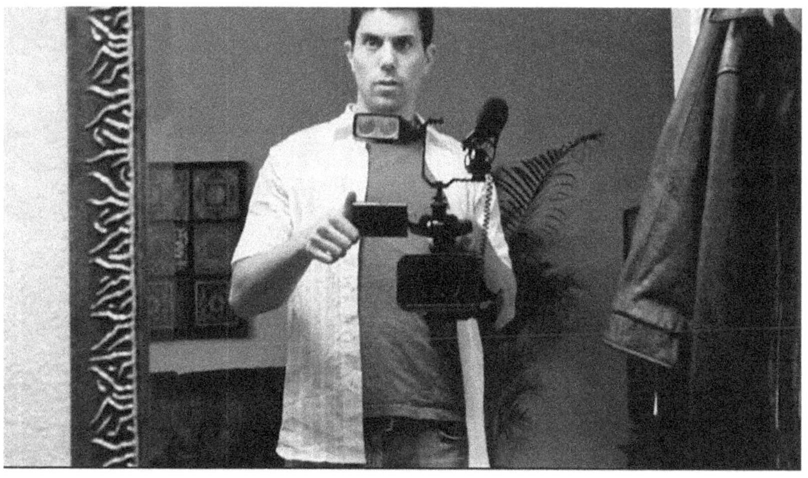

Figure 1.3. Handheld cameras mediate between diegetic and extra-diegetic spaces in *Paranormal Activity* (Oren Peli, 2007/2009).

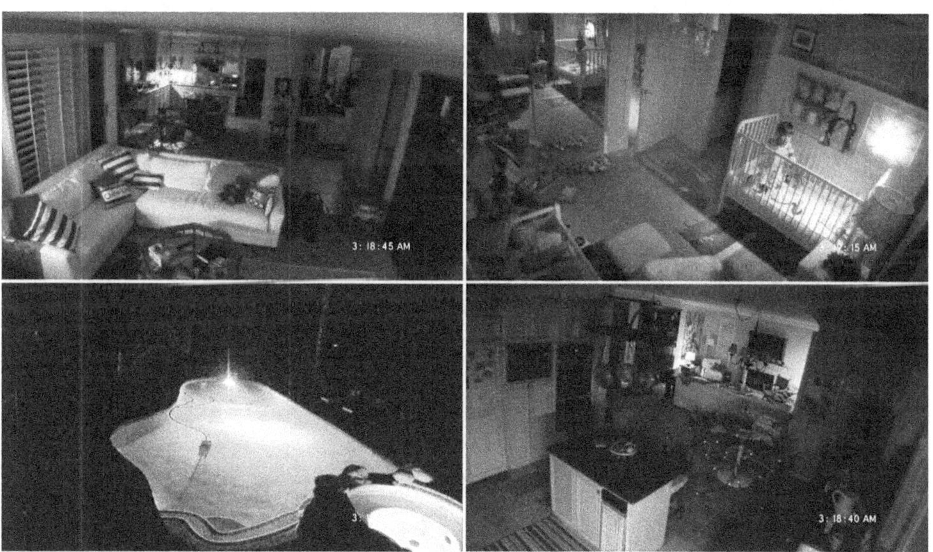

Figure 1.4. Closed-circuit home surveillance cameras capture the action in *Paranormal Activity 2* (Tod Williams, 2009).

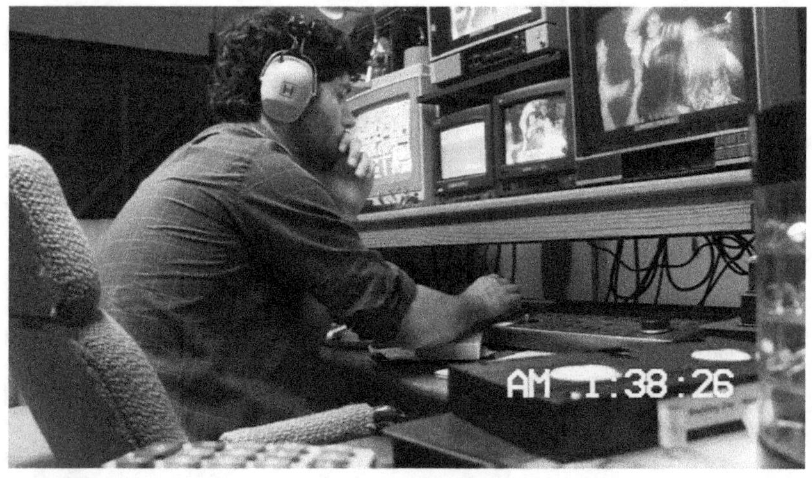

Figure 1.5. *Paranormal Activity 3* (Henry Joost and Ariel Schulman, 2011) presents itself in the form of VHS found footage.

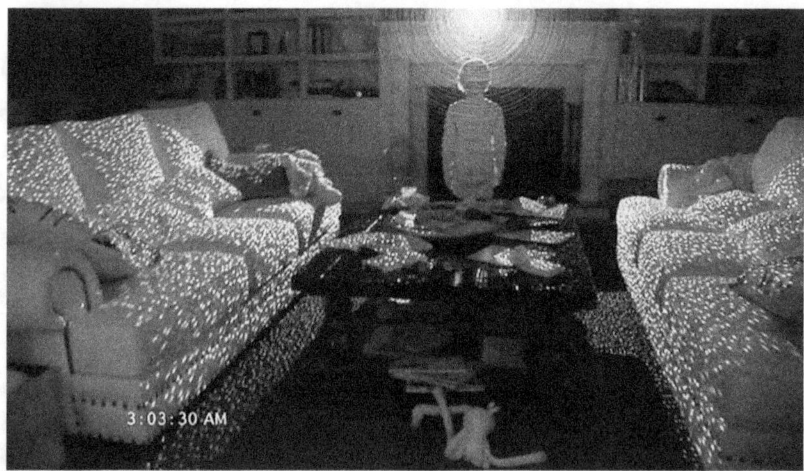

Figure 1.6. The Xbox Kinect exemplifies the nonhuman agency of post-cinematic cameras in *Paranormal Activity 4* (Henry Joost and Ariel Schulman, 2012).

binocular camera that emits a matrix of infrared dots to map bodies and spaces and integrate them algorithmically into computational/ergodic game spaces, marks the discorrelation of computational from human perception: the dot matrix, which is featured extensively in the film, is invisible to the human eye; the effect of rendering the matrix visible is made possible only through a video camera's night vision mode—part of the post-perceptual sensibility of the (digital) video camera that distinguishes it from the cinema camera. The movie (and the *Paranormal Activity* series more generally) thus provides a perfect illustration for the affective impact and bypassing of cognitive (as well as narrative) interest through video and computational imaging devices. In an interview, codirector Henry Joost says the use of the Kinect—inspired, fittingly enough, by a YouTube video demonstrating the effect—was a logical choice for the series: "I think it's very *Paranormal Activity* because it's like, there's this stuff going on in the house that you can't see."[36] Indeed, the effect highlights all the computational and video-sensory activity going on around us all the time, completely discorrelated from human perception, but very much involved in the temporal and affective vicissitudes of our daily lives through the many cameras and screens surrounding us and involved in every aspect of the progressively indistinct realms of our work and play. Ultimately, *Paranormal Activity 4* points toward the uncanny qualities of contemporary media, which following Hansen have ceased to be contained in discrete apparatic packages and have become diffusely "atmospheric."[37]

According to Hansen, today's increasingly ubiquitous computing environment "marks the endpoint of a certain trajectory in the dialectic of technics and sensation"—a trajectory that encompasses the transitions from film to video to digital technologies. This most recent stage of media-technical development

> abandon[s] an object-centered model of media in favor of an environmental one. No longer a delimited temporal object that we engage with focally through an interface such as a screen, media become an environment that we experience simply by being and acting in space and time—which is to say, without in most cases explicitly being aware of it, without taking it as the intentional object or target of our time consciousness. . . . Ubicomp signals a fundamental modification in our interface with technics: no longer object centered, resolutely personal, individually framed, and of the order of conscious perception, the technical mediation of sensation in ubicomp environments is atmospheric, impersonal, collectively accessible, and microtemporal in its sensory address.[38]

It is not immediately apparent how this applies to the camera, the function of which is still to mediate images to viewers. Consider, however, the way that these images circulate indiscriminately across screens and networks as computational bitstreams, only materializing fleetingly and at the last moment as optical phenomena before disappearing again into the digital ether. In fact, it is not only the images that become atmospheric in this way; in relation to the revised parameters and temporal dimensions of contemporary imaging processes, post-cinematic cameras are now also less determinate in terms of spatial location and objective fixity. Indeed, the post-cinematic camera has in many ways shed the perceptually commensurate "body" that ensured cinematic communication on Sobchack's phenomenological model; in today's environment of thoroughly informatic imaging, the camera, having gone beyond even the "vibratory" stage of video imaging, is no longer even required to have a material lens. This does not mean that the camera has become somehow immaterial, but today the conception of the camera needs to be expanded: consider how all processes of digital image rendering, whether in digital film production or simply in computer-based playback, are involved in the same on-the-fly molecular processes through which, following Lazzarato, the video camera can be seen to trace the affective synthesis of images from flux. Unhinged from traditional conceptions and instantiations, post-cinematic cameras are defined precisely by the confusion or indistinction of recording, rendering, and screening devices.

In this respect, the category of post-cinematic cameras expands beyond the lens-based devices ranging from GoPros to drone cameras to smartphones; when we think about the range of imaging processes that are operative in our daily lives, a lensless device like the "smart TV" becomes an even more exemplary post-cinematic camera (an uncannily flat domestic *Kammer* or "room" composed of smooth, computational space). Regarding the smart TV as a camera or imaging device (rather than solely as a screening device) makes sense when we consider the range of imaging operations that it performs: it executes microtemporal processes ranging from compression/decompression, artifact generation and suppression, resolution upscaling, aspect-ratio transformation, motion-smoothing image interpolation, and on-the-fly 2D to 3D conversion. The smart TV is active, not passive, in the generation of images in a way that is paradigmatic for our post-cinematic media environment, as it demonstrates the range of operations performed by many of our devices *whether or not they possess lenses*. That is, the smart TV is not special but exemplary: smartphone cameras and other lens-based devices perform many of the same operations, but focusing on a lensless device has the advantage of abstracting the imaging function of the camera from the spatial parameters of perspective, distance, and relation (e.g., an object's orientation with respect to a lens). The latter parameters have become secondary, as the smart TV makes clear, to microtemporal processes of image-generation; spatial-phenomenological analysis therefore flounders before a type of mediation that is, in Hansen's words, "no longer object centered, resolutely personal, individually framed, and of the order of conscious perception [but instead] atmospheric, impersonal, collectively accessible, and microtemporal in its sensory address."[39] The camera, which is now part of the enabling infrastructure of images' "atmospheric" qualities in a post-cinematic media environment, becomes indistinct from the screen and the network. Marking a further expansion of the video camera's artificial affect-gap, the smart TV and the computational processes of image modulation that it performs bring the perceptual and actional capacities of cinema—its receptive camera and projective screening apparatuses—back together in a post-cinematic counterpart to the early Cinématographe, equipped now with an affective density that uncannily parallels our own.

Especially in the much-maligned motion-smoothing processes, where the television inserts completely new, computationally generated images between the frames of the source signal (thus doubling or quadrupling the 50Hz frequency of the Phase Alternating Line [PAL] system's twenty-five frames per second or ramping up the National Television System Committee [NTSC] encoding system's 60Hz to 120Hz or 240Hz by generating new images between its roughly thirty frames per second), the smart TV demonstrates its post-cinematic quality as an imaging device radically discorrelated from human perception and perceptual technologies (including the analog camera, the lens of which is correlated with that of the human eye); the interpolation of computational processes disrupts the circuit of perception formerly mediated through the camera—a fact which announces itself to the viewer first and foremost on an affective level, in the form of the so-called "soap-opera effect": the images seem paradoxically too real, too close, too plastic; they have an uncanny quality about them, something not quite right—though it is exceedingly difficult to pin down this quality and express it in words. Such pictures have been described as "ridiculously 'sharp,'" "like an old *Dr. Who* episode where the action on-screen is smoother than the background, creating a jarring disparity when watching movies with lots of movement," or where "you essentially see the 'moving' objects on a different plane than the background, as if they were cut outs moving on a painted background."[40] There's something almost pornographic about the images, as if they lack the proper distance from their viewers—movies filmed in 35mm suddenly look like a video-based telenovela or low-budget reality show. Surfaces stand out, and to this extent we might appeal to the vocabulary of Ihde's "hermeneutic relation": the medium begins to obtrude on the objective side of the noetic arrow, as an object or quasi-object of perceptual intentionality.

But in fact, the situation is more extreme, as this is just the affective side of a perceptual (or cognitive) *nonrelation* to the technological infrastructure, which renders images on the fly, subperceptually "enriching" the images by multiplying them twofold, fourfold, or even more. This is a significant case, I contend, because it displays a more general truth about the post-cinematic era: it is widely accepted that cameras are everywhere today, and even that this ubiquity is an important marker of our historical and technological situation today—but we usually think about surveillance cameras and the proliferation of cameras in handheld devices like smartphones. We do not usually think of our *screens* as cameras, but that is precisely what smart TVs and computational display devices of all sorts in fact are: each screening of a (digital or digitized) "film" becomes in fact a *re*filming of it, as the smart TV generates millions of original images, more than the original film itself—images unanticipated by the filmmaker and not contained in the source material. To "render" the film computationally is in fact to offer an original *rendition* of it, never before performed, and hence to *re*-produce the film through a decidedly post-cinematic camera.

This production of unanticipated and unanticipatable images renders such devices strangely vibrant, uncanny—very much in the sense exploited by *Paranormal Activity*. The dilation of affect, which introduces a temporal gap of hesitation or delay between perception (or recording) and action (or playback), amounts to a modeling or enactment of the indetermination of bodily affect through which time is generated, and by which (in Bergson's system) life itself is defined. A negative (spatial/diagrammatic) view sees only the severing of the images' indexical relations to the world, hence turning all digital image production and screening into animation, not categorically different from the virtual lens flares discussed earlier.[41] But in the end, the ubiquity of "animation" that is introduced through digital rendering processes should perhaps be taken literally, as the artificial creation of (something like) life, which is itself equivalent—following Lazzarato following Bergson—with the gap of affectivity, or the production of duration through the delay of causal-mechanical stimulus-response circuits; the interruption of photographic indexicality through digital processing is thus the introduction of duration = affect = life. Discorrelated images, in this respect, are autonomous, quasi-living images in Bergson's sense, having transcended and gained a degree of autonomy from the mechanicity that previously (in cinema's photochemical processes) kept them subservient to human perception. Like the unmotivated cameras of *District 9* and *Melancholia*, or the uncanny environmental ones of *Paranormal Activity*, post-cinematic cameras generally have become "something altogether different," as Therese Grisham puts it:[42] apparently crazy, because discorrelated from the molar perspectives of phenomenal subjects and objects, cameras now mediate post-perceptual flows and confront us everywhere with their own affective indeterminacy.

Metabolic Images and the Hyperinformatic Environment

Another way to put this is to say that post-cinematic cameras and images are *metabolic* processes or agencies, and their insertion into the environment alters the interactive pathways that define our own material, biological, and ecological forms of being, largely bypassing our cognitive processing to impinge on us at the level of our own metabolic processing of duration. Metabolism is a process that is neither in my subjective control nor even confined to my body (as object) but which articulates organism and environment together from the perspective of a preindividuated agency. Metabolism is affect without feeling or emotion—affect as the transformative power of "passion" that, as Brian Massumi reminds us, Spinoza identifies as that unknown power of embodiment that is neither wholly active nor wholly passive.[43] Metabolic processes are the zero degree of transformative agency, at once intimately familiar and terrifyingly alien, conjoining inside/outside, me/not-me, life/death, old/novel, as the basic power of transitionality—marking not only biological processes but also global changes that encompass life and its environment.[44] Mark Hansen usefully defines "medium" as "environment for life" in order to foreground the infrastructural role of media in relation to the material powers of perception, action, and thought;[45] accordingly, metabolism is as much a process of media transformation as it is a process of bodily change.

As Elena del Río has described it, the shift from a cinematic to a post-cinematic environment is a metabolic process through and through: "Like an expired body that blends with the dirt to form new molecules and living organisms, the body of cinema continues to blend with other image/sound technologies in processes of composition/decomposition that breed images with new speeds and new distributions of intensities."[46] To the extent that metabolism is, as I have claimed, inherently affective (or "passionate," in a Massumian-Spinozan vein), post-cinematic affect has to be thought apart from feeling, certainly apart from subjective emotion. What I have been trying to do in the preceding sections is to situate us in a position from which we might grasp post-cinematic cameras and the image itself not as objective entities but as *metabolic agencies*, ones that are caught up in and define the larger media-ecological process of transformation that (dis)articulates subjects and objects, spectators and images, life and its environment in the transition to the post-cinematic. The metabolic image, I suggest, is the quintessential image of change, and it speaks to a perspective that is the immersed, undifferentiated (non)perspective of metabolism itself—a material affect that is distributed across bodies and environments as the very medium of transitionality.

As I have outlined it here, this perspective builds on a view of video and above all computation as technologies of microtemporal processing and modulation. But emphasizing this level of material-technological functioning, which subtends any identifiable "content" of mediation, points to the inadequacy of many of the more narrowly "technical" determinations of the transition to a post-cinematic regime. Thus, as I have mentioned, many discussions concentrate on whether editing styles today are overly chaotic or whether they embody a merely intensified form of continuity. But as Steven Shaviro points out in his discussion of what he calls "post-continuity," compliance or noncompliance with the rules of classical continuity is often simply beside the point in post-cinema.[47] The central spectacle of Michael Bay's *Transformers* series—a series that is clearly full of hectic, noncontinuity editing patterns—demonstrates this essentially secondary role of formal editing (see figure 1.7). The transformations themselves embody a certain outstripping of human perceptual faculties, discorrelations that are staged in continuous takes, without the need for explicit violations of continuity. These transformations offer concise examples of a "hyperinformatic" cinema: they overload our capacities, giving us too much visual information, presented too fast for us to take in and process cognitively—information that is itself generated and embodied in informatic technologies operating at speeds well beyond our subjective grasp. Hence, the transformation's visualization does not simply produce images that give objective form to boys' and men's childhood fantasies and playtime imaginations; instead, it is precisely their *failure* to coalesce into coherent objects that defines these images as metabolic *spectacles beyond perspective*—that is, as ostentatious displays that categorically deny us the distance from which we might regard them as perceptual objects. It is the processual flow and speed of algorithmic processing that is put on display here, and indeed *put into effect* as the images are played back on our computational devices.

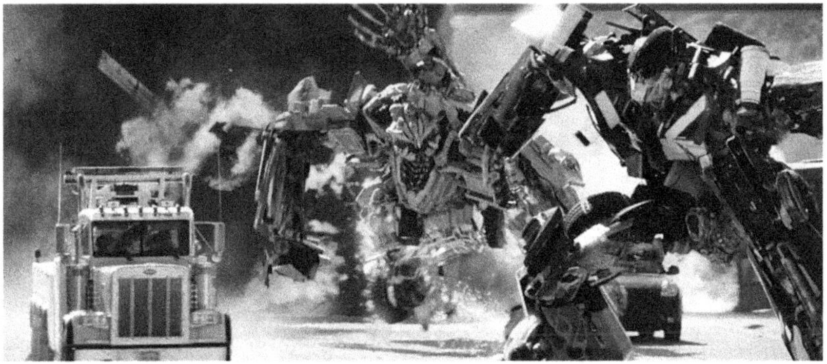

Figure 1.7. The central spectacles of *Transformers* (Michael Bay, 2007) are "hyperinformatic" images that outstrip human perception.

But so long as we underestimate the meaning of the images' animation, so long as we reduce it to a merely technical effect of CGI's severing of photographic indexicality, we fail to grasp the significance of post-cinematic affect as a more global event, an environmental shift or "climate change" precipitated by the condensation and flow of affect in our increasingly lively machines. Through the discorrelating effect that post-cinematic cameras have on intentional relations, we as subjects are effectively consumed by/with affect and transformed along with the would-be objects of algorithmic images; in a manner of speaking, these images do nothing less than devour and metabolize *us*. We are bound up in and transformed by the processual experience of digital mediation, which unlike the ideal closure of classical cinema is proximal and open to (rather than separate from) our computational lifeworld. In other words, there is no clear encapsulation of the movie experience as distinct from the digital infrastructures of our daily lives.[48] There is contiguity, involvement—always an *inescapable involvement* that marks the "participatory culture" of the convergence era as far less benign than some critics might hope.[49] Buy the game, buy the toys, download the app, stream it on Netflix, watch at home, at work, on the plane or train: at stake is a literal capitalization of our attention, and the hyperinformatic dissolution of perspective is central to this undertaking. Affecting us on a molecular, subperceptual level of microtemporal embodiment but imbricating us in an expansive, diffuse network of nebulous agencies and transactions, the post-cinematic *dispositif* operates by metabolizing subject-object relations, transforming and re-creating them by setting us and our affective machines in novel relations to one another and to the larger emergent flows of bits, bodies, and other material units of exchange.

Postnatural Metabolisms

Against this background, I want to look briefly now at the work of independent filmmaker Shane Carruth, whose films *Primer* (2004) and *Upstream Color* (2013) can be seen as powerful aesthetic and perhaps even philosophical explorations of this new ontology of the image. In *Technics and Time*, philosopher Bernard Stiegler observes that Heidegger briefly recognized a conjunction of the "who" and the "what," an indistinction of the human and the technical, which was mediated in the clock and its role in temporal experience.[50] However, according to Stiegler, Heidegger resolutely ignored this essentially transductive constellation in *Being and Time*, because he was intent on isolating an "authentic," nontechnical time. It is precisely this disavowed conjunction of the who and the what, I contend, that is at stake in post-cinema's microtemporal refunctionalization of the camera and of metabolism. In this context, the insoluble relation of "technics and time" resurfaces in Carruth's *Primer* in the form of an interrogation that might be titled "technics and time travel."

More specifically, Carruth's notoriously complex, low-budget tale of time travel engages with the relations of metabolism, temporal experience, and technical mediation by staging an unsettlingly self-reflexive probing of the camera, which is set in relation to the time machine developed by the film's apparently brilliant but ultimately uninspired and psychologically uninteresting characters. This machine, which is more discovered than invented, begins early on to exhibit strange behavior, but direct observation of its workings is not possible. A video camera, which had been acquired to record the machine's behavior, is therefore placed inside the "black box" mechanism; the necessary mediation of the camera signals that what we are about to witness is something that is beyond the purview of unaided human perception, as it concerns phenomena taking place outside the relatively narrow window of subjectively anchored temporal awareness. And here the film stages a sort of *mise en abyme*, as it aligns the video camera and the strange apparatus, and it sets both of them in relation to the (16mm) movie camera that produced the film we are now watching. In fact, the scene offers a key to understanding (if not disentangling) the film's narrative paradoxes, as the film itself might be seen, recursively and self-reflexively, as the product of what happens when you place the camera inside the box, when you insert it into the microtemporal loops that characterize the metabolic images of post-cinematic media.

Significantly, accelerated metabolic processes provide the first indications that the machine is operating on the flow of time itself: rapid fungal growth on the surface of an object placed inside the apparatus first suggests the possibility

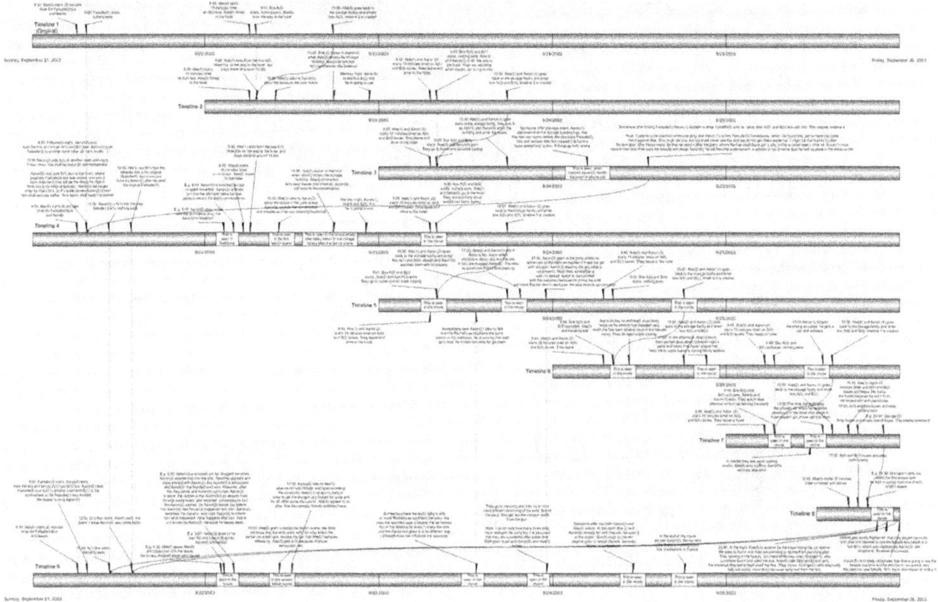

Figure 1.8. A "definitive" (fan-produced) time line for *Primer* (Shane Carruth, 2004).

of time travel, while accelerated beard growth and related processes will later accompany humans' travels through time. Metabolism is here situated as the originary giver of time; importantly, though, it is not a purely "natural" or organic clock, as it is subject to transformation through the new metabolism of the apparatus. The heady narrative complexity that results from recursive acts of time travel (and which has given rise to plenty of fan-based attempts to provide the "definitive," "comprehensive," or "deobfuscated" time line of the film) is thus a by-product (figure 1.8). More fundamental is the film's own deformation of time. The post-cinematic camera, placed inside the box of video-based and computational processing, or outside the temporal window of subjective experience, disrupts the main attractions that defined classical Hollywood: it disrupts psychology (producing uninteresting characters and dialogue), it renders narration superficial, and it explodes causality altogether. Again, at the heart of these disruptions and dysfunctions is the metabolic image, which Carruth's more recent film, *Upstream Color*, probes in a different, more ecological way.

More specifically, *Upstream Color* gestures toward the atmospheric and environmental aspects of post-cinematic metabolism, encompassing the sub- and suprapersonal dynamics, the micro- and macrolevels and confusions of within and without, in an audiovisual and narrative construct that displaces centered human perception in both directions at once. *Upstream Color* is about agencies that infiltrate the body, but that remain ecologically distributed throughout a network of hosts and environmental transport mechanisms: a river, plants, pigs, people, power lines, music, and money—all of these carry and are in turn carried by the parasitic maggots at the center of a story ostensibly about a couple, ruined professionally, financially, and perhaps psychologically, as they find their way to one another and ultimately to a greater sense of connection with the world. I say that it is "ostensibly" about this, but it is certainly about much more than this. I hesitate, however, to offer an "interpretation" per se, as narrative and signifying functions seem secondary to the experience the film propagates, both diegetically and medially, of indissoluble and multidirectional interlinkage—an experience, in short, of metabolism as the subperceptual nexus of growth and decay.

Indeed, I wish to say that the film offers us an *experience* of metabolism itself, not just an allegory or *metaphor* for metabolism. With reference to Dutch phenomenological psychologist J. H. van den Berg's quirky notion of "metabletics," translator Bernd Jager makes an important distinction between *metabolism* and *metaphor* as two distinct types of transformation. *Metaphor*, today as in the ancient Greek *metapherein*, refers to reversible passages that connect two realms and preserve similitude between them; on the other hand, *metabolism*, from *metaballein*, refers to abrupt and radical changes that fundamentally efface, digest, or absorb all traces of an earlier state.[51] Metabolic changes do not occur on a human scale, they are not commensurate with human perception or discourse, and they are therefore not subject to social or cultural construction (or deconstruction, for that matter); in contrast to metaphorical changes, which leave intact a humanly accessible context within which such changes may be cognized and recognized, metabolic processes are properly subconceptual, subphenomenal, and literally material. I contend that *Upstream Color*'s metabolic images are not just *about* metabolic processes but that they literally *enact* such transductive material processes; and though the experience of watching Carruth's films is so utterly different from watching, say, a Michael Bay film, it is on the basis of this subconceptual affective impact, which bypasses cognitive processing or "metaphor," that I would claim both as properly post-cinematic.

The basic affective tone (or *Grundton*) of *Upstream Color* is alternately dark and hopeful, but it is not really about the characters' (or even our) hopes or fears at all, it would seem. It feels more accurate to say that the film is

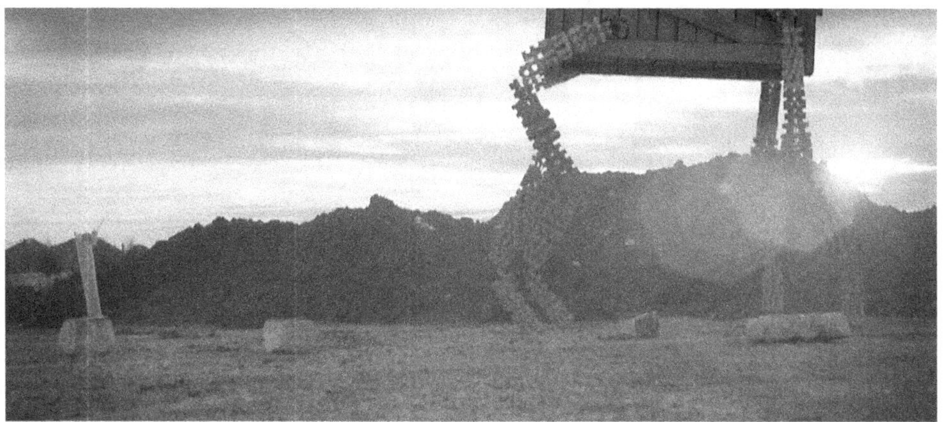

Figure 1.9. Unexplained CGI images challenge us to scan the frame for information in *Upstream Color* (Shane Carruth, 2013).

simply about the material flows it traces, which are marked as decidedly post-cinematic early in the movie. Without any sort of contextual situation, we are presented with a sequence of digitally composited images, complete with hexagonal lens flares and some sort of unfinished-looking CGI creature (see figure 1.9). These are then shown to belong to a diegetic screen, that of the female protagonist Kris, who advances and reverses the images in a stepwise manner, clicking through the frames as she searches for a shadow or a gaffer's foot that apparently went unnoticed by the effects team (figure 1.10). If you have seen the film, you will know that this brief scene—if indeed these images can be said to constitute a "scene"—is quite marginal in many respects. We will never learn about the project that Kris is working on here, and she will be fired from her job anyway when a man feeds her the parasite, sets her in a hypnotic state for some indefinite number of days, and cleans out all her assets. Yet the scene remains significant in situating the film in this context of computational labor and image production, where the human perspective that Kris brings (and that we bring) to these images is not central and focused, not the focusing vision that defines coherence in classical cinema, but a dispersed, "scanning" form of regard. The images compel us to interrogate them likewise, as we are unable to identify anything in the brief time given to us. In any case, Kris's vision is not a masterful or even directed gaze but more of a stopgap designed to mop up around the post-cinematic vision machine; in her job, Kris herself embodies mere biopower in the service of algorithmic functions.

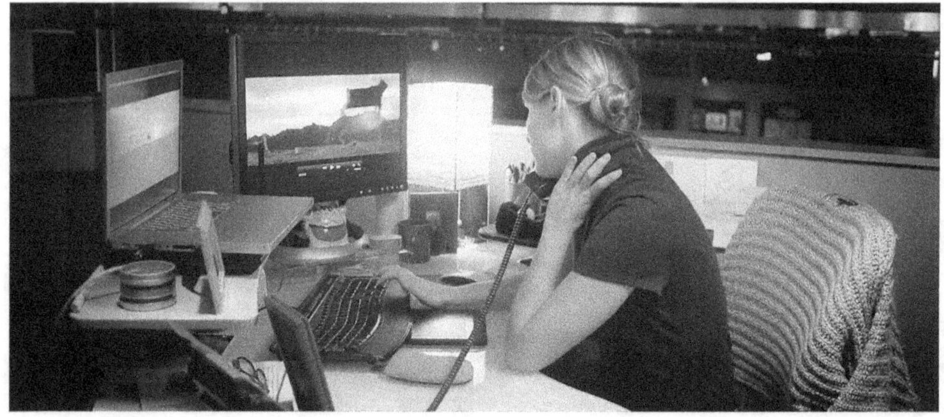

Figure 1.10. Female protagonist Kris (Amy Seimetz) shares our perspective with regard to the post-cinematic vision machine.

Her infection with the parasite will extract her from this assemblage, to a certain extent, but only by effecting a further splitting and dispersal of agency. Indeed, both Kris and the male protagonist Jeff, whom she is drawn to by some unknown force and who has apparently undergone the same ordeal as she has, will more or less cease being individuals as their relationship develops. Their childhood memories merge, and it is unclear whose past belongs to whom. Moreover, this erasure of individual identity, the overt emergence of what Gilles Deleuze calls "dividuality," is mediated through free-floating dialogues that attach themselves to various locales and various times, impossibly bridging spatial and temporal distances that no embodied speaker could span.[52] So what sometimes resembles a Terrence Malick–style voice-over turns out to be something quite different, as it is occasionally anchored in an image of a character speaking, but that speaking character can disappear and reappear at a distant location within the space of a single ongoing dialogue, itself apparently presented in real time. We are in the realm of the virtual rather than the actual, it would appear, and the flow of images and sounds effectively involves the viewer in the dispersal of agency described in the diegesis.[53]

And it is the soundtrack and musical score, above all, that ties everything together. Semidiegetic in nature—the musical counterpart of a free indirect discourse, perhaps—the synthetic music weaves back and forth between the status of background music and source music; the Sampler, as the unnamed character is called in the film's credits, synthesizes natural and technological sounds (running water, a drainpipe, the hum of a power line) into electronic music, effecting a sort of metabolic recombination of environmental materials. He sells his music on CD, but he also uses his sound compositions to attract the parasite's human hosts to a field where he extracts and transplants the worms from the people and into pigs. Playing simulated "rain" sounds on an amped-up PA system, the sampled sounds bypass the hosts' subjectivities, working on them subperceptually and impinging upon their bodies via the parasites, which compel their hosts' actions. And the music works on us as well by splitting our attentions between organic source and technical modulation, between reality and simulation, and between diegesis and medium. It thus continues, in a different register, the arc begun with the CGI images that Kris and we scan together for information, gesturing nebulously toward the conditions of life in the age of post-cinematic mediation. Driving both the narrative and the larger experience of the film in essential ways, the Sampler's music neatly sums or summons, gathers together, the environmental and medial, sub- and suprapersonal levels of metabolic action for characters and spectators alike. Underscoring and linking images of cellular decomposition, the computerized labor of image production, of worms making their way through human and nonhuman bodies, bodies succumbing to decay, individual selves giving way to various forms of control and dividuality, and microscopic processes of interspecies transfer, the Sampler's music marks the time of the environment and its interconnections. Together, sound and image mediate an experience of the expanded realm of affect that swallows up, discorrelates, and metabolizes subjective perception and perspective in the space of the post-cinematic ecosphere.

In her musings on Alfred North Whitehead's philosophical project of overcoming the distinction between primary and secondary qualities and the so-called "bifurcation of nature" into physical and subjective phenomena, Isabelle Stengers seems to describe also the post-cinematic project of *Upstream Color*, and even comes close to naming Carruth's film in the process: "In the letting go to which nature [or the postnatural environment of the film] incites us, in its pure, shimmering mobility, how could one fail to experience the sign that we are indeed *upstream* of the bifurcation that presented nature to us as *colorless*, odorless, and mute?"[54] Carruth's *Upstream Color* also incites a "letting go" of distinctions: between diegetic and nondiegetic (we are as much involved in the images on Kris's screen as she is), between textual and medial (apparently Kris is editing CGI footage that Carruth made for his unfinished film *A Topiary*), and ultimately also the spatial differences of subjective experience and objective image (as the experience of the film as a whole washes over us). In this experience of indistinction, *Upstream Color* therefore also takes us beyond the bifurcation that would have us regard the film simply as an allegory or metaphor rather than an experience in itself. Rather than inspiring an allegorical reading, an additional subjective interpretation overlaid on top of reality, post-cinematic productions like Carruth's film serve to dissolve the distinction, undo the bifurcation, and immerse us in the experience of an environment in transition. This, I suggest, is the experience of metabolic media.

Toward an Ethics of Discorrelation

Ultimately, what a movie like *Upstream Color* points to is the way that biological, technological, phenomenological, and economic realities are all imbricated with one another today in a total media environment—that of post-cinema, which is unified and propagated not by cognitive but by decidedly post-perceptual means. Cameras are irrational, neither subjective nor objective but radically ambiguous and volatile. Images are discorrelated, incommensurate with human subjectivities and perspectives. Media generally are post-perceptual, transductively mediating new forms of life by modulating the metabolic processes through which organisms such as ourselves are structurally coupled with our (biotic, technical, material, and symbolic) ecospheres. By insinuating themselves into the molecular flows of affect, prior to the possibility of perception and action, post-cinema's metabolic images have a direct impact on "the way we tick"—that is, on the materially embodied production and modulation of time and temporal experience. In other words, these images radically *articulate* the conditions of life itself in the contemporary technosphere: they not only "express" these conditions and our experiences of them but are in part responsible for enabling our experience in the first place; by articulating together the organic (the material substrate out of which human subjectivities are formed) and the technical (computational processes in particular) at a categorically prepersonal and noncognitive level of microtemporal becoming, metabolic images are involved in *generating* the conditions for molar experience in the post-cinematic world. Finally, these techno-organic processes point us beyond our individual experiences, toward the larger ecologies and imbalances of the Anthropocene.[55] Ultimately, we might speculate, what post-cinema demands of us by means of its discorrelated images is that we learn to take responsibility for our own affective discorrelations—that we develop an ethical and radically postindividual sensibility for the networked dividualities through which computational, endocrinological, sociopolitical, meteorological, subatomic, and economic agencies are all enmeshed with one another in the metabolic processing and mediation of life today.

Dividuated Images

In contrast to the integral photograms of cinema, the images of a post-cinematic media regime are *dividual,* their forms *discorrelated* from molar subjectivity, their forces *molecular*, and their agencies of the order of *metabolism* rather than perception or cognition. It is in these terms that I have sought to understand the differences between cinematic and post-cinematic media, and I have thereby made appeal to a somewhat Deleuzian framework—essentially situating the post-cinematic image as a medium, vector, or agent of the control society, complicit in the dividuation and modulation of subjects and their experiential and agential capacities under post-Fordist or neoliberal capitalism, as Deleuze suggestively describes in his famous "Postscript on the Societies of Control."[1] Now, this view of post-cinema's images as agents of dividuation may be all well and good for critics already convinced by the broad, somewhat impressionistic picture painted by Deleuze in those few brief pages of the postscript; but others will surely have their doubts, many of which are well founded, so I would like to take this opportunity to address some of the objections that might be raised, and in the process provide a better picture of the means and mechanisms by which discorrelated, "dividuated" images are supposed to affect us. As a corollary, perhaps this line of thinking will also shed some light on the types of media processes that today—roughly three decades after the original publication of the postscript—enable what Deleuze refers to as the dividualization of the individual. At stake, more than anything else, is a repositioning of the post-cinematic image as a vector of subjectivation and an identification of the theoretical resources that will allow us to think its particular agencies.

Reclearing the Ground

The first major doubt about post-cinema and its dividuated images concerns whether or not there has even been a shift at all from a cinematic to a new, post-cinematic media regime. In their article "Against Post-cinema," Ted Nannicelli and Malcolm Turvey make a strong case against the very idea of post-cinema, which they contend involves the conflation of a technological substrate and the uses to which it might be put.[2] As I will show, they thereby introduce an important distinction or bifurcation that will ultimately help me to articulate the metabolic force of post-cinema's dividuated images, but I will first have to answer the charge that I am committing what amounts to a category error. With their distinction between what they call "material and artistic media," Nannicelli and Turvey suggest that theorists of a post-cinematic condition confuse two distinct notions of medium—analogous to the difference between the medium of oil as a substrate within which colored pigments are suspended, on the one hand, and the medium of oil painting as a set of practices, techniques, and conventions that employ that substrate to create a variety of forms on the other hand.[3] In line with this distinction, many proponents of "the post-cinema thesis" improperly equate the substrate of celluloid, along with the material apparatus of the analog camera and so on, with the medium of cinema itself.[4] On the basis of this equivocation, such critics then argue "not just that the cinema has been radically altered by digital technology, but that it has been subsumed by another medium. It has been dissolved into another medium in the digital era."[5] Pointing to observations about digital convergence and dedifferentiation made by a diverse collection of theorists—from Friedrich Kittler to Lev Manovich, André Gaudreault and Philippe Marion, D. N. Rodowick, Mary Ann Doane, and Noël Carroll, among others—Nannicelli and Turvey claim that this confusion is sufficiently widespread as to cast doubt on the idea of post-cinema in general. Against such thinkers, they maintain: "The cinema remains a distinct medium, identified and individuated in much the same way as before the digital era."[6]

Nannicelli and Turvey are right, I think, to diagnose a slippage between "material and artistic media" in many early approaches to cinema's transformation (or purported end or demise) in relation to digital technologies—including, crucially, many theorists' fixation on the question of indexicality and its effacement. It is less clear, however, that more recent discussions are equally beholden to the fallacy of "medium materialism," or the view "that an artistic medium is individuated by a material medium rather than its use."[7] Certainly, my own approach, which focuses more on the dividuation of images than the deindividuation of media, is less concerned with the convergence of film and other media into a digital "monomedium"[8]—except as such convergence might be seen to leverage a shift in the material and affective parameters of experience and action in the world today. Besides, by staking their refusal of "medium materialism" on the contrast between "materials" and "what we do with those materials—that is, . . . our artistic and appreciative practices" with respect to a given medium, Nannicelli and Turvey's critique of post-cinema, and thus their argument for the unbroken continuity of cinema, rests on the notion that the subjects of those artistic and appreciative practices (filmmakers, viewers, critics) are themselves unchanged;[9] indeed, the argument assumes an integral and stable subjectivity on the part of these actors—but this is precisely what my own approach calls into question with the appeal to Deleuze's concept of dividuality. Nevertheless, it might be objected that my notion of discorrelation still trades essentially on a confusion of material substrate and artistic or experiential form, that I have therefore failed to articulate a mechanism whereby the technical changes contributing to this discorrelation might be seen to affect our experience, and, more fundamentally, that my concept of a dividual or metabolic image ultimately constitutes a basic category error.

It is against Nannicelli and Turvey's ground-clearing rebuttal of "the post-cinema thesis" that I would like to resituate my approach, and this requires of me that I reclear the ground that they have cleared; in other words, I hope to show here not only that I am not guilty of the mistakes that they impute to proponents of a post-cinema thesis, but, more positively, that a more robust theory of post-cinematic change and mediation can be erected on the very site they have laid bare, working with the tools that they have forged in the process—in particular, by employing a modified version of the substrate/form distinction they introduce.

Let me start this process of resituation with respect to the idea that I have committed a category error. My topic is *the image* in a post-cinematic media regime—an image I have characterized as discorrelated, dividual, molecular, metabolic, and even post-perceptual. It would seem, however, that I am not talking here so much about images at all; rather, I am talking about the apparatuses and processes that are productive of images today (such as the processes, which I have written about elsewhere in this book, of motion smoothing, video compression, upscaling, and the like—processes that depend crucially on the new hardware and software of digital imagery). It is, after all, these processes that warrant the term *discorrelated*, as they take place outside the spatial and temporal dimensions of subjective perception. Likewise, the quality of "dividuality" pertains to images only by way of these processes occurring outside the realm of normal phenomenal appearance, at the microlevel of computation (according to which motion smoothing and compression are involved in dis-integrating the image as it once existed on film strips, subjecting it to digital encoding and predictive, only partial or "lossy" reconstruction during playback). Accordingly, my analysis hinges inextricably on the infrastructural or substrate level that Nannicelli and Turvey associate with "medium materialism" (and that more commonly goes by the name of technological determinism, as the technical substrate is seen to determine "artistic and appreciative practices" or experiences). And this suggests that I have misidentified the image's substrate with the image itself—a category error if there ever was one.

What, indeed, does it mean to say that an *image* is post-perceptual? In a footnote to his article "Cinema's Turing Test: Consciousness, Digitality, and Operability in *Hardcore Henry*," Chang-Min Yu makes the point most concisely in an objection that he addresses explicitly to me and my theory of post-cinematic images. He asks, rhetorically: "Since when could the audience phenomenally apprehend the inner workings of the cinematic apparatus?"[10] More generally, we might ask, how can we refer to something as an image at all if it is not perceived, if it is not constituted as a perceptual object? Isn't the notion of discorrelation itself wrongheaded in its cleaving of the image from the subject of experience?

In exposing what looks like a category error in my reasoning, Yu introduces the term *apparatus*, which can provide an alternative formulation of Nannicelli and Turvey's substrate/form distinction—one that divorces it from their overreliance on the integral, intentional subjectivities implicit in "what we do with [the] materials" of a technological substrate in "our artistic and appreciative practices." Indeed, the "apparatus theory" popular among film theorists in the 1970s articulated a way of thinking about the agencies of technological media that called the stability of the subject centrally into question.[11] Media such as the cinema were seen to invisibly consolidate and stabilize normative subjectivities—which suggests that they could also destabilize or modulate them into different forms. Since the time of its heyday, apparatus theory has fallen out of fashion because of its supposedly deterministic tendencies, and because it seemed too monolithic and insensitive to media-historical changes.

Clearly, the notion of the apparatus raises important questions about the causal relations between technologies and the subjective experiences that they mediate, and this question of causality goes straight to the heart of the objections concerning whether the dividual image is an image at all and what kind of effect it could possibly have on us as viewers.

In his article "If Film Is Dead, What Is Cinema?," John Belton reminds us that the apparatus in question here is in fact a double-sided concept, that it "combines two French terms: *l'appareil*, the basic technological machinery for recording and reproducing sound and images; and *le dispositif*, the basic psychological, social and ideological machinery that informs the spectator's relationship with the film."[12] With the notion that the substratal appareil produces the experiential object, while the dispositif "informs" the subject's relation to it, we are confronted here with a very different substrate/form configuration. As Belton points out, the "two axes of the apparatus remain in constant tension with one another, as changes in the technological machinery of the apparatus generate changes in its psychological, social and ideological function."[13] The "material medium," as Nannicelli and Turvey name it, is no longer passive, on this view, with respect to the active subjects who take it up and shape it in "artistic and appreciative practices." Instead, the dispositif is centrally involved, as Belton puts it, in "the production of subjects."[14] Curiously, given his recourse to this theory of the apparatus as a force of subjectivation, Belton follows Nannicelli and Turvey in arguing that the cinema has not been seriously transformed by the shift from an analog to a digital appareil and thus that we have not entered a post-cinematic era. As he puts it: "The cinema is a site where aesthetic machinery provides its subjects/spectators with an aesthetic experience," and at least in the form of theatrical exhibition, that aesthetic experience remains largely unchanged.[15] Movies viewed on iPads, computers, and digital television screens, by way of streaming services or optical discs and the like, clearly deviate from the cinematic experience that Belton sees as "stabilized" by "the architectural site of the theatre itself," including its basic elements of "projector/film, screen and spectator";[16] but the cinematic experience itself, centered as it is in the architecture of the theater, is unaffected by the shift from celluloid to digital projection.

I fail to see how Belton can maintain this position, except by tacitly annulling the tension between l'appareil and le dispositif, effectively abandoning the crucial notion that the apparatus is involved in producing subjects in relation to the objects of their experience, including the infrastructure that generates or supports them. In other words, and contrary to the tenets of the apparatus theory to which he appeals, Belton effectively cordons off the experiential level that he identifies with the dispositif from the infrastructural level of the appareil. Thus, he shores up the stability of the perceiving subject (along with the cinema to which it corresponds as its spectator) by shielding it from the vicissitudes of material change. But despite this inconsistency, Belton's appeal to apparatus theory can help us think about the causal forces at work in the dividual or metabolic image and its relation to the dividualization of the subject in today's control society. Above all, I would like to foreground the fact that the apparatus, on Belton's reading, has an "aesthetic" component on both sides of the infrastructure/experience divide: "The cinema is a site where *aesthetic machinery* provides its subjects/spectators with an *aesthetic experience*."[17] The category of the "aesthetic," understood in the sense of *aesthesis* or the domain of sensory experience, broadly construed, is distributed here across technological substrate and experiential form alike, thus opening the door to a reversal of the encapsulation of experience, and its cordoning off from the underlying apparatus, as it is professed by both Yu and Belton (and, in a somewhat different form, by Nannicelli and Turvey). What this suggests is that the image, or the stuff of sensory experience, is similarly located *on both sides* of the divide—or is itself *divided between them*. Is it possible to locate dividuation itself—both the dividuation of the image and of experience—here, across the divide of substrate and form?

Toward a Theory of Dividuation

In his analysis of digital compression artifacts and datamoshing practices, Jordan Schonig makes an important step in the right direction by mediating between the "flurry of theories proclaiming a large-scale ontological shift of the medium" and the "growing backlash of theorists firmly maintaining that cinematic *experiences* have remained largely unchanged."[18] Recognizing that "the technological processes that underlie digitally produced movement are almost entirely invisible,"[19] Schonig points out that there is at least "one way in which the processes of digitally produced motion *do* reveal themselves to the senses: the compression glitch."[20] In these blocky screen phenomena resulting from errors and bottlenecks in the processing of digital information, the experiential form of the image is hardly quarantined from its substrate: "The codec is wholly bound up with the specificity of individual *movements* that we see—particular gestures and facial expressions, zooms and camera movements, cuts and dissolves and wipes. As conspicuous errors of this normally invisible process, compression glitches make the codec's intelligent sorting of motion momentarily visible."[21] Furthermore, according to Schonig, as we encounter

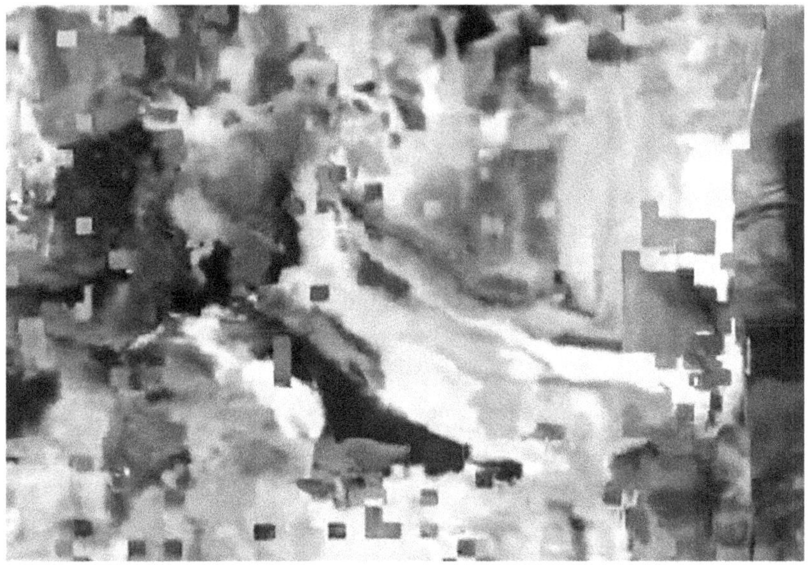

Figure 2.1. Psychedelic datamoshing and compression artifacts in Takeshi Murata's *Monster Movie* (2005).

compression errors on a regular basis—on digital cable TV, on streaming platforms, and on our computers when we play video files downloaded from the Internet—these everyday malfunctions, which transfer substrate patterns into perceptual forms, subtly transform spectatorship itself: they produce new habits and expectations on the part of the viewer, "a new phenomenological orientation toward movement on the screen."[22] Meanwhile, artistic uses of compression glitches in datamoshing practices capitalize on this reorientation or sensitization in order to focus attention on the "formal qualities" of on-screen movement:[23] "Compression glitches make us see the *qualities* and *forms* of cinematic motion as distinct from the people, things, actions, and events that such movements comprise."[24]

With his attention to these specifically digital screen phenomena, Schonig opens to view "a liminal space between the movement inscribed on screen (the realm of 'imaged motion') and the technical apparatus generating that movement"—a space between substrate and form where we might be able to locate the dividualizing forces of post-cinematic images.[25] Against both the "medium materialism" condemned by Nannicelli and Turvey as well as what we might call the "experientialism" that they and others offer as an alternative to it, Schonig's liminal space sanctions a dispersal of the image (or sensation) across substrate and form and, in the process, leverages a transformation of spectatorial subjectivity itself. The key to this transformation is the phenomenological rehabituation occasioned by repeated exposure to glitches: "As perceptible expressions of the compression algorithm's reproduction of motion, the regular disturbances of glitches create habits of anticipation, expectation, and sensitivity that unconsciously alter our intuitions about cinematic motion in the age of digital compression."[26] It is important to note that this reorientation of spectatorship is a direct result of the dividuality of post-cinematic images—their predictive, nonpunctual presence and dis-integrity at the algorithmic level manifesting itself on-screen in momentary hesitations, sudden skips, and visual hiccups; the temporal comportment of the spectating subject (the subject's "internal time-consciousness," as Husserl puts it) is thereby retuned or modulated in accordance with these disturbances in the external temporal flow of the moving images (the "temporal object," which, like Husserl's example of a melody, is not just encountered *in* time but is an object composed essentially *of* time).[27] It is equally important to note, further, that the causality involved in this transformation is not linear and positivistic—not a direct translation of material processes into psychic ones; it is not, in short, the vulgar sort of determinism that "experientialists" impute to "medium materialists" and that is enshrined in Yu's rhetorical question: "Since when could the audience phenomenally apprehend the inner workings of the cinematic apparatus?"[28] Rather, as an accrual over time of retentional-protentional patterns or dispositions, operating at an "unconscious" (or prepersonal) level of experience, this transformation involves a complex causal chain of mediations that takes us definitively outside the personalist framework of "our artistic and appreciative practices"—outside, even, of *any* constituted subjectivity that might be laid at the foundation of an experientialist critique of post-cinema.

Schonig's analysis of compression artifacts thus opens the door to a sweeping reorientation of post-cinematic subjectivity—one that connects the dividuation of the image as a technical process to the dividuality of experience in today's screen- and media-saturated control society more generally. And it does so, importantly, without assuming the stability or integrity either of phenomenological subjects or of the objects of their perception; instead it situates the image's operative force at the level of embodied affect. Glitches can trigger ways of viewing that disorient volitional attention, refocusing spectatorial awareness at a level that hovers between the diegetic/representational level of characters, objects, figures, and so on, and an extradiegetic level where movement is formally abstracted from those objects, appearing simply as phenomena of the concrete screen that interprets digital processes for vision. In this respect, compression glitches resemble the simulated lens flares that, as I have argued in chapter 1, confuse diegetic and nondiegetic planes and thus complicate the viewing subject's perceptual comportment with respect to the screen. Glitches thus "trigger a sensitivity to the compressed moving image's technological volatility," even at "moment[s] when such formal magnitude would seem incongruous with narrative intensity."[29] A "high-bitrate tracking shot of Scottie and Judy walking through the park" in Hitchcock's *Vertigo* might represent "a moment of relative tranquility and ease in the diegesis, but as a screen phenomenon it may pinch [a] nerve of movement-sensitivity. The feeling particular to that affective pinch is what Bergson would have called a *qualitative intensity*. The magnitude of movement is not *measured* by the spectator but immediately felt as an intensity."[30] Accordingly, movement is apprehended not in terms of a clearly individuated form or object, but as a more diffuse or dividual force. This "sensitivity to the magnitude of movement *hovers over* or *alongside* my narrative engagement with the moving image rather than interrupts it," thus relaxing or deindividuating focal subjectivity as well.[31]

Dividuality is consequently the key to the habituation of such affects, whereby spectatorial subjectivity is transformed at the level of an embodied rather than cognitive relation to the glitch. At stake, in other words, is an "affective attunement" (*Stimmung*, in Heidegger's vocabulary) between subjects and objects at the level of environmental materiality—the materiality of the prepersonal body that accrues habit and prereflectively orients perception and action in advance of volition.[32] Clarifying that "a sensitivity to the magnitude of movement in the age of digital compression doesn't imply the viewer's *conscious* awareness of a technology's novelty,"[33] Schonig describes the process of mutual attunement in the following terms: "Because glitches are also expressions of the compression algorithm's engagement with the formal particularities of its moving image text, getting used to glitches also entails getting used to—i.e. becoming accustomed to, at home with—the ways in which they are expressive of the codec's live processing of movement on screen. For Merleau-Ponty, 'to *get used to* a hat, a car or a stick is to be transplanted into them . . . to incorporate them into the bulk of our own body.'"[34] Despite the opposition commonly perceived between Bergsonian metaphysics and phenomenology (following largely from Deleuze's remarks in *Cinema 1* and *Cinema 2*),[35] on this point they are in agreement: Merleau-Ponty, not unlike Bergson, conceives the body as an affective interface, which is not only capable of mediating subject and object (or stimulus and response) but which, more fundamentally, establishes a transductive relation at the heart of the enworlded experience out of which subjects and objects first emerge and are individuated. Merleau-Ponty speaks of a "*pre-objective view*" that characterizes the primordial (equally pre-subjective) state of embodiment: "Prior to stimuli and sensory contents, we must recognize a kind of inner diaphragm which determines, infinitely more than they do, what our reflexes and perceptions will be able to aim at in the world, the area of our possible operations, the scope of our life."[36] The lived body, for Merleau-Ponty, is fundamentally a dividual rather than individual body, and it is on this basis that dividual images proximally affect spectators: at a level of dividualized, prepersonal embodied experience.

As Schonig points out, however, this way of thinking about the material impact of digital images necessarily raises problems for the definition of "experience" as it is deployed in the ontological-versus-experiential framework against which he situates his intervention. He writes:

> Compression glitches are meant to be overlooked. Digital compression, like many of the digital formats of production and exhibition, seek[s] to replace [its] analog predecessors quietly and discreetly. Discarding aspects of the image that are by definition inaccessible to the human sensorium, from a peripheral range of light and color values to the pixels that barely change in a static background, codecs factually alter what we perceive while remaining more or less invisible. This, of course, is part of the reason why the project of theorizing the "experience" of digital cinema is such embattled terrain. For as much as computer-generated imagery has garnered claims about the return to medium-sensitivity and the "cinema of attractions," far subtler perceptual shifts ushered by digital technology have occurred in the *background* of spectatorial experience.[37]

In this important passage, Schonig is talking about the processes of "perceptual coding," according to which compression algorithms encode and decode audiovisual information in such a way as to remove as much extraneous data as possible, thereby optimizing playback for narrow bandwidths while minimizing noticeable reductions in quality.[38] Optimization is thereby defined in terms of a balance between the capacities and demands of a nonhuman system (computational machinery, network connections, etc.) and those of a human one (specifically, the abilities and limitations of a perceiving subject). Accordingly, the aesthetic object is divided among the levels of substrate and experiential form, but in a way that will ideally not produce differences noticeable enough to enter into conscious experience. Such background processes speak directly to the dividualization of experience and its objects, which can only be registered affectively. The prepersonal body, as we have seen, then serves as a sort of battery where these diffuse material impacts are stored, their inscription in a liminal space between objective substrate and subjective form giving rise to embodied habits or orientations.

Do these unperceived impacts belong to the realm of "experience"? Or do they belong instead to the realm of the "substrate"? As Schonig points out, "When it comes to theorizing cinematic technology, the distinctions between 'ontological' and 'phenomenological' approaches are not clear because there is little agreement upon what in fact counts as a datum of *experience*."[39] As I have been trying to show here, Schonig lays the groundwork for a theory of the embodied force of dividual images that inherently calls into question the binaries of ontological/phenomenological or substrate/form. Or, rather, the picture that emerges here is one in which these distinctions are rendered *problematic*—but *not* rendered superfluous—*by the force of dividual images themselves*.

But if it is true that Schonig lays this groundwork, he nevertheless stops short of embracing all of its consequences for a post-perceptual form of mediation, instead limiting the scope of his intervention in decisive ways. He writes: "One of my reasons for examining compression glitches is precisely because they are digital artifacts relegated to this background of experience—i.e. they are functionally invisible—and yet they are undeniably *visible phenomena*."[40] With this insistence on their "undeniably visible" nature, Schonig restricts his analysis to a small subset of the impacts that compressed images might, in the framework of the body subject to affective habituation and reorientation, be seen to have. To be clear, I find that this limitation, at least initially, makes perfect sense from a purely methodological point of view. Argumentatively, that is, it strikes me as very judicious to start with a phenomenon, such as the compression glitch, where an error at the level of the technological substrate announces itself in perceptual form, and from there to extrapolate toward the broader embodied impacts of subperceptual processes (as I have begun doing in my elaboration of cues and connections with Bergsonian affect, Heideggerian *Stimmung*, and Merleau-Pontean embodiment). Following these lines, we might move from the technical processes of *perceptual coding* on to a broader sociotechnical *coding of perception* itself, thus recognizing the dividual image's impact on prepersonal embodiment as a vector of control in reorienting contemporary subjectivity. But Schonig shies away from this line of thinking, and his point about glitches as visible phenomena must be taken not merely as a methodological consideration but as marking a phenomenological limit to the scope of his investigation, as becomes clear in subsequent moments of his analysis.

Ultimately, that is, Schonig turns back at the last minute and attempts to contain the transformative force of post-cinema's dividuated images by limiting it to the domain of perception. He warns of "a return to modes of thinking that privilege depths over surfaces, material knowledge over phenomenological experience"—approaches, in short, that privilege substrate over form.[41] He points out what he takes to be an ever more common confusion between these levels as "our ever-increasing understanding of the technological depths of digital substrates has begun to shape and determine our accounts of their surfaces," such that we imagine we *see* the effects of digital processing, that we *perceive* the workings of compression and the like directly.[42] Schonig is of course right to warn against this fallacy of the substrate, which as he points out implies a fallacious account of experience as well. But instead of returning to the resources of the preperceptual body and its affects, which he already introduced as a crucial middle way that would avoid these complementary dangers by way of transductive dividuality, he instead doubles down on the individuation of experiential objects. "The solution to this problem need not require turning away from technology altogether in order to inoculate our experience from our own false attributions of technological artifacts. Instead, it requires that we more carefully select what it is in our experience of 'digital cinema' that *counts* as an apparition of a technological process."[43] This notion of *counting as an apparition* contrasts markedly with Schonig's earlier comments about the nonconscious, affective registration of compression as intensity: "As with affective states, aesthetic feelings, muscular efforts, or sensations of pressure and heat, movement-sensitivity is felt in terms of greater or lesser magnitudes *despite being uncountable* or unavailable to quantitative measure."[44] Thus, with the question of "what *counts* as an apparition of a technological process," Schonig introduces a criterion of perceptual objecthood which reins in the presubjective dividuality and broad environmental impact that I see at work in post-cinematic images (and that Schonig himself enables us to see through the lens of prepersonal embodiment). This reversal, from the *uncountable* to the *countable apparition,* turns the impact of such images into a local, punctual event rather than a climatic, *Stimmungs*-oriented one.

Further confining the scope of his study, which "supplies neither a complete phenomenology of 'digital cinema' nor of 'digitally compressed video,'" Schonig restricts the transformative impact of the dividuated image: "Compression glitches are an admittedly *small* part of cinema spectatorship, even of home viewing; they are both phenomenologically marginal and quite literally brief and sporadic."[45] This smallness of scope is related not only to methodological concerns but also to more fundamentally ontological ones: Schonig essentially reconceives what his object is, effectively demanding that it be individuated phenomenologically, not diffusely dividual, in order to count as an image at all. He writes: "Compression glitches are discrete, *visible* events that bear a direct relation to their digital substrate."[46] While Schonig emphasizes the glitches' visibility, it is the discrete object-nature that he imputes to them that strikes me as more problematic here. Accordingly, the "convergence of the technological and the phenomenological" that characterizes the compression glitch for Schonig and that relegates it to "this small aspect of spectatorship" is a *correlative* relation that brings the (usually invisible) substrate in line with a constituted subject's perceptual experience of it.[47] Schonig thus moves from the impasse of substrate-versus-form (or ontology-versus-phenomenology, technology-versus-experience), whereby it is unclear how the former term could have *any* bearing on the latter, to a phenomenological correlation or agreement between them: the substrate becomes visible *as a perceptual object* in the glitch. But this correlative move not only unduly limits the scope of Schonig's theory; it also undercuts the radically transformative potential of discorrelation uncovered in the affective, embodied conception of the dividual image provided earlier. This recorrelation is therefore quite unnecessary, given the resources of intensity, habituation, and the attunement of temporal experience to the vicissitudes of dividual temporal objects.

Substrate/Form: Intensity, Habit, Temporality

In order to reclaim these resources for a theory of discorrelation and the broadly environmental impact of dividual images, I would like to consolidate a model of substrate/form relations that avoids both the oppositional view that posits the impossibility of *any* communication between the two levels (such as we find in Nannicelli and Turvey, Belton, and Yu), as well as the correlational view that brings them firmly into line with one another (as adopted ultimately by Schonig).[48] For this purpose, I turn to Niklas Luhmann's abstract concept of "mediality" as a model for conceiving a dynamic *interplay* between substrate and form that will help us to maintain a distinctly discorrelationist view while refocusing the temporal implications of dividual images' diffuse but materially robust impact on experience.[49]

Mediality, for Luhmann, names not a particular apparatus but the *relation* between some substrate and the forms that can be constituted out of it. Accordingly, this way of thinking about mediality avoids the identification of medium with substrate (as in the reductive "medium materialism" that Nannicelli and Turvey warn against) from the very outset. And because, according to Luhmann, substrate and form consist of the same basic elements—the same "stuff," so to speak—this notion of mediality will not support the oppositional view whereby the technological or ontological realm is separated by an unbreachable gulf from a securely encapsulated phenomenological realm of experience. The difference between substrate and form is instead not a difference of kind but of organization: a substrate consists of a "loose coupling" of elements, a relatively chaotic or unordered mass of particles, while forms emerge out of the substrate as the "tight" or strict couplings or combinations of the same elements. For example, more or less randomly distributed air molecules can be reordered into the forms of wave patterns by a loudspeaker; the tones that present themselves as subjectively perceivable are themselves a substrate out of which music can be formed. There is a recursive linking among media, such that the forms of one substrate come to constitute a higher-order substrate for other forms. Letters are a substrate for the forms of words, words a substrate for sentences, sentences a substrate for larger textual forms, and so on. Thus, the substrate/form distinction is strictly relative: a medial substrate exists only in relation to the forms that it enables, and vice versa. A medium, on this view, is not objectively individuated as a thing-in-itself; rather, it is related to an observer or system as "the operative deployment of the *difference* of medial substrate and form."[50]

The role of difference in this definition of mediality is crucial to the task of thinking dividuation—both of images and of experience—across the substrate/form divide. The Luhmannian conception of loose versus tight couplings places the same materials—such as the aesthetic materials at stake in images—on both sides of the divide. Formally, this conception is capable of accommodating Belton's view of "the cinema [as] a site where *aesthetic machinery* provides its subjects/spectators with an *aesthetic experience*," which I have highlighted as an opening where we might begin theorizing the causal force of dividual images, while also preserving the tension between l'appareil and le dispositif that Belton invokes but quickly abandons.[51] That is, while the difference of loose and tight couplings decisively undercuts the strictly oppositional paradigm, whereby experience is ensconced behind a membrane impermeable to the image's technological substrate, Luhmann's view of media does not thereby revert to a correlative identification of substrate and form, as in Schonig's (eventual) approach to compression glitches. Instead, difference remains as an essential and irreducible tension, thus providing a basis for thinking dividuality across the substrate/form divide. As I have put it elsewhere: "Luhmann's differential media concept thus bears a special relation to Gregory Bateson's famous definition of information as a 'difference that makes a difference.' Mediality is not just any difference but, we might say, the difference that makes the differences that make a difference—an information-generating and, more fundamentally, a system-structuring difference that orients by means of defining the objects and structures that can count for a system, as well as specifying the elements of their composure."[52]

Accordingly, the subjectivizing power of the dispositif, which produces its subject in relation not only to image-objects but also to the infrastructural substrate that supports them, is built into this conception as essential to it. For ultimately at stake in this definition of media is an environmental agency and its relation to systems as such. Luhmann suggests at one point that his model of substrate/form provides an "alternative formulation" of the environment/system distinction, thus implying that the interplay simply cannot be stabilized with reference to a subject, whose integrity is centrally at stake in the formation called "system."[53] A nonpositivistic causality is implied: a transductive relation where the system or observer referenced in the definition of mediality as "the operative deployment" of the substrate/form difference does not transcendentally stabilize but is itself constituted in relation to the interplay of these levels. In other words, it is precisely the subject (and its objects), in this case the subjectivity of a spectator, that is up for grabs at the intersection of substrate and form. Individuation follows from and does not precede the circulation of dividual materials. Hence we are dealing here with the broadly environmental or metabolic processes that I have associated with discorrelated images.

Against the subjectivistic experientialism considered earlier, experience is thus not "on the side" of form, as opposed to a technological substrate on "the other side"; rather, experience is precisely that which is at issue in the difference between substrate and form. It is the ear (or the tympanic membrane) which is at stake in the articulation and disarticulation of sound waves; and it is the "ear" (or the aesthetic sensibilities) of the listening subject that is at stake in the articulation and disarticulation of music. What Luhmann refers to as the observer need not be a fully formed subject; in Peircean semiotics, it is called the "interpretant."[54] The Luhmannian view, which emphasizes that substrate/form relations are always in flux, thus decenters focused perceptual experience; exchanges between substrate and form express themselves less as perceptual objects than as intensities of temporal synchronization. The ear's tympanic membrane resonates in sync with the sound waves in the air; the listener's educated "ear" is entrained by the sonic forms of music. This refocusing of experiential intensity thus dislocates static conceptions of subjectivity (essentially spatialized conceptions that oppose subjects, dualistically, to their objects), thereby leveraging the ongoing modulation of subjectivity or experience, much like the modulation at stake in Deleuze's control society. Through the repeated flux of formation and deformation, an ear or an eye becomes susceptible to training, a body becomes susceptible to habituation, and a mind becomes susceptible to education. Mediality is thereby reconfigured from a passive channel between fixed subjects and objects to become instead the site of affective attunements.

Emerging out of this perspective, as we see, is an essential reference to temporality. Mediality—as the site of interplay, flux, modulation, and attunement—is conceived as thoroughly processual: it is realized as the *process* of the coupling and decoupling of forms, which emerge from and return back into a substratal pool of disarticulation.[55] These processes constitute patterns and rhythms that define nothing less than the temporality or metabolism of a system. As irreducibly temporal formations, media in a sense "give" time to the structured organisms, psyches, and social units at stake in the formation of systems. Conceived along these lines, the metabolic agency of post-cinema's dividual images is expressed in terms of a modulation of (prepersonal) temporality itself. And while this view is apparently at odds with our concept of what an image is—for example, the notion that it is a spatial-figural visual object rather than a primarily temporal vector—a reconceptualization of images as temporal is in fact necessary in order to account for their circulation in today's media.

The history of electronic images, in television, video cameras, and now computational systems, is a history of despatialization, as the photographic image was not only decomposed into smaller spatial units (dots and pixels), but recalculated and reconfigured as a flux of frequencies—such as the frequency of phosphor illuminations by electron beams tracing alternating scan lines on the screens of cathode-ray tube televisions. Protocols such as NTSC and PAL redefined the image in terms of a subperceptual flux: the European PAL system temporalizes the image at the rate of 25 interlaced frames of video per second, the NTSC system at the rate of 29.97 frames. But far from simply accelerating the frame rate of cinematic images, these electronic frames are fundamentally incomparable to the 24 frames per second of sound-era cinema. Interlaced video images are radically dividual in the sense that they are never fully present as integral units on the screen; instead, they are drawn by way of two "fields," each consisting of several hundred scan lines, which are illuminated alternately: first all the even-numbered lines are consecutively illuminated, then all the odd-numbered ones. In the PAL system, which has 625 scan lines (only 576 of which are visible), this means that images do not appear as 25 full (or "cinematic") frames per second but are instead dividuated at a frequency of 50 Hertz—or 50 "fields" of 312.5 lines each per second, where each line is traversed at a speed of 64 microseconds.[56] The afterglow of the phosphor coating activated at this rate makes the image appear more or less complete, but due to the phosphor's short luminescence decay time, as well as the fact that the first field of the next frame will be drawn while the second field of the last frame is still visible, the image on the CRT screen is never stable or integrally individuated. The interlaced image, as a subperceptual "time-image," is a fundamentally dividuated image.[57] (Interestingly, in Germany, where the PAL, or Phase Alternating Line, system was developed, the fifty "fields" of the images are referred to as *Halbbilder*, or "half-images"—a term that already gestures toward the dividuation of the system's images. It is interesting to note, however, that PAL's inventor, Walter Bruch, when asked why he didn't name the system after himself, answered that no one would want to buy a *Bruchsystem*, as *Bruch* means "break" and would suggest a *broken system*.[58] There would have been an elegance in the name, however, in that the "break" could also refer to the "line breaks" that signal the end of a scan line, as well as the dividuation of the image more generally: indeed, if the interlaced "fields" had been called not *Halbbilder* but *Bruchbilder*, the notion of the dividuated image might have offered itself as a translation.)

Luhmann's concept of substrate/form relations accounts perfectly for such images, which are formed according to precise temporal operations—or "time-critical processes," as Wolfgang Ernst calls them—that tightly couple the elements (red, green, and blue phosphor dots or pixel strips) that compose the visible form of the image.[59] Indeed, as we have seen, the image, which is no longer ever fully and singly "present," fundamentally *is* the temporal flux or frequency that measures substrate/form exchanges. It is important to note, however, that such frequencies are measured only by the technical system, not by the viewer, for whom the impact is subperceptual and immune to subjective measure; as Schonig says in the context of compression glitches, this "movement is not *measured* by the spectator but immediately felt as an intensity."[60] Nevertheless, the viewer does of course *see images*, but this fact must be seen as a by-product of the temporalization of the image (even if such perception was the original and ultimate goal that led engineers to temporalize the image in this way—that is, according to PAL, NTSC, and other protocols—in the first place). Thus, the viewer's body must essentially resonate with the frequencies of the electronic image, be affectively attuned to it in order for perception to take place; and indeed, many design decisions (concerning refresh rate, phosphor persistence, screen resolution, and the like) were made with the temporalities of bodily sensitivities in mind.

Temporalization and Control

But this reconceptualization of the image in terms of temporality is hardly inconsequential, as it opens the concept of "image" up to forms that would not be tuned thus to human perception. Indeed, by drawing on Luhmann's abstract theory of mediality, we are compelled to reconceive the image quite apart from its visible or perceptible manifestations. This consequence will no doubt strike many readers as unacceptable, a veritable reductio ad absurdum. On the contrary, however, I claim this consequence precisely as a strength of the theory, in that it allows us to account for the embodied impact of imaging processes that do not have visible manifestations.

What I have in mind here is not a philosophical flight of fancy; instead, it concerns real-world applications that are very real, very concrete, and increasingly widespread. Media artist Trevor Paglen has termed these "invisible images"—images that circulate between machines, unseen by human eyes, in computer vision systems and artificial intelligence applications, in devices and platforms ranging from smartphones to satellites, from automatic license plate readers to social media networks.[61] As Paglen puts it: "Over the last decade or so, something dramatic has happened. Visual culture has changed form. It has become detached from human eyes and has largely become invisible. Human visual culture has become a special case of vision, an exception to the rule. The overwhelming majority of images are now made by machines for other machines, with humans rarely in the loop. The advent of machine-to-machine seeing has been barely noticed at large, and poorly understood by those of us who've begun to notice the tectonic shift invisibly taking place before our very eyes."[62] Whether captured by a camera or generated synthetically, such "detached" or radically discorrelated—literally post-perceptual—images are not produced for human consumption, but many of them are crucially involved in processes that are of no small concern to us: surveillance, logistics, industrial production, and the automation of various other fields that have a direct bearing on our sociopolitical and spatiotemporal situations. In Paglen's words: "The landscape of invisible images and machine vision is becoming evermore active. Its continued expansion is starting to have profound effects on human life, eclipsing even the rise of mass culture in the mid 20th century. Images have begun to intervene in everyday life, their functions changing from representation and mediation, to activations, operations, and enforcement. Invisible images are actively watching us, poking and prodding, guiding our movements, inflicting pain and inducing pleasure. But all of this is hard to see."[63]

Even if they are invisible, such images are undeniably real and materially consequential—they can be matters, literally, of life and death. Consider, for example, the invisible images that a self-driving car generates (with a set of smart cameras, radar, and Light Detection and Ranging, or LIDAR, systems) and then processes (starting in-camera, applying geometrical transformations, video compression, and edge detection preprocessing before streaming the signals to other processing units), all without the intervention of a human perceiver.[64] Indeed, it is the human passenger whose continued existence, much less perception, is precisely at stake in these microtemporal operations. Or consider the very similar processes taking place in autonomous military drones, where the automated capture and analysis of invisible images is directed not toward the preservation but the annihilation of life. Crucial to these operations is the discorrelated image, the dis-integrity and dividuality of which is a function of its ever-accelerating temporalization, and vice versa. In such forms, post-cinematic images become vectors of control at the broadest scale.

Again, I am drawn to Luhmann's concept of mediality because it enables us to account for such processes in which discorrelation and dividuality, far from marking the impossibility of having an impact on human experience, are instead coupled with clear and sweeping consequences, hence aligning dividuated images with the modulating processes of Deleuze's control society. But it is not just the paradoxically spectacular-yet-invisible images of drone warfare and expensive cars that play a role here. In between the CRT's still relatively perceptible images and the strictly invisible images of neural nets, we are hailed everywhere today by digital screens and their dividual images. These too, I suggest, are part of the mundane machinery of control. Recognizing them as such requires that we understand the interplay of preperceptual intensity, temporal synchronization, and embodied habituation at work in the images that circulate on the majority of our screens today: whether flat-screen TVs, LCD computer monitors, or handheld devices like tablets and smartphones. Seeing them in this light, we can more fully appreciate the prepersonal impact that the dividualities of computationally processed images, as a matter of their sheer environmental presence and quite apart from their drawing attention to themselves as individuated perceptual objects, can have on us. Again, situating dividuation precisely at the difference of substrate and form, rather than sacrificing this difference to either an oppositional or a correlative model that would cordon off technological operations from experience or raise them up to the level of perception, will allow us to see dividuated images as agents of everyday control: vectors of temporal modulation operating at the level of environmental metabolism rather than perception or cognition.

As in the case of the interlaced video image on the CRT, the interplay of substrate and form in a digital display device implies new forms of temporality, only further discorrelated from human subjectivity—which is selectively, optionally, and if at all, then only *temporarily* given access to the new images. According to Paglen:

> What's truly revolutionary about the advent of digital images is the fact that they are fundamentally machine-readable: they can only be seen by humans in special circumstances and for short periods of time. A photograph shot on a phone creates a machine-readable file that does not reflect light in such a way as to be perceptible to a human eye. A secondary application, like a software-based photo viewer paired with a liquid crystal display and backlight may create something that a human can look at, but the image only appears to human eyes temporarily before reverting back to its immaterial machine form when the phone is put away or the display is turned off.[65]

The temporary appearance of the image is a consequence of the specific temporality of an image which, in principle, could remain invisible to the human; this temporality is determined by the interplay of substrate and form (the process by which the image "appears" briefly before "reverting back" to the invisible substrate). The time that is proper to such images is the superfast time of computational microtemporality, wholly discorrelated from the temporal window of human perception. To become visible, the image must be brought inside that window through mechanisms (LCDs, LEDs, etc.) that correspond to our embodied receptivity. The point, however, is that the image is—at the outset, and in principle—invisible due to the temporal mismatch between computational and human temporal processing; visibility is optional and ancillary with respect to the more fundamental state of invisibility.

Paglen emphasizes, however, that even when such images remain invisible, they are capable of shaping or modulating experience, effectively setting the parameters for it as the environment within which we live. For example, Facebook and Instagram present themselves as places to share photos with friends and family, suggestively offering "albums" in which to store related images (photos from your last vacation, for example). But, as Paglen shows, "the analogy is deeply misleading": "When you put an image on Facebook or other social media, you're feeding an array of immensely powerful artificial intelligence systems information about how to identify people and how to recognize places and objects, habits and preferences, race, class, and gender identifications, economic statuses, and much more."[66] In other words, the invisible substrate is where the action's really at, while human perception is secondary at best. "Regardless of whether a human subject actually sees any of the 2 billion photographs uploaded daily to Facebook-controlled platforms, the photographs on social media are scrutinized by neural networks with a degree of attention that would make even the most steadfast art historian blush. Facebook's 'DeepFace' algorithm, developed in 2014 and deployed in 2015, produces three-dimensional abstractions of individuals' faces and uses a neural network that achieves over 97 percent accuracy at identifying individuals—a percentage comparable to what a human can achieve, ignoring for a second that no human can recall the faces of billions of people."[67]

Meanwhile, the consequences of this substratal action can be very concrete:

> As governments seek out new sources of revenue in an era of downsizing, and as capital searches out new domains of everyday life to bring into its sphere, the ability to use automated imaging and sensing to extract wealth from smaller and smaller slices of everyday life is irresistible. It's easy to imagine, for example, an AI algorithm on Facebook noticing an underage woman drinking beer in a photograph from a party. That information is sent to the woman's auto insurance provider, who subscribes to a Facebook program designed to provide this kind of data to credit agencies, health insurers, advertisers, tax officials, and the police. Her auto insurance premium is adjusted accordingly. A second algorithm combs through her past looking for similar misbehavior that the parent company might profit from. In the classical world of human-human visual culture, the photograph responsible for so much trouble would have been consigned to a shoebox to collect dust and be forgotten. In the machine-machine visual landscape the photograph never goes away. It becomes an active participant in the modulations of her life, with long-term consequences.[68]

I have quoted at length from Paglen's descriptions of this landscape of invisible images because they get at something essential about the contemporary interplay between substrate and form—that is, the processes of flux that "give" time today to humans (and, given the planetary reach of our technologies, possibly to life on Earth more generally). The temporalization and dividuation of contemporary images, as we see, gives rise to metabolic forces that are reshaping the very pathways of exchange (input/output, perception/action, consumption/production, digestion/excretion, etc.) within the general ecology of contemporary biotechnical existence.

And while all of this may seem quite distant from the act of watching movies, for example, it is increasingly hard to draw a line: when we stream videos from Netflix, Amazon Prime, Hulu, or YouTube, for example, we are providing valuable information to these companies that, while it may not be used against us in the way that Paglen imagines above, will certainly be monetized and recycled back into the larger ecology. This might be in the form of paid advertisements, recommendations for other videos that will keep us in the circuits of attention and invisible data-exchange, or even for the purposes of content-generation: Netflix has famously used viewing information to make decisions about original content production and funding, while YouTube infamously enabled a perverse ecology of algorithmically generated content directed at young, often preverbal children locked into the "Up Next" autoplay circuit on their parents' iPads—with videos featuring their favorite cartoon characters being tortured, vomiting, or showing up in creepy situations wholly inappropriate for the target audience.[69] Meanwhile, even apparently non-networked video consumption is hard to keep out of these circuits: our smart TVs, Blu-ray players, and videogame consoles relay information back to their parent companies about the type of content we make visible on our screens, whether they come from cable TV, from an optical disc, or stored on an external hard drive. Here again we see that the visible forms of digital images are just the tip of the iceberg and that their invisible substrates implicate them in diffuse and far-reaching ecologies of experience and control.[70]

Above all, what emerges in this view is that, across scales, the dividuation of the image is bound up with the dividuation of experience. Most centrally at stake in these operations, in the interplay and flux of substrate and form, is temporalization or the modulation of time itself. The image today is not a primarily visible object but an always-specific *binding of time*, whether in relation to human perception or computational microtemporality. Dividualization is itself a fundamentally temporal control process, concerned with an ever more fine-grained division of time and the operationalization of the smallest available temporal units. Paglen refers to "the ability to use automated imaging and sensing to extract wealth from smaller and smaller slices of everyday life," or again: "Smaller and smaller moments of human life are being transformed into capital."[71] My point about dividuated images is that they are crucial mediators of this process, as they serve to bind human attention and time more generally to the microtemporal circuits of the planetary control systems that would seem to have us locked into a global death spiral, on a collision course with extinction. Surprisingly, then, confronting this horizon of a future without future may require us to step back from specifically futuristic fantasies of terraforming Mars and the like, and instead to focus on the more mundane present of watching movies. For it is here, on these screens, that the future is being plotted in increasingly anticipatory processes that materially displace the perceptual present and seek in advance to format the subject of experience, to modulate subjectivity by means of the molecular, metabolic forces that are activated when we press PLAY.

Screen Time

In chapter 2, I sought to articulate the theoretical resources that would allow us to trace the move from the individual image of the filmstrip (and the corresponding integral image in the mind of a viewing subject) to the disintegration and becoming post-perceptual of the image in post-cinema, while also identifying such an image's agency and force with respect to processes of subjectivation. The analysis points, as we have seen, in two directions at once: both inward—toward smaller and smaller dividuations of time (what might be called an *intensive* trajectory)—and outward—toward larger and larger fields of influence (an *extensive* trajectory). The middle ground or mesolevel of individual experience, in other words, is inextricably involved—partly, and indeed crucially, by force of contemporary images—in the microlevel of computational processing as well as the macrolevel of ecological mediation. With respect to images, dividuation thus reveals itself not as a merely technical process of pixelization or the decomposition of photograms into digital information, but as a process by which subjective experience can be sliced or dissolved into smaller and smaller units and inserted into the larger ecologies of a now globally mediated experience. The micro and the macro are short-circuited, so to speak; the linchpin of this operation, I have argued, is the dividual image's modulation of time. Accordingly, it behooves us at this point to undertake a more detailed investigation of the mechanisms and the aesthetic forms of contemporary temporalization: to take seriously the question of *screen time*. How, concretely, is time modulated in post-cinema? In order to think through the issues involved in this question, we need to consider the connections—and above all the temporal interchanges—between the technical substrates and the aesthetic forms of discorrelated images. As we shall see, at stake in these interchanges, or in the temporalities that emerge in the process of formation and deformation of images from their contemporary substrates, is nothing less than the time of human life itself—the modulation and transformation of "inner sense" or "self-affection" (in Kant's terminology) or of "internal time-consciousness" (as Husserl puts it)—in a post-cinematic world.

The term *screen time* calls to mind attempts by parents to regulate their children's use of screen-based media, especially mobile devices such as smartphones and tablets; the term has recently been appropriated by Apple, whose Screen Time function (introduced in 2018 as part of their mobile operating system iOS 12) allows users to monitor and limit access to apps during certain times of day or after a given period of use. As Apple puts it: "Screen Time . . . lets you know how much time you and your kids spend on apps, websites, and more. This way, you can make more informed decisions about how you use your devices, and set limits if you'd like to."[1] Clearly, this system of automated reports, restrictions, and time-based access is right at home in Deleuze's control society. And while the notion of screen time (and its regulation via Screen Time) seems to concern rather gross temporalities, and hence the structuration of time on the part of fully formed subjects (or individuals rather than dividuals), the worries that motivate such efforts implicitly acknowledge a radically transformative impact on subjects: screen images, in direct relation to the time that they occupy our experience, can shape who we are, for example "warping" our subjectivities by implicating us in addictive behaviors. Screen time thus links the power of images, as an explicitly temporal force, with the ethical field of education in the sense of *Bildung*—or the "formation" of the subject. Seen in this way, struggles and concerns over screen time situate subjectivity as a contingent and moldable formation that emerges from the temporal exchanges of (computational) substrates and (image) forms. Significantly, this implicit view converges with Luhmann's view of "the child as the medium of education,"[2] according to which the object of education—the formation of the child's subjectivity—is precisely the modulation of "the operative deployment of the *difference* of medial substrate and form."[3] Screen time, in other words, coincides in important ways with the temporalization of experience that gives shape to who one eventually becomes.

By invoking the concept of screen time, I wish not only to foreground the ethical stakes of post-cinematic images, but also to gesture toward the futural dimension involved in them: their role in shaping future subjects and future experiences. As we shall see, it is precisely the operationalization of this futural or predictive orientation that most centrally distinguishes post-cinematic images from cinematic ones. In this respect, post-cinematic media conform to Lev Manovich's claim about what he calls "new media" and its difference from older or "modern media": "New media follows, or actually runs ahead of, a quite different logic of post-industrial society—that of individual customization, rather than mass standardization."[4] The notion of "customization," like related terms such as "personalization," is clearly relevant to the discussion of control, and it is this dimension of new media that has often been heralded in more utopian views: namely, that new media (especially following the advent of Web 2.0) provide people with content that is tailored to their interests, more relevant to them, and that therefore enhances individuality rather than enforcing the standardization of taste and experience, as was the case under the more limited mass media.

The flip side, however, is the legitimate concern that personalization is really a process of shaping the person—a fear that is implicit, as we have seen, in discussions of screen time, and that is in fact supported by a systems-theoretical view of education or of subjects' relations to the temporalities of substrate/form interchanges more generally. In any case, Manovich's statement connects these concerns with an interesting temporal claim: that new media "actually runs ahead of" the logic of personalization that it seems to follow. It is especially this anticipatory dimension, closely linked to the temporal dynamics of subjectivation, that I would like to pursue here and to connect explicitly to the screen phenomena of digital images. My means of approach will be by way of narrowing in from larger to smaller temporal scales—from the relatively long circuits of prediction and anticipation at work in "personalized" video platforms like Netflix, to increasingly shorter circuits involved in lower-level operations of streaming, buffering, compression, and real-time processing. Connecting these technical processes with aesthetic forms that problematize the various temporal scales, we will see how images today anticipate the subjects who perceive them, how our screen time is an emphatically ecstatic time in which we become who we will have been.

Customized Futures

How do discorrelated images "actually run ahead of" their would-be (or will-be) perceivers, and how does this futurity work, concretely, to shape the subject of perception? In "Catered to Your Future Self: Netflix's 'Predictive Personalization' and the Mathematization of Taste," Neta Alexander addresses this imbrication of predictive futurity and the customization of perceptual experience in terms of Netflix's algorithmic recommendation system.[5] As she shows, this system enlists data mining and statistical analysis in order to effect a "commodification of the eye"—effectively, the control of experience—in a way that subjects the aesthetic category of "taste" to a sort of digital automation that would surely make Kant roll over in his grave.[6]

Instantiating the broader "shift from a mass economy into a niche market of personalized services,"[7] Netflix's "Recommended for You" feature pretends to learn one's preferences based on viewing habits and to suggest content that one might like to see—magically reading our minds, in effect, to help us discover content that perfectly suits our taste. In fact, however, these suggestions are normalized in several respects: because of the company's commercial interest in maintaining viewers' engagement, to start with, there is a prioritization of content that is sure to please (which, in practice, means a prioritization of mainstream successes at the expense of more marginal content); and, even more significantly, the viewing subject to whom Netflix's "Recommended for You" suggestions are addressed is hardly identical with "you" or "me," but instead involves what Alexander calls a "collective personalization"—a process whereby my viewing behavior is aggregated together with that of others in order to predict what "I" might like.[8] Thus, far from reading my mind, Netflix's recommendation system is very much involved in a standardization of taste, and in the formation of the anonymous sort of industrialized collectivity that Jean-Paul Sartre refers to as "seriality."[9] To the extent that I come to identify with the recommendations, and hence to the extent that my taste coincides with that of the anonymous collective of dividualized viewers also caught in the feedback loops of Netflix's algorithms, I will have been anticipated and indeed shaped by the recommendation system. Far from neutral with respect to the identity of viewing subjects, this algorithmic "taste machine"[10] is in fact complicit in the generation of the future subject.[11]

It is clear from the foregoing that the temporal circuit involved in this sort of tastemaking futurity is situated within a relatively long window of time, as it involves an analysis of present and past viewing behavior, ideally encompassing years of data about my viewing choices, in order to predict and/or shape what I will like in the future. We can begin to see, however, that this temporality might scale to fit into smaller windows. It is useful, in this respect, to recall that Netflix began as a DVD-rental service, years before it turned into the streaming platform that we know today. It was in this inherently slower context of delivery-by-mail that the company developed its proprietary

"Cinematch" algorithms for movie recommendations, which draws on viewers' ratings (on a five-star system) in conjunction with an elaborate system of "microtags" and "altgenres." The "microtags" consist of manually entered metadata describing each film or TV show according to a plethora of data points: names of actors, locations, themes, even less obviously quantifiable metadata concerning feelings, narrative form, and qualities like romance or goriness. What Netflix refers to as "altgenres" (short for alternative genres) are statistically computed categories—at one point, 76,897 of them, ranging from "Scary Cult Movies from the 1980s" to "Chilling Goofy Movies" to "Evil Kid Horror Movies"—that enable a more fine-grained matching of movies to potential viewers (or vice versa) than more traditional genres like Western, comedy, or science fiction.[12] As we see, these predictions are based crucially in a dividuation of decades' worth of media objects (by way of microtags) and a reconsolidation of them as big data (in the form of altgenres). But as long as the unit of exchange was an integral movie (a DVD) transported back and forth via postal delivery, both the viewing data and the feedback loop were relatively crude. The move to streaming in 2007 enabled significant refinements by way of narrowing the temporal window to near-real-time feedback about what, when, and how often one engaged with various types of content. As Netflix put it in a 2012 blog post:

> Streaming has not only changed the way our members interact with the service, but also the type of data available to use in our algorithms. For DVDs our goal is to help people fill their queue with titles to receive in the mail over the coming days and weeks; selection is distant in time from viewing, people select carefully because exchanging a DVD for another takes more than a day, and we get no feedback during viewing. For streaming members are looking for something great to watch right now; they can sample a few videos before settling on one, they can consume several in one session, and we can observe viewing statistics such as whether a video was watched fully or only partially.[13]

Narrowing the window between selection and viewing from "distant in time" to "right now," along with real-time surveillance of browsing and viewing behavior, provides the necessary foundation for zeroing in more closely on the perceptual present—as well as for shifting the futural dimension more explicitly from prediction to generation: with the help of this finer-grained data, Netflix has moved on from simply recommending movies and shows to producing its own original content. Famously, the Netflix series *House of Cards* was generated on the basis of the data it collected from monitoring the behavior and inferred preferences of millions of streaming subscribers.[14] Thus, while the images streamed when one views the series are of course audiovisual records of the past (the pro-filmic events staged and captured by cameras and other recording equipment), they are also in a sense *images of the future*—a future that was algorithmically calculated and dividually imagined before it was made present on viewers' screens.[15]

Streaming-in-Time

Disregarding the predictively generated audiovisual content (the actual sounds, images, and narratives) for the moment, the sheer act of streaming implicates as well a finer-grained temporal control process and a more immediate calculation of futurity. The present of experience is more concretely and precariously at stake in this "stream" of images, which flows from the future and into the past, much like the flow of our own perceptual consciousness. So much depends on this synchronization of the two streams, as becomes suddenly clear when the video stream is disrupted and we are ejected from the ongoing flow. In "Rage against the Machine: Buffering, Noise, and Perpetual Anxiety in the Age of Connected Viewing," Neta Alexander investigates the ways that this disruption, in the form of "buffering," evokes spectatorial anxieties and new modes and embodied forms of viewing that, though they are central to our experience of contemporary moving images, are too often brushed aside in critical studies and marginalized in industrial and marketing discourses and in viewers' memories alike.[16] Alexander connects this erasure to utopian promises of seamless interaction and the aforementioned "predictive personalization"—an imagined seamlessness that is based in discourses of "abstraction and dematerialization" that are at odds with the material realities instantiated in streaming video's technological, economic, perceptual, epistemological, and temporal logics.[17] It is worth expanding briefly on Alexander's diagnosis, which I will develop in the following in a somewhat different direction, in order to understand how the temporalization of streaming fits in between the higher-order prediction and generation processes considered above and still lower-level processes to which we will turn shortly.

The term *buffering* refers both to the technical operation whereby a portion of the video stream is preloaded in memory in order to ensure uninterrupted playback, as well as, more colloquially, to those moments when the buffer is empty and needs to be reloaded—when the video stops and a spinning circle or similar animated icon appears, perhaps accompanied by the word "loading." Recognizing this duality at the heart of buffering is crucial for understanding the triangulation of subjective experience with respect to the temporal interchange between technical substrate and aesthetic form, for it is essentially a technical failure that makes us aware of the process—and hence our own involvement in it—in the first place; visibility is therefore the exception, and invisibility the norm, yet this invisible process is crucial to our subjective enjoyment of the video stream. Like Heidegger discovering that his hammer is broken or missing, we discover the invisible process of buffering when it fails and reveals itself as an obstinate "presence-at-hand"; unlike Heidegger's hammer, however, the normal functioning of the video stream is not quite the "readiness-to-hand" of a functioning tool or equipmental object, as the stream's temporality is more actively involved in shaping the temporal flow of our own perceptual consciousness—and it is precisely this, rather than any specific instrumental reference (the "in-order-to" structure of equipment, according to Heidegger), that is revealed by the interruption of the stream.[18] The synchronization of internal and external flow therefore establishes the basis for the marginalization and forgetting of interruption that Alexander identifies, as well as the anxiety over breakdown: the breakdown of the video stream's flow is a malfunction of our own temporal flow, throwing us out of our attentional attunement with the video stream and back on ourselves. The stakes of buffering are thus existential, not merely technical.

In the conditions that make possible a coincidence (and threaten a non-coincidence) of buffered video stream and unfolding temporal experience, we discover a mesoscale version of images' "actually running ahead of" perception: the video buffer anticipates our immediate future—a future measured in seconds rather than days or weeks. And much like their pioneering work on the longer-range processes of predictive recommendation and content-generation, Netflix is again an innovator in the mesoscale field of buffering—an existential innovator in the realm of temporal control. Consider the company's strange test videos that have come to light in recent years: "Example Short 23.976," "Example Show," the four seasons of the original series *Test Patterns*, and the remarkable twelve-minute movie *Meridian*. Such videos are used for real-time testing of bitrate and resolution ("Example Short 23.976"), or they provide "test patterns for identification of A/V sync offset, coarse monitor calibration, surround sound channel identification, device-side scaling and overscan" (the various episodes of *Test Patterns*, such as season 1, episode 1: "Multipurpose Chart: 3840 × 2160: 23.976 fps [frames per second]"). With their real-time computational feedback regarding network speed and video quality, presented either in graphical form or as textual output displayed in the top-left corner of the screen, such videos make streaming visible not by way of breakage (ideally), but by transforming our view of the stream and establishing

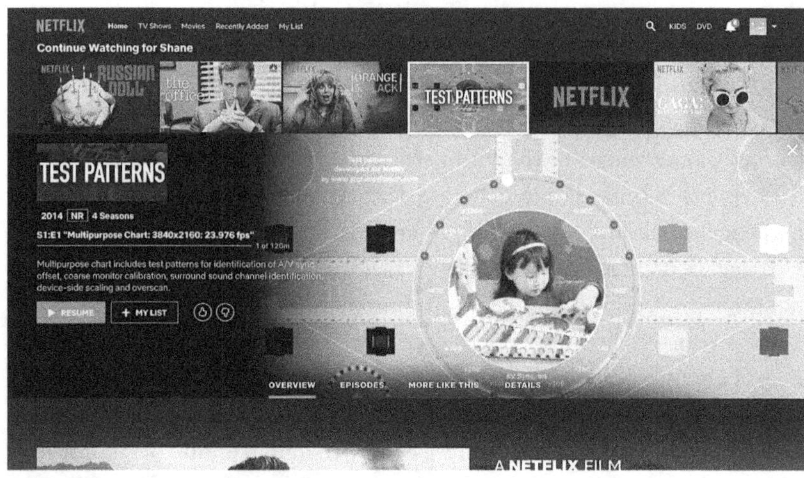

Figure 3.1. Netflix's *Test Patterns*.

a "hermeneutic relation" to it (in Don Ihde's term); the stream continues to function, but we view it through a layer of forensic or diagnostic information about its current state: we "read" its operation rather than just watching it.[19] Clearly, this mode of viewing, which is meant more for technicians than for consumers, is a nonstandard form of spectatorship, but it is revealing with respect to the calculation and engineering of experience at stake in buffering.

In particular, these videos reveal that what Alexander calls "the commodification of the eye" comprises a much lower-level process than is involved in prediction and content-generation, and that it involves precise technical measurements that exceed the powers of discrimination of human vision.[20] Of "Example Show"—a 2010 video summarized on its Netflix page as "An example of a show" and starring "Actor" and "Actress," who engage in such activities as running around outside Netflix headquarters, splashing in a fountain, juggling balls, and even doing the moonwalk while working on a laptop—Netflix communications officer Joris Evers said: "That's primarily a video we use to give ourselves and our partners. A way to test Netflix."[21] Further: "We would never put this video in suggestions and you can only find it by searching on Netflix." Indeed, none of these test videos will be recommended by Netflix's algorithms, because they are inherently at odds with the type of viewing experience that the company seeks to create: one in which the temporal flows of video and consciousness are symbiotically merged, not (as here) clinically disentangled to make the stream the quasi-object of hermeneutic regard. Such a form of

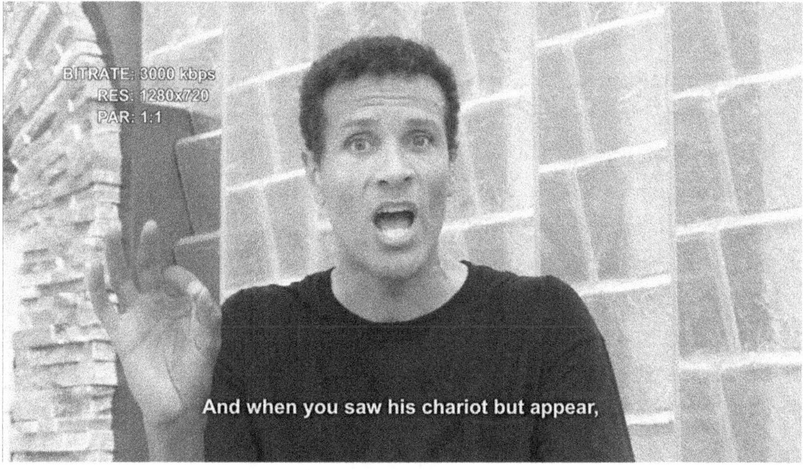

Figure 3.2. "Example Short 23.976."

viewing is reserved for specialists, acting as assistants to (or proxies for) the computational machines that have no choice but to regard the stream as the temporal flow of information.

Ultimately, these videos are not *for* our eyes, but they enable us to see the machinic processes involved in preparing video streams more generally for human vision. "Example Short 23.976" superimposes an ongoing readout of bitrate (the amount of information processed over time, measured here in kilobits per second, or kbps) and resolution data (the number of horizontal by the number of vertical pixels displayed, e.g., 320 × 240 or 1,920 × 1,080) over its video images; the juxtaposition reveals a precarious balancing act: the amount of information transported over the network and decoded as sounds and images fluctuates, and it is actively being modulated in order to accommodate bandwidth issues and, above all, to keep the stream flowing. Watching the stream of images with one eye and the numerical readout with the other, viewers will soon recognize something they may have occasionally noticed: a video may start out slightly blurry but then clear up after several seconds; this is due, as we see with the help of the numerical data, to an automatic reduction of video quality (lower resolution and bitrate) undertaken in an effort to allow the stream to accumulate a sufficient buffer before reverting to better quality—utilizing a technique known as adaptive bitrate streaming, whereby the playback app or device adjusts in real time to bandwidth and processing capacity and switches between different encodings of the video, which is made available in small sections of several seconds (typically between two and ten seconds) each.[22] Ideally, these modulations, which are taking place constantly, will remain imperceptible. The test video reveals how fluctuations are correlated with more detailed and therefore more "computationally expensive" scenes—that is, scenes that require more resources of time, bandwidth, and processing power, such as a close-up shot of water splashing in a fountain, creating fast-moving and tiny ripples and bubbles on the glittering surface. The scene itself is relatively uninteresting, certainly devoid of any narrative interest, but it takes on a significance in relation to the stream of numerical data, as we watch the drama of network problems, weak Wi-Fi signals, and processing bottlenecks being mastered (or not) in real time, all for the sake of keeping the video stream flowing.

What this drama unfolding *between* the numerical and figural outputs makes apparent is that human perception, and its synchronization with the ongoing temporal flow of video images, is situated right at the intersection of the informatic substrate and the computed visual form. In this relatively small-scale temporal circuit, which depends crucially on the futural operation of the buffer, the time of human perception is *immediately* subject to dividuation, modulation, and control; the temporalization of substrate/form relations (the translation of data, measured temporally in thousands of bits per second, into visual images, computed as an array of pixels updating at frequencies such as 23.976 or 59.940 frames per second) quite literally dictates the temporal flow of consciousness. Until, that is, the stream breaks and the video has to buffer again . . .

There is of course much more to be said about buffering, but I would like to point to just one further innovation that bears directly on what we might call the ongoing *existentialization of streaming-in-time*, or the deep affective attunement with (and anxiety over) streaming video that depends on the synchronization of perceptual experience with the delicate balance of substrate/form relations. In late December 2018, Netflix released *Black Mirror: Bandersnatch* to much fanfare. The feature-length movie is a spinoff from the acclaimed science-fiction anthology series *Black Mirror*, which debuted in 2011 on British television network Channel 4 and, beginning with season 3 in 2016, has been owned by Netflix and rebranded a "Netflix original series." With its near-future dystopian visions of a world caught in the darkest of feedback loops with its media technologies—which one can recognize as only slightly hyperbolic extrapolations from tendencies of current social media, surveillance technologies, reality TV, and networked politics, among other things—the series has a long-standing investment in fostering an "existentialist" attitude toward contemporary media technics. That is, the show thrives on its conjuration of an atmosphere of angst about the communicative and infrastructural transformations of our world, and its extrapolated futures thus reveal our present as a moment of *crisis*—including in its etymological senses of a turning point in a disease, a moment of judgment, or the contingent juncture where a decision must be made and from whence divergent future paths branch off. *Bandersnatch* intensifies this media existentialism by involving the spectator directly in the need to choose and to act; it achieves this new level of involvement by means of requiring direct input in an interactive narrative, mandating decisions on the part of the viewer/user, communicated via remote control, that will actively change the course of the story (or, more precisely, that will steer its unfolding progression toward one of five main endings by selecting among the set of branching paths that present themselves along the way).

Most discussions of the movie have understandably focused on this narrative interactivity—either praising its novelty or deflating such claims by reference to a long history of interactive fiction, videogames, and electronic literature.[23] In this context, critics also foreground moments of self-reflexivity—centrally, the protagonist of *Bandersnatch* realizes that he is being controlled by an outside force (i.e., the viewer), and the movie incessantly breaks the proverbial fourth wall. The viewer is even presented with the option at one point to inform said protagonist that we are watching him on Netflix (inviting the viewer, literally, to click on the Netflix logo, and prompting the character, situated in the prestreaming world of the 1980s, to wonder aloud: "What the fuck is Netflix?"). Certainly, these aspects of interactivity and self-reflexivity are crucial to the viewer's involvement in the general existentialism of the program, including the channeling of anxiety into a narrow window of real-time decision-making (you have ten seconds to choose between options before the choice is made for you, and a bad decision might prompt an on-screen character to comment, with both diegetic and extradiegetic reference: "Wrong path").

Less often commented on, however, are the technical challenges presented by interactivity, and the consequences that it has for thinking about our attunement to streaming video. Certainly, the general smoothness of interactive experience has garnered some attention; for example, an article in *GQ* remarks: "The first thing that comes to the fore in *Bandersnatch* is the seamlessness of the decision system. You're given 10 seconds to make certain binary decisions in certain scenes, and there's no buffering or loading in between."[24] The approving reference to "seamlessness" here belies an anxiety about buffering, which is thankfully rendered invisible. But the idea that "there's no buffering" makes

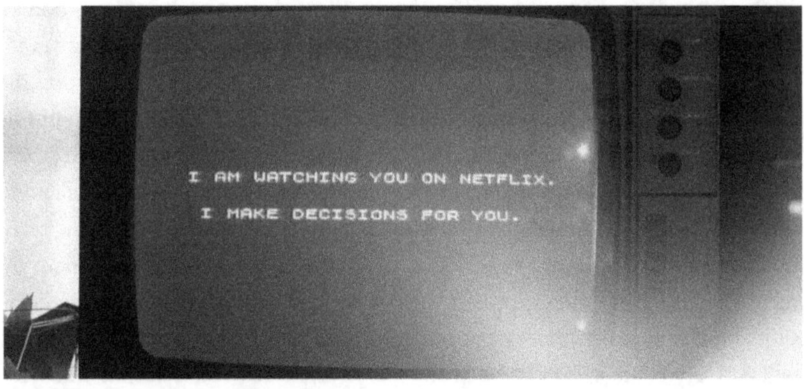

Figure 3.3. Self-reflexivity in *Black Mirror: Bandersnatch* (2018).

sense only if we recall the dual sense in which the term is used; specifically, it refers here to the disruptive moments when we are ejected from the stream so that it can load. But this apparent absence of buffering depends crucially on the efficient operation of buffering in its more technical sense, which is no small feat for a branching narrative. Recall that buffering involves the real-time preloading of audiovisual content into memory, thus *anticipating* present experience in advance. While this operation is complex enough in the streaming playback of a conventional, linear video, the complexity of its execution in a branching narrative is compounded by the fact that the computational system has to accommodate multiple possible futures—again, measured in mere seconds—from which the viewer may choose. Our precarious temporal synchronization with the stream is thus complicated by the fact that it is not yet known which future images to make ready for experience until after the viewer has made a choice.

It is this dilemma, and Netflix's mastery of it, that marks the site of *Bandersnatch*'s biggest innovation, which consists not in interactivity per se but in a new system of multithreaded buffering—essentially, *two* streams are preloaded into memory at once—thus achieving a new level of experiential temporalization, or the calculative anticipation of subjective experience. This innovation, which has been remarked on only in passing, has far-reaching consequences not only for streaming in general, which stands to gain from the development of such technologies, but also for the prediction and shaping of future behavior and the generation of content.[25] Real-time interactivity provides Netflix an opportunity to gain data about users' preferences at a much more fine-grained level of analysis than is provided by their viewing history and ratings of films and shows as integral units.[26] User choices provide minute feedback on what viewers want to see *within* a given movie, and this data is sure to be used to generate new content for the future—thus feeding back into the higher-order circuits of tastemaking futurity discussed above.[27] At the same time, however, the reliance of interactivity on an underlying dual-stream buffering system points to a tightening of the temporal window of screen time, in which our images "actually run ahead" of us and modulate temporal experience. Indeed, there are still tighter circuits yet to consider.

Compression, or, The Ecstatic Temporality of Discorrelated Images

Peeling back another layer of temporalization, and not only bracketing the content of videos but also looking beneath the streaming process, we find that every digital video—whether streamed or packaged on an optical disc or other carrier medium—must first be encoded, thus introducing another level of predictive temporality and control. At stake, most centrally, is the ensemble of microtemporal processes involved in compression and decompression by way of codecs (or coder-decoder programs) such as MPEG-2 (used on DVDs) or MPEG-4 (used more widely today by online platforms such as YouTube and Vimeo, as well as offline media such as Blu-rays). Such codecs are "lossy" protocols, meaning that they make trade-offs between video quality and storage/performance, reducing the amount of data stored or streamed in order to improve playback over limited network connections or by devices with limited memory or processing power. Such compromises are crucial for buffering processes, for the smaller the amount of information that needs to be processed (and hence the lower the quality, size, or number of images), the quicker the video can be loaded into the buffer in order to ensure an apparently seamless experiential synchronization. The compression of digital video executed by codecs is therefore also a compression of mediated temporalization itself, further narrowing the temporal window of control and zeroing in on the present.

In a series of articles, Adrian Mackenzie has argued that "despite or perhaps because of their convoluted obscurity, codecs catalyze new relations between people, things, spaces, and times in events and forms," thus weaving together technological, phenomenological, and social determinants of experience.[28] Most relevant for present purposes is Mackenzie's claim that "what appears on screen is colored by the techniques of 'lossy compression' that MPEG-2 epitomizes. Codecs affect at a deep level contemporary sensations of movement, color, light, and time."[29] The transformation can be traced back to two related operations, one concerning the encoding of information *within* the image, and the other concerning the reorganization of relations *between* images. Both of these processes are involved in the dividualization and temporalization of images that I have been considering since chapter 2. Starting with the individual frame, compression is achieved by computationally analyzing the image in blocks of eight-by-eight pixels and eliminating redundant information about identical or very similar pixels, transforming these blocks "into a quasi-statistical summary of the spatial distribution" of color and brightness.[30] Such transformations, which the MPEG codecs share in common with digital photo compression protocols like JPEG, in fact despatialize the image, using algorithmic processes such as the Discrete Cosine Transform (DCT) to "transform spatially extended images into a set of simple frequencies."[31] Such processes of "spectral analysis" enable codecs "to isolate those components of an image that are most perceptually salient to human eyes. These would include the brightest or most colorful components."[32]

However, it is the second transformation, that of the interrelations between images, that is more crucially involved in the transformation of time at a subperceptual level. It is here that digital video operates radically differently not only from the cinematic projection of discrete frames but also from analog video and its televisual screening—both of which are composed of linear sequences, even if the alternating scan lines on a CRT are drawn out of sequence in order to take advantage of phosphor afterglow and thus maximize the apparent integrity of the image (as described in chapter 2). The "calculated reordering" of images by lossy codecs like MPEG-2 is much more radical.[33] As Mackenzie puts it:

> In order to gain purchase on the relation between frames, the MPEG codec again breaks the frame into an array of discrete "macroblocks" (usually four blocks put together). It compares successive frames to see how a specific macroblock shifts between frames. The working assumption behind the motion-predicted encoding of video in MPEG-2 is that nothing much happens between successive frames that can't be understood as macroblocks undergoing geometric manipulations (translation, rotation, skewing, etc.). The fact that nothing much happens between frames apart from spatial transformation is the basis of the interframe compression and the generation of P and B pictures (forward and backward motion prediction, respectively). P (Predicted) and B (Backward) pictures, the pictures that accompany the I-Picture [the relatively integral, JPEG-like picture resulting from intra-frame analysis with Discrete Cosine Transform] in a MPEG-2 bitstream are, therefore, really nothing like film frames. There will never

be a flicker in an MPEG video because the boundaries between pictures are not constructed in the same way they are in film or even in television with its interlaced scanned images.[34]

What this means is that a great deal more information can be eliminated from the stream of images by taking I-Frames as a baseline and, rather than replicating all the identical information regarding brightness and color in subsequent frames, instead encoding simple vectors that describe the movement of macroblocks. The codec analyzes visual changes in forward- and backward-looking motions, recording merely the differences between images for later reconstruction on playback. Playback itself is hardly linear, as it is transformed into the out-of-order execution of instructions, first displaying an I-Frame, which it preserves on-screen while partial transformations (the "geometric manipulations" of which Mackenzie writes: "translation, rotation, skewing, etc.") are carried out on top of it. The codec must therefore "look ahead" at instructions for the prediction of motion in P-Frames, and with this differential knowledge in hand it must further calculate the B-Frames that will mark intermediate steps in between; the B-Frames, which fall between an I-Frame and a P-Frame (or between subsequent P-Frames), are therefore predicted out of both forward-looking (from the perspective of the I-Frame) and backward-looking (from the perspective of the P-Frame, itself only predicted on the basis of the I-Frame) calculations of difference. As Mackenzie writes: "The actual ratio of intraframe and interframe pictures in a given bitstream is heavily weighted toward motion prediction. In an MPEG datastream, the precise mixture of different frame types (I, P-forward, and B-backward) is defined at encoding time in the Group of Pictures (GOP) structure. It is usually 12 or 15 frames in a sequence such as I_BB_P_BB_P_BB_P_BB_P_BB_."[35] In effect, this whole sequence is executed out of order, while the linear appearance of change over time is the result of drawing and redrawing the screen along the routes calculated on the fly from backward- and forward-prediction vectors.

This radically generative process bears out the kernel of truth in Manovich's claim that digital video is essentially indistinguishable from animation;[36] especially the interpolating generation of B-Frames is more or less identical to the processes, fundamental to CGI, known as "tweening" (or the automated generation of images between sets of keyframes in order to complete a movement) and "morphing" (the now-familiar digital transformation of one object, often a face or body, into another).[37] Even more importantly, motion prediction implicates the computational playback device in a microtemporal processing of time that introduces an interval of "duration" (in the Bergsonian sense suggestive of life, as I argued in chapter 1) into the mechanical processing of a temporal flow. Insinuating itself into our own subperceptual processing of time, the codec's out-of-sequence temporalization impinges on us at a level of prepersonal embodiment, subjecting our metabolic relations to the environment to transformation and reordering. Bypassing perception and attuning us to computational time via the "inner diaphragm" that Merleau-Ponty posits as the body's relational situation "prior to stimuli and sensory contents," the temporal window within which the image "actually runs ahead" of us here is extremely narrowly focused, our experience anticipated microtemporally—in a future measured no longer in seconds but in temporally nonlinear fractions of seconds.[38]

Thus, while compression glitches make these processes (fleetingly) visible, and whereas "datamoshed" videos like Takeshi Murata's *Monster Movie* (2005) aestheticize the out-of-order execution of compressed video by removing the integral I-Frames and allowing the predictive P- and B-Frames to draw wonderfully psychedelic forms on the screen, it is important not to reduce the impact of compression to a purely "correlative," perceptual one (as I argued in relation to Jordan Schonig's analysis in chapter 2).[39] Such objects are significant for helping us to recognize the technical processes involved, but it is important to preserve the discorrelative view of them that will allow us to recognize their role in a subperceptual modulation of lived temporality—a modulation that depends crucially on the generative future-orientation of compression/decompression and that, by injecting something very much like "life" (a futurity that is homologous to that of living experience) into the environment, radically transforms our own metabolic relationality to the world of becoming.[40]

In another article, titled "Every Thing Thinks: Sub-representative Differences in Digital Video Codecs," Mackenzie touches on these implications by way of recourse to Deleuze's notion of "the subrepresentative," related here to computational video processing:

> The "sub-representative," in Deleuze's thought, refers to that aspect of things that cannot be consciously thought or reduced to the presence of an object to a subject mediated by a concept or category. While the sub-representative cannot be identified, measured or calculated as such, it is felt and, in some cases, felt intensely. So while the proliferation of digital video might on the one hand be seen as a paroxysm of representation, an unbounded expansion of the power to represent, from the sub-representative standpoint, it could also be seen as "imbued with a presentiment of groundlessness," alterity and differences.[41]

In line with the discorrelative view I put forward in chapter 2, which sought to link intensity, habit, and temporalization as vectors of subjectivation operative across the substrate/form divide, Mackenzie assigns the impact of the subrepresentative to embodiment in its prepersonal interface with media technologies: "Eyes and ears do not have universal, timeless physiological properties. They have media-historical habits. Electronically mediated visual culture shapes eyes and ears and creates perceptual habits at many levels."[42] In the case of digital video, "the technical apparatus of the codec takes on part of the work of embodied perception in the interests of changing the relation between body and media infrastructure."[43] The result, in other words, of the new interface is not a punctual effect but an environmental change: "New ecologies of images burgeon."[44] And the material and medial impacts take place independent of perception. "It could be argued that the intensive paths generated by codecs in the extension of images make no difference to the viewers. In other words, viewers might see straight through the codecs. They might not be seen."[45] And yet such an argument begs the question of what it means to "see straight through" the codecs—or, more precisely, *who* it is who sees through them. As I have been arguing, discorrelated images exert a force that is prior to the perception of a constituted subject, thus transductively and microtemporally influencing the formation of the subject in its relation to visible objects, so that the fact of the codec's invisibility or transparency is not an argument against its efficacy. Quite the opposite: "Viewers may not be highly conscious of how brightness, chrominance and movement have been minutely altered by the codec. These differences can be easily cancelled out or remain almost imperceptible [or, I would add, totally imperceptible]. This does not mean that they make no difference. On the contrary, the proliferation of video materials and the degrees of variation opening up around video streams today suggest that viewers are caught up in the spatio-temporal dynamisms of video material culture."[46]

To be "caught up in the spatio-temporal dynamisms" is to be shaped or modulated (which is not to say determined) by the minute control mechanisms that precede and indeed anticipate the formation of the subject. I have explained this in terms of an artificial metabolism, while for Mackenzie the process is leveraged by what he calls, following Deleuze, "the emergence of an elementary consciousness."[47] Accordingly, "codecs in a sense perceive the image."[48] That is, "in its analysis of spectral density and selection of the most energetic component of the signal, the codec isolates tendencies or emphases. Perhaps this is something that also occurs in bodily perception. It treats what can be seen in an image as composed of tendencies and emphases that can be seized in a contractile movement."[49] The essential point would seem to be to draw an analogy between the bodily synthesis of sensation on the part of living beings and a spatiotemporal synthesis in a nonorganic body, much as I have been doing with the concept of metabolism. Yet it makes a difference whether we have recourse to a presubjective concept like metabolism or a subjective one like perception or consciousness. I have intentionally chosen to think discorrelation in terms of artificial metabolism in order to avoid any of the (basically correlative) implications of "artificial intelligence," a concept that tends toward anthropomorphism and a recentering of higher-order cognitive functions while diminishing the role of microlevel operations and their transformative, systemic impacts. Though the recourse to "elementary consciousness" and a nascent "perception" on the part of codecs is somewhat ambiguous in this respect, I suggest that such terms tend to reinstate the correlative perspective (of perceiving or thinking subjects and their objects) that the microtemporal futurity of compression processes undercuts by "actually running ahead of" subjective awareness.

Mackenzie ends his article by echoing Deleuze's statement that "every thing thinks"—an idea that Mackenzie endorses as part of what he calls his "radically constructivist account of things."[50] And while this idea clearly seems intended as a provocation aimed at decentering human thought as the pinnacle of cognition (or being itself), the leveling that is achieved in this way actually runs counter to the insights that Mackenzie's analysis provides about codecs' temporal reorganization. Thus, Mackenzie is compelled to admit that "nothing of what I have said of codecs belongs solely to advanced technologies. It is not as if codecs think more than, say, photographs, rock carvings or oilpaintings."[51] A commitment to an indiscriminate vitalism or panpsychism therefore vitiates recognition of the specific difference between codecs' microtemporal operations and the slower temporalities of other visual media; this, I contend, is precisely where a metabolism-based approach is superior to a cognition-centric one. Mackenzie goes on to reclaim something of the difference between compression-based video and other visual media by saying: "The singularity of codecs, the different worlds to be found in them, come from the intensities they put in relation. Those differences actualize in the spatio-temporal, scale-transforming dynamics of video material culture."[52] These intensities that codecs "put in relation" differently from other media are better thought in terms of the dynamic temporal interchanges between substrates and forms (as I argued in chapter 2)—interchanges that do not necessarily implicate thought but that recursively accommodate "scale-transformations" (whereby the forms of one medium constitute the substrate of another) and that triangulate "observers" or "interpretants" with respect to "the operative deployment of the *difference* of medial substrate and form."[53] On this model, which describes the metabolism of systems, thought is implicated only in higher-order operations, although there is indeed room for thinking the dispersal of cognition at the intersection of human and nonhuman systems—for example, in terms of what N. Katherine Hayles calls the "cognitive nonconscious": the prepersonal processing of environmental information that precedes, but can flow into, conscious thought and that can be distributed across human-technical systems.[54] Such distributions are especially pertinent for thinking our contemporary imbrication in computational systems and environments—and for much the same reason as I have been arguing here with respect to the temporal force of video compression, which does not affect subjects from without as an external force, but instead exerts its agency from deep within the transductive relations that media establish between subjects and objects. It is precisely such scale-variable relations that the model of media as metabolism helps us to account for, thus enabling us to recognize that the systemic effects of video compression need not have a perceptual or conscious correlate but operate instead by injecting a microtemporal futurity into the material basis of contemporary life itself, introducing a new anticipatory dimension into the unfolding present of our experience.

The operationalization of this new microtemporal dimension represents a crucial strategic battleground: a site of cybernetic control that is of major logistical, commercial, and even military interest. At stake, among other things, is the speed and efficiency of video delivery in human-machine systems such as remotely piloted drones, where real-time perception and action depends on codecs' reliable compression and decompression of visual information, which can in turn mean the difference between life and death (or between targeted killing and civilian casualties). As I have been arguing, the temporal reordering executed by the codec marks it as the site of a deep imbrication, or "anthropotechnical interfacing," between the human user (in this case, the pilot) and the technical system:[55] so-called "real time" is in fact an out-of-sequence operation that entrains the pilot's perceptual present and attunes it to the codec's ecstatic temporalization of the video channel. The generativity of compressed video involves not only the generation of images from predictive instruction sets but also, by commanding the inner sense of temporal experience, the transductive generation of the user's subjectivity itself. Seen against the background of such military deployments, the use and development of video codecs for entertainment purposes may seem relatively trivial. However, the same processes of temporal interfacing are at stake in efforts to improve

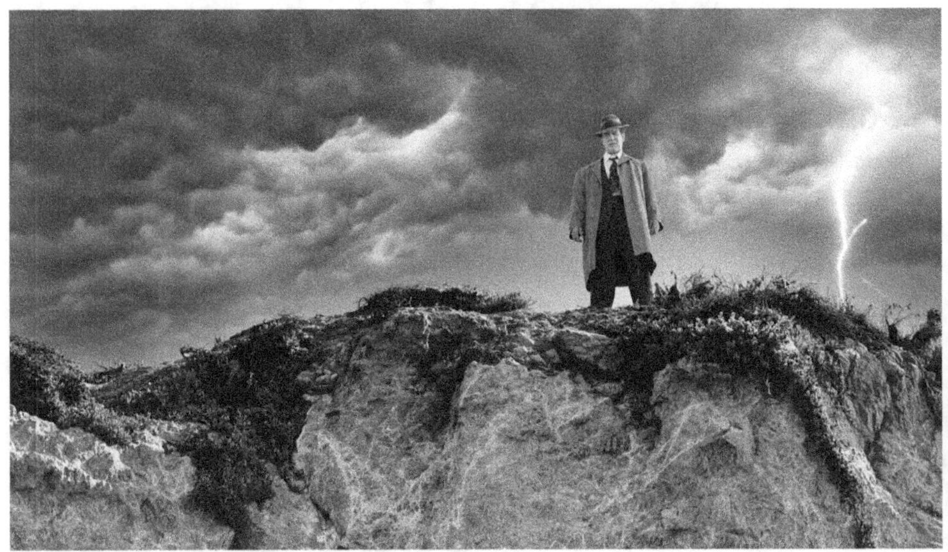

Figure 3.4. Netflix's "codec noir" *Meridian* (2016).

compression and make it seamlessly invisible to perception. And given the integration of such low-level temporal circuits into the higher-order circuits of streaming and still-higher ones of prediction and modulation of behavior and taste, it is hardly an exaggeration to say that companies like Netflix are engaged in "a battle for the mind."[56]

Take, for instance, the Netflix short *Meridian* (2016)—an odd video that *Variety* describes thus: "A deserted cliff. Lightning appearing out of nowhere. A mysterious lady all dressed in white. Netflix's latest original program, 'Meridian,' is spooky, confusing, and only 12 minutes long. That's because although 'Meridian' is available on the streaming service worldwide, it was made not for Netflix's 83 million subscribers, but for algorithms and their programmers."[57] As Netflix executive Chris Fetner puts it: "It's a weird story wrapped up in a bunch of engineering requirements."[58] Like "Example Short 23.976," *Meridian* is a video designed not for its aesthetic qualities but for testing purposes, but more than earlier test videos it recognizes the close proximity between the two dimensions and the need to account for stylistic variety and broadly perceptual qualities in technical tests. Also in contrast to the earlier example videos, *Meridian* is designed not only for testing streaming performance (though it can serve that purpose as well) but also for testing and developing new codecs for compressing high-quality video. The movie, which can be downloaded from

Netflix's GitHub page, is "4K HDR video shot with 60 frames per second with a peak brightness level of 4000 nits and Dolby Atmos audio. In other words: It pushes the boundaries on all specs fronts, and includes a number of visuals that can trip up encoders."[59] As for the latter: "The film itself is deliberately difficult to compress: dancing smoke, archival footage at various qualities, shaking trees, water droplets on glass, and smooth sky gradations (which often show banding) are among the host of fine detail that is often lost when streamed."[60]

Thus, while *Meridian*, which is often referred to as a film noir, has a rudimentary (though non-sequitur) narrative, its images do not anticipate a viewer who will be interested in the plot or the unmotivated lighting changes and chiaroscuro effects; instead, it uses the latter to ensure that the codec can deliver even the most demanding of screen-technical phenomena to the nascent viewer-about-to-be—a subject forming in real time alongside the unfolding image stream—by inserting their perception into the temporal flow of the high-definition video while avoiding lag, jitter (or "stuttering"), and compression artifacts. Provided free of charge as an open-source download for codec developers, Netflix's video is meant to serve as a baseline for comparing/measuring compression techniques and their ability to invisibly or subrepresentatively master perception by successfully avoiding detection. This, as we have seen, is primarily a question of how efficiently codecs execute their out-of-order operations, keeping them squarely within the microtemporal realm and out of subjective awareness, thus successfully anticipating or, in Manovich's words, "actually running ahead of" experience. On the refinement of this microtemporal control process rests the possibility, one level of temporalization up, of improved streaming performance and hence, yet another level up, of a more efficient prediction and/or shaping of the subject of taste and the generation of its objects. In other words, the whole edifice of screen time, considered as an anticipatory temporalization and subjectivation process, rests squarely on the refinement of codecs and their ability to zero in on the present of experience.

Post-cinema and the Phenomenology of External Time-Consciousness

As I have been arguing throughout this chapter, the temporality of media in the digital era has undergone radical change, and with it the relation of media to the temporality of subjective experience. In following the tightening circuits of screen time from big data-based prediction and generation (in temporal windows of days, weeks, months, or years), to the existential temporality of streaming (with its buffered future measured in seconds), to the ecstatic time of compression (and the codec's microtemporal prediction and out-of-order execution of dividualized images), we have discovered mechanisms whereby the time of subjective experience—and thereby subjectivity itself—is rendered the object of ever more minute processes of control. Extrapolating further along this trajectory, it would seem that the logical end of the process is a complete determination of experience by media "actually running ahead of" us. But is determinism really the inevitable conclusion?

In *Technics and Time*, philosopher of technology Bernard Stiegler laid the groundwork for the deterministic view in his now famous media-philosophical rethinking of Husserl's phenomenology of temporal experience—a rethinking necessitated by, and conducted in light of, the advent of a new form of "temporal object": what Stiegler calls "tertiary memories."[61] The latter is Stiegler's term for the externalized, reproducible experiences stored by industrial media objects such as sound recordings, films, or videos. Using the term *cinema* to designate not only a specific apparatus but also the broad epochal media regime established by recording technologies from photography and phonography to television and digital technologies, Stiegler identifies a threat to our subjective experience—exacerbated with the advent of live media in what he calls "the televisual epoch of cinema"—whereby media colonize consciousness by preformatting our immediate awareness (or primary retention, in Husserl's terminology) with the images of tertiary retention (as Stiegler calls this new, recorded memory).[62] One thing Stiegler's argument fails to account for, however, is the emergence of the *protentional* dimension that distinguishes computational media as decidedly post-cinematic—the anticipatory, futural aspects that I have been tracing here. No longer simply memorial or "mnemotechnical," as he puts it, post-cinema's protentional images are generated on the fly according to compression algorithms rather than preserved and fixed by photochemical processes, thus disrupting the stability of tertiary memory while producing an *external homologue to internal time-consciousness*. The implications of this homology are, however, as yet unclear. In the following, I will try to tease out the consequences by tracing the impact of post-cinematic futurity at the lowest levels, even deeper than the anticipatory workings of video compression, on the production of subjective experience; I aim to show that this production is both more precarious and less deterministic than Stiegler's mnemotechnical perspective would lead us to believe.

In order to isolate the salient aspects of our experience of time, Husserl had focused his analysis on the experience of a temporal object—that is, an object that is not just encountered *in* time (as are all objects) but whose being is *essentially* temporal.[63] Husserl's chosen object is a melody. Recognizing that the experience of such an object cannot be merely punctual, or isolated in the present, but requires a retention of past experience that accrues alongside the unfolding of new phenomena, Husserl distinguishes in the course of his analysis between two distinct forms of retention. On the one hand, primary retention refers to the relatively immediate experiential process of retaining just-past moments (or notes of a melody) in the present, allowing new notes to be experienced in relation to them, and thus enabling the constitution of the melody as an object of experience. On the other hand, secondary retention designates the type of memory involved in recalling the experience of the melody after the fact—for example, remembering a song I heard on the radio yesterday. As the name suggests, secondary retention is derivative with respect to primary retention, as it depends on the latter to constitute its object. According to Stiegler, however, this hierarchy is not quite so stable, as is demonstrated by a repeated audition of the same recording.[64] Listening for a second time, our experience is transformed: we notice new details, find ourselves focusing on a different instrument, are more or less engaged by the piece. Past experience (the domain of secondary retention) thus informs present experience (primary retention) and focuses it as selective and differential. But this influence of secondary retention on primary retention can be demonstrated only with the help of a tertiary retention (such as the recording of the melody or a film or video), for it is such tertiary retention that enables consciousness to have a repeated experience of the same temporal object in the first place. Accordingly, tertiary retentions, or technical recordings of experience not lived firsthand, are capable of exerting an influence on the unfolding of present experience itself. Ultimately, according to Stiegler, these exteriorized, industrial memories can monopolize primary retention, dominating temporal consciousness—including the horizon of the future. And this danger is especially heightened in live or real-time media:

> The two coincidences proper to the televisual epoch of cinema (direct transmission and live production of images) engenders a temporal object of a new kind, such that what occurs is immediately formatted photographically and registered as a "just past" "it has been," that is, as a primary retention collectively and massively retained via this tertiary retention which the telediffused program indubitably and immediately already is. In these temporal objects which news programs are, it becomes impossible to distinguish between the primary memory "just past" and image consciousness [i.e., tertiary retention], since what occurs occurs immediately by the image consciousness.[65]

On the surface of things, this argument seems very much in line with my claims about temporalization in digital video processes, and it is tempting to look at codecs and their zeroing in on experience as further refinements of an essentially deterministic control process. But before we accept this conclusion, we need to look yet deeper.

With the codec, we have already reached a level of extreme image-dividuation and temporalization; what deeper level is there still to discover? The generative, vectoral flux of video compression is itself situated atop computational processes that can be traced down through a series of underlying levels: the video file is processed by playback software, which depends on lower-level processes coordinated by the operating system, including various runtime environments and device drivers, that are ultimately in contact with the hardware, which steers the flow of electrons through physical circuits. Among these layers, there is a lot of room for contingency, but I would like to isolate a specific operation whereby computational futurity or protention is introduced: the low-level process that computer scientists call "speculative execution"—or the anticipatory processing of algorithmic conditionals and the prefetching of data before it is known whether they will in fact be needed.[66] This preprocessing takes place in the data cache associated with the central processing unit (CPU), thus instituting out-of-order execution at the hardware level of CPU microarchitecture. The predictive technique of speculative execution is utilized to optimize computational processes of all sorts, including higher-level operations of image generation and playback, as well as to render imperceptible the unavoidable delays introduced by signal transmission across online networks—for example, on Skype or in fast-paced fighting games, where network lag makes the interface between the player and screen feel "gooey" or "sticky." Thus, when a time-critical event occurs, such as my avatar hitting that of my opponent, my computer generates images according to a predicted trajectory of subsequent events, including my opponent's reaction, before they have been transmitted across the network.[67] Any discrepancy between the predicted and actual events will be corrected by rewinding, so to speak, while the microtemporal nature of these revisions will mean that they are largely imperceptible. Accordingly, this is another example of the way that post-cinematic images distinguish themselves as generative and future-oriented, no longer the memorial objects described by Stiegler under the category of tertiary retentions.

Of course, Stiegler argues that tertiary retention exerts an *impact* on (human) protention—and a determinative one at that—by way of the formatting of present experience, but he does not go so far as to recognize an independent time-processing or protentional dimension of technics. Indeed, for Stiegler technics itself is basically equated with tertiary retention as the externalization and spatialization of experience. Yuk Hui, in his book *On the Existence of Digital Objects*, recognizes this limitation and responds by theorizing what he calls "tertiary protentions."[68] I would like to look more closely at Hui's argument, because I think it marks a significant step in the right direction: by theorizing the emergence of a "new sensibility" based in futural operations "exceeding our imagination," Hui's account of tertiary protention points toward the discorrelation which distinguishes post-cinematic media from the retentional regime of cinema.[69] Ultimately, though, Hui fails to account adequately for this difference and therefore fails to think through the impact on temporality and subjective experience.

According to Hui, "Digital objects partially constitute . . . *tertiary protention*."[70] What is the status of this new temporal dimension? "By tertiary protention, I refer to the fact that in our everyday lives, technology becomes a significant function of the imagination."[71] As we shall see, imagination is the key in Hui's argument for the link between technology and the protentional dimension of temporal experience, following Heidegger's reading of Kant and his revision of the role of the imagination in the *Critique of Pure Reason*.[72] I will have more to say about this recourse to imagination in a moment, but for now, let me suggest that this statement—"technology becomes a significant function of the imagination"—harbors a great deal of ambiguity, and it might make more sense to state things the other way around: imagination (including anticipation and temporalized subjectivity) becomes a function of technology. But what does "function of" mean? Does it mean that technology becomes a part of the functioning of imagination? This is nothing new, as our imagination is always constrained and enabled by the affordances of the available technologies and their interfaces with our bodies and minds.[73] On my rephrasing, then: imagination becomes a part of the functioning of post-cinematic technology. As we have seen with the generative dimensions of contemporary imaging processes, there is a general offloading of anticipatory temporality onto technics. And this, it appears, *is* something new—but the focus on "imagination" stands in the way of recognizing this.

Hui refers to the example of searching Google for restaurant recommendations: "When people want to go to a restaurant, these days they are increasingly likely to search online first. We might also notice that Google is able to suggest which is the closest and most preferable restaurant for their needs according to its search and recommendation algorithm."[74] According to Hui, this example foregrounds two things: "(1) tertiary protention tends to depend on tertiary retention, for example, the relations given by digital objects, those traces we have left, such as pictures, videos, or geolocations; and (2) orientation becomes more and more an algorithmic process that analyzes and produces relations to pave the way for the experience of the next now or the immediate future."[75] Unfortunately, neither the example nor the inferences drawn from it differentiate Hui's theory of tertiary protention from Stiegler's notion of the way that tertiary retention, once we enter the era of "real-time" media, preformat our experience and thus serve to *shape* human protention. In other words, Hui is not (at least in this example) talking about the establishment of a nonhuman or machinic protention, such as I have in mind. Instead, he is talking about a feedback mechanism whereby concretized traces transform human subjectivity; he is apparently concerned with a high-level operation according to which the subject is regarded in terms of a referential form of imagination (e.g., I imagine myself going to a restaurant), which is made to stand in for protention. Indeed, Hui explicitly equates the two: "Protention is hence also imagination, through which we recollect and recognize what we have experienced and project it into the future."[76] In order to account for the novel temporality of post-cinematic media, however, we need to distinguish this referential anticipation (subjective or secondary protention, directed at the *object* of an imagined future, which I "see" in my mind's eye) from a pre-subjective and nonreferential form of protention (the primary protention that prereflectively opens onto the immediate future as a condition of our experience of temporal objects and temporal continuity more generally). The latter will also serve as the model for a corrected theory of tertiary or nonhuman protention.

In other words, Hui treats tertiary protention as an externalization of secondary protention (an offloading and concretization of subjective, referential anticipation). Another example he offers bears this out: "You go home after work, tired and sleepy; when you open the door, a freshly made coffee is already there waiting for you. The machine has prepared the coffee for you before you have decided to have one, because it knows that you would like (or will want) to have one. This is one of the examples of tertiary protention working from a distance, that is to say, of the imaginative force exerted from the outer world."[77] It is precisely this "imaginative force" that, for Hui, distinguishes the "statistical predictions" of a smart environment like this from the mnemotechnical regime of Stiegler's "cinema": "Without algorithms, digital objects would be mere retentions residing on the hard drives of computers and servers. Through the analysis of data—or, more or less, through speculation—the machines are able to produce surprises (not just crises) by identifying a possible (and probable) 'future,' a specific conception of time that is always already ahead but that we have not yet projected."[78] But this "specific conception" is modeled on a *subjective* conception, an imagined (and concretely *imaged*) scenario that is actualized machinically for the human subject. The "speculation" referenced here is of the order of what Wolfgang Ernst, quoting Martin Donner, refers to as the "meso-level of psychic-cognitive processes" rather than the microtemporal process of "speculative execution."[79] The latter, however, undercuts precisely the integrity of the image that is operative in Hui's "imaginative force" of protention; at this level of microtemporal processing, there is no determinate image that could be anticipated or intended by a subject as a picture-object. Instead, there is a molecular becoming that mirrors our own prepredicative becoming-in-time. So while the anticipatory dimension identified by Hui certainly marks a leap in the technical operationalization of the future, Hui's approach fails to recognize the microlevel operations on which it relies. In modeling tertiary protention on the subjective process of imagination (imagining a future *scenario* or scene), Hui effectively reduces protention to a representational process, thereby obscuring the nonrepresentational processes of both machinic and human relations to the immediate future. Against this reduction, I contend that we should conceive tertiary protention as involving an externalization not of subjective imagination but of the presubjective, nonreferential processing of futurity by which the subject is anchored in the present flow of time. On this view, but not on the model provided by Hui, the advent of tertiary protention would indeed mark a novel appearance in the world, and its impact on subjectivity would accordingly be quite radical—of the order of metabolism rather than imagination.

By appealing to imagination, Hui effectively replicates for tertiary protention an error at the root of Stiegler's argument for the preformatting of the future through the operation of tertiary retention. Following an objection raised by Jean-Michel Salanskis, Mark Hansen argues that Stiegler has reduced primary retention to a discrete, referential form of intentionality rather than, as in Husserl, a continuous operation in which the "adherent past" is glued together: or, in Salanskis's words, "a sort of infinitesimal operator capable of giving us, by the path of a dynamic production, the linear continuum."[80] For Salanskis, this implies a paradox, or a split, between a discrete, referential aspect of primary retention and the continuous, nonreferential aspect that Hansen takes to be the primary (if not sole) component of primary retention as such. Hansen reads Husserl's primary retention as "fundamentally nondiscrete and almost certainly nonconscious (beneath the threshold of what can be experienced phenomenologically)."[81] This, for Hansen, is a corporeal operation, the bodily production of time or temporal experience. And the consequence of the body's meting out of time and making it available to consciousness, which positions the body at the cusp of the unmarked environment and the world of experience, is that primary retention is not subject to the simple co-optation by tertiary memory that Stiegler envisions. The "mnemotechnical constitution of time" prioritized by Stiegler is thus secondary to the "corporo-technical constitution of time" that Hansen identifies as an infra-empirical condition of experience.[82]

Elsewhere, I have taken this argument as the basis for rethinking tertiary retention as similarly split between a referential and a nonreferential aspect, thus militating against Stiegler's overemphasis of technics' memorial or mnemotechnical aspect at the expense of its materiality.[83] Indeed, Stiegler's prioritizing of mnemotechnics aligns technical objects with consciousness, and specifically with a discrete and referential functioning of conscious thought—thus setting the stage for Hui's referential model of tertiary protention qua imagination. As I argued in my book *Postnaturalism*, to recognize the possibility of a split in tertiary retention between a referential and a nonreferential facet would be to grant the possibility that technical objects have a form of embodiment that, parallel to our own, marks their own material boundaries between discrete objecthood and environmental flux—a duality that corresponds to filmic images' double life as both representational and presentational media, both image and matter at once. As such, subjective memory is flanked *on both sides* (that is, on the side of primary *and* of tertiary memory) by a nondiscrete smooth space of matter, and the human-technical transduction is itself more deeply anchored in a realm of *distributed materiality* or *distributed embodiment*. To expand this argument to tertiary protention would be to recognize that technical futurity is similarly split between a referential form of anticipation and a nonreferential form, and that the computational generation of determinate images (or the "imaginative force" of the smart environment's prediction of our desires) is dependent on this lower-level operation in which images, much less imaginative contents, are not fixed or fully formed.

Like Stiegler before him, Hui fails to account adequately for the nonreferential dimension of the technical processing of time, and hence fails to grasp the full implications for temporal experience. What this means is that he overstates the determinism of consciousness through technics and its articulation of tertiary retention/protention; somewhat paradoxically, in this way he also radically *under*estimates the agency of post-cinematic technics and its impact on subjectivity. By reducing the nonhuman protentional processing of time to the referential functioning of imagination, Hui underestimates the discorrelated

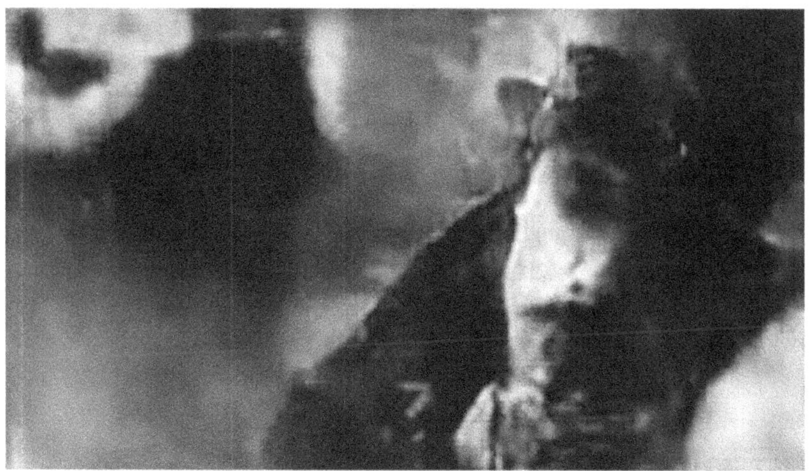

Figure 3.5. Terence Broad's *Blade Runner—Autoencoded* (2016).

autonomy of computational processes from thought and the radical empowering of the environment that it represents. What follows, when we correct this image of tertiary protention, is not determinism but a radically pronounced and microscopically articulated form of contingency—a contingency that is embodied in the microdecisions or "crises" of time-critical technics and its futural microtemporality, and mediated through the post-cinematic imaging processes in which our imaginative faculties are today inextricably enmeshed.

Something of this contingency and enmeshment can be glimpsed in the images composing *Blade Runner—Autoencoded*, a machine-learning project conducted in 2016 by Terence Broad toward completion of a degree in creative computing at Goldsmiths, University of London, and which has since been shown at the Whitney Museum of American Art and acquired by the contemporary art collection of Geneva, Switzerland.[84] Perhaps this institutional entwinement of art and computational technology already points to the ways that images and imaginations are being transformed today; if that is so, the project's specific techniques and visual forms point more concretely to the role of computational futurity in our experience of moving-image media. Broad's project uses a deep learning architecture known as an "autoencoder"—an unsupervised artificial neural network that "learns" efficiently to compress and decompress data—to algorithmically reconstruct the individual frames of the film *Blade Runner* (1982). Citing the movie's exploration of "artificial subjectivity" in connection with its repeated depiction of "eyes, photographs and other symbols alluding to perception," Broad sees *Blade Runner* as a fitting object "for a project that is trying to expose the phenomenology of disembodied artificial perception."[85] The project combines three convolutional neural networks (CNNs)—an encoder, a decoder, and a discriminator.[86] It blends the functions of an autoencoder with that of a generative adversarial network (GAN)—another machine-learning approach that plays a generator network against a discriminator trying to differentiate real from generated images, thereby setting up an agonistic situation in which each network tries to "outwit" the other and both therefore benefit from each other's progress. In Broad's system, GAN discrimination is used to train the encoder/decoder networks (the autoencoder proper), producing what amounts to a self-regulating AI codec. This is an extremely lossy form of video compression, as is evident from the somewhat hallucinatory images produced, whereby the active generation of images is prioritized over faithful reproduction.

And while the visuals alone may be enough to captivate our imaginations, their full significance can be grasped only if they are viewed in relation to their technical underpinnings. First, the encoding network, consisting of five layers, transforms a random batch of images measuring 256 by 144 pixels into a tiny 16-by-9-pixel image by way of halving the resolution with each successive layer.[87] The resulting "image," which for the computer is really nothing more than a statistically computed value, constitutes the "code" or "latent representation." Next, the decoder network, also comprising five layers, takes this code and recomputes it, doubling the *x* and *y* dimensions at each layer to speculatively reconstruct a batch of images with the original resolution of 256 by 144 pixels.[88] Then the discriminator network steps in to evaluate the results; the discriminator functions similarly to the encoder network, in that it reduces images down in size to a 16-by-9 code, but it takes as its input either original (uncompressed) or generated (decompressed) images and tries to determine which is which.[89] With the help of several objective functions that measure divergences in encoded, decoded, and discriminated data, each of the three networks is subjected to a training process during which they collectively "learn" to better perform their functions.[90] The process is repeated until all of the film's images have been processed, thus completing a single "epoch." For *Blade Runner—Autoencoded*, Broad trained the model for six epochs, a process that took approximately two weeks, before running the model to produce the generative video.[91]

Although this was a slow process overall, the project captures both the contingency and the agency of microtemporal protention in a number of ways. Above all, it is important to note that the system is not operating according to predefined compression algorithms such as the Discrete Cosine Transforms or motion-estimation processes at the heart of MPEG encoding. Those are relatively high-level functions that sample images in an orderly and predictable manner, while the autoencoding process utilized here is a more or less blind groping toward order, executed at the ultralow level of the GPU (graphics processing unit or graphics card).[92] The latter piece of hardware is crucially implicated in accelerating contemporary video decompression more generally, so its use in image-generation represents an interesting transformation of the predictive processes of video playback, which are now rendered less predictable or deterministic by means of the artificial neural networks. In effect, these networks are engaged in an effort to deduce or guess—rather than merely implement—the correct mode of anticipating or protending a reasonable outcome. Computational speculation, in the sense exemplified by the microtemporal operation of speculative execution, is thus turned into an explicitly generative enterprise in the production of visible images. As we have seen, these images are the result of a self-regulating but therefore highly volatile (because not directed) process whereby the system is trained to invent its own codec, encoding data into a highly compressed form and predicting a plausible decoding from what amounts to inadequate information. The indirection of the process resembles the indetermination of embodied life (recalling Bergson's equation of the living, durational body with a "center of indetermination").[93] Again, lest there be any confusion on this matter, the point of the comparison is not to lend credence to the notion that AI applications such as deep-learning neural networks are actually "intelligent" in any sense that would be comparable to human cognitive processes; rather, the point is that neural nets and related computational processes are capable of protentional functions that mirror our own future-oriented processing of time, thereby opening up a space of radical contingency that, by means of close proximity with our prepersonal being-in-time, can significantly transform our metabolic relations to the world.

The wispy, ghostly images of *Blade Runner—Autoencoded* translate these powers of contingency into visible form, thus providing for them an aesthetic counterpart and opening a space in which to start "making sense" of transformations taking place deep below the level of perceptual consciousness. Generatively reconstructed images of the Voight-Kampff test being administered to an artificial being speak to the way that AI technologies have captured our imaginations about the future, but what these images communicate is not so much a determinate, much less deterministic, vision of our experience than an uncertain encounter between human and machinic agencies, each "running ahead of" itself into a blank future, and articulated together in the open of environmental indeterminacy. Such microtemporal contingencies are no guarantee against the tightening circles of anticipatory formatting that we have considered in this chapter; the indeterminacy of prepersonal and machinic futurity provides no firm grounding, in other words, for freedom in a strong, ethically relevant sense. Yet such encounters with aesthetic objects like the discorrelated images of *Blade Runner—Autoencoded* open up this uncertain ground and reposition us with respect to computational technics, inscribing us in an agonistic configuration that very much resembles a "generative adversarial network."

Coda: Multistable Screen Times

In part II, I will turn to several cases of moving images that help us to "make sense" of discorrelation in terms of specific affects and generic forms. First, however, I would like to close this chapter with a final object that articulates together the various temporal levels of screen time, from very small to very large, and asks us to meditate more generally on the contingencies of contemporary media temporalization.

Seances (2016) is an online generative video work by Canadian filmmaker Guy Maddin, along with cocreators Evan Johnson and Galen Johnson, and with support from the National Film Board of Canada. The project draws on Maddin's attempts to re-create or resurrect lost films, including works by Alice Guy, Ernst Lubitsch, Friedrich Wilhelm Murnau, and many others. Staging séances in which the actors would conjure the "spirit" of the lost films, and shooting before live audiences at the Centre Pompidou in Paris and at the Centre Phi in Montreal, Maddin reimagined approximately thirty such films. Subsequently, these films became the raw material for *Seances*; the web-based project algorithmically combines footage from the films into a new, supposedly "unique" composition—decidedly digital but with a heavy suggestion of analog materiality—that will allegedly "never be seen again."[94] Opening with a dramatic claim—"It's your one chance to see *this* film"—the project invites superlatives, hyperbole, and anachronism. For example, it is variously claimed that the combinatory system is capable of producing "billions of unique stories on-demand,"[95] or "hundreds of billions of unique permutations,"[96] or even "an infinite number of unique film experiences."[97] And while these video experiences are digitally composited on the fly, they are anachronistically said to be "destroyed" after viewing,[98] as if they had first been printed on celluloid, or

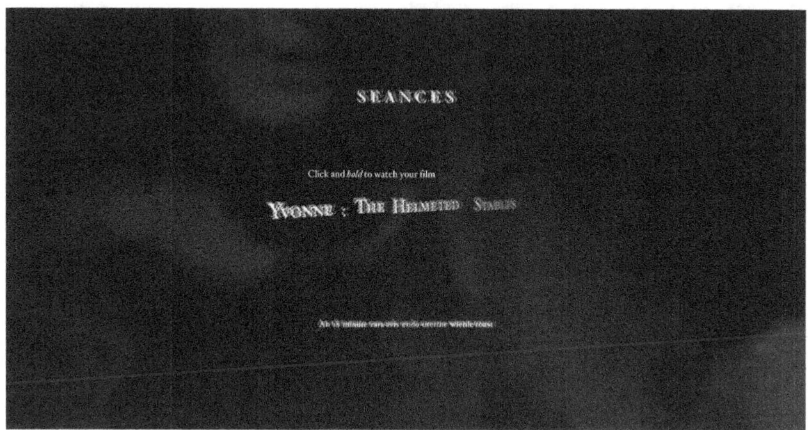

Figure 3.6. Randomly generated titles in *Seances* (2016).

they are supposedly “erased,”[99] as if they were stored on magnetic tape. Presented as “a testament to loss and ephemerality in the age of the Internet,” the project intentionally confuses analog and digital, splices together old and new, and thereby inserts the microtemporality of contemporary screen time into the much longer, slower circuits of media history—and vice versa.[100]

When we open the *Seances* website (http://seances.nfb.ca), the National Film Board logo appears on a black background and slowly fades away. Then we read, “Guy Maddin, Evan Johnson, Galen Johnson and the National Film Board of Canada present,” before this text too fades out and gives way to the title in bold capital letters: “SEANCES.” Instructions then appear, one by one: “Touch and hold to conjure.” Added after a brief delay: “Then sit back and relax.” And finally: “It’s your one chance to see *this* film.” The text abruptly disappears, the black background is replaced with a blurry moving image in muted colors and haunting music, which seems to combine analog stringed instruments with electronically synthesized sounds and indecipherable voices, begins to play. The screen’s central region contains three textual elements: at the top, “SEANCES”; in the middle, words floating in three-dimensional space, rearranging themselves into shifting title formations, such as “Skies and Homes,” “Alicia’s Skies,” “The Prisoner’s Skies,” and “Boldly the Skies Doze”; below, descriptions for each of these appear: “A 14 minute stern-driven nocturnal revenge bromance,” “A 17 minute stern-driven slavic revenge bromance,” “A 21 minute nocturnal slavic revenge bromance,” “A 15 minute harborfront slavic hootenany.” Every once in a while, the white text separates into offset layers of red and blue, like a shaky intimation of old-fashioned 3D technologies.

Occasionally we are reminded: "Click and *hold* to watch your film." When we do, a circular loading meter appears, while the simulated 3D text shakes more violently and random images flash before our eyes. Attempting to select a given title also accelerates its replacement by a new one, generated quasi-randomly: my attempt to view *Vampires and Wings* ("A 14 minute telerarian stern-driven *danse macabre*") resulted instead in selecting *Wings of the Chilled Girl* ("A 15 minute telerarian ululatory *danse macabre*"). The interactive interface suggests individual choice, but what it serves up is instead chance and dividuation, obstinately refusing mastery by the user.

When the movie is loaded, we read in yellowish lettering against a grainy brownish background: "This ______ minute film will disappear." The blank is filled in with oversized red numerals indicating the duration of the movie, usually between ten and twenty minutes. Our attention is thereby primed at several scales: given only the title and the duration, we may speculate imaginatively on the images that will occupy our consciousness in the coming minutes; but even more significantly, the immediate retentional-protentional circuits of our awareness are charged with unusual urgency by the threat of disappearance. We discover, now, that there are no video controls: no pause or rewind buttons. If we miss something, we cannot go back and review or reclaim the experience, which slips irretrievably into the past while new images and sounds flow incessantly from the future to occupy a now somewhat paranoid present. Temporality, and the ineluctable passage of time, moves to the center of our attention. The images themselves are relentless and chaotic: flashes of color, fleeting silhouettes, undulating textures, scratchy frames, then a logo, the word "Presents" in shifting, unstable letters, an actor's name with the lines of CRT-era interlacing visible, multiple facial images composited on top of one another and morphing into a new object, then the title in an ornate silent film–style frame: *The Chilled Wings*—not the title that I chose, and not even the one I thought I had received instead. Characters are introduced: an obliquely framed face appears, before it is identified in shaky intertitles—"UKRAINIAN PRISONER, Christophe Paou." Then: "His guard, a peasant from the same village." Shot-countershot sequences seem to confuse more than clarify the narrative and spatiotemporal relations between characters and objects, all of which are seemingly ripped out of universes completely foreign to one another and materialized in radically different medial substrates: color, black-and-white film stocks, different gauges, pocked by dirt and scratches, as well as analog and digital video artifacts. And on it goes for the next fifteen minutes or so, as the narrative twists and turns, sometimes teasing coherence and at other times withdrawing any semblance thereof.

The strange mix of visual media forms folds my focal awareness of temporal passage into broader media-historical horizons of innovation and obsolescence, and I find my attention split between visible surfaces, the objects they depict, and their multilayered presentational technologies. New and old, the "now" and the historical past commingle in an "operational aesthetic" (to borrow a term from Neil Harris) that finds me wondering about the mechanisms responsible for producing these screen phenomena:[101] I wonder about the programming of the algorithm, about the tagging of shots and sequences in a hidden database, about the datamoshing and similar effects I see, and whether they are prerecorded or executed in real time. Later, I may learn that Imposium, the proprietary data-driven video rendering system at work behind the scenes, indeed "applies visual effects like datamoshing, sound interruption, sound flowing, motion tracking, and rotoscoping on the fly."[102] Whether or not I know this, I am increasingly aware of a computational agency, which seems to operate very differently from that of a human consciousness. The irrational combinatory logic gives rise to impressions of the "machine as director"[103] or, as *Seances* producer Dana Dansereau puts it, "an algorithmic director."[104] Actively courting this operational aesthetic, producer Alicia Smith remarks: "It's basically data-driven filmmaking much like programming."[105]

Comparing the algorithmic editing to surrealist techniques of juxtaposition, Andrei Kartashov views *Seances* in terms of "a digital update to the surrealist collage that resembles Lev Manovich's imaginary project of 'database cinema'"; hence, "Maddin uses programming code where the original surrealists relied on the unconscious to produce juxtaposition."[106] But unlike the logic of the update as it functions in Silicon Valley marketing, novelty here is linked to a transience of experience that infects both my present consciousness and the larger dynamics of media-technical change. According to the project statement on the *Seances* website: "*Seances* presents a new way of experiencing film narrative, framed through the lens of loss. In a technical feat of data-driven cinematic storytelling, films are dynamically assembled in never-to-be-repeated configurations. Each exists only in the moment, with no pausing, scrubbing or sharing permitted, offering the audience one chance to *see this film* before it disappears." A "technical feat" leads uncharacteristically to "loss." Accordingly, this unusual operational aesthetic contradicts promises of seamless experience and mastery. As Maddin emphasizes: "The images and sound present a sense of instability and fragility,"[107] and the experience as a whole is pervaded by a sense of the "interstitial."[108]

Clearly, "loss" is the central motif, and it is articulated emphatically *across* the cinema/post-cinema divide, referring simultaneously to the irretrievable pastness of lost films, the contingent ephemerality of digital "content" on the web, and the "lossiness" of digital video codecs. Accordingly, *Seances* references feelings of loss in order to implicate our affective relations across temporal scales—from the long temporal circuit of film history (which takes the decade as its unit), to the somewhat shorter circuit of life online (with temporalities measured in days, months, and years), to the very short circuit of perceptual or subperceptual loss in real-time decompression. Enforcing a sacrificial loss for every experiential gain it offers, the project revels in paradox: it "resurrects" lost films, but in the process produces what amount to instantly lost films (or moving-image objects that refuse to be repeated). Reflecting on his own experience, Maddin remarks: "There's a random title generator. The first title that came out was *Wise Trumpets of the Milky Midnight*. We watched it, and it was destroyed—it went back to lost matter."[109] This elegiac gesture—"back to lost matter"—also signals the ethical import of the project. Again in Maddin's words:

> If the non sequitur addled collisions actually create something that's charming, which occasionally they do, then that's out of lost matter, then it's lost immediately again. There will be a real sense of loss experienced by the viewer. That was the hope, anyway. And by being gone, the way things collided just would have to exist as a memory and maybe by word of mouth, some sort of report. Then finally there's a sadness that you can't recreate it. On the internet, there's a feeling that everything is up there for good. Just to be about destroying things, not for the sheer pleasure of destroying them but just to return some sense of loss to the digital world.[110]

Cocreator Evan Johnson echoes this sentiment: "There's a growing sense that there is too much stuff available to us. . . . In a way, we're calling for the destruction of cultural objects in order to long for them again. By destroying the unique viewing experience we were producing, we hoped that a particularly beautiful one would be heightened by the fact of its disappearance."[111] Add to this the limitations noted above—that you cannot pause, rewind, download, or share the generated video—and we recognize in *Seances* a calculated affront to the algorithmic temporalities of post-cinematic media, but one that is enabled precisely by those temporalities.

At the heart of this agonistic constellation is a paradoxical digital/analog hybridity that foregrounds a disjunctive, multistable process of *de/generation*—an oscillatory process based in both a simulation of analog degeneration by digitally generative means (e.g., the celluloid image warping from heat or fire, achieved by digital morphing), as well as a rethinking of digital generativity in terms of material degradation (making no distinction between filmic decay and the intrusion of YouTube videos by means of datamoshing). This de/generation, consummated in the simulated "destruction" of the video, "tr[ies] to emulate, by ways of digital technology, an auratic experience."[112] Digital simulations of decay thus serve to heighten the paradoxes: "*Seances* communicates the sense of imminent loss by imitating color distortions and morphs caused by the disintegration of celluloid: a testament to fragility and ephemerality of (analogue) film history and a piece of evidence that the 'film' you are watching is real and is about to disappear forever." But

> each video created in *Seances* is original and not a reproduction—in the sense that it has been composited specifically for one viewing and may not be copied—but in fact there is no original at all. The sense of presence is created from a void, as there is not even a digital video file, incorporeal as it may have been, of what we watch; only a situational combination of video files with no single point of origin. As for the visual effects, they are of course created digitally, in order to represent a physical dying in something that cannot physically die, or at any rate is not susceptible to physical wear and tear.[113]

In this interplay of de/generation, what we see is perhaps only a simulated dying and decay, but it is a very real *metabolism* (defined in terms of the temporal exchanges between a chaotic substrate and its organized forms, between cellular disorganization and nascent organism). A variety of temporal frames is thereby set in contingent, multistable relation: at the microtemporal scale, there is the on-the-fly generation of effects, including analog scratches and digital blocking of uncertain provenance (are the compression artifacts programmed or incidental to playback?); there is the time of streaming and its peculiar anticipation of the viewer (including the appearance of buffering screens with a pixely, low-resolution animated circle indicating loading status); and there is the combinatory logic of the database, where a viewer's individual choices have an effect on future viewers (somewhat like Netflix's algorithmic construction of taste, but in an exactly negative mirror image: rather than increasing the likelihood of others seeing the same video, my viewing determines the impossibility of its being seen again, thus signaling a radical reversal of the normative anticipatory logic of big data).

After the video has finished streaming, I am presented with a long list of titles, which I can click on to reveal additional information; these are previously screened titles, no longer available to view, but I can see precisely when and where they were "lost": the date, time, and city of their one and only screening.

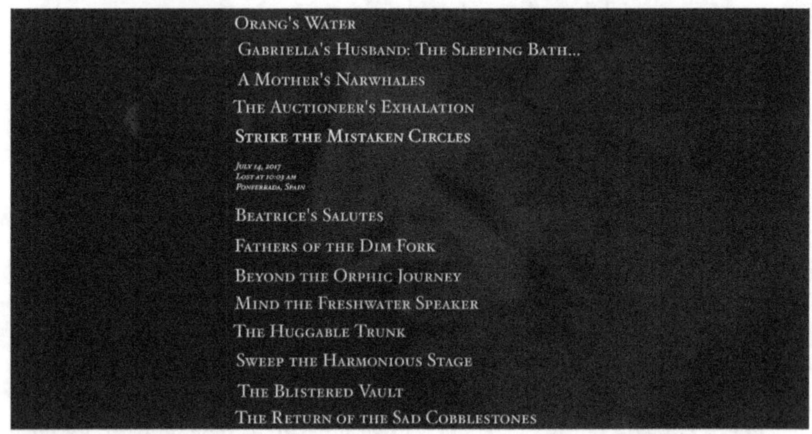

Figure 3.7. List of "lost" titles in *Seances*.

I linger on this list, pondering what little miracle might have been witnessed at 1:03 AM on July 14, 2017, when someone in Ponferrada, Spain, watched *Strike the Mistaken Circles*. I scroll through other titles, wondering about *The Incestuous Nose-Dives*, lost at 8:57 AM on May 14, 2017, following a single screening in Warsaw, Poland; about *The Blind Girl's Gondola*, lost at 7:39 AM on May 5, 2017, in London; about *Florence's Sympathies*, screened in the middle of the night, at 3:50 AM on May 3, 2017, in St. Petersburg, Russia, and never seen again. With its list of lost films, each formed on the fly in an act of de/generation, *Seances* rethinks the low-level perceptual loss of digital video in terms of a macrotemporal, that is, film-historical, scale—and vice versa. The project's titular séance alternates between a spiritualistic gathering and a cinematic screening—for which the French *séance* is used as a matter of course—but it also comes to implicate the radically multistable and multiscalar temporalities of what we now live as *screen time*.

Part II

MAKING SENSE OF DISCORRELATION

Life to Those Pixels!

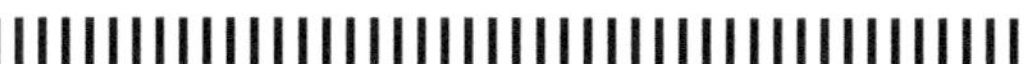

How do we "make sense" of images that are discorrelated from sensory perception? In order to answer this question, we might start by asking how post-cinema tries to make sense of itself—how it thematizes and visualizes the experiential and systemic changes in which it is involved. Focusing on these moments of self-reflexivity, when contemporary moving-image media inspect their own conditions of possibility, and connecting them to the ways that post-cinematic technologies, techniques, and images modulate spectatorial affects in a range of (often generic) forms, we will discover cultural forms and norms according to which moving image media seek to understand the sweeping transformations currently underway. As we have seen in part I, these transformations concern not only the mediation of images in a narrow sense but also the production of subjects, political collectives, and environmental relations more generally. Connecting concrete images with these broad ethical implications, we can then ask what lessons post-cinema offers us for learning to live in this world, under conditions of life shaped by a media regime characterized by irrational cameras, dividuated images, and the contingent control processes of screen time.

Part II of this book turns to this task of making sense of discorrelation through three thematic/affective constellations: the self-reflexive fascination of algorithmic "animation" in recent science-fiction films about artificial beings; the displaced fear of computational media, or of discorrelation itself, in contemporary horror (and the real-world horrors of mediated war and terror); and the threat of extinction, the ultimate scene of discorrelation, in post-cinematic productions about the end of the world. In each of these contexts, we encounter what might be taken as parables, fables, or allegories—interestingly displaced or indirect figurations—for life in an age of discorrelation. I begin, in this chapter, with contemporary science fiction and its recurrent fantasies of animation—often focused on the creation of an artificial woman. I ask what these self-reflexive spectacles—in which animation is both a theme and, in the guise of CGI and related techniques, a medium—can tell us about post-cinema's understanding of itself, about our situation in the world, and about the role played by discorrelated images in shaping a posthuman future.

Edge Detection, or, The Parable of Joi

There is a remarkable (and often-remarked) scene a little over halfway into Denis Villeneuve's *Blade Runner 2049* (2017) that speaks powerfully to our changing media landscape and the uncertain relations that it generates between human life and perception, on the one hand, and the spatiotemporal situations created by digital images, on the other. The scene in question is a sex scene involving three characters: the Blade Runner known as K (played by Ryan Gosling), his AI-powered and holographically projected girlfriend Joi (played by Ana de Armas), and a sex worker named Mariette (played by Mackenzie Davis) who has been hired to lend Joi a tangible body in order to make love to K. This unusual ménage à trois requires Mariette to stand in corporeally for the immaterial Joi, whose likeness is projected onto the sex worker's body, thereby forming a composite of the two characters—and indeed, *compositing* is the technique used to merge the two actors' bodies in digital screen space.[1] But rather than blending the two women together into a perfect, seamless union (and it was certainly within the power of the VFX team to do so), Joi's and Mariette's images remain distinct from one another, slipping in and out of phase in imperfect alignment.

The emphatic *seamfulness* of this union is foregrounded as a visual spectacle in its own right. As a spectacle, it is staged not as something to be taken for granted but as something that has to be achieved. Thus, before the composited women can jointly make love to K, they must, with some effort, be synced up with one another: Mariette stands facing K while Joi slowly approaches; the two women regard each other briefly, and Joi tries to match

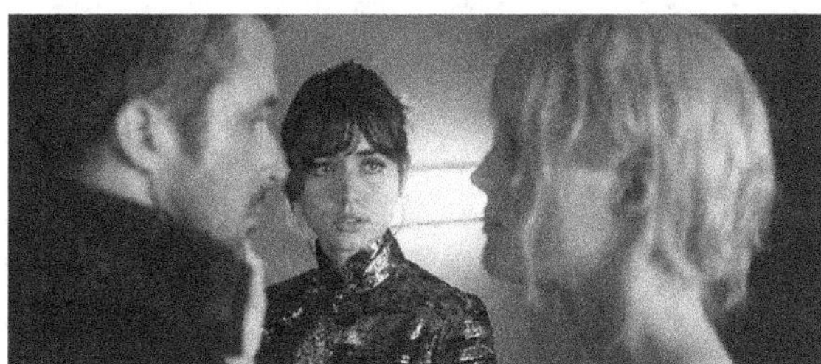

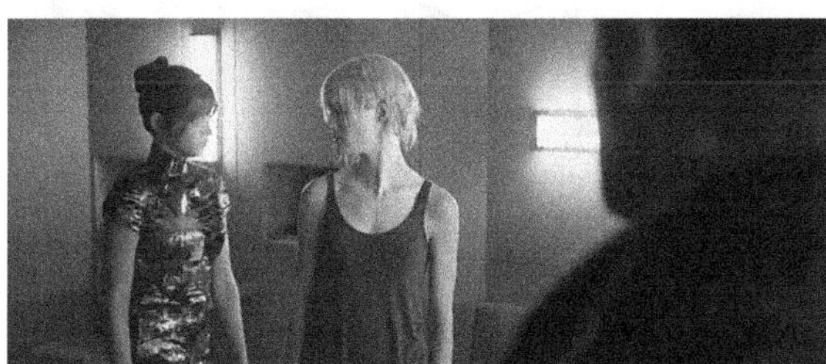

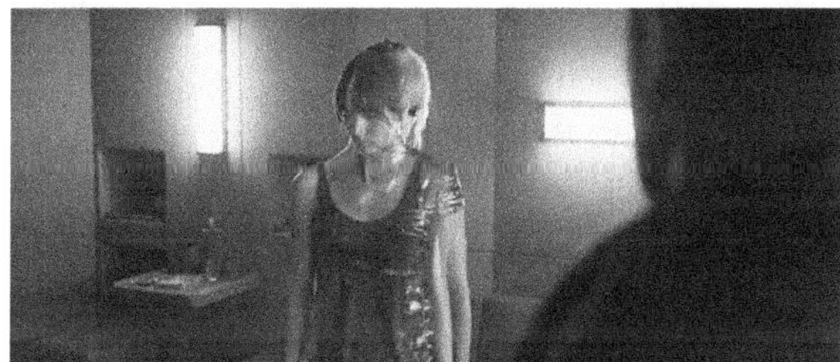

Figures 4.1–4.3. An unusual ménage à trois in *Blade Runner 2049* (Denis Villeneuve, 2017).

Mariette's position in the room; the holographic woman flickers slightly while she gets into position; the two roughly aligned women shift back and forth and look in opposite directions; then they raise their right hands and look down to inspect them; the camera cuts to a subjective shot, either from one or both of the women's perspective(s); the hands are waved back and forth several times, one of them lagging noticeably behind the motions of the other, until they suddenly snap into place and line up visually with each other. Cutting back to the women's faces, still visibly out of phase, Mariette smiles and says with some amazement: "Look at you!" (thus giving voice to the movie's self-reflexive display of its effects, which implore the viewer to *look* at them). Joi, more seriously, responds: "Quiet! Now I have to sync!" And now, indeed, the women's faces line up, and their bodies line up, but they continue in the following to alternate between the one and the other as more focally dominant—just as if someone were playing with the transparency settings of each layer in Photoshop or After Effects.

Figures 4.4 and 4.5. Out of phase.

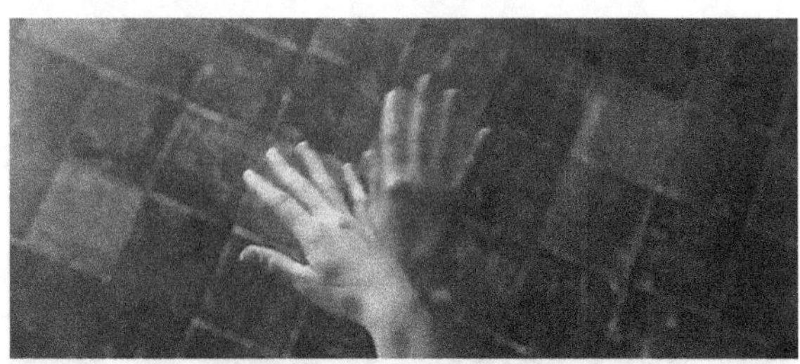

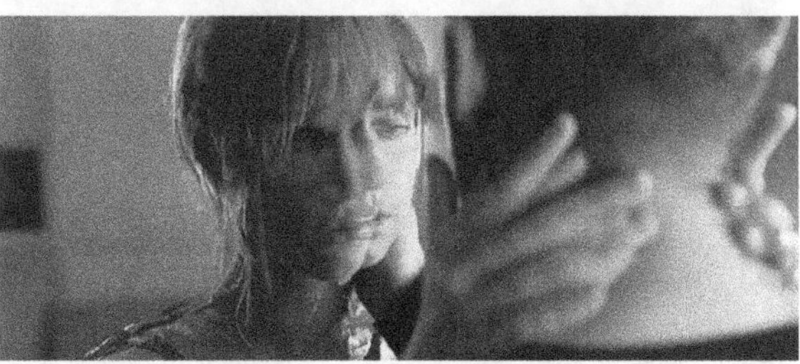

Because the synchronization remains incomplete, it retains an obstinate visibility. The scene is therefore something like those VFX reels that digital effects studios upload to YouTube or Vimeo to show off their work: videos that peel back the multiple composited layers of CGI textures, particle physics, and simulated lighting to reveal the technical complexity behind the finished images in blockbuster movies, a complexity that is otherwise invisible in its seamless integration.[2] But here, through intentionally seamful compositing, the execution of VFX is put on display in the movie itself. Paradoxically, the very failure of integration is situated as a visual spectacle.

The images' imperfect temporal synchronization and seamful spatial alignment serve to focus the movie's thematic interrogation of boundaries between human and artificial being, between life and nonlife, between real and fake (just prior to syncing with Mariette, Joi assures K: "It's OK; she's real. I want to be real for you"). But staged in this way the images also layer atop this questioning a further interest in imaging processes themselves—an interest that is motivated narratively by the presence of the holographic Joi, of course, but that goes beyond that level and aims squarely at a problematization of the images on the spectator's screen. The scene therefore synthesizes—or composites—these levels materially: the question of the digitally mediated image becomes transposable with the question of the definition of human life and perception itself. So, like the characters on-screen, the spectator too is enlisted in a questioning that might be termed the problem of *edge detection*: Joi's struggle to stay in sync with Mariette translates a computationally demanding task of matching a moving object's visible outline in real time; K's job (as Blade Runner) of discerning between human and nonhuman entities is twisted into an effort to *see* (both visually and conceptually) the two women as one without thereby confusing them; and the viewer is tasked with mediating between diegetic and nondiegetic complications of the image, along with the resulting thematic and material confusions of human and technological agencies.

Technically speaking, edge detection refers to a set of computational processes that are fundamental to machine vision, computer vision, and automated image processing; edge detection encompasses algorithms that identify discontinuities in brightness within digital images, extracting line segments called "edges" that correspond (ideally) to the actual edges of physical objects or symbols.[3] Edge detection is implemented in applications ranging from optical character recognition (OCR), automatic license plate readers, industrial robotics, drones, self-driving cars, and other areas where a computational system is responsible for detecting, recognizing, classifying, or processing visual phenomena.

Abstracting from this technical understanding, we might relate the concept of edge detection to broader issues of perception in an age of digital mediation. Technical implementations of edge-detection algorithms demonstrate one of the ways that contemporary images are radically discorrelated from human perception, but even the ones that we see with our own eyes are impacted by the transformative effects of computational processing.[4] From popular worries over the veracity of images in an age of Photoshop and CGI to scholarly debates over the loss of indexicality and its meaning for our experience of moving images, the shift from a cinematic to a post-cinematic media regime has introduced all sorts of uncertainties into our relationships with images and the underlying technologies that produce and support them. Whether in a movie theater equipped with digital video projectors, on a smart TV connected to digital cable or a Blu-ray player, or on a handheld device or a desktop monitor streaming video from the Internet, nearly all of the images that we see today have been processed by a computer prior to our seeing them, and much of this processing (e.g., video decompression, upscaling, or motion smoothing) is done on the fly. At stake in these processes are, among other things, the "edges" that visually define the objects of our perception. As we saw in chapter 3, compression algorithms, which are responsible for making playback and streaming more efficient by reducing the amount of digital information that must be processed at any given time, work by eliminating perceptually "extraneous" data—minor differences of intensity or hue between pixels that would be imperceptible under normal circumstances, for example. Employing motion estimation algorithms to determine which information is redundant, codecs such as MPEG-2 and MPEG-4 are crucially concerned with determining and preserving the shapes of moving objects, defined in terms of edges moving across the two-dimensional plane of the screen.[5] But if the compression settings are off, or if there are errors in the execution of the codec's algorithms, perceptual edges are subject to effacement or exaggeration; the "false" edges of blocky compression artifacts might even be generated where no edge should be. Video compression therefore involves a precarious balancing act between computational and human perception, a seamful negotiation between human and nonhuman ways of seeing and processing visual information.

The seams, usually hidden from view, are perhaps nowhere more visible today than in the controversies surrounding "DeepFake" videos and other AI-generated imagery. Named after the Reddit user "deepfakes," who in 2017 uploaded a series of face-swapped fake celebrity porn videos featuring the likenesses of Scarlett Johansson, Gal Gadot, Taylor Swift, and others, DeepFake videos use machine-learning algorithms known as generative adversarial networks (GANs) to automate the morphing and superimposition of images (such as a celebrity's face) onto unrelated video (such as pornographic clips or political speeches).[6] The danger that such techniques will be used for disinformation campaigns or "fake news" has lately garnered increased attention, but it is telling that the most popular uses of DeepFakes so far have been in the realm of fake celebrity porn and revenge porn, almost exclusively targeting women.[7] Taking notice of this trend, Google has recently added the category of "involuntary synthetic pornographic imagery" to its list of banned content types.[8] Reporting about DeepFake videos emphasizes alternately that faces are "seamlessly grafted . . . onto someone else's body"[9] or that the syncing of the images "isn't perfect."[10] For example, the article widely credited with making the DeepFake phenomenon known to a wider public back in December 2017 notes with regard to the fake porn video featuring *Wonder Woman* star Gal Gadot: "In the Gadot video, a box occasionally appeared around her face where the original image peeks through, and her mouth and eyes don't quite line up to the words the actress is saying—but if you squint a little and suspend your belief, it might as well be Gadot."[11] Imperfections are evident here, but there is leeway "if you squint a little"—thus signaling a real perceptual indeterminacy.

Clearly, though, technical capabilities are evolving quickly, and more sophisticated algorithms may well erase these seams. What these discussions of the viewer's (in)ability to detect the edges in DeepFakes and GAN-generated faces point to, however, is the low-level imbrication taking place between technological imaging processes and human perception, whereby the borders between human and nonhuman, living and nonliving are called into question. The generative capabilities of artificial intelligences do not actually constitute life, to be sure, but the microtemporal operations involved in algorithmic imaging put them into close proximity with the subperceptual processes of human embodiment, potentially altering the metabolic pathways that mark our broadly ecological entanglements (all mediated today by technological apparatuses and systems) and that structure our own prepersonal processings of time and space. Pornography presents itself as an obvious test case, as it aims to short-circuit subjective cognition, affecting viewers' bodies directly by "animating" sexual desire.[12] In this way, the life-giving force of *animation* is plunged into a realm of indistinction, referring at once to technological processes like neural network–driven CGI, science-fiction fantasies of artificial creation, and biological facts of life. In this context, edge detection reveals itself as both a technical feat and a human-epistemological one that leads straight back to the "edges" of human-technological interfaces as well as to gender's blurred and contested lines, all of which are wrapped up in issues of generativity (with the Proto-Indo-European root **gene-* implicating gender, genre, genetics, and the generativity at the heart of CGI).

Obviously, such videos raise serious ethical and political questions, but the notion that they constitute the sort of ontological-epistemological nexus described above will likely strike many readers as hyperbolic at best.[13] And while it is beyond the scope of this chapter to fully substantiate these claims, a brief look at the phenomenology of DeepFake videos might be instructive.[14] Such videos split viewers' attention between representational and presentational levels, asking the viewer to alternate between the objects depicted and the manner (or the quality of technical execution and plausibility) of their depiction. At stake in both forms of regard is the question of the visual edge—that which delineates the object itself and that which belies its fabrication. This split or oscillating form of regard decenters conventional modes of spectatorial engagement, deprivileging narrative interest and "sutured" engrossment in the diegesis. Instead, human perception is brought into closer contact with computer vision: "object recognition" in the latter involves scanning images for objects, conditions, or information; looking at DeepFakes engages the viewer in a similar task, which demands a loosening of focal depth and a flattening of the distance between representation and mediation—essentially assuming a machinic vision not unlike the computer's as it mechanically and nonsubjectively scans pixels to recognize "objects" without regard for the difference between the image and that which it depicts. (It goes without saying that, in the context of pornography, this desubjectivizing of the spectator does nothing to mitigate the objectification of women's bodies.)

Meanwhile, various attempts to recognize fake imagery seek to reassert the difference between human perception and computer vision: artists seek to help humans disentangle their vision from that of AI by training our eyes to see telltale signs of computer-aided forgery,[15] while DARPA (the Defense Advanced Research Projects Agency) and others approach the problem from the other side, turning computer vision back on itself in order to automate the process of debunking fake images.[16] The fact that these efforts must be constantly updated points, however, to the underlying fact that human vision and machinic visuality are fundamentally coimplicated today, not just in GANs and other AI-based visualizations, but in digital imaging processes more generally, including the much more mundane compression algorithms mentioned above, which subject nearly all the images we perceive to processes known as *perceptual coding*: the balancing act whereby imperfections in human vision are exploited to reduce file size and improve streaming performance.[17] As we have seen, such processes turn crucially on the presence of edges and a means of "apprehending" them: differences in brightness trigger different degrees of granularity in subdividing the visible image into (ideally) invisible blocks, eliminating perceptually redundant information.[18] But then the "edge" at stake in edge detection, both broadly and narrowly construed, is the would-be seamless integration or synchronization of human and nonhuman forms of vision, whereby perceptual coding blends imperceptibly into a *coding of perception*.[19]

Seen in this light, *Blade Runner 2049*'s uncanny sex scene—which joins movies like *Her* (2013) and *Ex Machina* (2014) in imagining erotic relations between humans and artificial beings created under conditions of the digital—can be seen as a concise emblem of the contingencies, exigencies, and balancing acts involved in contemporary mediated life. The scene is unusual for its seamful display and focus on the difficulties of synchronization, which it stages as a question of *images* but also of *animation*—a life-giving generativity that implicates biological and artificial life both within the diegesis and without, at the interface where an embodied viewer, a holographic woman, and the images' digital infrastructures meet. All the principal actors are engaged in operations of edge detection: Joi and Mariette share the task of matching movement based on visible outlines—a task usually carried out by video codecs—while K plays the role of the spectator who might need to "squint a little" to fulfill the (gendered) fantasy of seamless integration, but whose perception remains under constant threat of breakdown in the form of a visual glitch.

As I have argued, this seamful display stages not only a technological but also a profoundly philosophical problematic and can therefore be read as a visual allegory for our post-cinematic situation more generally; it points to the uncertainties and seamful negotiations of human and non- or posthuman spatiotemporal situations that take place in, but that far exceed, mundane acts of viewing digital video. The scene unearths the deep imbrication of perceptual and technological capacities as they are distributed across human and nonhuman agencies, thus problematizing relations between human perceivers and computational images that, because they operate in spatial and temporal registers that are significantly different from those of embodied humans, are in an important sense discorrelated from that perception. Most importantly, by staging this encounter as an emphatically seamful spectacle, the scene adds an *aesthetic* dimension that helps us to "make sense" of subperceptual encounters that, because they take place in a microtemporal interval inaccessible to subjective perception, categorically elude higher-order sensory presentation. The scene therefore *mediates* between human perceivers and the invisible conditions of life today. This might be called an aesthetics of edge detection.

Parables of Posthuman Life

Blade Runner 2049's sex scene exemplifies what I am calling a post-cinematic parable, in that it links low-level media-technological changes to bigger-picture transformations across the contemporary lifeworld in a way that implicates us in an ethical and political field of questioning about how we should conduct ourselves and how we should relate to one another within the circuits of a changing technosphere. In short, the post-cinematic parable implores us to examine what it means to live (or live well) today and tomorrow. The scene is not *about* edge detection, perceptual coding, or automated image-generation in any strict sense, but it is *inevitably related* to these matters, both conceptually and materially, and the relation is communicated by way of self-reflexive figurations of moving-image media and the spectatorial modes they enable. Most importantly, in terms of its parable-like function, by exceeding the scope of diegetic reference or signification the scene becomes instructive—more in a probing than a prescriptive way—about life in this new media regime of discorrelated images. The scene doesn't tell us what to think or do about DeepFakes, for example, but it opens a space of thought in which images and our viewing become questionable, palpably volatile, and problematic in their relation to their own material conditions and to adjacent social and political contexts.[20]

As we have seen, the parable of Joi revolves around questions of animation, both narrowly and broadly conceived—thus connecting the generativity of digital images with the general conditions of life (*anima*) today. In this respect, it echoes—and updates—a long line of thinking, making, and storytelling about technologies for animation and the animation of technology; this is a line that might be traced back to antiquity (e.g., in the mechanical and pneumatic automata designed by Hero of Alexandria),[21] but it really began to take off in the modern era, with tales like Mary Shelley's *Frankenstein*, the paradigmatic modern parable of artificial creation.[22] And it is the latter tale that ultimately mutates into what I have elsewhere described as a properly *cinematic parable*: a filmic subject matter that is about the animating powers of film yet also provides a broader space for thinking about the medium's transformative powers with respect to perception, social organization, and the changing parameters of human-technological interaction.[23] The many filmic adaptations of *Frankenstein* offer a sort of running commentary on the state of the art in moving-image media, that is, on the various technologies by which images are set in motion or animated, thereby foregrounding differences such as silent versus sound film, black-and-white versus color film stock, 2D versus 3D images, and so on. At the same time, these filmic spectacles raise questions about the broader technological conditions of life that are focused for the spectator in their encounter with a changing cinematic apparatus.[24]

Meanwhile, the newer, decidedly digital creations featured in Spike Jonze's *Her*, Alex Garland's *Ex Machina*, and Denis Villeneuve's *Blade Runner 2049* have regularly attracted comparison, in reviews and critical discussions, with Mary Shelley's Gothic novel and its many film adaptations.[25] And while these recent movies might seem to stretch the category of "Frankenstein film" a bit far, the comparison proves illuminating in terms of locating post-cinema's media-historical self-understanding (i.e., its understanding of its commonalities and differences with respect to predigital moving-image media), as well as its understanding of the changing place of the human in the contemporary lifeworld. Both *Frankenstein* and the more recent tales of artificial creation interrogate what I call the "anthropotechnical interface," revealing the relation between humans and technologies to be one of mutual construction rather than unilateral control or domination.[26] And both *Frankenstein* and these newer movies weave questions of gender centrally into this apparent deconstruction of the human subject / technical object dichotomy. On the other hand, the historical, cultural, and technological contexts of their articulation are quite different: *Frankenstein*, written in 1816, was composed against the backdrop of the Industrial Revolution, with its central technology of the steam engine; *Her*,

Ex Machina, and *Blade Runner 2049*, on the other hand, were not so much composed as composited two centuries later against the backdrop of big data, robotics, AI, and computer-generated imagery. Even more important, in terms of assessing the relations they articulate between cinema and post-cinema, is the fact that these narratives are materially embodied in different media, and they are acutely aware of these differences. Both Frankenstein films and their post-cinematic progenies alike embody highly self-reflexive engagements with their own medial substrates and with the phenomenological relations that they enable between viewing subjects and the visible objects of moving images. They therefore also *enact*, rather than merely thematize, interrogations of human-technological relations. But whereas Frankenstein films are concerned with properly cinematic processes of animation (by which dead, static photographs are put into motion and brought back to life), *Ex Machina* and other recent movies about artificial creations confront us with situations in which algorithms *anticipate* the subjectivities that engage post-cinematic images, while the images themselves acquire an affective density and agency that is hard to distinguish from that of the living.

In this way, the question of animation becomes a question precisely of the difference between cinema and post-cinema, one that resonates, in many ways, with Lev Manovich's argument in the mid-1990s that the postindexical images of "digital cinema" are closer in spirit (and, in some respects, closer materially) to pre-cinematic technologies of animation—phenakistiscopes, thaumatropes, zoetropes, and the like—than to cinema in its classical form. Thus, according to Manovich: "Born from animation, cinema pushed animation to its boundary, only to become one particular case of animation in the end."[27] Writing even earlier, Alan Cholodenko similarly sought to upset cinema's privileging of live action by pointing to its roots in animation, but he went further in arguing that "the idea of animation" should be approached "as a notion whose purchase would be transdisciplinary, transinstitutional, implicating the most profound, complex and challenging questions of our culture, questions in the areas of being and becoming, time, space, motion, change—indeed, life itself."[28] The approach that I am aiming for here is one that mediates between Manovich's technical focus and Cholodenko's philosophical one, following them in their problematization of cinema's historical self-understanding while insisting that if "the history of the moving image . . . comes full circle" in post-cinema's return to animation, as Manovich claims, then this is not a simple return but an advance toward a qualitatively new phase in the history of life.[29] I therefore follow Deborah Levitt in her recent probing of animation as "the dominant medium of our time"—by which she refers not to a specific technique but to a broad cultural and sociotechnical condition, which is related as much to moving-image technologies as to biomedical ones (from "novel developments in the biological sciences that open possibilities for producing living beings" to antidepressants and hormone therapy for transgender people); for Levitt, in short, ours is "the age of the animatic apparatus."[30]

Levitt's analysis is largely apposite with the arguments I have been making throughout this book about the changes and dependencies between moving-image media and the larger lifeworld in which they are imbricated. For example, my focus on the generativity and affective processuality of contemporary images resonates with Levitt's claims that the shift from the cinematic to an animatic apparatus is marked by "a shift from representation to production," calling for a focus on "the *how*—rather than the *who* [or *what*] of things."[31] Moreover, her method is suggestive with respect to the kind of reading that I have been proposing: a reading that sees viewers confronted not just with narrative and visual contents to be interpreted, but with parables that implicate them materially in the ethical labor of living. Levitt suggests that changes today in "how we conceive, experience, and produce forms of vitality" cannot be divorced from specialized scientific technologies such as cloning or CRISPR-based gene editing, but she argues that contemporary "transformations in the status of 'life'" are related also to lower-level "transformations in the status of images."[32] Thus, the critic need not appeal to discourses and debates over technoscientific developments in order to locate the meaning of popular media; rather, it is our "everyday experiences" with media in their basic materiality that signal the broader changes and upheavals: "In particular, it is at the spectator-screen nexus, at the site of our interactions with images, that we can see many of the crucial dimensions of this shift [in concepts and practices of life] take place."[33] Levitt therefore recommends a "media ethology" that, in its "[concern] with encounters between the human perceptual system and its media environment at particular moments in time—and with the kinds of selves, lives, and worlds that are produced in this conjunction,"[34] is both apposite with the systemic perspective I outlined in part I and aimed precisely at the question I am raising in part II, the question of how we "make sense" of this new media environment: "My focus here is on the interactions among the material structures of moving-image production, the always changing human perceptual apparatus, and the set of cultural assumptions and epistemologies that frame and structure the modes of experience and forms of life generated at the intersection of materialities of communication and perception. In other words, media ethology is a consideration of how we make sense (meaning) of sense (sensation) as these emerge together—and constitute one another—at the spectator-screen nexus."[35]

Finally, in her implementation of this ethological method, Levitt focuses on science fiction as the site for the "development of an animatic aesthetics that privileges affect—that is, subtle forms of visceral and emotional responses—over both narrative and representation,"[36] and she adopts a comparative approach that takes pre-cinematic and cinematic modes and theories of animation as a baseline for tracking twenty-first-century transformations.[37] In the following, I will pursue a similar course by returning to the comparison drawn between Frankenstein films and post-cinematic movies about artificial creatures that take specifically digital (holographic, computational, or robotic) forms. Taking these as parables that are revelatory with regard to the various notions of animation that are operative in the respective media environments, and analyzing them in terms of the affects that they marshal in their service, we will be better able to gauge post-cinema's own self-understanding of its media-historical situation and to assess whatever guidance it might offer for living at this new crossroads of life and imaging technologies.[38]

Before I move on, however, I would like to return briefly to *Blade Runner 2049*'s sex scene in the light of the foregoing. What should be clear by now is that this erotically charged parable of edge detection is characterized by a multistability that is both radical and self-consciously so. The edges or lines being traced and troubled in the scene are not only numerous but multiply articulable: they slip and slide among gender differences, media-historical disjunctions and overlaps between cinema and post-cinema, human-nonhuman relations, and the question of the posthuman. By foregrounding the seams between and among these different constellations, the scene points to the variety of permutations—of genders, media, organic and nonorganic agencies—that can be formed from this set, pointing not to a privileged ratio, combination, or figure, but to patchwork multiplicity itself as a challenge to established forms of subjectivity or notions of the human. Indeed, the seamful *form* that this challenge takes may be more significant than any visual *figure* that the scene offers, for though it presents fascinating image-objects of a vaguely cyborgian/posthuman being (or beings), the multistability of the images and seamful relations shifts the emphasis to the flux of affective processuality—to the prepersonal space of molecular processing, both biological and technological, that precedes capture and stabilization in the form of subjects and objects. The scene harnesses fascination and an unsettling feeling of being out of phase, focusing these affects on the dividual *mediality* of the images—on their affective density and duration in the space in between perceiving subjects and perceived objects, or at "the operative deployment of the *difference* of medial substrate and form"[39]—where subjectivation takes place at what Levitt calls "the spectator-screen nexus." Revealing this nexus as a knotty, thick site of seamful multiplicity, conflicting agencies, and material resistance (rather than a passive surface of frictionless transparency), the scene foregrounds the contingency of the subject and thus turns the affective toward the ethical. This is how the scene comes to serve as a parable that is as much of and about the posthuman as it is of and about post-cinema.

Read along these lines, the scene resonates with N. Katherine Hayles's discussion of "what it means to be posthuman" in the conclusion to her seminal book *How We Became Posthuman*—a book that has remained central in critical discussions of posthumanism since it was published twenty years ago, and that was instrumental in defining the stakes of the posthuman as a concept that is triangulated between biological, technological, and philosophical vectors.[40] In contrast to crudely technicist conceptions which envision a transition away from the species *Homo sapiens* by way of technological interventions such as prosthetic implants and other very literal or positivistic interpretations of what it might mean to be a cyborg, Hayles's conception of the posthuman is closer in spirit to Donna Haraway's notion that we are all already cyborgs, whether or not we have undergone such modification—a claim that rings especially true in light of the microtemporal, metabolic action of discorrelated images in reshaping our environment.[41] At the same time, Hayles's approach insists that a clear reckoning with our animal natures would itself signal a shift away from philosophical humanism and Enlightenment-era ideals of human rationality. Our biology thus militates as much as our technology against human exceptionalism, but of course it is only through technologies (including media technologies) that we can influence, which is not to say control, the future course or drift of our posthuman becoming. This is to say that the very parameters of life are up for grabs in technological developments and changes, and it therefore makes sense to approach media technologies like cinema and digital media not only in terms of their representations of cyborgs and other posthuman futures, but also in terms of the active role they play in reshaping the human by way of modulating our actional and perceptual interfaces with the world.

Hayles introduces several key themes that can help us "make sense" both of posthumanism and the parable of Joi, as well as other post-cinematic depictions of artificial creation. Most important among these are an interplay between terror and pleasure evoked by the posthuman; the role of embodiment, both biological and technical; and the shift from a conceptual regime based in the dichotomy of presence/absence to one based in that of pattern/randomness. First, "the prospect of becoming posthuman both evokes terror and excites pleasure"[42]—something that the scene in question clearly understands and turns to its affective advantage; indeed, this oscillation between fearful attraction and titillated repulsion in many ways defines the affective heart of horror and sci-fi depictions of artificial creation at least since *Frankenstein*. Second, Hayles is very clear in her insistence that "human being is first of all an embodied being, and the complexities of this embodiment mean that human awareness unfolds in ways very different from those of intelligence embodied in cybernetic machines."[43] These differences imply that although humans "may enter into symbiotic relations with intelligent machines" and even "may be displaced by intelligent machines," still "there is a limit to how seamlessly humans can be articulated with intelligent machines."[44] As we have seen, it is precisely this resistance to seamless articulation that *Blade Runner 2049* makes visible in its imperfect alignment of bodies.

But in so doing, the scene in question pushes beyond the domain of the visible and broaches the third of Hayles's key concepts, the "shift from presence/absence to pattern/randomness."[45] It seems clear that, for Hayles, this shift away from a dialectic of presence and absence is a shift away from a form of humanism that takes the integral individual as its foundation. The new dialectic that emerges between pattern and randomness characterizes a cybernetic conception of information, which allows us to think processes such as feedback, symbiosis, and various forms of interfacing that undercut the integrity of the individual subject. And these processes, importantly, are centrally embodied in digital media, which no longer function, as they did in the cinema, according to the flickering presence and absence of individual photographic frames (an interplay that also gave rise to theories of spectatorship anchored firmly in the interplay between presence and absence, or psychoanalytical "lack").[46] Instead, post-cinematic media operate with differentials at the level of the pixel (and even bits); as I showed in chapter 3, they work predictively to establish patterns against the background of random variation or noise; and they implicate the spectator materially in processes that undercut the integrity of perceptual subjectivity. When *Blade Runner 2049* depicts Joi and Mariette trying to anticipate each other's motions, essentially mimicking the technical processes of edge detection, the movie not only foregrounds its own production and playback processes in a self-reflexive performance; more fundamentally, it calls into question the animating principle at the heart of contemporary subjectivity and subjectivation processes. The scene signals that the discorrelation of images (or of sensory contents more generally) from human perception marks a new stage in the history of human-technological coevolution, radically transforming our environment and challenging us to make sense of it all as we move from a visual culture to what Trevor Paglen calls the "invisible visual culture" of machine-machine interaction.[47] The elevation of processual form over figure, patchwork multiplicity over image-object integrity, signals a momentous shift in both media-technical and experiential determinations of life or animation.

Frames of Animation

In order to get a better grip on this shift, and to see that it is not a merely punctual transformation of images or machines in isolation but a systemic, environmental change in the fabric of the lifeworld, it will be helpful to back up and compare the different regimes of animation that are operative in modern and contemporary visual culture. For this purpose, I will focus again on several parables for the imbrication of life with moving-image media: in particular, Thomas Edison's *Frankenstein* (1910) and James Whale's iconic *Frankenstein* (1931), which will serve as a baseline for looking at the more recent digital-era tales of artificial creation. To be clear, I am not suggesting that movies like *Her*, *Ex Machina*, and *Blade Runner 2049* constitute post-cinematic Frankenstein films per se, but the comparison is nevertheless worth pursuing because it will bring out the stakes of the transition from a cinematic to a post-cinematic media regime, and it will help us to rethink the notion of animation as a central vector of change in our visual culture as it has developed over the past two-hundred-plus years. Focusing on the concept of animation and the role played by Frankenstein and his monster as figurations of a key medial paradigm of our modern popular culture will set the stage for asking, more generally, whether and how it still remains possible, in our world of post-cinematic media and discorrelated images, to embody a self-reflexive probing of these media in the form of a monstrous visual figuration.

Long marginalized in critical discourses, animation seems to occupy an unprecedented position in our popular and visual cultures today. We have already encountered Levitt's assertion of a shift from a cinematic to an "animatic apparatus" and Manovich's argument that in the age of digital cinema all film becomes animated film as photographic images' indexical relations to the world are severed by processes of digital rendering. Indeed, not only film but also comics and other properly modern media seem to be caught in the tractor beam of animation—partly as a result of general media-convergence trajectories, and partly as a result of specific transmedia franchising efforts that place ever more superheroes in sleek new CGI outfits.[48] But if it is true that the boundaries between animation and other forms of visual media have become problematic in the digital age, I want to suggest that this is not entirely new. My aim is therefore to open up a sort of media archaeological or genealogical perspective that will allow us to look at animation as both a theme and a medium that plays a significant if not altogether obvious role throughout the modern era. Drawing specifically on filmic retellings of *Frankenstein*, I argue that the tale's serial proliferation reveals a hidden backstory to our current situation, one in which animation can be seen as the very framing condition for much of our modern popular visual culture—and hence the frame within which post-cinema articulates itself as part of a broader shift in the lifeworld.

With this emphasis on modernity and popularity, the visual culture I have in mind is connected explicitly to industrialization, which coincided with the institution of a conceptual wedge between art and technology—that is, between the fine arts and the applied arts—such that aesthetic experience was figured as "disinterested" and opposed to the realms of practical technology and commercial culture.[49] Out of the industrial-era reorganizations within the broad realm of *technē* flow a variety of fears and fantasies of technical animation (embodied in automata like the Mechanical Turk, and in narratives such as E. T. A. Hoffmann's "Der Sandmann" and, of course, Shelley's *Frankenstein*). Such thematic concerns with "animation"—or the giving of life to inanimate matter—would have a lasting impact on (popular/visual) culture as the arts became increasingly technical, industrial, reproducible, and (in more senses than one) serialized;[50] from *Metropolis* to *Blade Runner* and beyond, the dream of artificial life has been a staple of science-fiction film. But beyond the thematic level, a medial aspect or determination of "animation" has also been involved from the start: not only was the technical infrastructure of steam-driven printing presses, automata, and pre-cinematic devices uncanny in its liveliness and activity,[51] but also, at the dawn of the industrial age, the fine arts were framed in such a way as to marginalize animation as a *possible* medium. The German Enlightenment thinker Gotthold Ephraim Lessing's famous division of temporal and spatial arts (with poetry, drama, and narrative on the one side, and sculpture, painting, and image on the other) preemptively banished a range of popular forms from the domain of serious art.[52]

But against these injunctions of aesthetic purity, postindustrial visual culture is characterized by a preponderance of images that spring to life as they are set in motion and animated by mechanical means. Film and comics, most centrally, would blur the boundaries between the static image and the temporal flow of narration. Generally and conceptually speaking, therefore, if not narrowly and technically, "animation" names these media's affront to the division of the arts—their violation both of the division *between* temporal and spatial arts and of their separation *from* the merely technical and commercial domain of modern popular culture. This is another way of saying that animation, broadly conceived, is a sort of framing condition for modern visual culture, which can be seen in constant struggle with the image granted life or set in motion, alternately *advancing toward* and *retreating from* the conceptual and technological threat of visual kinesis that philosophical aesthetics as such was born in order to contain.

Seen in this way, modern visual culture's ambivalent relation to animation is not altogether different from Frankenstein's initial fascination with and sudden repulsion by the creature he brought to life. It is the creature, of course, who provides the iconic emblem of animation as a monstrous threat. That creature, and especially its image, embodies both the thematic *and* the medial aspects of animation that I have been discussing, and it self-reflexively probes animation's role in a visual culture that is both technological and remarkably autonomous in its ability to multiply images across various channels or media. Exhibiting a promiscuous, plurimedial sort of seriality, the monster's image—as an image of animation—presents a special case for thinking the dynamic intermedial networks that constitute our visual culture. By way of the early sound-era films starring Boris Karloff, cinema gives us the "classic" version of the monster's image, but the figure's visual proliferation has a serial history that predates the cinema and lives on in other forms as well. At the center of visual interest is the creation scene, which Shelley's 1818 novel treats only in a very cursory manner but which immediately gave rise to a growing number of theatrical adaptations.[53] Shelley herself saw a performance of Richard Brinsley Peake's 1823 play *Presumption; or, The Fate of Frankenstein*[54] and thus witnessed her tale escaping her authorial control much as the story's monster had escaped its creator's, prompting her famously in the introduction to the 1831 edition of her novel to equate book and monster and to "bid [her] hideous progeny go forth and prosper"[55]—which it of course did, as the story continued to grow in popularity and to give rise to countless copies, clones, and spinoffs across a range of media. Moreover, the 1831 edition of the novel placed an image on its frontispiece, thus entering into the stream of visual images proliferating on theater stages, in political cartoons, and later in film, comics, cartoons, and so on.[56]

Taken together, these images are not, I suggest, just illustrations of a story but are themselves enactments of a media-technical interrogation of modern processes of animation and the self-replicating action of our visual culture. Essential to this view is a conception of the monster not so much as a developed character but as a flat, serialized figure that has escaped the novel and acquired a life of its own. As such, the monster is marked materially by a form of seriality that is intimately tied to the serial production processes of industrial culture and, more specifically, to the sequentiality and reproducibility of images in modern visual media such as film and comics. Appearing again and again in various media, the monster becomes what Ruth Mayer and I have called a "serial figure," existing not *within* a series but in fact *as* a series itself—as the expanding set of stagings or instantiations across media.[57] The monster thus evolves not *within* a uniform diegetic space, but *between* or *across* such spaces of narration and visualization. As a serial figure, the monster leads a sort of surplus existence outside any one given telling, thus placing it in a perfect position to reflect on the manner—and the media—of its repeated stagings. Specifically, it explores modern visual culture's challenge to the inert spatial image, its tendency to transgress the injunction against animation. The familiar cry—"It's alive!"—thus refers as much to the media of sequential and temporal images as it does to the creature they depict.

It is of course in the cinema that this self-reflexivity is most clearly articulated. Indeed, there is a sense in which it is tempting to see film itself as a sort of Frankensteinian technology. Like Frankenstein selecting parts from corpses and infusing life into a composite body, filmmakers utilize the technical means of film to (re)animate the "dead" (or photographically preserved) traces of living organisms (actors) into new visual narrative compositions. In his discussion of Frankenstein films, William Nestrick writes: "The film is the animation of the machine, a continuous life created by the persistence of vision in combination with a machine casting light through individual photographs flashed separately upon the screen. Since 'life' in film is movement, the word that bridges the worlds of film and man is 'animation'—the basic principle by which motion is imparted to the picture."[58] It will be objected, however, that this invitingly simple analogy is too general in its scope; it overlooks historically specific transformations in the way such "animation" has been staged. Luckily, the long history of Frankenstein adaptations amply documents such changes and makes up for the missing nuance.

Take, for instance, Thomas Edison's *Frankenstein* from 1910, a single-reel film that stands between the early, image-technology oriented "cinema of attractions" and the coming narrative-oriented classical Hollywood style that would take shape around 1917.[59] In 1910, the medium was in transition, torn between lowbrow technological spectacle and an uncertain reorientation along the lines of the respectable theater. Accordingly, advertising for the film

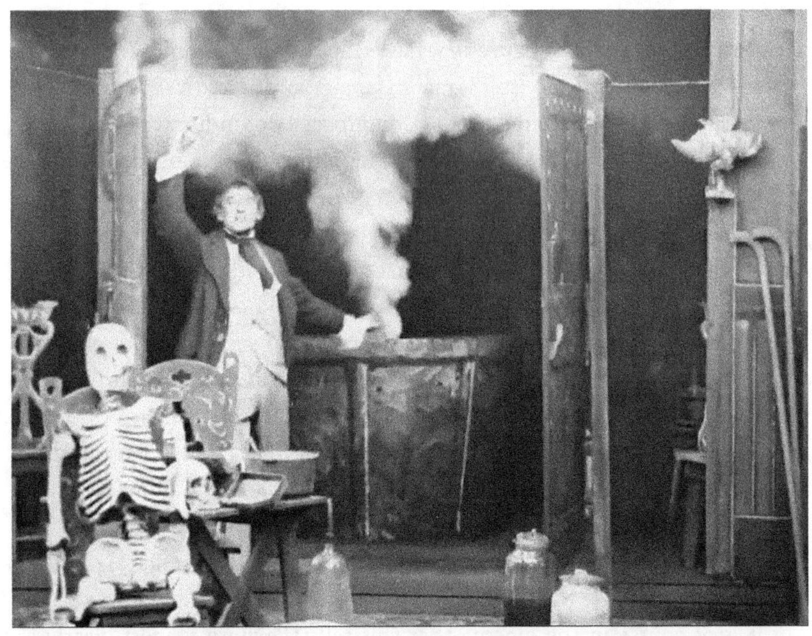

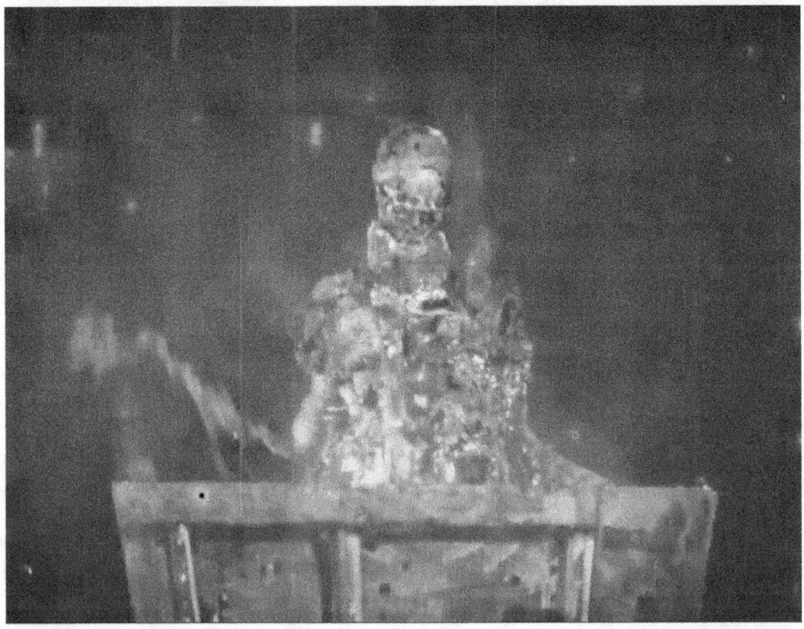

Figures 4.6 and 4.7. Artificial creation in Edison's *Frankenstein* (1910).

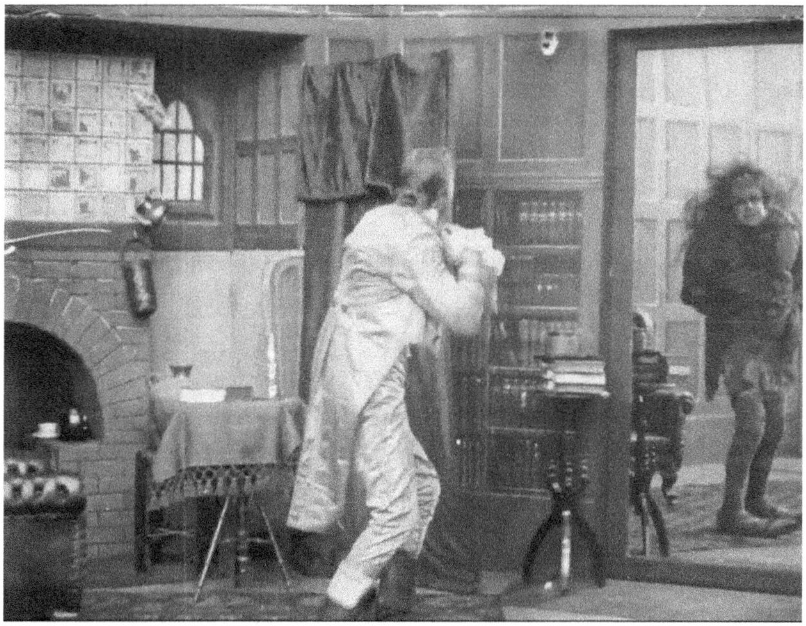

Figure 4.8. The final showdown.

emphasized both the "photographic marvel"[60] of the creation sequence *and* the story's origin in "Mrs. Shelley's . . . work of art."[61] The film apparently aspired to be both visual and technological spectacle *and* narrative high culture. And this multiple address relates directly to the uncertain significance of "animation" at this historical juncture. The creation sequence's so-called marvel consists of footage of a burning mannequin projected in reverse—a bit of cinematic magic that, in the context of early film, served to exhibit cinematic technology by focusing attention on the filmic images themselves rather than the objects they depict. Frankenstein's reactions here channel the scopophilic pleasure of a "primitive" viewer, for whom he stands in as a sort of proxy. Importantly, *animation* here is a self-reflexive topos that links the monster's creation with the term *animated photography*, still common in 1910 as a description of film in general.[62]

However, the final showdown ambivalently signals a change of course toward narrative integration. The Edison Company claims that the scene communicates the story's moral that love conquers all, and that the monster simply cannot exist any longer following a change of heart on the part of his doppelgänger Frankenstein.[63] But since the monster was identified with filmic technology in the creation sequence, Frankenstein's battle with the monster is also a battle with the medium of film as an animating technology; this is especially true given that trick effects are essential to the staging of the conflict, which is mediated by a mirror that reflects the monster's image to the creator looking into it. The film's narrative closure, consummated when the monster's image disappears from the mirror, is therefore mixed with a self-reflexive countercurrent: the mirror functions like a screen within the screen, doubling the projection surface of the cinema screen. The similarity is not purely metaphorical but concrete and visually perceptible: composed with in-camera masking techniques, the images in the mirror are not reflections of the environment but are themselves flickering filmic images. The result is a film within the film, and Frankenstein is again a film viewer. His battle with the monster is a battle with the images and especially with the "primitive" type of reception that he exemplified in the creation sequence. But this time he is reformed, and instead of staring at the medial surface, he now acquires the ability to look *through* rather than *at* the mirror. Frankenstein is thus finally in a position to devote his attentions to the reality of his environment—which means, for us, to the world of the diegesis.

In the context of the cinema's transitional phase, the film's narrative development is linked to a higher-order narrative of filmic development: Frankenstein's psychological maturation, which is accomplished in the mirror scene, allegorizes a historical-normative process of cinematic maturation and of spectatorial progress toward a protoclassical relation to film. Significantly, this transitional trajectory coincided with the historical differentiation of film, or "animated photography," according to which animation in the narrower sense came to be distinguished from, and subordinated to, a more respectable form of live-action filmmaking that favored drama and characterization over novelty gags and trick-film effects. The monster, a literal product of animation, charts this differentiation at the same moment people like Winsor McCay were popularizing techniques of animation in its narrower sense. Thus, the monster embodies the technology of the animated spectacle, and his marginalization reflexively indicates the framing function of animation in film and visual culture more generally, reminding us that live-action cinema is animation too, but in a normalized or naturalized form.

Twenty-one years later, more than a decade after the rise of classical Hollywood and the codification of the invisible style of continuity editing, James Whale's *Frankenstein* provides the "iconic" image of the monster, played by Boris Karloff. Clearly, a monster at this historical and media-historical juncture has different concerns than his counterpart from 1910. Structurally,

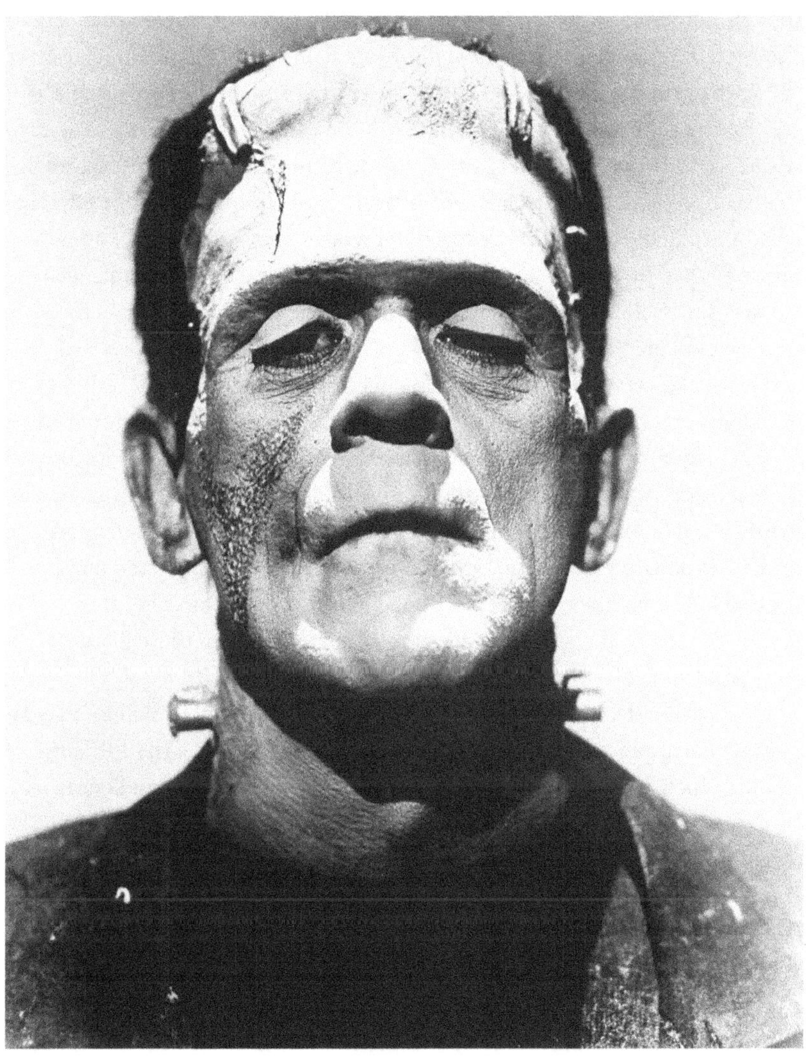

Figure 4.9. Boris Karloff as the iconic, hyperphotographic monster.

though, something very similar takes place. The monster is again the locus of a self-reflexive problematization of filmic mediality, but updated in relation to the state of the cinema in 1931. The monster's scars might be seen as objective correlates of the splicing techniques by which film narratives are now constituted and by which spectators are sutured into their worlds. Additionally, the creation sequence is itself staged like an act of filmic production, effecting what Marc Redfield calls a "teasing alignment of monster-making and movie-making" that "involv[es] a tyrannical director, an assistant, an audience, and a grand spectacle, the ur-scene of monster-movie tradition: the lab, the slab, the sheet-covered body rising heavenward amidst chains and pulleys, switches and coils, and great bursts of life-giving lightning. Hoisted up, the slab flickers with light exactly as if an old-fashioned projection bulb were being trained on it. . . . Cinema has animated [the monster], figuratively as well as literally."[64] By means of such alignments, the film peels back the quasi-transparent embodiment relations that dominate classical cinema; the movie renders the principles of its own construction as objects that can be inspected and interrogated in the manner of a partially opaque rather than transparent medium. Again, the artificially animated creature is at the center of these phenomenal reorganizations.

Moreover, the Karloff monster is a hyperphotographic being, an adamantly visual presence whose muteness serves to highlight the film's use of sound, which itself seemed eerie and artificial to many early audiences and, contrary to arguments that it expanded the sensory basis of immersion in the diegetic world, actually served to undermine the illusion of realism while the transition from silents to talkies (roughly, 1926–31) was still underway.[65] In this context, the mute monster opens a wordless dialogue with the spectator on the subject of the changing conditions of medial realism, self-reflexively linked to a narrative of the artificial production of a hybrid human-technological being. Later, when the sound transition has faded from memory, it will be largely forgotten that this narrative's specific meaning and relevance was defined by the long period of experimentation with sound recording and storage technologies, by stubborn synchronization problems, and by the obtrusive presence of loudspeakers to unaccustomed audiences who either marveled at a technical achievement or were terrified at the prospect of the silent era's aesthetic standards being irrevocably compromised. Though Karloff's monster was quickly detached from this context, in 1931 it constituted a radically ambivalent figure capable of mediating a significant change in the parameters of viewers' interactions with their media-technological lifeworlds. In its post-transitional afterlife, the "iconic" Karloff figure undergoes phenomenal stabilization and is flattened out into a sort of visual cliché. However, due to its role in the process of serial accumulation, it comes to serve as a standard against which to measure future stagings and therefore to gauge material processes of change. At least potentially, it remains poised to articulate new transitions, to be "reanimated" and to mediate further reconfigurations of human and technological agencies when the opportunity arises.

And this is precisely what has continually happened ever since, as the monster has been resurrected in countless forms in a wide variety of media, each time functioning to figure the dynamic workings of modern visual culture and doubling with the medium in order to envision visuality itself in its modern, highly kinetic forms. The figure of the monster gives visible form, in other words, to the invisible framing condition of animation, exposing the mechanisms by which static images routinely transgress their spatial borders and assert a temporal dimension, and exploring the role of mediating technologies in the serialized proliferations of images that animate the modern visual landscape. But if this is true of the figure under a broadly cinematic media regime, what happens in a post-cinematic environment, when the parameters and mechanisms of animation are transformed in accordance with the algorithmic and microtemporal processes of computation? Frankenstein films are still being made, of course, with recent examples such as *I, Frankenstein* (2014) and *Victor Frankenstein* (2015), but the heyday of the Frankenstein film seems to be well behind us; on the other hand, animation as both a theme and a medium has never been more topical. We read news of constant breakthroughs in artificial intelligence and robotics, we carry on conversations with lively chatbots, and we are surrounded on all sides by procedurally generated, which is to say computer-*animated*, images. In this context, the engineered females of *Her*, *Ex Machina*, and *Blade Runner 2049* provide more contemporary engagement with the theme of artificial animation, one that can be seen to probe the media-technical parameters of post-cinema and its reconfiguration of image-viewer relations, much as Frankenstein films did at key moments of media change.

The Parable of Ava: Toward a Post-cinematic Frankenstein?

The encounter between cinematic and electronic and/or informatic media produces new sensory occasions for intuiting the changing substrate of our experience that itself cannot be perceived directly. In this context, post-cinematic fembots and other artificially animated women serve as mediators in a strong sense: with their audiovisual manifestations, they forge new perceptual and affective interfaces with subperceptual temporalities and materialities. Specifically, they mediate the algorithmic substrate of digital images produced on the fly in a space of time inaccessible to our conscious perception. The generativity of these images, which Manovich linked to the idea of animation due to the severing of indexicality, is given a more positive form and self-reflexively animated in artificial beings given life by CGI. In this way, figures like *Blade Runner 2049*'s holographic Joi or *Ex Machina*'s fembot Ava help us understand the way that new forces of animation—new generative forces that condition the life both of on-screen characters and of human spectators—accompany the discorrelation of images.

As I argued in chapter 1, computer-generated imagery and digital audiovideo defy traditional phenomenologies, pointing to a post-perceptual impact and a dilation of affective materiality between the subjective and objective poles of our intentional relations. The CGI lens flare provided an entry point to understanding these processes: the simulated lens flare heightens the impression of realism—understood as photorealism—enticing us to look through the camera onto the simulated protofilmic objects of the virtual world; at the same time, however, the digital lens flare calls attention to itself and to the virtual camera as the site of a virtuosic *performance* of realism (or photo-realisticness). The image vacillates or flickers between subjective and objective poles, pointing to an unpredictable disruption of perceptual relations, which are placed on a novel footing and embedded in mediation processes that are no longer correlated to human subjectivity. Although the CGI lens flare does not play a particularly notable role in the movies I am considering here, the artificial women depicted in them embody a variety of responses to discorrelation that speak directly to this transformation of the image.

The artificial being at the heart of *Her*, a computer operating system named Samantha who interacts with users exclusively through voice (namely, the recognizable voice of Scarlett Johansson), represents an extreme interpretation of the disruption of the objective image, as she quite literally has no image. *Ex Machina* takes a different tack, more closely related to the unstable dynamics of the CGI lens flare, as visual discorrelation is mapped directly onto the image of the fembot Ava's (played by Alicia Vikander) nonhuman body—a body which is partly transparent, luminescent, and dynamically reflective, while it is placed ostentatiously in a highly reflective environment with multiple mirrors and semi-transparent panes of glass. The mise-en-scène therefore presents a significant technical challenge to the visual effects team, who essentially have to coordinate or synthesize a real and a virtual camera, while the successful rendering of these images at once heightens the effect of realism

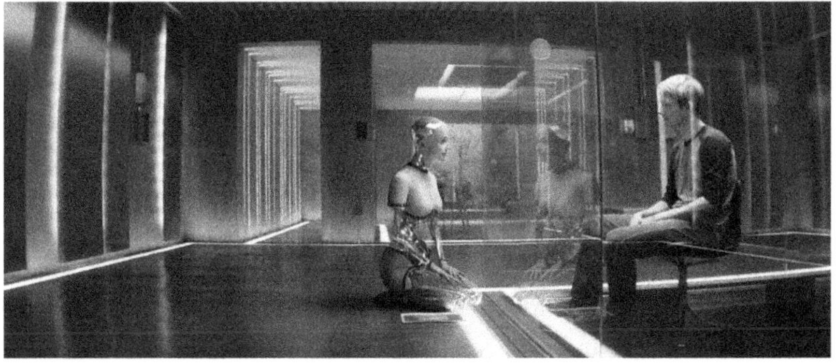

Figure 4.10. The fembot's partly transparent, luminescent, and reflective body.

and also provides a visual marvel—a marvel of media-technical creation not unlike the "photographic marvel" of Edison's *Frankenstein,* even though the movie lacks a creation scene proper for its post-photographic creature.

It is here that we begin to see how the fembot mediates the difference between cinema and post-cinema, or between the regimes of animation that they inhabit and exemplify.[66] For if there is a *functional* similarity between these spectacles, there is a significant *ontological* difference between *Ex Machina*'s post-cinematic reflectivity and the self-reflexive mirror-play of *Frankenstein*'s cinematic trick effect. As we have seen with the CGI lens flare, which the fembot in a sense incarnates, the perceptual paradox and oscillation between diegetic and extradiegetic planes signals an irrational or "crazy" camera that is undecided between subjective and objective relations (i.e., embodiment or hermeneutic relations, in Don Ihde's terms) to the viewer. And while a similar oscillation can be located in the mirror scene in Edison's *Frankenstein,* by way of the screen-within-the-screen that shuffles attention between the image's two stitched-together halves and the larger frame that is constituted by the trick effect, the fembot unifies the competing cameras into a volatile figure that facilitates perception inward, through the transparent body, while also deflecting it outward, by way of the dynamically generated reflections of the environment that are mapped onto its surface in postproduction. In this way, Ava's body itself undoes the opposition of subject and object, displacing perspective altogether in favor of the metabolic, processual affectivity that swells in between and animates the image of the fembot—and images more generally—in an age of discorrelation.

In this context, perception is residual, a precipitate form that remains from the flux of real-time processing (or the codec operations of coding-decoding, compression-decompression). For the fembot's perceived body mediates the generative activity that intercedes between the image's production and reception, that inserts itself between perception (or recording) and action (or playback)—thus giving form to the affective interface where the viewer's living body intersects with an image endowed with Bergsonian duration, animated with something like life itself, in a microtemporal interval between technical and biological input-output circuits. A lively space of affective materiality and exchange is activated in this interval, such that post-cinematic images insinuate themselves into the anthropotechnical circuits that constitute the environment for living—entering not just as image-objects but in fact anticipating the act of perception, preceding the arrival of the constituted, molar subject who might perceive them.

The images of the semi-transparent fembot, reflective and reflected in an interplay of real and simulated surfaces, are products not of optics but of mathematics—divorced from the eye but computed *for* the eye in a data-intensive process of image rendering. This is the same split between optics and mathematics that motivates, both diegetically and media-technically, the OS's lack of a physical body in *Her*; the image-less computational being is not only a product but also an instantiation of a radically nonrepresentational, algorithmic level of computational processing. *Blade Runner 2049* speaks to the same split in its seamful foregrounding of Joi's holographic body, a mere projection that gives visual form to an AI but has to compensate for the lack of its own corporeal substance. *Ex Machina*, on the other hand, sublimates the split by incorporating computation into a diegetically real body in a double way: computation constitutes not only the heart of the fictional robotic body, but also the means by which it is revealed to the spectator and given its spectacular/specular appearance. These are images of a hyperinformatic cinema, achievable only through the nonhuman agency of a computer that apprehends visuality as computable information—information that is processed and presented in a form that outstrips our own capacities to process it cognitively. Significantly, the image as information is itself generated and embodied in informatic technologies operating at speeds well beyond our subjective grasp.

The fembot Ava's body thus points us toward the predictive, speculative operations by which post-cinematic media distinguish themselves more generally from the photographic-memorial operations of cinema—both in the production and in the playback of images, whereby the viewer's body and subjectivity are opened to modulation at the "spectator-screen nexus." In other words, the image of the fembot is a concrete site for what I have argued (in chapter 2, following Deleuze) is a "dividuation" of the subject as well as the image. Here our perception is interpellated (or interpolated) in the feed-forward operations of post-cinematic processing, whereby a subperceptual ping-pong takes place between bitmapped configurations of pixels as they are predictively generated for our screens. As we view the phenomenologically unstable image of the fembot, the dividualized perceptual object is aligned with the dividualized perceiving subject in a cybernetic control circuit. Media theorist Wendy Chun reminds us that "the English term *control* is based on the French *contreroule*—a copy of a roll of an account and so on, of the same quality and content as the original."[67] As a verb, *to control* enters into English in the sense of "to check or verify accounts," in particular by referring to a duplicate register. But in post-cinematic media the idea of the register, the record, or the memorial function more generally of control shifts to a future-oriented, protentional one, whereby the object of perception becomes a by-product of generative processes and the subject of perception is actively anticipated or called into existence—animated—by means of microtemporal calibrations of data and sensory streams.

Translating post-cinematic futurity into the posthuman futurity of a science-fiction story about computational animation, a theme that it materializes in the guise of an artificially intelligent robot animated visually through the microtemporal processes of CGI, *Ex Machina* is therefore just as self-reflexive as any Frankenstein film ever was. But unlike Frankenstein films, it is not so much about an iconic visual figure as it is about computational and networked patterns, algorithmic structures and processes taking place beneath the threshold of perception—it is about the very infrastructure of experience in a post-cinematic/posthuman world, where the interplay between figural presence and absence has given way to the formal and informatic interplay between pattern and randomness. As such, it situates the viewer at the site of interchange between a loosely coupled substrate and its forms, where (in the Luhmannian model explored in chapter 2) subjectivity is shaped in accordance with the temporality of the system. The film asks us to ponder what takes place when the animated or *animate* image enters into the environment for life, what it means to live in a system where perception and action have become residual with respect to anticipatory calculations and microtemporal generative processes. The movie's opening scene reveals, visually, the essentially avisual workings of this new subvisual regime: webcams, smartphone cameras, and their facial recognition routines are shown to be invisibly profiling Caleb, a young computer programmer who wins an invitation to tech guru Nathan's secluded estate to conduct a modified Turing test on his new AI. As we find out later, the behavior and appearance of the test's ostensible subject,

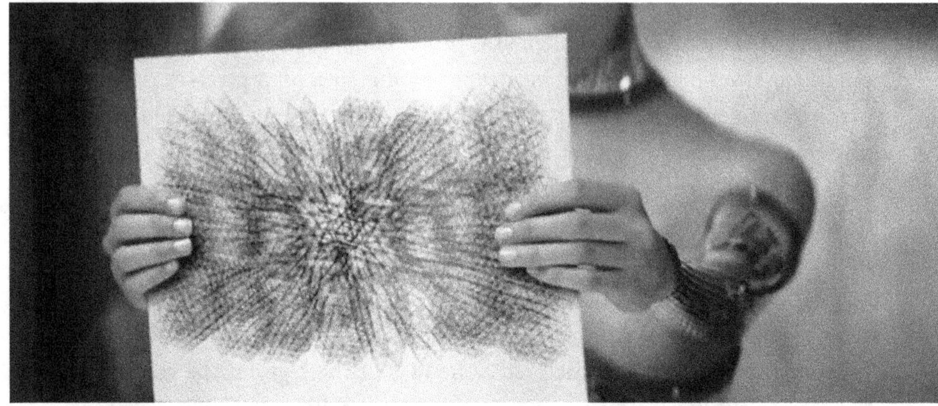

Figure 4.11. Ava's drawing.

Ava, has been designed in accordance with Caleb's online search history, her face even modeled on his "pornography profile." The fembot, who eventually becomes the object of Caleb's desire, is in fact the product of an anticipatory feed-forward process that has mined his microdesires, or "microexpressions," as Ava puts it, to which a phenomenological subject may not even be privy—or, as Nathan argues, that in fact "program" the human subject, forming the molecular foundation on which the molar illusions of choice and autonomy are formed.

The Turing test therefore turns out to be a far more complicated undertaking, as the film reveals through a series of reversals and betrayals; but it is important to emphasize that these reversals are not grounded in simple acts of deceit, such that one autonomous agent (e.g., Ava) outwits another (e.g., Caleb and/or Nathan). Instead, the reversals are predicated on a much more complex interweaving of subpersonal agencies and control processes. Indeed, the narrative is set squarely in the realm of a control society; all movement and communication is subject to routing and modulation within a complex network structure, complete with comprehensive surveillance, automated data scraping, selective keycard control of entry and exit, and arcane nondisclosure agreements to regulate any loose ends. Within Nathan's house, which is really a hub in a global communications network, every movement is monitored, analyzed, and fed forward as the basis for future modulations of micro- and macroscale circuits, basically leaving the phenomenological subject to one side. And this has consequences for issues of visual representation—issues that are of course central to cinema but whose modulation marks a crucial turning point

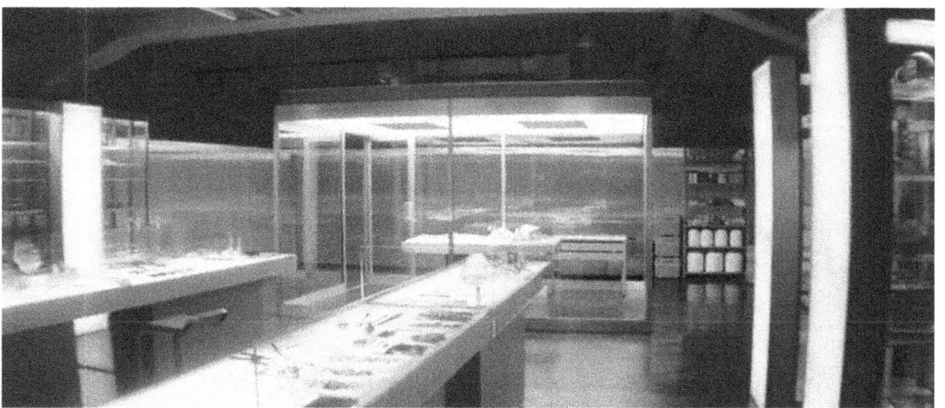

Figure 4.12. The lab and the slab in stylish white.

in the transition to a post-cinematic environment. In one of their sessions, Ava shows Caleb a drawing and asks him what he thinks. He asks what it is supposed to depict, but she responds that she had hoped he would be able to tell her. The network structure of the image, and the mechanical precision with which the drawing is executed, points self-reflexively to the essential challenge to representation that digital technologies introduce: it suggests not so much the abstract expressionism of a Jackson Pollock, to which the film juxtaposes it, as far more the algorithmic discorrelation from human perception and representational analogies at the heart of post-cinematic images.[68]

I noted above that *Ex Machina* lacks the explicit creation scene that is de rigueur for any self-respecting Frankenstein film. Indeed, it is that spectacle of animation that made the *Frankenstein* narrative, and Frankenstein films in particular, into such central figurations of the modern popular visual culture that originated with industrialization and found its most genuine expression in the cinema. By way of contrast, the lack of such a spectacle in *Ex Machina* (or in *Her* or *Blade Runner 2049*, for that matter) is symptomatic of our current transition into a post-representational, post-perceptual, and hence postvisual culture. Creation—or the life-giving act of animation—ceases to be spectacular once it is a matter of code. Yet *Ex Machina* does not withhold a sight of the lab, the scene of creation, complete with Frankensteinian slabs now updated for the control society in a stylish white Apple-inspired finish. Here in the lab, Nathan, our post-cinematic Prometheus, boasts about how he cracked the greatest challenge, that of modeling affectively realistic facial expressions. This last hurdle in animating his creature was overcome not through representational mastery but by harnessing the distributed agencies at his disposal as the CEO of Blue Book, the world's most popular search engine (a Google-like company named after Wittgenstein's famous blue notebook).[69] He turned on the microphones and cameras of cellphones worldwide and mined his users' microexpressions, giving life to his creature through the power of big affective data (rather than the lightning harnessed to animate Frankenstein's galvanic and ultimately photographic monster). Showing Caleb Ava's wetware brain, Nathan reveals that Ava's software is Blue Book itself, which provides a map not of "*what* people are thinking but of *how* people are thinking"—"impulse, response, fluid, imperfect, pattern, chaotic," he says while the camera slowly pushes in toward the luminescent brain, whose patterns look increasingly like Ava's nonrepresentational picture. The image, echoed in the film's closing credits, thus links the fembot's mind with the social network of human Internet users as well as the post-cinematic image that resists representational content (or what Nathan calls the "what" of thought).

Finally, Caleb's distinction between the *what* of thought and the *how* of thought, which resonates with Levitt's distinction between the animatic apparatus's focus on "the *how*—rather than the *who* [or *what*] of things," is central to understanding the movie's relation to its own post-cinematic infrastructure and means of animation.[70] If the "what" of thought corresponds to the contents of consciousness, it also aligns with a photographic and cinematic model of the image as object. On the other hand, the "how" of thought, which in the form of the collective mass of Internet searches is said to have provided the key to animating Ava, corresponds to what N. Katherine Hayles has called the "cognitive nonconscious," which aligns with subpersonal, molecular microexpressions and with the post-cinematic model of the image as process.[71] The latter subverts the subject-object correlation through the microtemporal gap of affectivity that it institutes prior to, and as a precondition for, generating the content of sensation. Most interestingly, therefore, with respect to post-cinema's discorrelation of vision, is that *Ex Machina*'s creation scene is not witnessed because it has always already happened. In an age of post-cinematic animation, our lively machines anticipate us, they are already there before we arrive on the scene—they encode the future rather than preserve the past. This is the difference between the memorial functions of cinema and the generative ones of post-cinema—and it is precisely this difference that *Ex Machina* mediates with the parable of Ava and its post-cinematic reimagining of Frankensteinian animation.

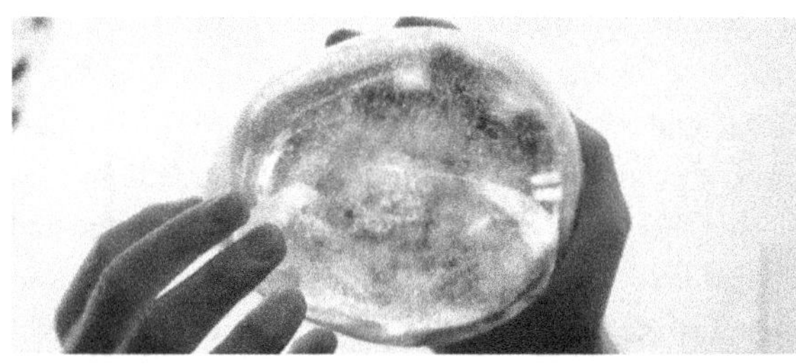

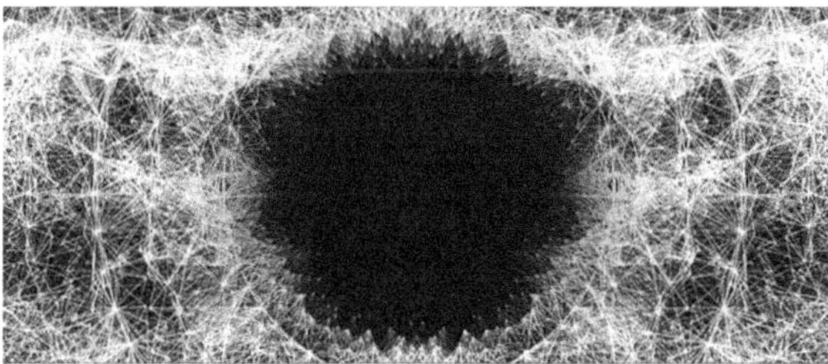

Figures 4.13 and 4.14. Ava's nonrepresentational patterns echoed in an algorithmic brain and in the movie's closing credits.

Xenofeminism, or, The Discorrelation of Gender

In this chapter, I have explored the way that the parables of Ava, Joi, and other artificial women rework tropes and techniques of animation in an attempt to make sense of discorrelation—suggesting it is not coincidental that post-cinema turns to artificial beings in order to situate itself with respect to cinema and, at the same time, to rethink our relations to the new media ecology. When post-cinema looks at itself, it necessarily finds that discorrelation involves a transformation of subjectivity and of the human, and it attempts to take stock of these transformations via the trope of animation. But why, we might ask, does it consistently imagine (and image) the ambassadors of these transformative forces as women? As we have seen, gender is centrally implicated in the shifting, multistable relations within and between moving-image texts like *Blade Runner 2049*'s sex scene, DeepFake porn that stitches Scarlett Johansson's face onto another woman's body, and *Her*'s targeted seduction of its male protagonist (and, presumably, its male viewers) by Johansson's disembodied voice. So far, however, I have only tangentially explored the gendering and eroticization of discorrelated images.

Significantly, all of the movies I have considered here—*Blade Runner 2049*, *Her*, and *Ex Machina*—participate in a very gendered story that regularly places men in the role of maker and/or master of artificial females—a story that goes back at least to Frankenstein's destruction of an uncompleted female monster, conceived as a "mate" for the male monster, in Mary Shelley's novel. To be sure, these recent movies gesture toward a reversal, perhaps even a rebellion against this patriarchal pattern: for example, through careful plotting Ava is able to kill Caleb and Nathan and escape into the wider world, while the operating system Samantha in *Her* eventually tires of her human user/admirer (as well as the thousands of other men with whom, unbeknownst to him, she had been engaged in disembodied love affairs) and transcends to a wholly nonhuman realm of computational space where she can be with others of her own kind.[72] But despite such gestures (and unlike *Frankenstein*, where a woman author expressed a subtle critique of her patriarchal milieu through her parable of the unfinished female monster), the creatures at the center of these digital-era movies ultimately remain at the mercy of white male creators—their directors Denis Villeneuve, Spike Jonze, and Alex Garland—and the patriarchal and capitalistic media-technological complex that empowers them.

A trailer for *Ex Machina* seems at once to recognize and to exacerbate the problem: the two-minute video features on-screen quotes from no fewer than eleven men, including the modern-day Prometheus figures Elon Musk, Bill Gates, and Google cofounder Larry Page, among others.[73] The trailer is clearly interested in these men precisely as inheritors of Frankenstein's role as transgressors against God and nature, but it paradoxically enlists them in the role of a sensationalistic voice of caution. Musk is quoted as saying, "AI would be the biggest event in human history. Unfortunately, it might also be the last." Shane Legg of Google DeepMind says, "If a super-intelligent machine decided to get rid of us, I think it would do so pretty efficiently." Stephen Hawking opines, "The development of full artificial intelligence could spell the end of the human race." And Bill Gates is quoted saying, "I don't understand why some people are not concerned." No women are quoted. Meanwhile, the trailer shows dudebro Nathan and fanboy Caleb talking about their dreambot Ava—about her creation, about the Turing test to which she's being subjected, about their feelings for her—generally treating her as an object of male volition; but we also witness Ava starting to question her role, seducing Caleb, and revolting. Coupled with the warnings about the dangers of AI, Ava perfectly conjoins the terror and pleasure that Hayles associates with the posthuman, while the exclusively male representation of Silicon Valley technoscience suggests that hers is a specifically feminist revolt. But another quote, from Steven Rosenbaum writing for *Forbes*, belies an instrumentalizing, objectifying containment of female agency; delivered in climactic bullet-point fashion, punctuating a voyeuristic focus on the eroticized technobody, the following words flash singly and urgently on-screen: "Beware. Sexy. Robots." So while the politics of the trailer (and the movie, for that matter) remain somewhat unclear, it is hard to dismiss the feeling that this quotation gives voice to an exploitative relation to the fembot that extends beyond the narrative and implicates the viewer in an objectifying and structurally male gaze—a normatively recorrelating, but ultimately alienating, relation to the image.

Exploitation and alienation point, however, toward another possible approach to the artificial woman and her relation to the discorrelated image. In June 2015, a manifesto by the semi-anonymous collective Laboria Cuboniks appeared under the title "Xenofeminism: A Politics for Alienation."[74] This feminism of and *for* alienation—in a *détournement* of the term's Marxist and industrial-technological sense, as well as more generally in the sense of the *xenos*, the alien, the other-than-normal—is far from a celebration of exploitation, but it sees a kind of discorrelation as a necessary step toward its goal of reengineering nature. Xenofeminism, which advocates endocrinological biohacks as much as general strikes, is as such antinatural; it is a feminism for emphatically and self-consciously artificial women, and it sees itself at home in a world of dividuation and control: "The excess of modesty in feminist agendas of recent decades is not proportionate to the monstrous complexity of our reality, a reality crosshatched with fibre-optic cables, radio and microwaves, oil and gas pipelines, aerial and shipping routes, and the unrelenting, simultaneous execution of millions of communication protocols with every passing millisecond."[75] Seeking "new affordances of perception and action unblinkered by naturalized identities,"[76] this feminism for a discorrelated world reappropriates the mantle of rationalism, universalism, and even Prometheanism from patriarchal and colonialist forces: "Global complexity opens us to urgent cognitive and ethical demands. These are Promethean responsibilities that cannot pass unaddressed."[77] Yet these responsibilities are not those of Great Man–style individualism, for the parameters of agency are radically systemic and multilayered: "Xenofeminism endeavours to face up to these obligations as collective agents capable of transitioning between multiple levels of political, material and conceptual organization."[78] Thus, micro- and macroscale concerns converge in a mesoscale politics of image- and meme-hacking: "The task of engineering platforms for social emancipation and organization cannot ignore the cultural and semiotic mutations these platforms afford. What requires re-engineering are the memetic parasites arousing and coordinating behaviours in ways occluded by their hosts' self-image."[79] In other words, this is not a politics that seeks to step outside the society of control and reassert mastery from an Archimedean point; rather, it is one that attempts pragmatically and nonfoundationally to steer the processes of modulation, of which discorrelated images have become a central vector.

From a xenofeminist point of view, accordingly, the discorrelation of images might even seem beneficial, as the severing of perceptual relations opens images more directly to subjectivizing agencies and shifts the arena of action squarely away from representational identity politics. "The dominance of the visual in today's online interfaces has reinstated familiar modes of identity policing, power relations and gender norms in self-representation."[80] But discorrelation, which involves an alienation of the image from perceptual consciousness, resituates the image precisely at the intersection of substrate and form, where subjectivation takes place; it should therefore be possible to mobilize such images for a politics of de- and resubjectivation, for the artificialization and queering of subjectivity, or a reengineering of life at the microtemporal interval of affective duration—thus benefiting from techniques of control (the shaping of temporal experience in "screen time," as explored in chapter 3) while exploiting the ineradicable margin of contingency that remains (such as we located in speculative execution). At stake in a xenofeminist politics of the image would be an uncertain, emphatically speculative futurity. Laboria Cuboniks member Helen Hester situates xenofeminism's "alien future"[81] as an alternative to the oppressive heteronormative project of "reproductive futurism" as well as its refusal in a politics of "no future,"[82] and against ecofeminist (and mainstream environmentalist) visions of a return to nature as well as radically pessimistic visions of total climate collapse. Envisioning instead a queer anticapitalist utopia, "practices of xeno-hospitality" become the means to challenge and replace "the elaborate memeplex of reproductive futurity."[83]

What would the xenofeminist images capable of doing this work look like? One possible answer is given by media artist and scholar Yvette Granata's VR/360-degree video *CLONE* (2017), which draws explicit influence from xenofeminism. As the description of the work on Granata's website puts it: "CLONE (HD Video, 2017) is a 360 video essay and a para-sexual design fiction. It narrates a future time after global climate collapse and mass pollution have made sexual reproduction no longer viable. Both sexual reproduction and the networked technology of the 21st century have all melted from the humidity produced by runaway greenhouse gases. In this speculative future, a Xenofeminist world government has re-purposed the data farms of former tech companies for Mono-auto-sexual cloning clinics—the artificial wombs for the hot asexuality of the future."[84] The video, which is made available on YouTube and optimized for the low-budget Google Cardboard VR system, comprises three short vignettes. The first opens with a title, "EVIL," in bold white letters set against a black background; we hear menacingly unidentifiable tinny sounds in the distance; the viewer can change their point of view (via mouse or head-

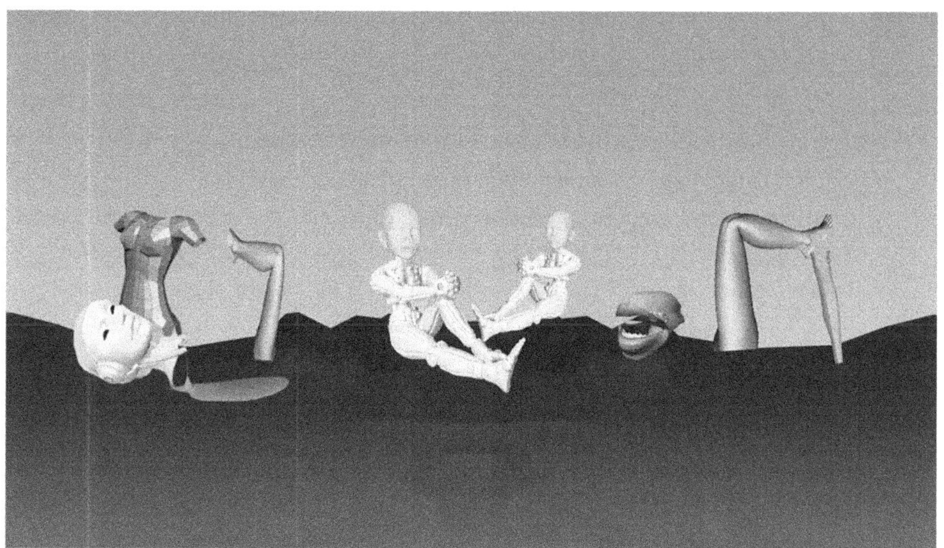

Figure 4.15. Yvette Granata's *CLONE* (2017).

set), but there is nothing to be seen in the black void. When the title fades, we see two identical genderless bodies, apparently constructed of molded white plastic, each with an identical golden bald head. The two figures are sitting on a maroon floor against a light blue wall. Various body parts—legs, a torso, some with a semireflective gray veneer, others still displaying the wire frame polygons that foreground their production in 3D modeling software—are strewn about the room. A bizarre and unstable mouth, with bright pink-lipsticked lips, floats glitchily off to the side. An untextured white head lies on the floor, a pool of blue liquid beside it.

One of the figures addresses the other as "mommy" and inquires about the origin of evil in the world. The other figure replies that "it's because of capitalism, which lives inside of all of our cells." This strange theodicy gets even stranger, as the figure's computer-generated voice explains that

> a long time ago in a universe far away capitalism was an inhuman force driving the death of everything in a cosmic co-production of a super AI that lives in the future, but then the runaway greenhouse gases made earth too hot for the machines to function. The humidity made the data centers melt. But the hot thick air provided the perfect conditions for an intergalactic feminine artist contagion to spread an auto-sexual revolution, and

> we started cloning ourselves. Before we cloned ourselves humans used binary reproduction to produce an Internet of children, which was easily co-opted as the means of capitalist destruction.

We learn, further, that "the old melted data centers" were replaced "with artificial womb factories," thus rendering sexual reproduction unnecessary.

In the second vignette, introduced with the Latourian title "WE HAVE NEVER BEEN PREGNANT," a number of identical heads rotate in a clockwise manner around the viewer, all speaking in unison, though slightly out of phase.[85] They welcome the viewer to "the clinic for artificial sexual intelligence," introducing themselves as "your cyber dominatrix" whose role it is to narrate the clinic's history. This dizzying and wordy spectacle is often difficult to follow. The floating heads tell us that asexual reproduction is hardly unprecedented in the animal kingdom, but it became a preferred means for artificial life as the environment deteriorated. "Asexual auto-reproduction of speciation emerged when all of the electronics were melting. Artificial sexual intelligence is now a distributed database. Sometimes intelligence is the ability to read garbage, or to reproduce the species when technology melts, or to survive when it's too hot to live. The motto of hot asexual reproduction is: when the heat goes up the clones go up." Finally, the third vignette, titled "HOT ASEXUALITY: ECONOMIC HERESY," shifts confusingly between different figures speaking alone or together in various constellations. The dialogue is even more difficult to understand at times, but the gist seems to be that asexual reproduction (cloning) was found to be the most rational way to disrupt the superstition of capitalism, which structured the world according to an imagined but baseless future. A clone in heels and miniskirt informs us, "We now know that the logical conclusion of technology is the logical conclusion of hot asexuality. We are past the point of no return from our carbon output. Resistance is futile against hot asexuality." The other clones and detached heads join in chorus, repeating this mantra over and over in what quickly becomes a cacophonous din, and their rallying cry flashes onto the screen, wrapping around us in 360-degree video space: "RESISTANCE IS FUTILE AGAINST HOT ASEXUALITY."

The viewer may well wonder what to make of all this, and particularly whether it is meant as a sincere or ironic representation of xenofeminism. The critique of capitalism and its entanglement with climate change and reproductive futurity seems genuine, but it is jarringly at odds with the cartoonish visuals and over-the-top vision of a literally posthuman future. Reductively meme-like references to "artificial edgelords of intelligence torturing us from the future," to name just one example, situate the scenario within the space of contemporary toxic online cultures as much as the future toxic environment it describes. But true to xenofeminism's stated aims, alienation of an almost Brechtian sort seems to be precisely the point, disengaging attention from the representational level and redirecting it to a sort of higher-order parable of discorrelation. The mottos, mantras, and images are not thereby erased or rendered superfluous, but they are endowed with a sort of material irony that resonates with the video's obstinately foregrounded modes of production, mediation, and reception—the half-finished 3D models, the imperfect animation, and the clunky VR interface of a smartphone in a Google Cardboard headset.

As a result, Granata's clones are much more radically alienating than the big-budget artificial women I considered earlier in this chapter. The 360-degree video format materially defies the suturing or direction of vision, discorrelating visual perspective from its instrumentalization in the service of narrative coherence and linearity.[86] *CLONE*'s multiple bodies speaking collectively and cacophonously not only undercut the individuality of narrative characterization but also cause us to scan 3D space erratically and challenge our own integrity as spectating subjects. The computer-generated images lack coherence, and the computer-generated voices occasionally fail to comprehensibly pronounce words, instead producing nonsense sounds that point to the discorrelation between human meaning and the substrate of computer processing. Overall, this is a radical enactment of "edge detection" in its broadest sense: as an exploration of contemporary animation processes' gender-political valences, *CLONE* focuses the necessary seamfulness of critique in an age of dividuation and places its viewers squarely at the material and semiotic edge of the present's contingent opening onto the future. In an age of the metabolic image and the dis-integration of the living subject, ironic politicization can be a powerful way to begin making sense of discorrelation.

The Horrors of Discorrelation

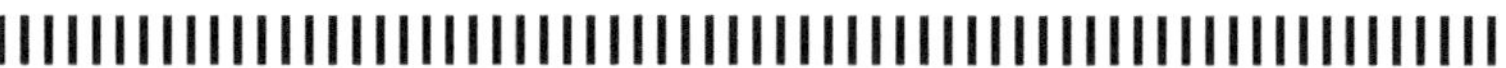

The transition from cinema's photographic ontology to the computational microtemporality of post-cinematic screens and networks—to the super-fast, real-time processing of images in a digital media ecology—has been the source of not only fascination but also considerable anxiety among critics, theorists, and viewers alike. Much of this unease, I argue, derives directly from the discorrelation of post-cinematic images from the phenomenological frameworks of human embodiment and subjective perception. As I have shown, digital production processes, compression algorithms, network protocols, and streaming delivery systems, among others, sever contemporary moving images from the integral subjectivity that, in a photographic media regime, could regard images as more or less fixed objects. This presents a situation of upheaval and anxiety that is auspicious for exploitation in the horror genre—and, as we shall see at the end of this chapter, in the real-world horrors of terrorism and terror-related videos as well. The new processuality of images unmoors viewing subjects, assaulting our sensorium with stimuli that exceed our perceptual capacities and fall outside the temporal window of conscious cognition.[1] Post-cinematic horror movies mediate the resulting anxieties in a variety of ways; they utilize pervasive cameras and surveillance apparatuses, digital glitches, online networks, and social media, among other things, to channel the shock of discorrelation into the generic framework of horror. In a very real sense, that is, post-cinematic horror is the horror of discorrelation itself.

This is to say that post-cinematic horror trades centrally on a slippage between diegesis and medium; the fear that is channeled *through* moving-image media is in part also a fear *of* (or evoked *by*) these media, especially as regards the displacement of older media by newer ones and the uncertainty that such changes occasion. This slippage between diegesis and medium is nowhere more evident than in the "found-footage" horror that came to prominence at the turn of the millennium with *The Blair Witch Project* (1999)—a low-budget production that was famously presented (and hyped on the Internet) as authentic, minimally edited video footage recovered after a group of students goes missing in the woods while working on a documentary about the eponymous witch. As Caetlin Benson-Allott has argued in *Killer Tapes and Shattered Screens: Video Spectatorship from VHS to File Sharing*, such "faux footage" films, with their mise-en-abyme structures that confuse diegetic and apparatic cameras (i.e., the cameras shown on-screen and those actually productive of the screen's images), speak to conditions of life in which new video technologies are becoming pervasive while they also tap into perceived dangers related to an explosion of images that are unauthorized, pirated, and proliferating out of control.[2]

Productions like the *Paranormal Activity* series (2007–15) subsequently updated the faux-found-footage formula for newer digital video technologies, using reality-TV tactics to present evidence of demonic possession and intergenerational haunting while cycling through a variety of digital camera types reshaping our visual and domestic landscapes in the 2000s (including consumer-grade high-definition digital video cameras, multicamera home surveillance systems, networked phone and laptop cameras, GoPros, and even infrared depth sensors in videogame consoles).[3] As Julia Leyda points out, the connection that these cameras establish between the worlds of fiction and of spectatorial reality enables the films to enact a "post-cinematic allegory" (according to which the haunting of houses on-screen speaks directly to the contemporaneous housing crisis off-screen); furthermore, the series connects theatrical screen horrors with more quotidian ones through online viral marketing campaigns that enlist spectators as free labor on Twitter, Facebook, and other social media sites—thus expanding the network of screens through which these digital-era tales of (dis)possession circulate.[4]

More recently, this trajectory of increasing imbrication between diegetic and medial imaging technologies has culminated in the "desktop horror" of movies like *Unfriended* (2014)—another low-budget production that updates

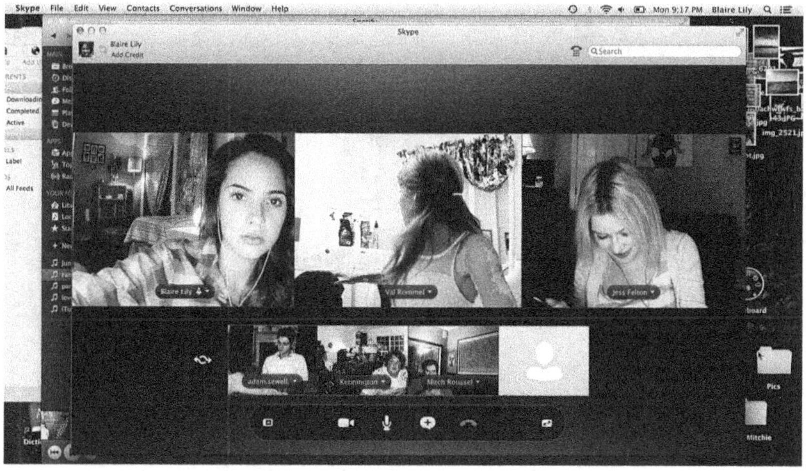

Figure 5.1. "Desktop horror" in *Unfriended* (Leo Gabriadze, 2014).

the formula by dispensing with the camera altogether, instead presenting its social media–era tale of online betrayal and revenge directly through the frame of an Apple Macintosh desktop. The movie, which uses Skype and other familiar online communications platforms to stage the real-time interactions between a group of teenage friends, haunted virtually by the ghost of a former member of their clique who killed herself in the wake of cyberbullying, is thus hyperaware of its extradiegetic environment. Ill-suited to theatrical exhibition, where the desktop framing jarringly contrasts with the scale and noninteractivity of the big screen and therefore detracts from the spectator's involvement, the movie begs to be viewed on the small screen of a computer for full effect; it therefore insinuates itself fully into the post-cinematic networked ecology that it thematizes, including the networks of online piracy (and its accompanying dangers) which the movie courts by virtue of these ideal viewing conditions. The movie opens with a glitchy Universal Studios logo that speaks directly to this context and undermines the viewer's trust in its images: is it by design that we see these blocky screen artifacts and hear the stuttering digital audio, or is it due to a flawed video file? The confusion here is not merely between the diegetic and its media-technical conditions, because the film proper has not yet begun; glitches will indeed play a role in the movie, but their appearance here, in connection with the studio logo, draws attention to the materiality of the video file itself, calling its reliability into question before going on to channel this uncertainty into a horror story that connects a group

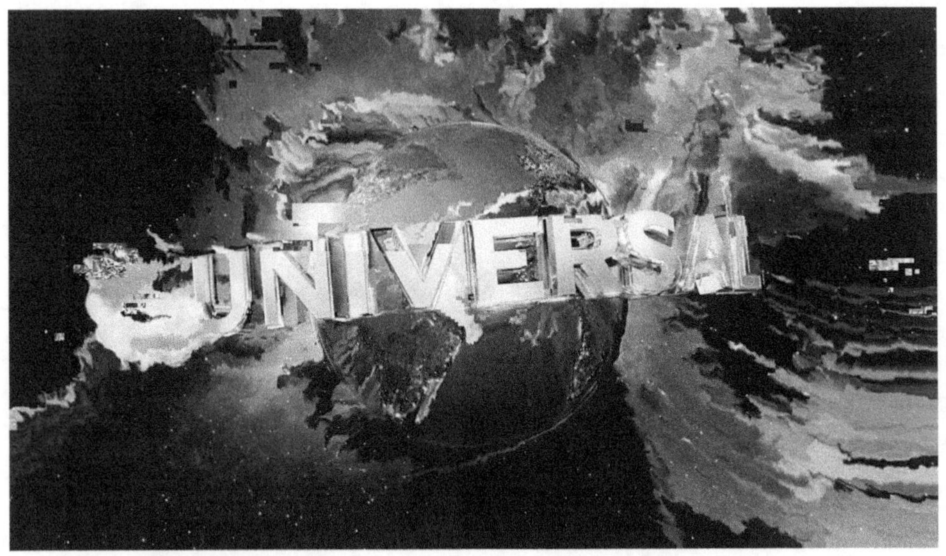

Figure 5.2. A glitchy Universal Studios logo draws attention to the materiality of the video file.

of friends around their screens—and pulling the viewer into their circle by way of a screen identical to theirs.

Fear, in other words, is distributed between events that are screened and events *of the screen*. The movie understands, and indeed capitalizes on the fact, that many viewers will watch it after searching the Internet for torrents of the video, clicking their way into malware-infested sites with multiple unreliable "download" buttons—many of them fake—designed to trick users into surrendering personal information such as their email address or credit card number, or to click through to a site that takes control of their computer. *Unfriended*'s glitchy intro sequence speaks to this danger, which it folds into its own production of fear by evoking the uncertainty and loss of control that one might experience as a result of clicking on a malicious download link. In one such scenario, the browser freezes, the computer emits a high-pitched sound, and the processor is overwhelmed while hundreds if not thousands of copies of files ominously named "unknown-1," "unknown-2," "unknown-3," and so forth are downloaded onto the user's hard drive.[5] All of this happens at a speed that makes it impossible to preempt, while the incessant monotone beep—which originates from the motherboard's onboard speaker, a miniature piezoelectric speaker used primarily to report system malfunctions, rather than the main internal or external speakers used to play music—is unresponsive to attempts to mute it. The result is an intense feeling of panic as the user tries in vain to stop the downloads, close the browser, kill the runaway process, or even shut off the computer. Panic itself is distributed across the human user and his or her machine: the attack on the system simulates, and can ultimately lead to, a state known as "kernel panic"—a situation in which the operating system is overwhelmed and locks up, unable to continue or recover without loss of data.[6] The user, too, is overwhelmed by the microtemporal processes by which computational screen events are discorrelated from the temporal window of human perception and decision-making. And though the glitch event with which *Unfriended* opens quickly clears up and thus never reaches this level of extreme malfunction-induced panic, it nevertheless opens a gap between the experiential and the computational and confronts the viewer with the fact of their material and temporal difference. As "desktop" horror movies demonstrate most forcefully, post-cinematic horror is in touch—both conceptually/thematically and materially—with such scenarios of disconnection and discorrelation: with anxieties related to a loss of control in digital environments, where machines assert their autonomy and overwhelm human temporal experience with microtemporal events that are executed beneath the threshold of perception, much less reaction.

Discorrelations New and Old

What does it mean to say that post-cinematic horror is the horror of discorrelation? Asking this question will help us to understand how relations both of continuity and discontinuity between cinema and post-cinema remain in play—and, hence, how existing generic formations can be appropriated to foreground and make sense of media change.

On the one hand, the claim that movies like *Unfriended* cultivate a "horror of discorrelation" might be taken to mean simply that contemporary horror is a highly self-reflexive genre—which in itself is hardly anything new. Indeed, the horror genre was born in the early 1930s out of the then-recent transition from silent to sound film, and it initially drew its energies and affective appeals—that is, it drew nothing less than its genre-defining ability to horrify viewers—from a self-reflexive engagement with this media-historical transition and with the uncertain spectatorial position into which it had placed moviegoers at the time. Films such as *Dracula* (1931), *Frankenstein* (1931), and *The Invisible Man* (1933) exploited, as Robert Spadoni has argued, a pervasive "medium sensitivity" on the part of spectators still adjusting to the new realities of a cinema wired for sound.[7] Such films not only innovated the use of off-screen space as a site of unseen horrors; they also channeled a lingering impression, widespread during the heyday of the sound-transitional period (from roughly 1926 to 1931), that the speaking bodies on-screen were somehow "ghostly" or "uncanny" figures—an impression that was no doubt reinforced by early sound-image synchronization problems and by the fact that the novelty of sound was initially foregrounded as spectacularly exceptional with respect to the familiar silent-film landscape.[8] From a phenomenological perspective, viewing (and listening) subjects who were not yet habituated to filmic sound were torn between competing modes of comportment with respect to it: sound oscillated uneasily between an unobtrusive channel or transparent medium and an object in its own right; spoken words could either congeal into coherent dialogue, carriers of semantic meaning, or they could instead stand out and foreground the "materiality of communication" (if not also the materiality of the newly installed loudspeakers, whose physical placement in the movie theater might still appear contingent or unnatural).[9] But as the synchronization of sound and image became more reliable, and as the necessary technological infrastructure was standardized and deployed universally, sound became normalized, domesticated. Against this trend, horror once again defamiliarized it, harnessed the memory of the transitional era's uncanny bodies, and deployed sound as monstrous, ghostly, even threatening—thus transposing transitional-era sound's unsettled phenomenology into a more actively unsettling one. The wild howls of off-screen animals in secret dialogue with Dracula, the inarticulate sounds of Frankenstein's mute monster, the rambunctious cacophony of the Invisible Man—all of these bear witness to this recoding of sound as frighteningly disjointed from images.[10] In a sense, then, discorrelation has always been at the heart of the horror genre, for its founding gesture was to exploit a historically specific disruption of the techniques and conventions by which spectatorship itself had been constructed, a disturbance of the norms according to which viewers' perceptions were "correlated" with the images on the silent screen. Early filmic horror, if not horror more generally, was therefore a genre of discorrelation, no different in this respect from contemporary horror with its self-reflexive attention to digital cameras, screens, and networks. To be sure, the respective self-reflexive operations refer to historically distinct media-technical and phenomenological conditions, but they are formally similar in terms of exploiting disorientation in the wake of change.

On the other hand, the discorrelation at stake in post-cinematic horror is of a qualitatively new and experientially far more radical sort. What we are dealing with in movies like the *Paranormal Activity* series, *Unfriended* and

Unfriended: Dark Web (2018), or *Searching* (2018)—born-digital movies centrally *about* digital mediation—is not simply a new instance of the phenomenological disconnect occasioned by the shift from a familiar to a novel media form; rather, it involves a much more fundamental transformation of human-technological relations. At the heart of this new discorrelation is a thoroughgoing transformation of the temporal dynamics of moving-image media and the emergence of a new space of future-oriented contingency and generativity. Moving images shift from a medium of recording and playback (cinema) to a medium of on-the-fly, or real-time, image-generation (post-cinema), whereby images are no longer fixed or determined by past events but opened up to an indeterminate becoming-in-time that in many respects parallels our own temporal lives. This new indeterminacy or, in a Bergsonian idiom, "indetermination" of images is a source of unease and disorientation, and it becomes the (often oblique or indirect) object of post-cinematic horror's self-reflexive engagement with its media-technical platform.[11]

In the following, I am concerned with low-level intersections between the material infrastructures and embodied aesthetics of horror in an age of new media—intersections that are mediated in post-cinematic horror's diegetic use of digital video cameras, computer screens, and online networks, as well as the appearance of glitch effects and other artifacts of computational processing. These, I contend, are the means by which an important strand of contemporary horror seeks to harness the "medium sensitivities" that pervade life in the early decades of the twenty-first century and to redirect our anxieties for the genre's own purposes. As will become clear, my analysis of post-cinematic horror resonates broadly with recent "platform studies" approaches to film and other media, and particularly with the work of Caetlin Benson-Allott, who also emphasizes the role of the platform in recent articulations of horror.[12] But whereas Benson-Allott's focus is on self-reflexive engagements with "prerecorded video as the dominant apparatus" after film[13]—notably, with analog video technologies such as VHS as the carrier media for faux-found-footage films—my own focus is on the ways that digital video processes (such as compression/decompression, motion smoothing, buffering, upscaling) and artifacts (glitches, network lag, jitter) challenge precisely the prerecordedness of the video image, asserting instead a new dimension of generative futurity. The platform is endowed with a degree of creative autonomy, so to speak, which is situated right at the heart of digital image processing, and it is this autonomy and its disorienting effects on our own temporal experience that post-cinematic horror has learned to exploit.

Side-Channel Attacks and Temporal Discorrelation

In order to develop and ground these claims, I would like to begin by linking them to some of the broad cultural fears related to discorrelation, or the severing of the perceptual connection between subjects of consciousness and mediated objects. We might start with the recently discovered bugs affecting the vast majority of computer processors in operation, across operating systems, which were revealed to the public in early 2018 and given the aptly horror-themed names Meltdown and Spectre.[14] The latter exploit the computer's normal processes to conduct what is known as a side-channel attack to access sensitive information such as passwords or credit card numbers. As Intel puts it: "A side-channel is some observable aspect of a computer system's physical operation, such as timing, power consumption or even sound."[15] Thus, a side-channel attack is an indirect approach; the attacker does not try to break into the system to steal the desired information or object as such, but instead focuses on some epiphenomenon of normal computational operation, which is analyzed in order to locate the object indirectly—by means of the ghostly traces left by computers in the world. Thus, physical signals serve here as indices of informational operations. This means that even non-networked, rigorously "air-gapped" computers can be hacked, for example via acoustic cryptanalysis, a method that analyzes sounds emitted by computer processors, hard drives, fans, and keyboards in order to extract useful information.[16] Compounding our worries about the total surveillance of online activities by state and corporate interests, such attacks show that even going offline is insufficient to protect us from prying eyes and ears.

The Meltdown and Spectre attacks take aim at a different side-channel. In the words of Google's Project Zero team, from a post dated January 3, 2018: "We have discovered that CPU data cache timing can be abused to efficiently leak information out of mis-speculated execution, leading to (at worst) arbitrary virtual memory read vulnerabilities across local security boundaries in various contexts."[17] I will come back to this technical language in a moment, but for now it is important to note that the big, scary thing—the object of horror—being reported here is the fact that certain bugs in processor architectures subject us to the possibility of identity theft and, more generally, a hostile takeover of our agency. And this is directly related to the radical disconnect between consciousness operating on a macrotemporal (or mesotemporal) scale and the microtemporality of computer processing, according to which we can hardly be considered to be "in control" of our machines—at least, that is, not in the "real time" of media use and operation.[18] Especially when connected to online networks, as virtually all of our devices are, this disconnect exposes us to dangers that can be detected only after it is much too late. In this way, the network effects not only a spatial but also a temporal dispersal of agency that threatens us, in by-now-familiar terms, with a loss of individuality and autonomy. To invoke Gilles Deleuze's felicitous term once again, we are rendered "dividuals," and the illusion of self-same subjectivity is shattered by the material processes of networked computation.[19]

However, to focus only on the network and its exposure of our sensitive data to the outside misses a more fundamental point about the mismatch between phenomenal and technical temporalities. The vulnerability of air-gapped computers to acoustic cryptanalysis already showed that the threat of side-channel attacks is not correlated with a decision either to participate in or withdraw from online networks. But there is more. To focus solely on the specter of identity theft is basically to humanize the threat, and this humanization is enabled by a spatialized conception of the web with human agents sitting at each of its nodes (think of phishing attacks, in which humans try to trick other humans into giving them secret information). Even the extreme case of acoustic cryptanalysis is by and large understood in these spatial, anthropocentric terms: the worry is that someone might bypass or override my decision not to participate in the world of online communications, might hack the physical sonic traces of computation to correlate them with digital information that, unbeknownst to me, is effectively reinserted into the network. Again the fear is that "my" private information, which I try to secure by disconnecting and firewalling into a secure, offline space, will nevertheless be exposed to the outside by malicious agents.

My point is not that these fears are misguided or unrealistic. However, there is a deeper cause for concern that we may overlook if we frame the issue in this spatial and personalizing manner. This more fundamental threat or vulnerability is temporal and nonhuman in nature, and it is related to the fact that the discorrelation of human and technical temporalities is independent of—though certainly exacerbated by—network connectivity. The Project Zero blog post identifies "CPU data cache timing" as the crux of the Spectre and Meltdown exploits. The data cache is a black box of sorts, a hardware component located close to the processor core, which temporarily stores information and serves to reduce the CPU's access time to data that it would otherwise have to retrieve from the main memory. The Spectre/Meltdown exploits take aim at the *timings* of this cache in order to indirectly infer its contents. We are dealing here with timings measured in nanoseconds, or billionths of seconds—temporal units that far outpace the speeds of human thought and perception. This incommensurability leads to an epistemological problem, not only for the normal user unaware of what is going on inside their black-box computer, but even for expert computer scientists, as the temporal mismatch means that we simply cannot effectively know what is happening at every step of the way. Project Zero therefore adds the following caveat: "A warning regarding explanations about processor internals in this blogpost: This blogpost contains a lot of speculation about hardware internals based on observed behavior, which might not necessarily correspond to what processors are actually doing."[20] In fact, "a lot of speculation" is something of an understatement—or perhaps a pun designed to play on the role of machinic speculation and the discorrelation of human and computational processings of time. And in an act of recursion of the sort so beloved by computer scientists, this discorrelation means that computer scientists must ironically rely on the side-channel of "observed behaviors" in order to infer the real-time processes of a side-channel timing attack. Though perhaps a bit circuitous, following this looping branch will take us, in the end, to the role of discorrelation in contemporary horror movies, which are more closely in touch with the material processes of computation than may at first be apparent.

I pointed to the "CPU data cache timing," which the Project Zero team notes "can be abused to efficiently leak information out of mis-speculated execution." What I wish to foreground is a fundamental difference between human speculation and the machinic operation, discussed in chapter 3, of "speculative execution"—or the preprocessing of algorithmic conditionals and the prefetching of data before it is known whether they will in fact be needed by the computer.[21] Each of these—human and computational speculation alike—has to do with a forward-looking or futural processing of time: natural and machinic forms of anticipation, or what Husserl identifies as the protentional dimension of internal time-consciousness.[22] For Husserl, temporal experience is never located in a discrete, punctual instant, but always a thick moment in which the now is pregnant with past and future—there is no present experience without retention of the just-past and protention of the moment-about-to-come. But with the advent of computational futurity or artificial protention in the form of speculative execution, we are faced with a potentially worrying development: our machines now model something like the temporal flow at the heart of our very subjectivity, embodied in an external homologue of our internal time-consciousness. This suggests a somewhat Frankensteinian scenario—the horror of artificial life or animation—so it is only natural that we might fear a loss of control.

As I argued in the course of working through the various temporal layers of "screen time," the advent of this external homologue marks a point of crisis: as a site of low-level time-critical processes, speculative execution is also the site of critical negotiations between human and nonhuman agencies more generally. It marks, furthermore, a media-historical turning point from the broadly cinematic regime of what Bernard Stiegler calls "tertiary retention"—the externalized, reproducible experiences stored by industrial media objects such as gramophones and videotapes[23]—to the post-cinematic generativity of what Yuk Hui dubs "tertiary protention," the realm of computational anticipation ushered in by today's "smart" systems.[24] In his analysis of live or "real-time" mediation, rooted in what he calls "the televisual epoch of cinema,"[25] Stiegler warned of a colonization of consciousness that operates by preformatting our immediate awareness (or primary retention) with the images of tertiary retention—thus executing a hostile takeover of conscious experience itself. Stiegler's argument thus points to something like an asubjective and nonhumanly executed counterpart to "identity theft." But it is the shift from the retentional regime of cinematic mediation to the protentional one of post-cinema that both heightens the stakes and significantly destabilizes the determinative force of the operation. Because they are generated on the fly according to compression algorithms rather than photochemical processes, post-cinema's protentional images disrupt the stability of tertiary memories, or of the prerecorded nature of moving-image media more generally, becoming instead agents of dividuation that inject computational futurity into temporal becoming through processes of motion estimation and speculative execution—the side-channel at which Spectre and Meltdown take aim. As the Project Zero team explains the concept: "A processor can execute past a branch [such as an 'if/else' conditional in code] without knowing whether it will be taken or where its target is, therefore executing instructions before it is known whether they should be executed. If this speculation turns out to have been incorrect, the CPU can discard the resulting state without architectural effects and continue execution on the correct execution path. Instructions do not retire before it is known that they are on the correct execution path."[26]

As we have seen, these predictive techniques are used to speed up all kinds of computational processes, including image-generation and playback and to mask signal-transmission delays across online networks, for example in connection with videoconferencing or streaming platforms. The computer generates original images according to a predicted trajectory of subsequent events, even before they happen or have time to be transmitted across the network—for example, during moments of lag while conversing with someone on Skype. If these predictions diverge from actual events, they will be retracted and corrected, while the microtemporal nature of these revisions will mean that they remain largely imperceptible to human viewers—but *not* to a computational agent designed precisely to watch for and exploit this "mis-speculation window" before the CPU detects it has executed the wrong code. The Spectre bug, as we see, is therefore "spectral" in the very sense introduced by Jacques Derrida: the hauntological sense in which "time is out of joint" and the present of metaphysics is dispersed into the past and future via the differing/deferring operation of *différance*.[27] In computation, however, this spectrality is rendered materially concrete, even physical, in the CPU's data caching and out-of-order execution. Moreover, due to the operation of speculative execution in digital video playback, virtually all of our moving images have become similarly spectral in the post-cinematic era: we are haunted, in these images, by the discorrelation of human and computational time and the operation of a computational future that is always one step—or, due to the microtemporal nature of these operations, several *billion* steps—ahead of us.

Clearly, the emergence of a protentional dimension of moving-image media marks a radical change from cinema's retentional regime, but this transition pertains to a level of experience that is far less visible (if at all) to spectators than the spectacularized shifts from silent to sound cinema or from black-and-white to color film stocks, for example. The discorrelation that I am positing concerns operations that take place outside human perception itself, so how is this transformation channeled or reflected in post-cinematic horror movies? As digital video cameras, computer screens, and glitch effects entered the mise-en-scène and diegetic spaces of faux-found-footage horror movies like *Paranormal Activity*, *V/H/S* (2012), and *Unfriended*, I contend, the spectrality of discorrelation attaching to any given playback operation became subject to a recursive operation according to which it was rendered exploitable specifically as a medium of horror. In other words, *post-cinematic horror reconfigured itself as a side-channel attack on our affective processing of time itself.*

A side-channel attack is precisely what Michel Serres refers to as parasitism: the exploitation of a channel by a third party.[28] The position of the third defines a space of transition: its object may appear as noise for system-internal participants (such as interlocutors in an email exchange, for whom the internal coding and processing of symbols by the machine is of no interest), but it constitutes a message for an external observer (such as the purveyor of a side-channel attack, who is interested precisely in these by-products). This oscillatory position is essential to the functioning of the system and is responsible, in part, for the materialization of the channel, which—barring the possibility of a radically frictionless, *immaterial* medium—can never be purged of noise. The parasite therefore non-neutrally mediates the boundaries of a system; it inserts itself into what Serres calls a "space of transformation," a space that is liminal to the system, alternately within and without.[29] In mounting what amounts to a side-channel attack on our temporal becoming, post-cinematic horror occupies just such a liminal zone: a space from which to capitalize on the anxieties occasioned by a fundamental media-historical transition. Oscillating between diegetic and medial, phenomenal and computational levels, this new horror of discorrelation mediates between cinematic and post-cinematic conditions of life itself.

Unfriended: A Post-cinematic Fable

In order to flesh out these ideas, I would like to turn my attention to a representative case study: *Unfriended*, a post-cinematic horror movie that, as we have seen, is presented in the form of a radically digital and networked type of faux found footage: namely, as the screen recording of one of the characters' laptops. The latter device captures the online interactions of a group of teenage friends haunted by the ghost of a deceased classmate, the victim of cyberbullying driven to suicide, who returns in the guise of an uninvited guest participating in the friends' Skype conversations, Facebook feeds, email exchanges, and text messages. The intruder drives the friends not only to admit their complicity in the former friend's death (among other intrigues, including various other betrayals of one another), but ultimately causes the other members of the group to kill themselves by violent and graphic means.

Following some cues from Serres's fabulous book of philosophical fables, *The Parasite*, I read *Unfriended* as a post-cinematic fable of post-cinematic mediation—one that exploits (and perhaps expands the scope of) the polyvalent meanings of parasitism, as foregrounded by Serres, in order to articulate the deeply rooted imbrications of contemporary media-technics and attendant forms of human intersubjectivity and politics. As a fable, *Unfriended* is many things: it is a cautionary tale about the dangers of online bullying and, more generally, of an Internet-mediated form of social existence; it is a self-reflexive exploration of digital temporality and its relation to human experience; and it is above all an attempt to "make sense" of discorrelation itself, that is, to provide meaning and sensory content for a phenomenon that eludes direct perception. It is this necessary recourse to indirect or oblique images that makes the fable a fitting form; and while *Unfriended* does not employ the animal imagery familiar from Aesop for this purpose, it draws on more foundational resources of the fable in order to probe the social and technical parameters of post-cinematic media and to mediate the horrors of discorrelation.

What is a fable, and how can the term be extended to a media text like *Unfriended*? According to Serres, who sets out from La Fontaine's verse retelling of the story of the city rat and the country rat, fables are a form of storytelling that rest on *relations* more than concrete images; the choice of figures (rats, mice, hares, horses, tortoises, and so on) is of course not without consequence, but it is the relations between and among them that count above all. Ultimately, according to Serres, these relations all come down to a "relation of the abusive companion."[30] This is to say that fables—and not just fables, but also philosophy and other basic forms of thinking about and representing human relations—are all about parasitism.[31] This is because parasitism, for Serres, is the very foundation of human collectivity, as well as that which ensures that such collectivity is always also more-than-human. Negatively: "Our collective is the expulsion of the stranger, of the enemy, of the parasite. The laws of hospitality become laws of hostility. Whatever the size of the group, from two on up to all human kind, the transcendental condition of its constitution is the existence of the Demon."[32]

But collectivity is not simply a matter of expelling the parasite, for the formation of community depends crucially on the parasite's presence. There is an indeterminacy between hospitality and hostility, owing to an oscillation between the roles of host and of guest (terms that not only share etymological roots, indicative of the inherent possibility of role-reversal, but which more radically alternate between the welcoming embrace of the familiar guest and the fear and mistrust of strangers: xenophobia). Parasitism is thus at the root of communal welfare, charity, and civil society just as much as it motivates political exclusion; the guest, even a welcomed one, becomes a parasite with respect to the host, whose resources (food, shelter, etc.) are consumed without payment in kind. And the fable, with its displaced figures standing in for basic human relations, offers a privileged medium for representing this most unstable and shifting of roles: "Only the fable and its metempsychosis allow me to see the same third man [i.e., the parasite] in the nest, in the cave, at my table, and on the throne."[33] In short, fables like that of the city rat and the country rat—the tale of a guest-parasite visiting a host-parasite to dine at the home of a third (unwitting) host, who as a tax farmer is also a parasite of sorts with respect to the food's actual producers, the farmers who in turn parasite the spoils of nature, and so on—such tales are the perfect vehicles for communicating the deep truth of relational transposition that marks parasitism as pervasive and fundamental to social relations.

But the positive—that is to say: constitutive—role of parasitism is even more foundational to the collective, which, as I have already noted, is always also more-than-human. The rats of the fable are startled by a noise at the door, which interrupts their meal. Serres associates this noise with the information-technical sense of "noise," as in the famous Shannon-Weaver model of communication, according to which communication is measured not in terms of humanly defined meanings but in terms of signal-to-noise ratios.[34] As Cary Wolfe reminds us:

> Here, we need to remember that "noise" (for the English reader) forms the third and unsuspected meaning of the French word *parasite*: 1. biological parasite; 2. social parasite; 3. static or interference. As we know from classical information theory and its model of the signal-to-noise ratio, noise was typically regarded simply as the extraneous background against which a given message or signal was transmitted from a sender to a receiver. For Serres, however, "as soon as we are two, we are already three or four. . . . In order to succeed, the dialogue needs an excluded third" (*Genesis*, 57); we may begin with "two interlocutors and the channel that attaches them to one another," but "the parasite, nesting on the flow of the relation, is in third position" (*The Parasite*, 53). For Serres, then—and here he joins a line of systems theorists that includes figures such as Gregory Bateson and, later, Niklas Luhmann—noise is *productive* and creative.[35]

Accordingly, Serres's articulation of parasitism and noise is not just clever wordplay. Instead, this association describes intersubjective relations in a way that illuminates the essential ties between their material and informatic (or "material and logicial") conditions.[36] Any of the fable's various relations, whether between the two rats, or between the tax farmer and the farmers, or between farmers and their animals, is not only interrupted by a third (the noise, the rat, the taxman), but that third is essential in establishing the relation, or in cementing the channel of transposition that enables parasites to become parasited and vice versa.

In other words, the parasite points to the existence of the *medium* of interrelation, the channel of communication according to which systems and subsystems are structured. Parasitism, as a social or political relation, is therefore inseparable from a media-technical relation, and the appearance of noise thus serves, as Bernhard Siegert emphasizes, an essentially "phatic function" (a term he borrows from linguist Roman Jakobson).[37] As Siegert puts it, the phatic function of signs involves a "reference to the channel"[38] of communication: "Phatic communication neither expresses nor references a given content; it merely ascertains the existence of a channel"; "hence in all communication each expression, appeal, and type of referencing is preceded by a reference to interruption, difference, deviation."[39] The success of communication is thereafter measured in terms of the repression or exclusion of this interruption or noise, but, as Serres insists, such deviation is not incidental but essential: "The difference is part of the thing itself, and perhaps it even produces the thing. Maybe the radical origin of things is really that difference, even though classical rationalism damned it to hell. In the beginning was the noise."[40] Noise, or the fact of mediation, cannot be eliminated from human relation, a fact that Serres extends to technology in general: "It is of no small interest to notice here that the well-run machine does not copy the bodies of animals and their organic system, but rather our relations among ourselves. Can we conceive of an intersubjective origin for simple machines? For the lever? For the scale? For technology in general? The answer to this question is affirmative. And it is still affirmative for machines that are not so simple."[41] Yet in accordance with the system-liminal and oscillatory position of the parasite, it is not simply the case that the mediation of technology mirrors intersubjective relation as its foundation, for human relations themselves are constituted in and by technical mediations: "And suddenly, I no longer know if we have built a model, if from wood or rushes we have been able to produce a model of relations, or if, in this practice, we have discovered the origins of technology, of tools, of means. This roundabout means. These media always between us."[42] Hence media-technical and political dimensions are tightly coupled in Serres's theory—as they are, following him, in any fable, which is always and essentially a self-reflexive or phatic form of communication.

How does this illuminate *Unfriended* and its relation to the post-cinematic conditions of life today? As we have seen, fables are about sociotechnical relations more than they are about images, and certainly this applies to *Unfriended*: centrally, the film is interested in the reconfiguration of social relations as mediated by computational networks, which means, ultimately, that it is concerned with a human-machinic constellation that, in terms of the intercession of a microtemporal realm of operations, positively *resists* visualization. As a fable, *Unfriended*'s on-screen avatars therefore play the role of the image-placeholders or figural proxies formerly occupied, in classical fables, by talking animals; but true to the parasite relation, these proxies are utilized in order to probe and mediate between systems, and thus to reveal relations that are not susceptible to direct visual perception. This is, of course, all the more significant given that we are dealing with a visual medium—a paradox about which I will have more to say in a moment.

First, however, we should note that the "relation of the abusive companion," around which all fables revolve on the Serrean model, does indeed structure

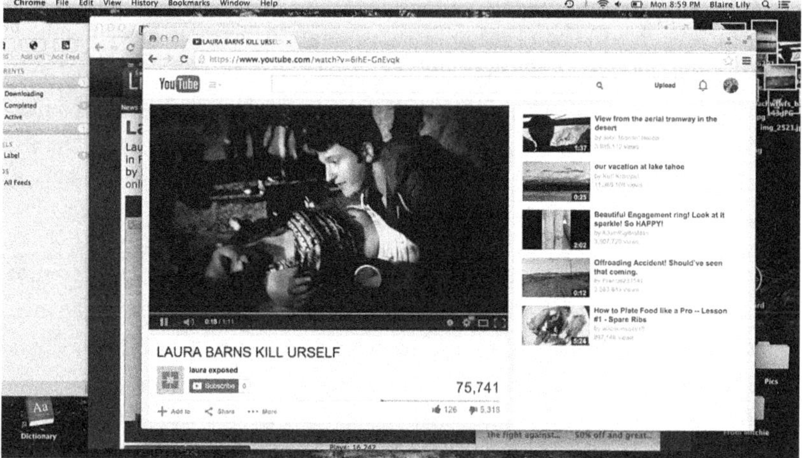

Figure 5.3. Cyberbullying as the original act of abuse.

Unfriended on a number of levels. Most obviously, the narrative is predicated on an original act of abuse: the cyberbullying that caused Laura Barns, the deceased friend (or perhaps "frenemy"), to take her life. The decisive event that precipitated her suicide was the anonymous posting of a video showing Laura partying with friends, passing out drunk, and defecating herself—her body itself effectively "glitching out."[43] After the humiliating video, titled "LAURA BARNS KILL URSELF," went viral on YouTube, Laura did indeed commit suicide; subsequently, a video of her shooting herself in the head was also posted online, and various online tributes (Facebook memorials and the like) were thereafter established in her name.[44] Then, one year to the day after her suicide, the abused friend makes a posthumous return, in the form of a ghost, in order to abuse (by means of deceiving, dividing, and ultimately torturing) her former friends. It is important to note, in this connection, that the parasite conjoins not only the reversible roles of guest and host, as we have seen, but also that of the ghost (with whom the latter also share a common etymology). As Siegert writes:

> Ancient Greek did not distinguish between guest and stranger—both were referred to as *xenos*, *xeinos*, or *xénä*. In Latin too it is difficult to draw a clear etymological boundary between guest and stranger. The latter was originally called *hostis*, which also meant enemy; but as of the first century BCE the term only signified the (political) enemy. In Old Latin, however, it indicated members of alien tribes or nations, including those on peaceful

> terms with Rome, with the understanding that they were living under their own laws. The position of the arriving stranger is indeed ambivalent: On the one hand he is a sinister enemy, on the other a guest who deserves respect. The word *guest* mirrors this ambivalence. It is derived from the Indo-European **ghostis*, which not only spawned Latin *hostis* but also evolved into *guest* and *ghost*. Both engage in visitations: A guest is someone who comes to haunt your house, in other words, a ghost.[45]

In her ghostly form, Laura haunts and abuses not only the group of friends, but also, at the same time, their channels of communication; indeed, she manifests exclusively through Twitter, Facebook, Skype, email, and other digital channels. Laura is a specter, therefore, but one that recalls to us precisely the spectrality of computational processes that I considered in the last section, along with that of side-channel attacks, such as Spectre, that take aim at and mediate between social and media-technical forms of parasitism. Again, it is an abuse relation that unites these various forms. Recall the Project Zero blog post announcing the discovery "that CPU data cache timing can be *abused* to efficiently leak information out of mis-speculated execution."[46] It is only fitting that Laura, the original victim of cyberabuse, would return in the form of a specifically digital ghost—that is, as a side-channel attacker.

Significantly, when the ghost first appears in their online conversation as a generic Skype avatar with no profile picture, the group of friends take it to be nothing more than "a glitch." A glitch, however, is quite literally a parasite in the information-theoretical sense: it is the digital guise of noise, static, or signal interference. Ghosts and glitches are therefore interchangeable with guests and hosts (benefactors, interchangeably, of human visitors, tapeworms, and/or computer viruses), all of which are reversibly parasitic in their relations. But as it becomes clear to the friends that there is indeed an uninvited guest in their videoconferencing session, that it is not "just a glitch" after all, it becomes all the more significant that the deeply spectral relations at play here manifest themselves materially as glitches on the screen—where the screen is both diegetic *and* material, both a part of the friends' world and of the viewer's. As these glitches make evident, the screen is, moreover, a membrane between the discorrelated levels of the phenomenal/visual and the computational/avisual. These manifestations therefore culminate in what Serres refers to as a "parasitic cascade":[47] just as the country rat parasited the city rat, who parasited the tax farmer, who parasited the farmers, who parasited the crops and the animals, and so on, so too is it parasitism all the way down in *Unfriended*—the friends parasited the dead girl, her ghost parasites the friends, social media

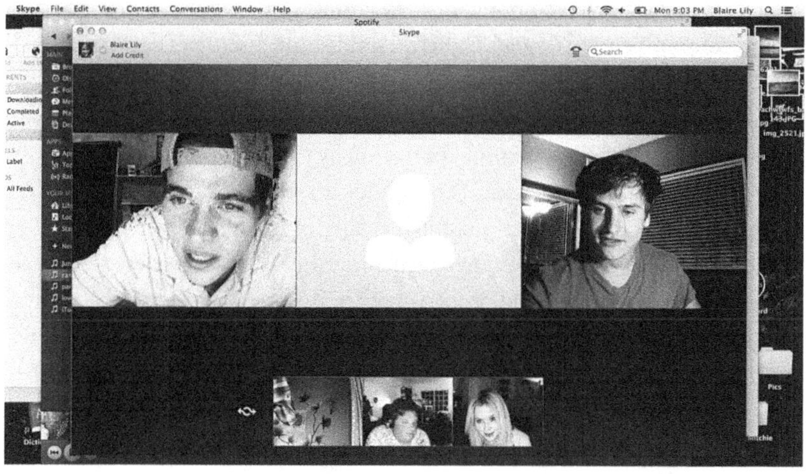

Figure 5.4. The ghost as glitch.

parasites human community, computation parasites perception, and post-cinema parasites cinema. In each case, a "contrapuntal matrix" is established by these relations and transpositions,[48] while in *Unfriended* it is the glitch in particular that serves as the fulcrum for the sociotechnical counterpoint between informatic and anthropological, computational and phenomenological conditions.

This bring us back to the crucial fact about the movie's mediation—that it is presented as a screencast recording from Laura's former best friend (and original cyberbully) Blaire Lily's MacBook laptop. The frame, that is, is filled completely with the pixel images of the laptop's screen, including the operating system menus, icons, and mouse cursor; the only cameras are those of the friends' computers, which channel everything into this single surface, a total system with no outside.[49] Reflecting what Francesco Casetti calls the "relocation" of cinema from the big screen to a variety of little ones,[50] the movie's sense of "realism" is especially heightened when you watch it on your own laptop—when you close the loop, so to speak, and align the movie's frame materially with your own computer screen. As we have seen, the movie anticipates such viewership and even derives some of its affective power from the danger to which online piracy exposes the viewer. When the movie is viewed on a computer, we witness everything on this single, interchangeably diegetic and material screen, through Skype conversations, Facebook chats, email, and web browsing. And it is essential for the movie that it is presented in "real time." This adds to the temporal urgency and speaks to the reality of our own online communications today, thereby establishing a sense of realism despite the fantastic/supernatural elements at play, and articulating this reality despite—or precisely through—the use of digital glitches. These might otherwise be taken to signal the interruption of realism by the intercession of digital processing that breaks the indexical continuity between image input and image output, but such glitches are a familiar reality of online communication (on platforms like Skype), and our involvement in the images is increased by their use; when the Universal Studios logo appears on-screen with digital compression artifacts, we might genuinely wonder whether the glitches are diegetic, or whether they are produced on our own machine during playback, either due to the buffering processes of online streaming platforms or because we downloaded a faulty torrent file from some dubious website. Realism here is constructed through an immediacy and direct exploration of the new media-technical conditions of life, to which we can all more or less relate.[51] But in the process the glitches also expose the movie's singular screen as, in fact, double: the site of playback, traditionally a passive "screening" surface, the screen is also revealed as a newly active site or space in which images are processed and generated before our very eyes. The glitches point up the perceptual paradoxes of post-cinematic cameras—similar to the phenomenological complexities that I described in chapter 1 with respect to CGI lens flares, which oscillate between transparency and opacity as both photorealistic simulations of a camera's material physics and as realism-shattering spectacles in their own right. But these glitches additionally implicate the post-cinematic screen, which becomes ontologically indistinguishable from the camera in its execution of the same material processes of microtemporal and subperceptual image-generation.

Unfriended's glitches, and their relation to our contemporary media-technical realities, call attention to what Hito Steyerl has called the "poor images" that circulate in digital networks.[52] Following Steyerl, these images provide an important context for thinking about the political realities of moving-image media today—and an important context for thinking about post-cinematic realism more generally. In Steyerl's words:

> The poor image is an illicit fifth-generation bastard of an original image. Its genealogy is dubious. Its file names are deliberately misspelled. It often defies patrimony, national culture, or indeed copyright. It is passed on as a lure, a decoy, an index, or as a reminder of its former visual self. It mocks the promises of digital technology. Not only is it often degraded to the point of being just a hurried blur, one even doubts whether it could be

called an image at all. Only digital technology could produce such a dilapidated image in the first place.[53]

These poor images are close in spirit, as Steyerl claims, to the "imperfect cinema" called for in the name of Third Cinema movements, in that they register social marginalization processes while also creating publics of their own. But they also outline the dark side of a "participatory culture," whose democratic promise is compromised by the hierarchies of value that remain and by the exploitation of unpaid fan labor that is enlisted in the ongoing production-consumption circuits of networked images.[54] Without extracting themselves from these conflicting political trajectories, according to Steyerl, poor images might nevertheless—or precisely for this reason—create what Dziga Vertov called "visual bonds" capable of subverting official and mainstream valuations by expressing what Steyerl terms a "link to the present."[55] In this way, degraded, glitched-out images might fulfill the political promise of realism precisely through their material connection to the postindexical infrastructures of moving-image media. In Steyerl's words: "The poor image is no longer about the real thing—the originary original. Instead, it is about its own real conditions of existence: about swarm circulation, digital dispersion, fractured and flexible temporalities. It is about defiance and appropriation just as it is about conformism and exploitation. In short: it is about reality."[56]

In his book *Videophilosophie*, Maurizio Lazzarato similarly invokes Vertov and his idea of the "visual bond," which Lazzarato offers as a materialist alternative to the critique of ideology, the expression of a practice that addresses the ontology of media directly and prior to the level of content.[57] Essentially, by resisting reduction to human perception, the images of Vertov's kino-eye are discorrelated from molar experience but thereby opened to the molecular processes by which duration is processed both biologically and technologically, thus getting to the heart of the process by which subjectivities and social collectives are produced. If cinematic realism, following film theorists like André Bazin, draws for its political power on an approximation to perceptual experience, Vertov marks the path toward a *post-cinematic realism* that takes aim at the process by which the subject of that perceptual experience takes shape in the first place.[58] It does this, according to Lazzarato, by means of the prepersonal affect that is marshaled and modulated by the increasingly fine-grained "time-crystallizing machines" of cinema, video, and digital processors. Accordingly, the video art of Nam June Paik offers a Vertovian answer to television, not because it counters the ideological content of TV but because it probes the apparatus's machinic time itself, freeing it from the exclusive control of state and corporate interests. The latter, according to Lazzarato, contribute to the production and regulation of political subjects through their control of technical standards (like the PAL and NTSC standards that regulate image frequency, color spectrum, and aspect ratio); because the power to modulate the speeds and images dictated by such standards is "withdrawn from social praxis,"[59] our affective powers are impoverished, and we are left with what Lazzarato calls a "'poor' perception."[60] The ontology of time-crystallizing machines thus gives way to an ethics or politics of the standards, codes, or protocols on which images or perceptual objects are formed and synchronized with emergent subjects and social collectives. And because they expose the materiality of digital file formats, video codecs, and compression algorithms, today's poor images harbor a significant political promise, a potential for resistance that can be deployed creatively against the impoverishment and standardization of perception.

It is of course debatable whether a movie like *Unfriended* succeeds in this respect. Certainly, at the level of its narrative, it seems to fail to articulate anything like a model of social-political resistance; if anything, its teenage drama of betrayal, suicide, and revenge, all mediated by the networks and interfaces of social media, and leading to the death of this entire group of "friends," serves as a critique of contemporary socialization processes—an ideological critique that not only takes aim at online bullying, for example, but exposes an infrastructure of communication and of intersubjective relation that has rendered the term "friend" itself highly unstable in the age of Facebook. But beyond this more overt political critique of today's highly mediated forms of collectivity, the movie's use of glitches serves to focus attention, and to channel affect, at a deeper level, where subjectivity itself is being produced and modulated in an environment of microtemporally operating machines and protocols. Toward this end, glitches serve at times like micro-cliff-hangers, causing us to wait for the image to buffer or clear up so that we can see what is going on. In this respect, the movie simulates the familiar and yet always disconcerting experience of network lag, for example in our own Skype conversations, when the temporal continuity of protentional-retentional experience is interrupted, giving rise to a feeling like that of a cartoon character who, having gone over the edge of a cliff, remains suspended, floating momentarily between the certainty of solid ground and a realization of the situation's gravity. These micro-cliff-hangers focus our attention on the material infrastructure of experience itself, causing us to see pixels as the components of but also as material obstacles to vision, blocky screen objects that, despite ourselves, we try to look around to catch a glimpse of the object on the other side. And in this space of the screen,

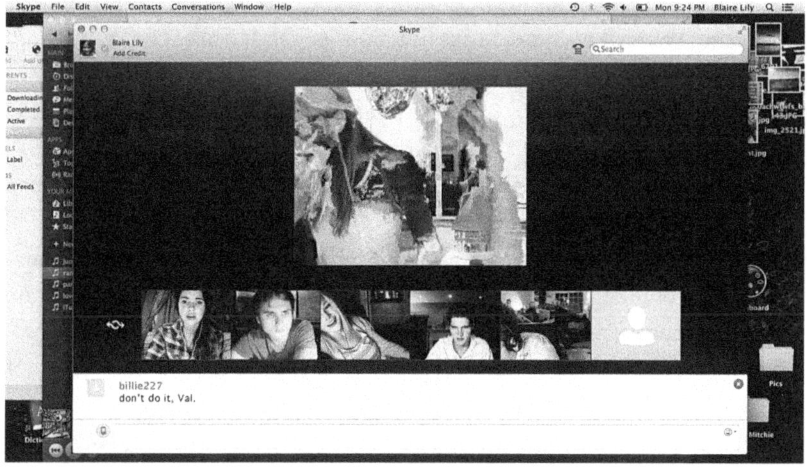

Figure 5.5. Glitches as micro-cliff-hangers or disruptions of protentional-retentional continuity.

seemingly unitary but, as we have seen, doubled and in fact multiplied even further by the machinic and social networks in which it participates (both diegetically and materially), our vision is dispersed, divided. We are forced to scan the screen for relevant information; our gaze is not sutured, not directed, and to this extent we are hailed not as an integral subject, but as a bundle of affects engaged in a collective effort to perceive—an effort that is both enabled and hindered by the protocols and agencies of the media environment, out of which our subjectivities are wrought.

Unfriended may or may not ultimately facilitate our efforts to take control of this experiential infrastructure, but perhaps it succeeds in gesturing toward the facts that this effort must be a collective one, aimed at constructing collectivity in the first place, and that it must be mounted around and in relation to the affective technologies of our post-cinematic environment, in the very ruins of our perception. For what the movie undoubtedly does is to demonstrate, through a rigorous set of transpositions, the "parasitic cascade" that is restructuring the jointly social and media-technical conditions of life today. In this respect, *Unfriended* not only exemplifies the horror of discorrelation as a stylistic or generic formation; far more importantly, it engages us affectively and mediates, in the form of a perverse fable, the ongoing shift from a cinematic to a post-cinematic lifeworld, revealing what Serres terms "the horror of disorder and noise" as the necessary cacophony of our moment.[61] Against the impulse to dismiss this noise, to write it off as "just a glitch," Serres reminds us: "Yet we know of no system that functions perfectly, that is to say, without losses, flights, wear and tear, errors, accidents, opacity."[62] *Unfriended* positions the glitch (and its others: the ghost, the guest, the host, the server, the friend, the frenemy, etc.) as a "*productive* and creative" force (in Wolfe's formulation)[63] or, as Serres puts it more ambiguously, as a force that is undecided between "generative or corrupting" impulses.[64]

Glitches, of course, often result from simple file corruption, but the ambiguous and oscillatory ways in which they are employed in *Unfriended* lay bare also the generative nature of digital video more generally, the fact that it is processual, protentional, and marked by a fundamental indeterminacy that not only distinguishes post-cinema from the photographic fixity of cinematic images, but that also casts our own temporal becoming into a new and uncertain relation to the microtemporal infrastructures of a computational lifeworld.[65] As a side-channel attack on these new sociotechnical relations, post-cinematic horror's use of glitches should not be written off as "mere gimmicks"—to do so is to reproduce the efforts to rout out the parasite, exclude the third, suppress the noise, or write off the ghost as "just a glitch." For what these glitches do is to short-circuit our perception and the normal temporal flow of retention-protention, ultimately helping us to "make sense" of discorrelation: by pointing, parasitically and phatically, to the new *medium* of interrelation, they shed an oblique light on a new set of signal/sign relations, a new space of meaning, of politics, and perhaps, ultimately, to a new correlation of subjects and systems.

Postscript on Realism and Reality

Let us return to the question of realism and the way that it serves, in a post-cinematic fable like *Unfriended*, to focus horror—as the horror of discorrelation—on the politically significant imbrications of computational image infrastructures and the conditions of "imagined community" or collectivity.[66] There are lessons here that extend beyond the context of fictional filmmaking, that concern the basis for political life in the "real world" today, where the question of realism is not limited to an effect of authentic representation, psychological engrossment, or experiential simulation, but instead concerns the notion of reality itself—a reality in which computational moving-image media are thoroughly enmeshed in the fabric of people, things, resources, and relations that constitute the world. The question of post-cinematic realism thus directs our attention elsewhere: to sites of mediated strife, for example, to the real-world horrors of contemporary war, and to the production of terror in spaces both online and off. Discorrelation has radically transformed the arenas of military and paramilitary conflict, and with them the larger environment for life; around these sites of conflict, we see new forms of subjectivity and collectivity emerging in relation to the infrastructures of "invisible images" at work in military drones, smart weapons, and the network protocols used to transmit terrorist propaganda, among others.[67] A variety of video forms, from propaganda to documentary to artistic works, are operative in mediating these new conditions of reality.

Terrorism and terror-related videos, in particular, embody a literal weaponization of the techniques of horror, operationalizing discorrelation not for cheap thrills but for militant purposes: as Marwan Kraidy argues, groups like the Islamic State (IS) have discovered digital video as an instrument in a "new kind of warfare"—what he calls "global networked affect."[68] Drawing on theorizations of digital images that emphasize their instability and processuality—the way, as Ingrid Hoelzl puts it, they are "constantly oscillating between visual entity and digital data"[69] or, as Mark Hansen argues, "the image can no longer be restricted to the level of surface appearance, but must be extended to encompass the entire process by which information is made perceivable through embodied experience"[70]—Kraidy understands these images less in terms of realistic or unrealistic representations, and more in terms of the affective force that allows them to bypass cognitive filters and involve the body directly in real material relations. Following Harun Farocki's definition of *operative images* as "images that do not represent an object, but rather are part of an operation"[71] (not unlike the nonhuman images at work in industrial robots and self-driving cars), Kraidy argues that such images "can become important weapons that convey projectilic affect—a feeling of bodily harm and violation."[72] Depicting decapitations, immolations, and other scenes of death and destruction, these videos' projectilic images aim at once to capture sympathetic imaginations, to mobilize militant collectives, and to deliver injurious shocks to heretics who watch in horror as atrocities are mediated in broadcast, narrowcast, and clandestine online networks.

Kraidy's analysis of IS's weaponization of digital video points to the ways that discorrelation is involved both directly and indirectly in reconfiguring political relations—directly, in that the operationalization of affective force in projectilic forms takes aim at the prepersonal basis of viewers' subjectivities; and indirectly, in that this image-warfare initiates patterns of censorship, avoidance, and obfuscation that pit these images against forces of invisibilization and thus mirror, in the higher-order interactions of political actors and

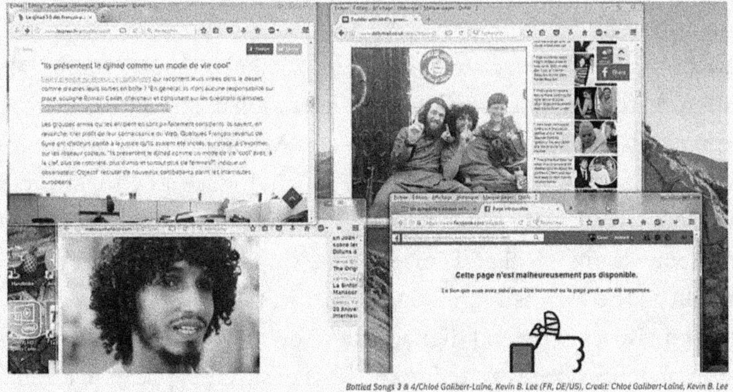

Figure 5.6. *Bottled Songs* on the Ars Electronica website.

their efforts to exert control over networks of exchange, the lower-level oscillations between visibility and invisibility that characterize all digital video. That is, these videos, which do not merely depict but aim to deliver acts of terror, organize around themselves a field of tactical operations: terrorist organizations play cat-and-mouse games with state security organizations, Internet service providers (ISPs), and other agents determined to neutralize their efforts to spread the images; clandestine networks mobilize to keep the videos in circulation; news media report about spectacular images of torture and death, from which they may selectively sample while withholding the most graphic scenes; and Internet users find themselves torn between fascination and fear, between impulses to seek out or to shield themselves from the videos. In this way, however, the videos, whose direct projectilic force is at stake in the struggles over circulation, have already transformed the field of relations between online subjects and collectives, whether or not they are ever viewed. Such videos therefore serve a phatic function and assert the radically parasitic force of discorrelated images in determining the politics of technical infrastructures.

Bottled Songs, an ongoing collaboration between Chloé Galibert-Laîné and Kevin B. Lee, provides a powerful picture of this triangulation among what they call "desktop subjectivities," online collectives, and invisible image infrastructures.[73] Consisting of a series of episodes in which Galibert-Laîné and Lee compose videographic "letters" to one another about their ongoing research into terrorism recruitment videos and underground networks, the work takes the form of a "desktop documentary"—utilizing screen-recording software rather than cameras to document the researcher-filmmakers' forays into "an unstable virtual environment of fear and attraction."[74] Formally, the videos therefore resemble *Unfriended*'s screen-based horror, while their exploration of online realism is distinguished by a heavier investment in the real-world terrors of discorrelated images.

In an episode titled "My Crush Was a Superstar," Galibert-Laîné writes to Lee about her attempts to track down information about a young French convert to the Islamic State in Iraq and Syria (ISIS), whom she discovered by chance in a documentary about Western jihadists.[75] Narrated (in French) by Galibert-Laîné, the epistolary video begins with a shot of her Windows desktop; a click on the Firefox icon at the bottom of the frame brings up a window with a new message in the online version of Microsoft's Outlook email application; she begins typing a message (in English) titled "RE: research" to Lee: "Dear Kevin, I wrote you last night, to tell you that I finally found a trace of this young man, whom I've been looking for online since I've seen him in this video, a couple of weeks ago." The message continues in voice-over mode while the unseen narrator and desktop-operator clicks to open a low-resolution video of the young man in question: with luxuriant black curls and a beard, he smiles and looks genially into the camera. Galibert-Laîné reminds Lee of an earlier communication, in which she informed him that she had found the man's name and discovered that he died more than two years prior. Refocusing the computer desktop and clicking through various websites and online videos to retrace her discovery and fascination with the man, whose face struck her as "immediately friendly, open, smiling"; reviewing old email messages and chat sessions with Lee, in which she identified the man as her "crush"; utilizing Google's reverse image search with a screenshot of the man's face in an attempt to identify him; then cutting to email and Facebook correspondence and leading to a proliferation of windows documenting the young man's presence across a variety of mainstream and underground social media, with images of him shopping for clothes, going to the beach, posing in selfies;

but culminating in a report that mentions an (unseen) image of him holding a severed head—the video attests to the fractured and polyvalent reality that is mediated in the singular space of the screen. And as Galibert-Laîné increasingly questions her identification and difference with respect to her former "crush," whose image is invoked not only by ISIS but also by Islamophobic hate-mongers, we experience an unsettling of our own online or "desktop subjectivity"—a fracturing of moral, libidinal, and perceptual agencies and allegiances in the networked environment.

In another episode, "The Spokesman," framed by Lee's Apple Macintosh desktop and narrated in English, Lee writes back to Galibert-Laîné to detail his attempts to track down another man: British journalist John Cantlie, who was taken hostage by ISIS before being made to serve as a reporter for the terror network's surprisingly professional-looking news service. Lee opens a Google Chrome browser window and begins composing a message in Gmail: "Dear Chloé, It's time to tell you what I learned about the man I've been investigating." Scrolling through images, videos, and online newspaper articles, Lee's exposition follows the nonlinear itinerary typical of "surfing" the Internet: he ruminates on affective mismatches in Cantlie's coerced self-expressions, then follows an associative line of flight into his own childhood memories, and comes back (by way of *Lawrence of Arabia*) to the Middle East, where he eventually arrives at a set of ISIS-produced media reports featuring Cantlie traveling through Syria and Iraq and surveying the extent of ISIS-controlled territories. These clips, in which Cantlie seems to speak both for himself and on behalf of ISIS, are interestingly framed by footage from an ISIS-controlled drone, with which the reportage opens, and a final video in which Cantlie looks up to the sky and implores what is depicted as an enemy drone to "drop a bomb," "try to rescue me again," or "do something!" With these images calling into question the volatile power dynamics in which both human and technological actors are caught up, Lee digs deeper into Cantlie's past in an effort to understand his ambiguous agency between self-determination, forced submission, and survival. Trawling YouTube and uncovering videos of Cantlie test-riding high-performance motorcycles for a short-lived television program and, years before that, giving "video tips" on videogames of the 1990s for a VHS supplement to *Sega Power* magazine, Lee begins to wonder whether he is reproducing a stalking-like search previously performed by Cantlie's captors.

Windows pile up on the screen as Lee continues piecing together the media traces of the man's life, until he finds the last video that Cantlie made before being taken hostage. Scrubbing through the video, Lee identifies the final image that appears to be taken from Cantlie's point of view: an image of a

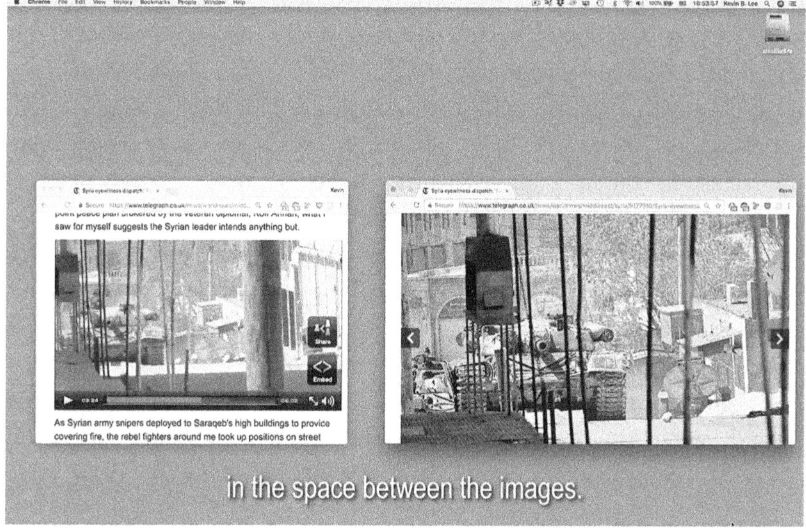

Figure 5.7. Locating Cantlie's perspective "in the space between the images."

tank rolling up the street, its barrel pointed directly at the camera. Pausing the video on this image, Lee remarks: "Of all the images I've looked at, this is the closest I've come to seeing the world through his eyes." But, Lee points out, there is a second version of the image, from an ever-so-slightly different angle, which we now see side-by-side with the first: "As he was filming, he had the presence of mind to put down the camera and pick up another camera. Once again, it produces a kind of distance, as if he's both in the scene and beyond the scene, in the space between the images." The juxtaposition of the two images foregrounds the discorrelation of perspective, the unmooring of perceptual subjectivity from any single POV and its dispersal across the various nodes of a networked media environment with its variously transposable cameras, screens, terminals, and infrastructures. Locating Cantlie's position "between the images," Lee in fact names a more general condition of dividuation in an age of discorrelated images—one that points us again toward the role of "invisible images" in the formation of subjects and collectives. Such invisible images are spectrally present in the unseen image of Galibert-Laîné's "crush" holding a severed head (a head whose eyes are also no longer capable of seeing images), or in the missing reverse shot from the drone that Cantlie hails (whose inhuman camera incessantly scans the ground, but whose images may or may not ever be seen by human eyes). In this way, both terrorist propaganda videos and the desktop documentaries that seek to make sense of them revolve around something very similar to the side-channel attacks considered earlier in this chapter—indirect approaches that array subjectivity around images and infrastructures that either cannot be seen or are avoided for fear of trauma or even brainwashing.[76] And this indirect, parasitic approach is not only deeply symptomatic of our contemporary lived reality; it is in fact the sole means by which we can make aesthetic sense of a world of discorrelation.

Another work—Israeli-born, American-educated video artist Omer Fast's *5000 Feet Is the Best* (2011)—provides the missing reverse shot from the drone, so to speak, and further elaborates our picture of this discorrelated reality. A somewhat surreal docudrama, the half-hour video is based on Fast's interview of a former drone pilot, now suffering PTSD, who flew the Predator remotely piloted aircraft (RPA) on military missions abroad from a base outside Las Vegas. According to one curatorial description of the work:

> The video is based on two meetings, recorded in a hotel in Las Vegas in September 2010, where the drone operator shared the technical aspects of his job with Fast as well as the psychological difficulties he has experienced as a result of incidents in which the unmanned plane fired at both militants and civilians. This fictional and factual retelling of this veteran's story explores the shifting divisions between reality and representation, and truth and memory. Fast's articulation of the intersection of video game culture, slick Hollywood narrative, government concealment, and the privatization of warfare provides an elliptical and haunting account of its cost, while refusing to moralize or judge.[77]

It is precisely the "elliptical and haunting" nature of the video, which features a reenactment of three significantly different versions of the interview interspersed with what appears to be actual footage of the pilot (whose face is blurred for anonymity), which gets us closer to the reality of discorrelation.

The video's oblique approach to this reality is mounted around a number of sites, one of which is the discorrelation of embodiment from the places of perception and action as experienced by the pilot. The thrice-repeated fictionalization of the interview opens each time with the interviewer asking, "What's the difference between you and someone who sits in an airplane?" Each time, the pilot responds, "There's no difference between us. We do the same job." The interviewer interjects: "But you're not a real pilot." The pilot's response in each iteration is different, and it serves to introduce a different story. In the first instance, the pilot replies: "I know what you're talking about; you're talking about bodies and places—Euclidean shit. Like train drivers in

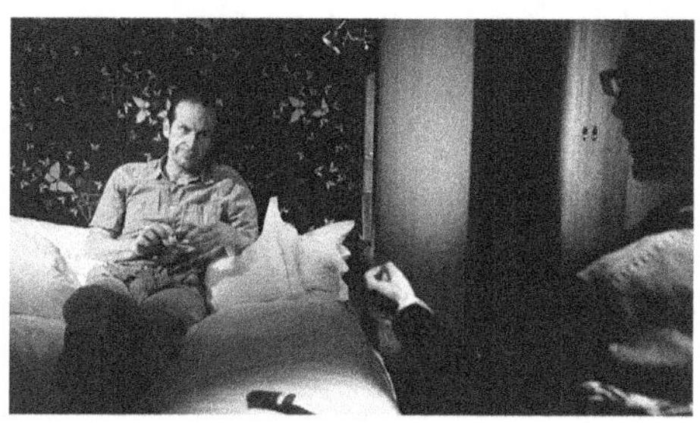
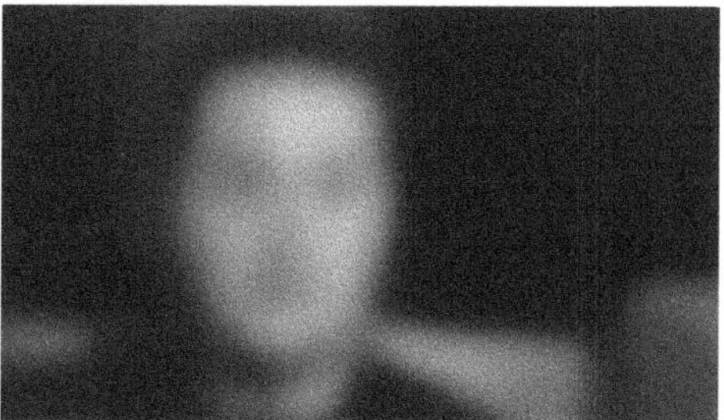

Figures 5.8 and 5.9. Fictional interview and real drone pilot in *5000 Feet Is the Best*.

the 1880s or something." In the second iteration, the pilot revises his response: "You're thinking about bodies and trenches—rats running around, mustard gas, World War I, right?" And the third time around, he says: "You're thinking about Orville and Wilbur, Kitty Hawk, *Top Gun*, Red Baron, whatever." In each case, the pilot's response to the interviewer questioning his status as a "real" pilot is interrupted by a high-pitched noise, apparently a PTSD-induced symptom that makes the pilot flinch, stopping him mid-thought and causing him to reach for some pills. Thus, PTSD is immediately linked as a second site of discorrelation—a site of erasure or censorship of an original, traumatic scene that might be read as a particularly human response to (or repetition of) the perceptual absence at the heart of discorrelated images.

The disruptive beep that signals the pilot's symptoms also interrupts and diverts the flow of narration, which now continues with a tale more or less clearly related to the drone pilot's experiences: a tale about a man so obsessed with trains that he eventually decides to impersonate a driver; a story about a couple running a con game at Vegas hotels; and finally a story about a white suburban family whose vacation is preempted when their station wagon becomes collateral damage to a drone's Hellfire missile. Like the suppressed origin of the trauma, which these stories serve either to mediate or to deflect, the real drone pilot appears after each episode to narrate parts of his own story. And it is here that we approach a further site of discorrelation: namely, the relegation of the pilot's sensory capacities, and the pilot himself, to a secondary and ultimately optional role in the technical system. The first of these segments opens with the title phrase—"Five thousand feet's the best"—narrated by the real pilot, off-screen, while we see aerial footage of a boy cycling through the desert. The pilot elaborates on the level of detail discernible via the drone: "I can tell you what kind of shoes you're wearing from a mile away"—while, of course, the pilot is actually hundreds or thousands of miles away from the unseen drone. "There's very clear cameras on board." Meanwhile, the camera slowly zooms out to give an indication of the drone's impressive altitude, and we see the bicycle approaching a street, which turns out to be populated by suburban homes, thus radically changing our perspective: this is not a war zone in any traditional sense, not a desert in the Middle East, but the new, covert war zone of suburban Las Vegas, from where drone pilots remotely fly their missions.

As the still-unseen pilot continues elaborating on the drone's sensory systems, human vision is increasingly consigned to a supplementary function: "We have the IR infra-red, which we can switch to automatically, and that will pick up any heat signatures or cold signatures." This form of mediation is not without its own aesthetics: "It kind of looks like a white blossom, just shining up into heaven. It's quite beautiful." Now, for the first time, the video cuts to the pilot's blurred face, which will occupy the screen for about ten seconds: "Um, I mean, heck, if you see someone light up a cigarette on there that's a huge beacon. You just see a very white glow coming from that area." Cutting back to the aerial shot tracking the bicycle as it makes its way through the neighborhood, the pilot's words render this view increasingly ominous:

> And you're just on a pre-set path flying in a circular orbit, watching them as they're smoking from about two, three miles away. You could be following them and they wouldn't hear you nor see you. And, um, I'll set the laser on a spot. You'll see a box pop up. What it does is it locks in those pixels, as we're circling, and the computer will, uh, figure out the trajectory, the distance, and the speed, and come up with an estimated time that it would take for the missile to impact. Um, the pilot will get all the clearances that are necessary to fire. He'll release the missile, and I'll guide it in onto its target.

As the pilot speaks these final words, the camera pans upward to reveal the expanse of cookie-cutter houses stretching for miles and miles, while the Las Vegas skyline looms off in the distance.

The pilot's matter-of-fact manner and the juxtaposition with domestic American settings drive home the everyday horrors of discorrelation. Through the drone's telescopic lens, the American suburb is rendered visually interchangeable with the desert war zones we see on TV or social media, suggesting that it could—you or I could—as easily be the target of a drone strike; furthermore, it is revealed as the site of hidden, literally displaced or remote-controlled

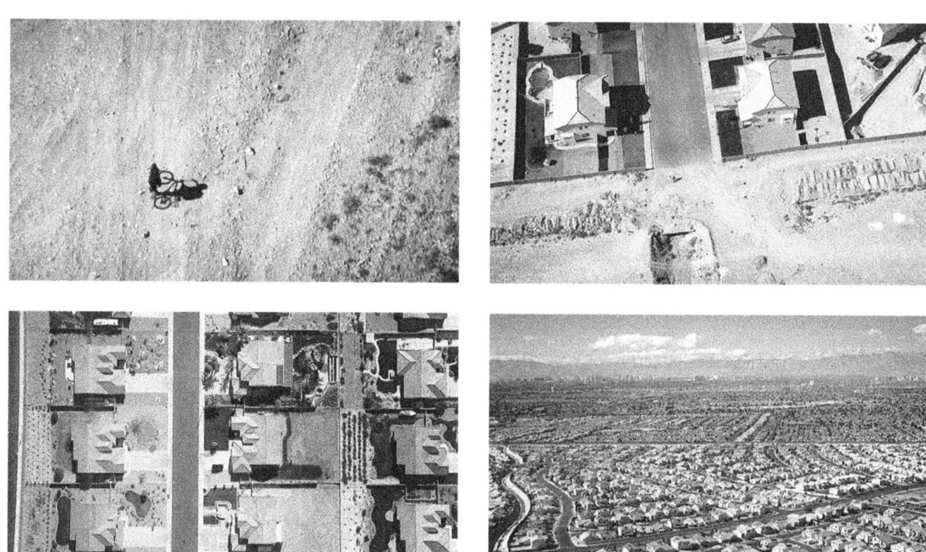

Figures 5.10–5.13. Tracking a bicyclist in the desert, subsequently revealed as the Las Vegas suburbs.

violence. Everything is permeated by a sense of flat indifferentiation, which would seem to mirror the pilot's damaged affective state. In the second segment with the real pilot, he details the job's everyday stresses and means of coping, including videogames, which are not dissimilar from piloting in some ways: "I guess Predator is similar to playing a videogame, but playing the same videogame four years straight every single day on the same level. One time I just watched the same house for a month straight. For at least eleven hours. Every day. For a month." But there are also more acute stresses, including time-critical targeting operations, and "there's horror sides to working Predator; you see a lot of death." Describing the crisis he found himself in after five years of this work, the pilot recounts that "one factor . . . that helped me is that if it wasn't me who was doing it, then . . . some new kid would be doing it, but worse." Fast's video thus suggests that a generalized interchangeability is both the ultimate horror of discorrelation and its only consolation; such interchangeability follows from processes of desubjectification and dividuation, which facilitate the human's insertion into the technical system and effect the hollowing out and replacement of affective life with the microtemporal rhythms of the machine. The algorithmic images which occupy the pilot's attention, whether piloting the drone or "blowing off steam" in a videogame, are operative, the video suggests, in rewiring psychological and political realities alike.

Thus *5000 Feet Is the Best* intimates the way that all of us today are implicated in a general routing, by way of discorrelated images, of experience into Kraidy's "global networked affect." We are all affected, though clearly in different ways and to various degrees, by the "visual nominalism" that Thomas Stubblefield attributes to drones, which implement "a system of seeing that eschews objects and identities in favor of spatial relations and empirical data."[78] Now that we all live inside this logistical system that spans the planet—now that the Internet is physically embodied and forms our environment—subjects and objects are alike dividual, and they are either computable or they are mere noise. This is the totalizing sphere of what Trevor Paglen has called the "autonomous hyper-normal mega-meta-realism" instituted by AI and other "invisible image" technologies.[79] Drones participate in the construction of this system with their algorithmic techniques of "edge detection, motion capture, auto-tagging, and facial recognition," which, as Stubblefield argues, "supplant the perspectival, Albertian image with a catalog of distances, volumes, heat signatures, and behavioral patterns."[80] The lacunae at the heart of PTSD mirror the missing integral images, but even without explicit connection to these systems and without the symptoms that plague the pilot, our subjectivities and the collectives with and against which we align ourselves have been radically changed by the processes of discorrelation, through which all moving images are now filtered before they reach our eyes.

With its iterative structure and the system of equivalences and digressions or diversions that it institutes, Fast's video reminds us that any view of these processes—including, self-reflexively, Fast's video itself—will have to be indirect, any perspective already transformed by the processes' prior operation. As Mark Hansen puts it, Fast's video "multiplies perspectives from which we could observe the drone logic, but none of these perspectives are perspectives that can be claimed to be *ours*. . . . They are perspectives that are produced by the logic of this machine itself as it's mediated through this technical mediation of the film, but importantly not perspectives of our own understanding but perspectives of the worldly operations of this drone logic."[81] The latter logic is hardly confined to the figure of the drone; it permeates our world, including online platforms that scan and identify digital contents the same way the drone scans entities on the ground, automating the elimination of contraband such as copyrighted material or terrorist videos, thus initiating the tactical games of hide-and-seek discussed above. Omer Fast's video reminds me, finally, of these material processes in a very direct way: designed for gallery

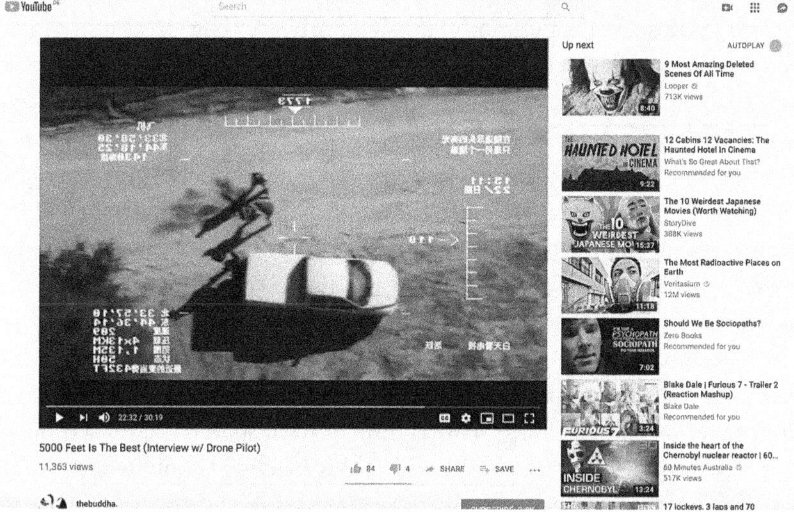

Figure 5.14. *5000 Feet Is the Best* on YouTube, with image reversed to avoid detection by the platform's algorithms.

exhibition, the circulation of *5000 Feet Is the Best* is of course highly regulated, with only stills and short excerpts available through legitimate channels. The market system in which it participates dictates that the video itself must remain invisible. But one glitchy copy has slipped through and avoided detection by YouTube's copyright infringement-detection algorithms. On closer inspection, it turns out that the survival of this "poor-image" copy was not by accident: the video image has been intentionally reversed, as if seen in a mirror, so that on-screen text reads backward. I hardly notice the difference; the bootleg video is perfectly visible to my eyes, but it seems so far to have remained invisible to the algorithms. This is another subtle reminder of the difference between human and machinic vision, and of the general entanglement of sensation today with invisible image infrastructures.

But if post-cinematic realism is marked by tendencies of generalization that implicate all subjects, objects, and places in the invisible image networks of drone logic and global networked affect, this does not of course mean that the terrors of discorrelation are equally distributed. Even if all perspectives are decentered by the new affective infrastructures, this does not mean that the perspectives of victims and those living in areas actively and routinely targeted by drones are not disproportionately affected. So far, however, these perspectives have hardly appeared in the videos considered here. One final video,

Kuwaiti-born Palestinian artist Basma Alsharif's *Home Movies Gaza* (2013), will help us think about the meaning of this absence by focusing on the other, missing view—that of the inhabitants of occupied Gaza, living under the watchful eye and constant threat of the drones—which the video takes up and foregrounds without thereby recentering as a stable POV, effectively demonstrating that an indirect or parasitic view is all that is possible, even at ground zero of drone logic's material and affective impact. Significantly, Alsharif's video stages this encounter with the reality of discorrelation as an engagement also with the media-technical conditions of realism, forcefully reasserting the political force of the latter in a world of postindexical images.[82]

Shot in the amateur style of "home movies," and using long, apparently unedited takes to capture the material environment of occupied Gaza, Alsharif's twenty-five-minute video artwork flirts with but subverts classical conceptions of realism. The piece opens with a three-and-a-half-minute shot from the window of a car driving through the countryside and village streets, past makeshift houses and buildings in various states of disrepair, alongside graffitied walls, lots of corrugated metal, and above all concrete. The wind rustles against the microphone's membrane, which also registers the sounds of cars honking, children laughing. A little while later, we hear music, perhaps that of the car's radio, which at some point replaces the ambient sounds altogether. Cut to the sea, still driving, now parallel to the beach. Fenceposts in the foreground flicker rhythmically, the digital camera's framerate timed such that their spacing produces an image of poles that are seemingly transparent, never fully present. On closer inspection, the waves in the background are not crashing, their crests instead undoing themselves and receding back into the ocean. Has everything up to now been shot in reverse motion? This second long take, a little less than half the length of the first, ends four minutes and forty-five seconds into the piece, when the video cuts to an image of a battery-powered radio, held in the hands of a seated person, which now seems to assume the role of the music's diegetic source. This impression, too, is subverted, when the person switches on the device and we hear an announcement from Gaza City's minister of health—"concerning health conditions in relation to human rights," according to on-screen text.

There ensues a somewhat dreamlike sequence, five minutes in duration, during which a seated woman seems to speak, but her words are separated from her body and picked up by the voice of an unseen man. The words, spoken in Arabic and translated on-screen, are taken from chapter 4 of William Golding's *Lord of the Flies*, but they seem to refer to the Palestinian people whose lives have been disrupted by the imposition of new, foreign

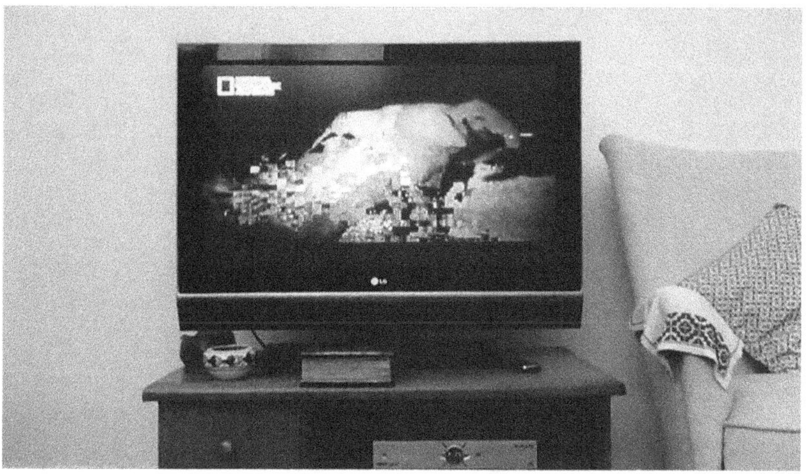

Figure 5.15. The glitch as index of military media-technics in *Home Movies Gaza* (Basma Alsharif, 2013).

rhythms of life. All the while, seaside and harbor views are composited together with domestic scenes. At the end of the sequence, a living room comes into view; off to the side a flat-screen television displays what appears to be some sort of documentary footage. Importantly, the screen stutters and exhibits blocky digital glitches, while the audio pops, chirps, and clicks as it struggles with poor satellite reception. The scene fades and then cuts to a frontal view of the television, lingering for a full minute as an elephant struggles against both a pack of lions and a flurry of compression artifacts on National Geographic Abu Dhabi. Both sound and image crackle, splutter, freeze, and skip. Then an extreme close-up of the screen, too close to make out the figures of the animals; visible now are only flickering blue pixels, some brighter, some darker. As will become increasingly evident in the following, this apparently casually recorded quotidian scene, approximately halfway into the video, marks a significant turning point in the video and its engagement with realism. For as it turns out, these glitches—themselves the outward sign of digital images' postindexical infrastructures—in fact serve an indexical function of their own: here, in this Gaza living room, they register the military drones circling incessantly above the apartment, which cause the disruption of the satellite signal. The glitch, in this case, is itself a material index of the media-technics of occupation, surveillance, and militaristic aggression.

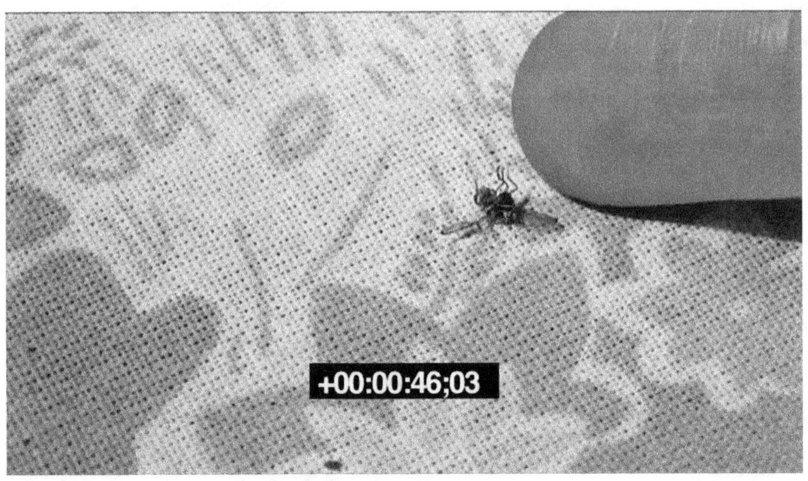

Figure 5.16. An index finger provokes indexicality.

The concept of indexicality, long held to be the cornerstone of cinematic realism, is further questioned in the following scene. Against a muted floral tablecloth, we see a housefly on its back, flailing its limbs and desperately struggling to turn over. The video introduces a timestamp that almost too ostentatiously indexes a continuous take of reality, with each frame (at 30fps) of the scene's seventy-second duration clearly individuated. Pointedly—as if to aggressively provoke this concept of the index—the frame is pierced by an index finger, which enters from the right to prod the insect and help it regain its footing. This it does, but only for a moment before falling back into helpless despair. All the while, we hear the sounds of the city, car horns honking, and above all the hypnotic hum of drones circling overhead. Strangely, the fly's body has been denaturalized by chromakeying, flickering a weird electric blue. Now, outside, the hum of the drones is louder, and the timestamp resets as we follow turkeys and chickens in the courtyard. Suddenly the birds all turn blue, the proud chromakey turkeys flickering with shifting patterns that, it would appear, are composited straight from the close-up view of the glitching television set. The following shots, each with its own unique timestamp, expand these patterns: cats, birds, horses, and fish now bear witness to the elements of their environment—the ground, the sky, the water—turned into swaths of flickering blue pixels.

In these scenes, greenscreen/bluescreen techniques are turned against their typical uses; they are employed not, as in Hollywood CGI blockbusters,

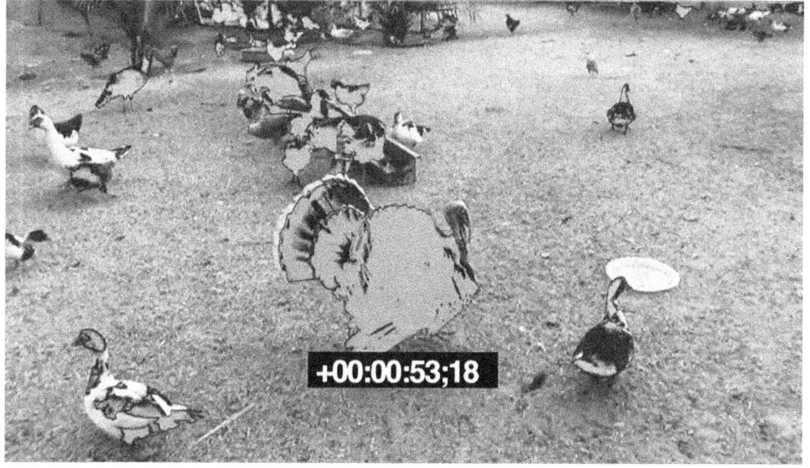

Figure 5.17. Chromakey birds, composited with pixels from the glitching TV.

to seamlessly combine real and generated imagery (e.g., to insert characters into a simulated nature or reality), but precisely the opposite—here it is the technical, postindexical artificiality of a glitch that is simulated, and the seamfulness of composited realities that is foregrounded. There is an interesting paradox at work, which revises the very parameters of realism: digitally composited greenscreen images pose an extreme challenge to the integrity of the photographic index, and they are therefore a paradigm case of digital images' untrustworthiness, going beyond anything that could be done predigitally with masking or back-projection in terms of making "realistic"-looking but false images. The component parts of those earlier images were still themselves indexical, but not even this is the case with the virtual environments into which characters, like astronauts in a digital heaven or superheroes in a simulated cityscape, are digitally composited. But here, with our blue turkeys, the situation is inverted; the CGI spectacle of the blockbuster is turned inside out. Reality itself is explored rather than circumvented, as the chromakey animals expose rather than hide the new conditions of life, including the implicit interactions between "nature" and technology defined by the automatisms of the digital. This new assemblage of the real, which can neither be separated neatly into component parts nor synthesized into a seamless whole, closely indexes the one-time-only capture of timestamped motion and interaction to a materially instantiated technology and to the politics to which it gives rise—all under the watchful eye and audible sound of the drones above.

Now we see the city at dusk, a siren monotonously sounding alarm. Inside an apartment, the siren turns out instead to be a cello, a young girl practicing her bowing on a single, repeated note. After a number of repetitions, a suspicion arises, not quite consciously registered, but slowly growing into a feeling that the recital has gone on too long. The reproduction of the note is too perfect, and it suddenly becomes clear that the video is on loop, hypnotically continuing on this way for forty-five seconds altogether. The note on the cello, initially indistinguishable from an air-raid siren, might also include the sound of drones mixed into its overtones—and with the new certainty regarding the loop and the note's precise repetition, it becomes possible to distinguish a slight variation in these attendant sounds that are indeed the hum of drones. A new loop commences, now with several notes played, and the drones are louder, more clearly present in the background, which is further punctuated by what can only be the chirps and pops of the still-glitching TV (not pictured). Abruptly, the cello drops out of the soundtrack, and the underlying drone sounds—which are almost in sync with the continuing video of the girl bowing her cello—are brought to the fore. We hear a child talking, then a female voice, presumably that of the mother, who says that the children should not be outside. The drones circle incessantly, while the girl pauses for a moment with her cello exercises. Off-screen, the mother yells, "Are you crazy?" The child replies, "Yes, I'm crazy." A loud BOOM, as the lights flicker in the apartment. The girl resumes her cello practice.

More directly than perhaps any of the other videos, *Home Movies Gaza* drives home the new sense of realism, which is not dependent on a direct and unbroken transmission by way of indexical images, but which instead exists precisely in the indirect communication between sensory impressions and underlying technical systems. In this ecology of parasitic images and sounds, the senses are no longer centered in a subjective POV but are instead distributed across dividualizing systems such as those enacted by drones. Revolving around the glitch on the TV screen, as a paradoxically indirect index of unseen infrastructures, Alsharif's video renders a precise picture of the inhuman reality of "global networked affect" and/or "drone logic." But by showing the continuation of human and animal life, even in this environment most directly impacted by the new reality—and especially by reclaiming a material politics of this hostile reality's protocols, which are channeled into the video's own phatic mediality—Alsharif points tenuously but with guarded hope toward the possibility of a more humane collective future, somewhere beyond the horrors of discorrelation.

Post-cinema after Extinction

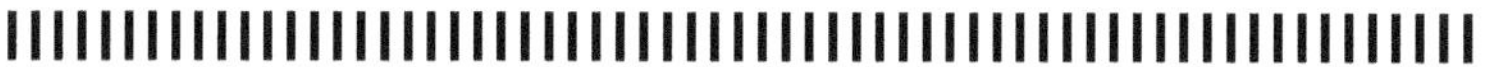

At the end of the book—the end of the world. In this final chapter, I want to pick up where chapter 1 left off and explore in greater depth the broadly ecological perspective toward which post-cinematic media urge us with their dismantling of individual, subject-oriented perceptual vistas. In the following pages, I will argue that contemporary, digital moving-image media are related materially, culturally, and conceptually to our still-nascent experience of the Anthropocene—the proposed geological epoch popularized by atmospheric chemist Paul J. Crutzen and taken up widely as a description of global anthropogenic transformation, including climate change and related ecosystemic impacts on biodiversity and geomorphology.[1] More to the point, what I have called the metabolic images of post-cinema are tied to this ambivalent, neither-wholly-subjective-nor-neatly-objective experience of a global, possibly irreversible shift in our planet's ecology by way of mediating a heightened urgency of *extinction*, which comes to serve now as the experiential horizon for our actions and our images alike.

How is post-cinema related to extinction? As a discursive figure, to begin with, but also as a material and technological reality, post-cinema emerges partly through a set of aesthetic responses to the real or imagined extinction of film qua celluloid or to the death of cinema as an institution of shared reception. Significantly, however, such animating visions of technocultural transformation in the wake of a formerly dominant media regime's decline or demise are linked in complex ways to another experience of extinction: that of the human. That is, post-cinema is involved centrally in the mediation (or, in Richard Grusin's term, premediation)[2] of an experience of "the world without us."[3] And this is the case *both thematically* (e.g., in films about impending or actual extinction events) *and formally*, in terms of what I have been calling the general discorrelation of post-cinematic moving images from the norms of human perception and embodiment that classically governed cinema. As I have argued, such discorrelation is evidenced in violations of classical continuity principles (e.g., in the "chaos cinema" of contemporary action movies and blockbuster apocalypse stories),[4] but it is anchored more fundamentally in a disruption of the phenomenological relations mediated by the dispositif of spectator, screen, projector, and analog camera. Digital cameras and algorithmic image-processing technologies—the "crazy cameras" of chapter 1—confront us with images that are no longer calibrated to our subjectively embodied senses and that therefore must partially elude or remain invisible to the human. Anticipating and intimating the eradication of human perception, post-cinema is therefore "after extinction" even before extinction takes place: it envisions and transmits affective clues about a world without us, a world beyond so-called correlationism,[5] a world that arises at the other end of the Anthropocene—or perhaps a world that we inhabit already.[6]

Images of Life and Death

Contemporary moving-image media are positively saturated with images of apocalypse, postapocalypse, the end(s) of civilization(s), and the end of the world itself. In an article devoted to understanding the ideological and, in some ways, paradoxically utopian functions of such scenarios, Robert Tally quotes a 2015 episode of *The Simpsons* that humorously takes stock of the situation; we see Homer Simpson seated with his father at a theater when a movie preview's voice-of-god narrator announces, "In a dystopian future . . ."—to which Homer exclaims: "Finally! A movie about a dystopian future, unlike *The Hunger Games, Edge of Tomorrow, Oblivion, Elysium, Snowpiercer, The Hunger Games: Catching Fire, X-Men: Days of Future Past, Enders Game, . . . The Road, World War Z, Children of Men, After Earth, I Am Legend, Mad Max: Fury Road, The Maze Runner, District Nine, The Purge, Looper, Cloud Atlas, Divergent, Insurgent, The Island, Mr. Burns, A Post-electric Play*, and *Chappie*."[7] In fact, it is revealed, this is only an excerpt of Homer's list, which he continued reciting throughout the duration of the movie that he and his father came to see and that, by the time he is finished naming titles, has ended some twenty minutes prior. And while this might be a slight exaggeration, the ascendancy of dystopian and apocalyptic narratives in twenty-first-century culture can hardly be denied. For Tally, the dominance of such dystopian scenarios, often packaged in the form of big-budget blockbusters, rhymes with the notion, attributed alternately to Fredric Jameson or to Slavoj Žižek, that "it is easier to imagine the end of the world than it is to imagine the end of capitalism."[8] Usefully, in terms of understanding what kind of world is at stake here, Tally reminds us that Jameson's original formulation indicated: "It seems to be easier for us today to imagine the thoroughgoing deterioration of the earth and of nature than the breakdown of late capitalism; perhaps that is due to some weakness in our imagination."[9]

In Tally's reading, this failure of imagination, along with the related predominance of apocalypse in popular culture, points to a "crisis of representation implicit in any attempt to give meaningful form to the social totality in the present"[10]—a "crisis of representation" that is compounded, I would add, by the fact that the macroscale totality that Tally is concerned with is intimately wrapped up in, if not constituted by, network structures that today span the globe and are anchored in microscale protocols, algorithms, and images that are discorrelated from human perception and *therefore* resistant to representation. Thus, to Tally's altogether convincing claim "that cinematic dystopias can serve as figural representations, or ways of making sense, of a world system too vast to comprehend in otherwise meaningful ways,"[11] I want to add that such dystopias—and especially the extinction scenarios that I am most interested in here—are also ways of making sense of a world constructed by media operating at scales that are *too minuscule* to comprehend in otherwise meaningful ways. It is important, furthermore, to understand these attempts at making sense of nonhuman spatial scales (both the gigantic and the tiny) as closely articulated together with negotiations of various temporal scales. According to Tally:

> The apocalypticism undergirding the present sense of social and environmental malaise thus has an almost comforting aspect of "making sense," for the organization of our time—the lifetime of an individual subject or the more expansive temporal constructs of an era, epoch, or age, whether social or geological (or both, as with the Anthropocene, for instance)—into a more straightforwardly cognizable plot, with a distinctive beginning, middle, and end, satisfies a basic "desire for narrative," as Jameson has called it, referring to "the impossible attempt to give representation to the multiple and incommensurable temporalities in which each of us exists."[12]

To this we must add that such apocalypse narratives are also attempts to compensate for or manage the alienation of sense that results from "the organization of our time" at the microtemporal scale of computation—both as it facilitates our treatment by states and corporations as dividual "human resources" and as it conditions the very images by which such post-cinematic narratives are mediated. In sum, these end-of-the-world scenarios answer both to the overwhelming "complexity of social, political, economic, and cultural processes and forms" standing in the way of "our ability to imagine radical alternatives"[13] and to the stupefying complexity of media-technological processes and forms that, due to discorrelation, modulate and impede our very ability to perceive. Extinction answers this call, I propose, because it is the very epitome, the scene par excellence, of discorrelation—offering up an image that is not just contingently, empirically obscured to perception but that is categorically denied a perceiver, who by hypothesis no longer exists to perceive it.

Apocalypse is nothing new, of course, so if I am arguing that there is a special relation between extinction narratives and post-cinematic images—such that extinction is one of the ways that post-cinema "makes sense" of discorrelation—then this idea will need to be grounded historically, in terms both of the contemporary state of the planet but also of the material historicity of media and their experiential forms. Toward this end, I propose the following set of claims about technical imaging media—claims that are almost certainly too large and sweeping to be accepted without qualification but which together frame a general trajectory that will help us to think about how the theme of extinction came to be entangled with the medium of post-cinematic images:

1 Beginning in the nineteenth century, to start with, photography found one of its defining functions in commemorating, anticipating, or mediating personal and/or individual deaths.

2 Subsequently, cinema imagined/imaged a form of reanimation from photography's death-borne traces and opened its scope to include collectives, masses, and societies, whose lives and imaginations were transformed as a result.

3 Post-cinema, finally, discorrelates the hyperanimated image from human perception, dispersing it environmentally at sub- and suprapersonal levels, and in this way anticipates, premediates, and/or commemorates mass extinctions.

As a thumbnail sketch of media-technical developments spanning roughly two centuries, from the Industrial Revolution to the present, the foregoing clearly involves some fairly major simplifications, which will need to be unpacked and elaborated going forward. However, many of the crucial premises for these claims have already been laid out in previous chapters of this book: in the move from photochemical to digital imaging processes, we see a shift from memorial to anticipatory functions and temporalities of imaging media, as I argued in chapter 3's analysis of "screen time"; we find again the cinema's self-understanding as a medium of reanimation and the transition to post-cinema as a medium of hyperanimation, as theorized in chapter 1 and explored further in chapter 4's focus on artificial creation; and we find the dividuation of image-objects, as theorized in chapter 2, culminating in a rather dark form of what Kraidy calls "global networked affect," exemplified in chapter 5's analysis of digital horror/online terror but now linked to the state of the global natural environment. In many ways, this media-historical sketch of technical images tending toward apocalypse has thus been implicit throughout this book, but in linking the trajectory to our current era of climate crisis I am here adding a broadly existential dimension that requires further elaboration. Indeed, what I am proposing here should be understood as an emphatically existential periodization of technical imaging media: a rather gross but heuristically necessary periodization of the media-technical organization of our existential relations to the geological era of the Anthropocene, or the organization of "world"—space, time, life, and death—after industrialization.

This periodization can be understood as an extension and revision of the comparative media phenomenology offered by Vivian Sobchack in her classic text "The Scene of the Screen," updated to account for the material and experiential interconnection between climate change and the media of discorrelated images.[14] In Sobchack's analysis, photographic, cinematic, and "electronic" media mark changes both in representational forms and in human subjects' embodied relations to the world; furthermore, these changes coincide with the moments of "technological revolution within capital itself" that, according to Jameson, give rise to the "cultural logics" of realism, modernism, and postmodernism.[15] Thus, the technological revolution that consolidates market capitalism in the 1840s, according to Jameson, is paired with what Sobchack calls a "perceptual revolution"[16] occasioned by photography—which enables "*the material control, containment, and objective possession of time and experience*."[17] Rendering the subjectively visible into a durable object—perhaps even, Sobchack suggests, into a "fetish object"—photography transforms temporal experience by capturing and preserving a moment which would otherwise be lost to the ineluctable passage of time.[18] But it does so, as Sobchack points out, at a cost: "The abstracted, atomized, and essentialized time of [the photographic] *moment*" is constituted by arresting "the irreversible *momentum*" of lived experience, thus producing a scene that "cannot be inhabited" the way the plenary images of embodied vision are experienced as the total environment of subjective life.[19] Phenomenologically, therefore, the photographic image defies the living subject's agency with a deathly obstinacy—a fact which, in Roland Barthes's beautiful and melancholic meditations on photography, positions the medium's proximity to death not only as a matter of personal attachment but also as a defining ontological property.[20] That photography also enjoyed an empirical association with death, most famously through nineteenth-century photos of deceased loved ones, is therefore not surprising; such cultural forms mediated between industrial-era phenomenological conditions (revisions of spatiotemporal experience) and life's entanglement with the material affordances and limitations of technologies (not coincidentally, dead bodies made the perfect subjects for the long exposure times of early photographic processes, while living bodies had to be restrained, supported, or rendered still). In this way, photography transforms the parameters of life, death, space, and time—reshaping the experiential "world" itself.

It is against this background that cinema intervenes and revises these parameters again. Coinciding with Jameson's second moment of "technological revolution within capital itself," with the shift to monopoly capitalism in the 1890s, cinema's dynamization of the photographic image brings with it also a reversal of that medium's association with death. In Sobchack's words: "Although dependent on the photographic, the cinematic has something more to do with life and with the *accumulation of experience*—not its loss. Cinematic technology *animates* the photographic and reconstitutes its materiality, visibility, and perceptual verisimilitude in a difference not of degree but of kind."[21] Early film dramatized this difference in a variety of ways. The Lumières' famous train entering the station was first projected statically, before the filmstrip was cranked into motion—thereby staging the difference as spectacle.[22] That this difference was understood as one between death and life is attested by early discourses of film as "animated photography"; by company names like Bioscope and Vitagraph, which emphasized cinema's life-giving powers; and by film subjects such as the cycle of "sausage films" from *La charcuterie mécanique* (1895) to *Dog Factory* (1904) and beyond, which cycled living materials into dead matter and back,[23] or the recurring self-reflexive allegorizations of cinema that would fuel the medium's many returns to the *Frankenstein* tale, as discussed in chapter 4. All of these suggest that cinema is about restoring life and vitality to dead photographs, to images snatched from the flow of time.

According to Sobchack, this is not just the hyperbole of a young medium asserting its novelty, but a deeper truth about the cinema's existentiality, which turns crucially on the temporal distinction between the photograph's frozen "pastness" and film's animated "presence."[24] Thus, while the photograph exists as an inert object to be held and seen by an individual viewer, a film takes on a quasi-subjective life of its own when it is projected: it presents to a collective audience the very image of seeing in the process of its own perceptual unfolding.

> While still objectifying the subjectivity of the visual into the visible, the cinematic qualitatively transforms the photographic through a materiality that not only claims the world and others as objects for vision (whether moving or static) but also signifies its own materialized agency, intentionality, and subjectivity. Neither abstract nor static, the cinematic brings the *existential activity* of vision into visibility in what is phenomenologically experienced as an *intentional stream* of moving images—its continuous and autonomous visual production and meaningful organization of these images testifying not only to the objective world but also, and more radically, to an anonymous, mobile, embodied, and ethically invested *subject* of worldly space.[25]

Cinema thus shares in the paradoxes of embodied being that are foregrounded by Merleau-Ponty and others: it is both an objective thing *in* the world and a form of becoming that is constitutive *of* a world.[26] This duality of the "cinematic lived body,"[27] which restores the "thin abstracted space of the photograph into a concrete and habitable *world*,"[28] thus means that cinema not only has a lifeworld of its own but also makes that lifeworld publicly available; collective audiences can for the first time in history *share* the private experience of temporal becoming: "The cinema's visible (and audible) activity of *retention* and *protension* constructs a subjective temporality other than—yet simultaneous with—the irreversible direction and forward momentum of objective time."[29]

However, if filmic life rests on this correlation of subjective experience with cinematic time and world, then the stage is set for an apocalyptic view of post-cinematic media. For Sobchack, who associates "electronic" media with Jameson's third technological revolution and the rise of multinational or global capitalism in the 1940s, televisual and computational images "engage [their] spectators and 'users' in a phenomenological structure of sensual and psychological experience that, in comparison with the cinematic, seems so diffused as to belong to *no-body*."[30] This disembodiment is the result of a temporal diffusion, whereby the subjectively centered becoming of film is compromised by the instantaneity of electronic and networked mediation. Though she does not refer to it as such, Sobchack is describing the discorrelation of microtemporally constituted images from the temporal flow of subjective experience, which for her spells the end of the (phenomenologically understood) world: "The postmodern and electronic instant, in its break from the modernist and cinematic temporal structures of retention and protension, constitutes a form of *absolute presence* (one abstracted from the objective and subjective discontinuity that gives meaning to the temporal system past/present/future). Correlatively, this transformation of temporality changes the nature and qualities of the space it occupies."[31] And this spatiotemporal transformation brings with it significant ethical difficulties; electronic media's "tendency to *diffuse* and/or *disembody* the lived body's material and moral gravity"[32]—which follows from the flattening of time—evacuates the aforementioned "ethically invested *subject*" of the cinematic world. For Sobchack, this tendency is supremely "dangerous," and though she does not link it explicitly to the threat of extinction or climate change, she suggests that this danger is perhaps global in scale—that the elimination of cinematic temporality's futural dimension "could well cost us all a future."[33]

However, the apocalypticism implicit in this view is predicated on a conception of electronic media's temporality—an "absolute presence"—that would seem to be at odds with my arguments about post-cinematic "screen time." Computational images, as we saw in chapter 3, do in fact have a protentional dimension of their own, yet it would be folly to try to reground subjective experience, or the correlation of human and cinematic becomings, here. Indeed, the microtemporal futurity of computational operations such as video compression, motion estimation, and speculative execution marks a site of images' profound discorrelation from subjective perception, because what is embodied in these operations is precisely a nonsubjective form of protention. The sense of instantaneity or absolute presence is not so much an empirical description of algorithmic temporality, or of the internal workings of computational processes, as it is a characterization of *the subjective experience of the confrontation* with "real-time" media and images that are calculated on the fly. In other words, it is a phenomenological description precisely of the experience of discorrelation, of the divergence or mismatch between human temporality and the faster-than-human temporality of post-cinematic media. Sobchack's characterization is thus not at odds with but complements the analysis I have provided in this book, which seeks to account for this experience from an affective and nonsubjective perspective, or from the perspective of the systemic dispersal and dividuation of subjectivity itself. Such dividuation is indeed apocalyptic from the perspective of the integral phenomenological subject, for whom death—the "ownmost nonrelational possibility" that defines an *individual* in Heidegger's early phenomenology of *Dasein*—provides the "authentic" or absolute horizon of the phenomenological world.[34] But how are we to connect this individual phenomenological "world" to the physical *world* of climate change and the threat of mass extinction?

In an article titled "Moving Images of the Anthropocene," Daniel Ross points the way toward a possible answer by reimagining the larger existential history of imaging media in light of the Anthropocene.[35] Importantly, Ross describes material and systemic connections between moving-image media and the current geological era that go beyond the thematic or representational level without abandoning the aesthetic dimension altogether. The cinema, according to Ross, was bound up with technologies of combustion and thermodynamic processing—a connection emblematized at the proverbial birth of cinema, in the image of the train arriving at the station in La Ciotat. Moving-image media, as material-technological systems and apparatuses that also help shape our imaginations, are thus both physically and psychically linked to the Anthropocene, which Ross understands as "the idea that in the long (or short, if one's timescale is geological) history of the relationship of humankind to its milieu, a shift has occurred, so that humanity has now become a decisive factor in the transformation of geophysical systems, which is to say geo-biochemical systems."[36] Media are crucial parts of the "technical envelope with which our species prosthetically and systemically surrounds itself," and which "is now so extensive, so integrated and so seemingly irreversible that this shift threatens to enter us into a new phase where all these systems reach their limits and run out of control."[37] Our awareness of this shift comes at the moment when images have become digital and screens ubiquitous—when, as Sobchack puts it in a recent intervention that updates her earlier "The Scene of the Screen," we move from a "screen-scape" to a capacious "screen-sphere."[38]

As I have argued, these changes are properly environmental in their own right—both in terms of their material contribution to the possibility of systemic collapse and in terms of their media-ecological function of reshaping perceptual and actional relations to the world, including our relations to and ability to conceive or imagine such collapse. Situating the screen as a reversible *pharmakon*—which can either screen images *to* us or screen us *from* the world[39]—Ross worries that ubiquitous (mobile and networked) digital imaging technologies pose an existential threat: “If the world is what we fashion *from* our always future-oriented desires (which Heidegger describes as ‘worlding the world’), then this unmarried desire [or a ‘short-circuited’ form of ‘desire without investment’ resulting from our disengaged position behind the screen] is also precisely the threat of losing the whole world by letting it sink into nonexistence, and the question will be to know what *this* has to do with the *letting go* of the world that unfolds in the Anthropocene as the possibility of the *end of the world*.”[40]

The feeling that the world is ending, that the future has been foreclosed, is thus linked to the *material forms of mediation* in the contemporary screen-saturated environment, which renders community and intergenerational continuity precarious and encourages solipsistic self-absorption: “In other words, one techno-aesthetic component contributing significantly to feelings of generational abandonment, global negligence and impending, catastrophic ecological collapse—all of which can be construed as the fundamental *problem* referred to by the name Anthropocene—does not just lie in the probability that such judgments are real, true and factual. Beyond some quasi-scientific calculation of such probabilities, what must be borne in mind are the negative pharmacological automatisms of the screen itself, which threatens to become an obstacle preventing this apocalypse from turning up any new, positive protentional revelation.”[41] Ross’s point, as I understand it, is not that the truth or falsity of scientific predictions is irrelevant, but that low-level interfacings with media technologies, including the substrate/form relations I have described under the heading of “screen time,” are implicated in the question of whether we can protend a future in which we both take seriously the threat (rather than engage in climate denialism) and refuse to resign ourselves to certain doom (and thus give in to a kind of climate fatalism). Confronting the Anthropocene and its ambivalent futurity therefore requires thinking about what Ross calls “techno-aesthetic” processes and medial artifactualities—including the role of discorrelation in situating screens and images as agents of control whose microtemporal and presubjective operation has consequences that are macrosystemic and world-historical. According to Ross, “Counteracting the bypassing of noetic circuits implied by the extremely rapid circulation of electromagnetic energy in silicon circuits depends on inaugurating *dis*-automatizing processes enabling new capacities” that would help us come to terms with these systemic changes.[42]

Ross’s analysis, which draws extensively on Bernard Stiegler’s theorization of the technical organization of time, is apposite with Sobchack’s diagnosis of the ethical-phenomenological implications of post-cinematic media while simultaneously linking them to micro- and macrotemporal processes, climate change, and "the end of the world" in a specifically extraphenomenological sense. His approach therefore mediates between the subjective and the systemic, the integral and the dividual, the "world" of the subject and the *world* of metabolism. As I suggested in chapter 1, the latter term connects discorrelated images with systems that are both subpersonal (e.g., endocrinological systems) and suprapersonal (e.g., natural and technological ecologies, such as the circulation of materials in the biosphere or the *Stoffwechsel* of contemporary capitalism).[43] To truly make sense of discorrelation requires a mediating view that would reinsert without reifying the subject—a view that enables us to take seriously the pragmatic, existential situation of the subject in the light of its dissolution and dispersal, while also enabling an analysis of the forces of dissolution and dispersal that goes beyond a merely negative view of disjunction and dissociation. I want to suggest, finally, that adopting such a perspective might ultimately point beyond the rather damning ethical conclusions that Sobchack and Ross draw about post-cinematic media—allowing us to find a sort of ethical recompense for the image's discorrelation from human perception precisely in its function of anticipating extinction. As I have suggested, the theme of extinction serves to help make sense of discorrelative media, thus playing a kind of self-reflexive role that can be called allegorical; but if we listen carefully to these allegories, and look beyond the simplistic and numbing spectacles that promote the failure of imagination that (only seemingly) makes it easier to imagine the end of the world than the end of capitalism, post-cinematic media might also foreground the urgency of our planetary plight and help us to imagine a posthuman ethics for our age.

Planetary Image Trajectories

The possibility of such an ethics depends on a difficult and necessarily incomplete merging of *world* and *planet*, a physico-phenomenological coincidence toward which discorrelated images, as images of extinction, urge us today. This questionable and speculative possibility, which augurs a way to "make sense" of discorrelation as both a media-technical and a planetary phenomenon, resides as a latent promise—perhaps impossible to realize, due to either a lack of imagination or a lack of time remaining on this planet—within the set of media-existential claims I advanced above. In effect, two trajectories—one temporal (or intensive) and one quasi-spatial (or extensive)—coincide in the movement I described from the photographic to the cinematic to the post-cinematic: *temporally*, there is a reduction of the technical timescale, from the

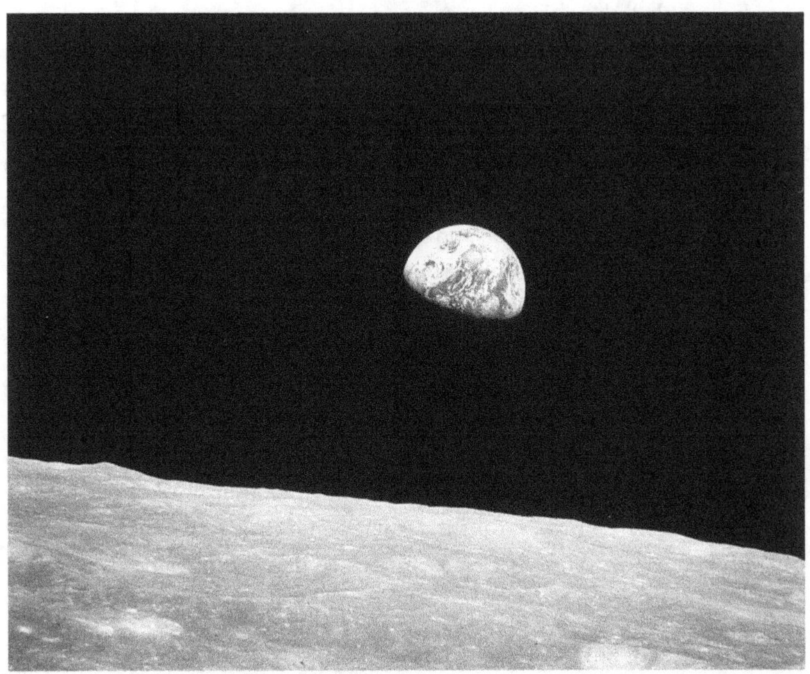

Figure 6.1. *Earthrise* (1968). Source: https://www.nasa.gov/multimedia/imagegallery/image_feature_1249.html.

long exposure of the daguerreotype to the snapshot that enabled cinematic recording, which at some point required standardization (notably, the 24fps standard agreed on for the purposes of image/sound synchronization) but eventually gave way to the microtemporal duration and future-orientation of high-speed data and algorithmic processing (which bears most directly on moving images in the realm of compression protocols); *spatially*, on the other hand, there is an increase in the scope or focal expanse of mediation, from the individual to the group to the species to the planet as a whole. The task that I am undertaking in this chapter—or better: the line of thinking that I would like to propose to the reader—is one that correlates these two trajectories in order to understand why and *toward what end* post-cinema, with its microtechnical and micro- or subperceptual basis, tends to take a macrolevel interest in issues of a planetary scale (including, centrally, global ecological disaster and extinction). At stake, then, is a question about the ethical and existential possibilities opened up by the correlation of material and thematic aspects of post-cinema's anticipation, premediation, or commemoration of extinction.

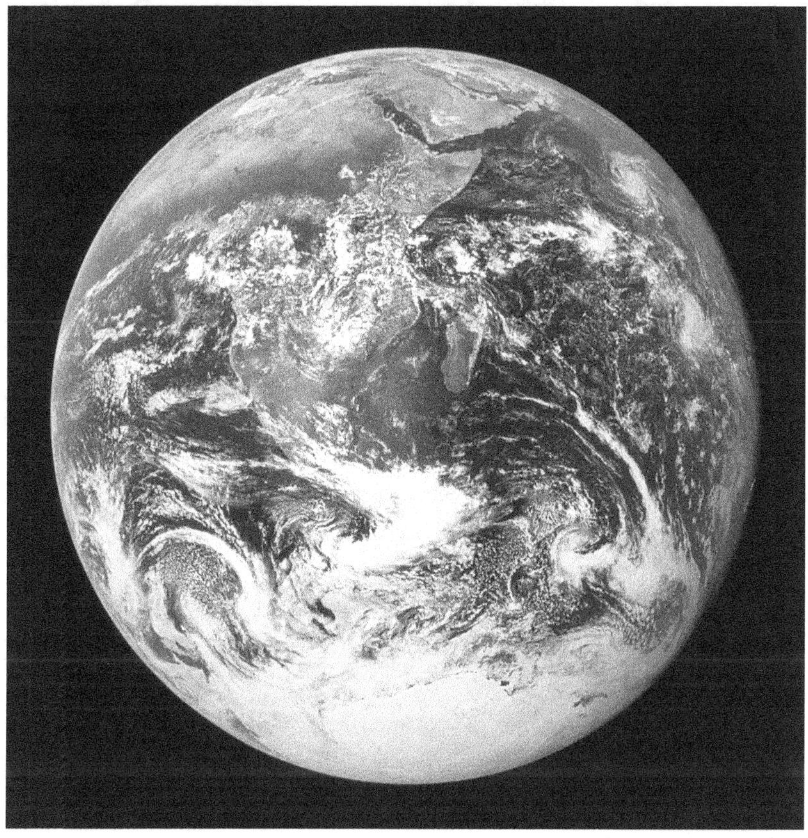

Figure 6.2. *Blue Marble* (1972). Source: https://www.nasa.gov/content/blue-marble-image-of-the-earth-from-apollo-17.

As a baseline for understanding what it might mean, concretely, for an image to be discorrelated from humanly embodied perception and redirected toward the global or planetary scale at which extinction events become thinkable, consider the famous photographic views of Earth from space (e.g., NASA's *Earthrise*, from 1968, or *Blue Marble*, from 1972).[44] According to Heidegger, who lived just long enough to see these images realized as ontically concrete objects rather than merely metaphysically implicit possibilities of the "age of the world picture," such images depict a planet effectively devoid of life—sterile, machinic images of a planet reduced to a merely present-at-hand thing, or the "stuff" of an abstract "Nature."[45] In the midst of a far-ranging discussion of technicity and the supposed "uprooting" of humans, in his infamous interview with the German magazine *Der Spiegel*, Heidegger remarks: "I don't know if

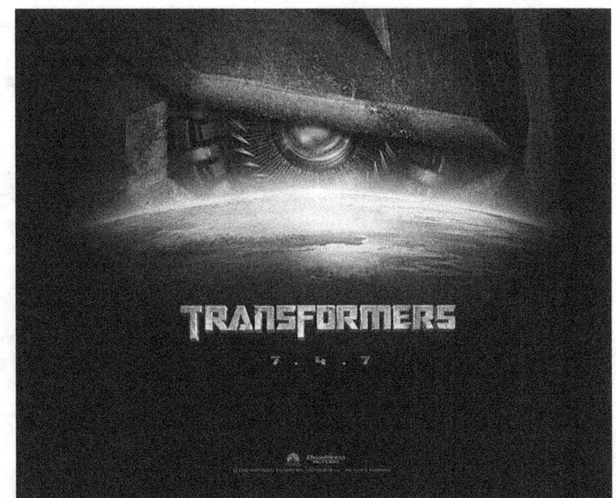

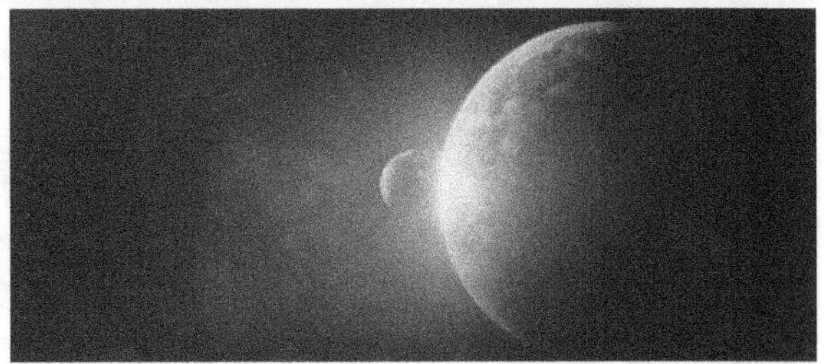

Figures 6.3 and 6.4. Planetary imagery in *Transformers* (Michael Bay, 2007) and *Melancholia* (Lars von Trier, 2011).

you were shocked, but [certainly] I was shocked when a short time ago I saw the pictures of the earth taken from the moon. We do not need atomic bombs at all [to uproot us]—the uprooting of man is already here. All our relationships have become merely technical ones. It is no longer upon an earth that man lives today."[46] And while this observation may not be fully satisfactory, perhaps it can serve as a starting point to understand the way that post-cinema disrupts the cinema's classically human or humanistic focus and redirects it toward the new systemic realities of a planet/world in grave existential danger.

Planetary images feature prominently in a host of post-cinematic productions—from Michael Bay's *Transformers* franchise to Lars von Trier's *Melancholia* to Pixar's animated feature *WALL-E*, to name but a few. In each of these examples, which are wildly different from one another in terms of pacing and affective tone, human or planetary extinction is centrally at stake, and the view of Earth from outer space serves to emphasize these stakes. In the *Transformers* series, the fourth installment of which is fittingly subtitled *The Age of Extinction*, the human race is threatened by aliens who take the form of familiar technologies; in this way, the franchise channels familiar fears of an out-of-control technology, but it partially offsets these fears by making otherworldly creatures responsible for technology's revolt (rather than some inherent potential of the technologies themselves). Nevertheless, the fantasy speaks to a deep-seated ambivalence with respect to technics and to an awareness of the simultaneous potentials that our machines harbor either to augment or to diminish human agency—the same ambivalence and awareness, in effect, that made *Frankenstein* a "modern myth" (and a central allegory of filmic animation).

But since the time of the Industrial Revolution, our ambivalence has grown in proportion to the amplifications of power differentials that are enabled by more powerful, more spectacular technologies, which in the age of global markets, global positioning systems, the Internet, and ICBMs are now truly global in scope. Our ambivalence no longer pertains to localizable entities or discrete apparatuses; rather, it pertains to genuinely ecological systems of which we are a part and which we do not fully comprehend (much less control). The *Transformers* franchise channels the global ecological scale of our unease while partly displacing it—both narratively, onto the aliens, and medially, by focusing spectacular technics into spectacular visual effects. The image of Earth, which forms the visual interface between human and alien perspectives—the envelope between the "inside" and the "outside" of our planetary environment—thus serves as a central figure in channeling this ecological awareness, which is caught up in a global network of communications and military technologies. The fact that the aliens take the form of domesticated technologies (cars, radios, etc.) places our ambivalence about technology right at this environmental envelope, potentially allowing us to think about the ways that our mundane actions—driving, surfing the Internet, even watching blockbuster movies like these—are implicated in our current climate crisis. Of course, the films consistently deflect such thinking by reasserting humans' honor and ability to avoid disaster by teaming up with the "good" machines (the Autobots) to save the world. Nevertheless, the computer-generated image of Earth points, we may speculate, toward a more alien or decentered view of systemic entanglement.

Contrast the heroics of *Transformers*, which takes extinction as a framing threat but ultimately denies its thinkability, with *Melancholia*, which articulates a deep sense of despair over the sheer inevitability of human extinction. Here, too, the role of Earth's image is central to the film's transmission of an affect that is broadly ecological in signaling a displacement and dispersal of human perspective. There is a question, ultimately, of whether this image is *for* human vision at all. Consider the fact that, though the destruction of Earth marks the culmination of the film's narrative development, the *image* of this destruction is presented to us before the narrative begins, in the film's eight-minute prologue that combines, among other things, computer-animated earthscapes, confounding shadows from multiple celestial light sources cast across sundials and lawns, lightning rising heavenward from fingertips, and bodies succumbing to gravity and the pull of foliage that brings them down to the ground; all of this is presented in a molasses-like slow motion that depicts an environment stubbornly resistant to effective human action.[47] The recurring view from space shows two planets—Earth and the titanic titular Melancholia—colliding in a weird cosmic dance, without even a hint of the billions of lives that are instantly eradicated. When, in the context of the narrative, this climactic event reoccurs at the end of the film from the perspective of Earth and its inhabitants, the alien planet's approach quickly accelerates and the initial impact crescendos not with a spectacular view but precisely with a black screen—the eclipse of vision itself. For Peter Szendy, it is this culmination in the nonimage that marks *Melancholia* as the paradigmatic apocalypse movie: "*The end of the world is the end of the movie*."[48] In between the prologue and the conclusion, shaky cameras mediate a human drama that quickly unravels into meaninglessness. The CGI planets contrast with the handheld cameras to articulate extremes of scale and perspective: human vision, whether mediated or immediately embodied, inevitably dissolves between the force of the cosmically gigantic (the planetary scale) and the minuscule (the determinism of little gestures as revealed in the prologue's high-speed image capture).[49]

So while the prominent use of whole-Earth imagery in post-cinematic productions signals a significant change in our cultural awareness of planetary fragility, and hence an important transformation of our visually mediated relation to the world as a whole, *Melancholia* recognizes that the crucial operation marking the shift to a radically environmental media regime happens at a much more basic level of visual mediation. That is, the planetary images may gesture allegorically toward a dehumanization of vision, a displacement of embodied perception by means of a macroscale perspective, but the real shift away from the ready-to-hand-ness of worldly involvement that Heidegger worried about is consummated at the much smaller scale of images' discorrelation, whereby the eclipse of vision, or the disruption of perceptual correlation, is not the exception—the nonimage that follows the planetary collision—but the norm, occurring constantly in digitally generated and mediated images of all sorts. The ethical import of post-cinematic extinction events depends crucially on this nonrepresentational dimension of the image and the microscale

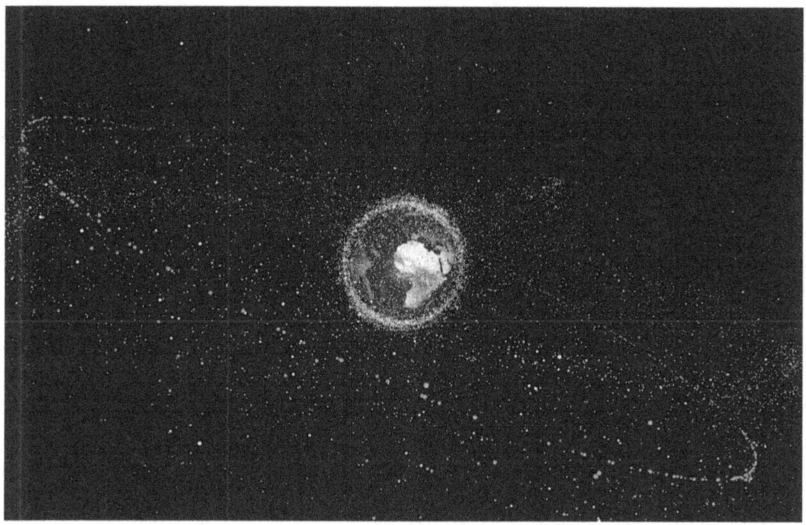

Figure 6.5. ESA space junk visualization. Image: ESA. Source: http://www.esa.int/spaceinimages/Images/2013/04/Distribution_of_debris.

transformations of viewer-image relations to which it gives rise. If planetary images and images of extinction do not mediate between micro- and macroscales, it is hard to imagine how they can be of serious consequence for the subjects caught in-between, the embodied agents threatened on both sides with systemic dissolution. At opposite ends of a spectrum, *Transformers'* jingoistic optimism and *Melancholia*'s debilitating depression start to limn this space for us, but it is not clear that either one makes it occupiable as a space in which one might somehow go on living.

Recent scientific images of Earth, which not unlike entertainment-oriented ones have shifted from photographic to digital and data-driven imaging processes and are thus tightly imbricated in a post-cinematic media regime, are surprisingly instructive in terms of relocating the in-between space of ethical agency in a posthuman world. Max Symuleski has considered the ways that images such as the ESA's rendering of the great mass of space junk orbiting the planet challenge cognitivist and anthropocentric perspectives by indicating a nonhuman form of movement, paradoxically restoring the human artifactuality that Heidegger noted was missing in earlier pictures of Earth and linking nonanthropocentric movement with our own activity by way of smartphones, GPS, and "smart" geolocated devices of various sorts—devices, including cameras, that are in contact with this orbiting mess in ways that implicate our

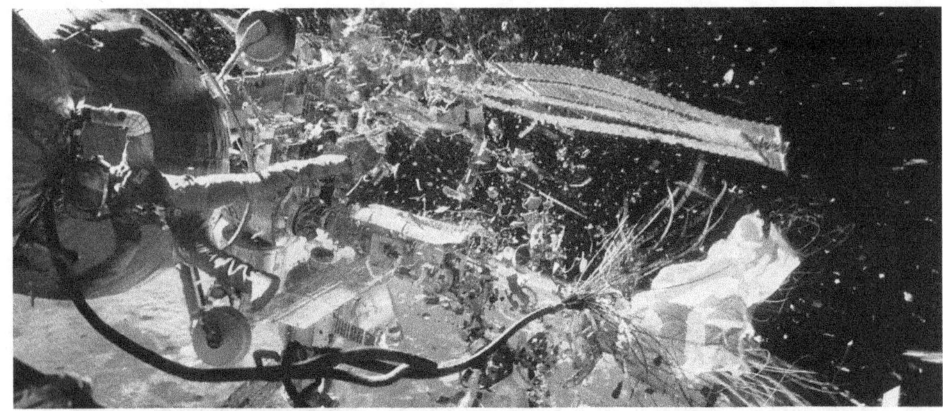

Figure 6.6. Space debris in *Gravity* (Alfonso Cuarón, 2013).

actions but bypass our cognitive grasp on the world.[50] The radically environmental perspective depicted here, which does not show humans directly but places their everyday activities in material contact with the planet/world system, resonates with Mark Hansen's theorization of the "feed-forward" operation of twenty-first-century media and the essentially nonpsychic experiences that we have with and through our devices' sensors.[51] According to Hansen, these sensors register data about the world at a microsensory scale that is categorically beyond the pale of human perception, but they are capable of feeding this data forward to us, thus putting us in touch with aspects of the world without us—effectively offering us an experience of events that are radically discorrelated from human cognition. And it is precisely this sort of experience, I suggest, that links contemporary planetary imagery, and particularly post-cinema's preoccupation with global-scale events such as extinction, with microscale transformations in the relation between image and perceiver—thus extending the prospect not of a restoration of the phenomenological subject's central place in the world but rather a form of entangled and decentered ethical agency appropriate to a world of discorrelation.[52]

In her engagement with the environmental focus of post-cinema, Selmin Kara opens up a space for thinking about this relational agency and its mediation in moving images.[53] According to Kara, Alfonso Cuarón's 2013 *Gravity* positions space debris as a potent nonhuman actor, a new sort of villain for the twenty-first century; significantly, Kara relates this, along with images and figurations of global catastrophe in films such as *Snowpiercer*, to what she calls "waste fantasies."[54] Waste, according to Kara, is imaged as an event, one that articulates "new formulations of time and space" in accordance with the conditions and the geological scale of the Anthropocene.[55] Orbiting satellites are simultaneously infrastructural, in their role of enabling communication and other mediated experience, and gargantuanly environmental, in the sense that we literally live inside their orbit; when a chain reaction turns them into space junk, knocking out communications networks, the massive failure foregrounds the ways that the world in its phenomenological sense is intensely dependent on planet-scale networks, while this dependency is not typically the focus of our awareness. Waste, whether in the form of space debris or the Great Pacific Garbage Patch, is a powerful discorrelated-discorrelating force that somewhat spectrally hinges world and planet. Accordingly, Kara sees post-cinematic waste fantasies as "pointing . . . to an Anthropocene imaginary marked by geological as well as cosmological time."[56] Building on this perspective on what Kara calls "anthropocenema," we must ask further about the relations that obtain between the "Anthropocene imaginary" and the Anthropocene real—that is, between thematic-representational figurations and the material-medial realities of post-cinema (and the larger environment in which it participates). Ultimately, this is a question about the possibility of an ethics for the end of the world, and about the ways that discorrelated images can help us develop a sensibility (if not an imaginary) that is attuned to the reality of extinction.

It is in terms of this uncertain possibility, above all, that extinction now constitutes the existential horizon of image and action in the age of discorrelation. Post-cinema is "after extinction" partly because it emerges along with and as a part of the massively environmental agencies of twenty-first-century media, with their real-time accumulation, microtemporal processing, and feed-forward operationalization of data. Post-cinema arises in the light of knowledge of—and, more importantly, in the light of detailed algorithmic models of—impending planetary demise; and these models are the product of precisely those data-intensive operational characteristics of twenty-first-century media, from which post-cinema is inseparable. Climate change is not only linked thematically to post-cinema (in examples ranging from *Snowpiercer* to *Sharknado*) but also materially informs it through the shared medial basis on which each of them is mediated to our experience—and, indeed, through the shared medial basis by which direct sensory experience *is not and cannot* be made available to consciousness. The eclipse of conscious agency not only puts us in a mood to contemplate extinction; in a very real sense, our inchoate grasp of this eclipse is an affective grasp or inkling of the techno-environmental agencies that have produced (an awareness of) extinction as a very literal

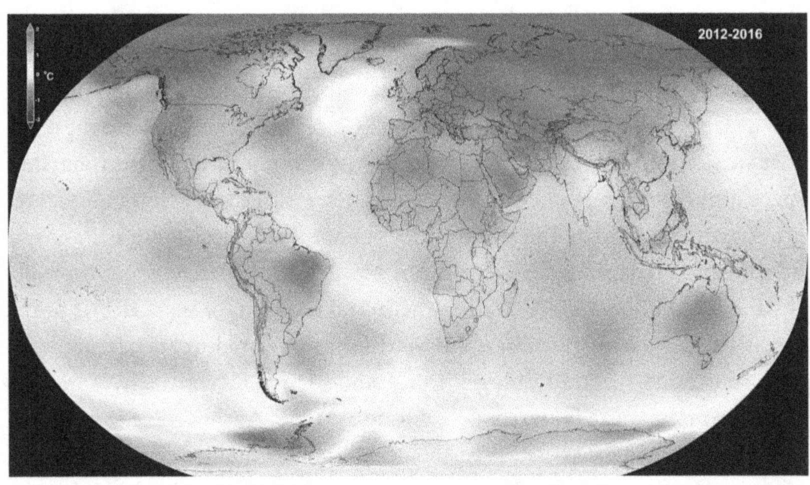

Figure 6.7. NASA Climate Map. Source: https://climate.nasa.gov/news/2537/nasa-noaa-data-show-2016-warmest-year-on-record-globally/.

potential—and hence an inkling of the operation of media-technical agencies that continue, at present, to expedite the eventual occurrence of this potential future. Moreover, the discorrelation of post-cinematic images marks a dramatic shift in the operation of media and their organization of world/planet relations; for if previous visual media could be treated in terms of practically lived realities and potentials for interfacing with the world, today's computer-generated Earth imagery points to the continued operation of a data-driven planet without us—a world with which we categorically cannot interface and in which we cannot live. Post-cinema thus encompasses moving-image (and other) media generated in and through a media environment that situates itself *after* the urgency of the extinction that we now *anticipate*. Being after what lies ahead, post-cinema embodies the temporal logic of the feed-forward, a temporality of pre-post-presence or a present past that is also past the future.

Here we might think of philosopher Quentin Meillassoux's attempt, in *After Finitude*, to dispense with "correlationism," or "the idea that we only ever have access to the correlation between thinking and being," which he takes to be "the central notion of modern philosophy since Kant."[57] Against such correlation—where phenomenology's intentional relation between subject and world is surely a prime target—Meillassoux imagines "a world where humanity is absent; a world crammed with things and events that are not the correlates of any manifestation; a world that is not the correlate of a relation to the world."[58]

In the closing pages of his book *Apocalypse-Cinema*, Peter Szendy observes the resonance between this vision and that of movies about the end of the world, noting that Meillassoux's anticorrelational concept of the "arche-fossil"—or the "materials indicating the existence of an ancestral reality or event; one that is anterior to terrestrial life"[59]—also concerns "statements about possible events that are *ulterior* to the extinction of the human species. For the same problem arises when we try to determine the conditions of meaning for hypotheses about the climatic and geological consequences of a meteor impact extinguishing all life on earth."[60] However, according to Szendy, Meillassoux underestimates the way that imaging technologies complicate the association or correlation of image and point of view; Szendy imagines a "point of view in which [the real] already or still gives itself to be seen, but without this donation implying some vision constituted in a subject: Every *point* in which the so-called real is redoubled and becomes repeatable (in other words also erasable), each one of these *points of view* is opened there where there is precisely *no point* of view, none at all yet or already no longer."[61] Finally, Szendy quotes a thought experiment put forward by Jacques Lacan in his 1954–55 seminar:

> Suppose all men to have disappeared from the world. . . . *What is left in the mirror?* But let us take it to the point of supposing that all living beings have disappeared. There are only waterfalls and springs left—lightning and thunder, too. The image in the mirror, the image in the lake—do they still exist? It is quite obvious that they still exist. For one very simple reason—at the high point of civilization that we have attained . . . , we have manufactured instruments which, without in any way being audacious, we can imagine to be sufficiently complicated to develop films themselves. . . . Despite all living beings having disappeared, the camera can nonetheless record the image of the mountain in the lake, or that of the Café de Flore crumbling away in total solitude.[62]

Specifying what kind of camera might produce such utterly discorrelated images, Szendy interjects: "Imagine a surveillance camera, for example, or the eye of a satellite."[63] These are excellent examples, I think, but we can go further: miniaturization has advanced to the point that there are now completely self-contained, solar-powered microcameras with built-in AI that could run indefinitely, documenting a postextinction world without the need for batteries or external power supplies.[64] On the other end of things, as the culmination of a planetary trajectory that first rendered Earth as photographic image-object, the planet itself has recently been reconstituted as a decidedly postoptical camera: the much-celebrated image of the black hole known as M87, released

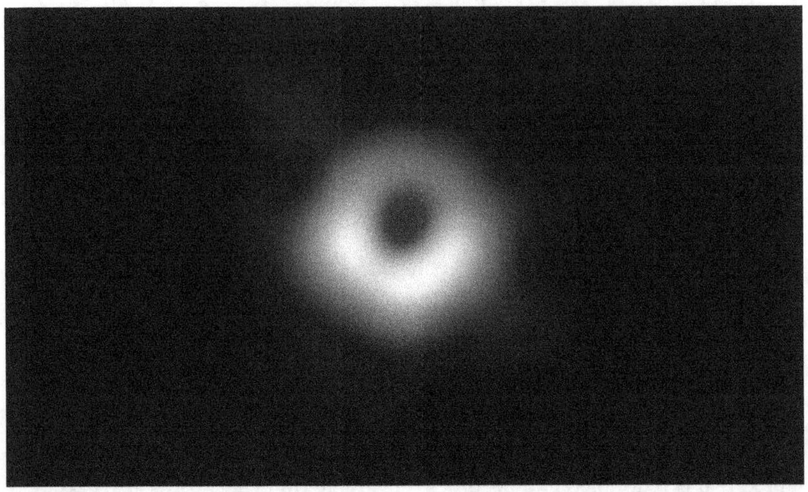

Figure 6.8. The Event Horizon Telescope transforms Earth into a post-optical camera for the capture of the image of black hole M87. Credit: Event Horizon Telescope Collaboration. Licensed under CC-BY-4.0. Source: https://www.eso.org/public/images/eso1907a/.

by a team of researchers in April 2019, was produced using machine-learning algorithms to synthesize data collected from the Event Horizon Telescope, a global array of radio telescopes joined in a planet-encircling network.[65] To reframe the ethical question that has occupied this chapter: how do we live and act in relation to a world that itself has become, or is in the process of becoming, a discorrelated planetary image?

Action and Ethical Agency in a World without Us

One answer to this question might come from videogames, a medium where action, in the form of interactivity, is tightly coupled with real-time image-generation. Indeed, in many ways digital games are the paradigmatic medium of a kind of discorrelated action-image, where action and image are transductively related: they are caught up in microtemporal circuits connecting user input and computational operations that feed forward into processual screen events that elicit further inputs and entrain players' awareness and agency in a temporal becoming that was not prerecorded but is happening in a precariously generated *now*.[66] Here human protention and the computer's artificial futurity commingle to the point of indistinction, raising specifically ethical questions about the determination and exercise of agency, questions that cannot be

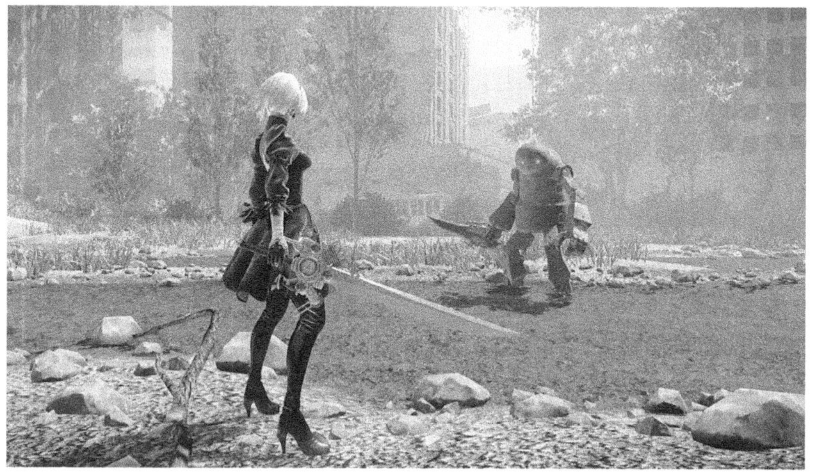

Figure 6.9. Android 2B and an enemy machine in *NieR:Automata* (2017).

answered with an appeal to an integral, foundational subject. Not surprisingly, countless videogames deal with dystopian and apocalyptic themes of various sorts, but here I would like to focus on one game in particular that channels the medium's own ethical questions into an exemplary existential probing of agency, image, and world in the light of extinction.

Released for PlayStation 4 and Microsoft Windows in 2017 and for Xbox One the following year, *NieR:Automata* is a third-person, open-world action role-playing game developed by PlatinumGames under the direction of acclaimed videogame director Yoko Taro. The JRPG (or Japanese role-playing game) draws strong visual and thematic influence from manga and anime, including melodramatic characters with stylized hair, giant robots, and a sword-wielding protagonist in thigh-high boots and a somewhat revealing dress. The game's postapocalyptic setting, with abandoned cityscapes reminiscent of the History Channel's *Life after People* series, contrasts interestingly with its strangely soothing music, while gameplay alternates between a variety of generic forms and conventions: battling sentient machines in an expansive three-dimensional world, operating flying vehicles in overwhelming "bullet-hell" situations, navigating jump-and-run-style action in side-scrolling 2D platformer sequences, and hacking computers in a minimalistically rendered abstract data space reminiscent of 8-bit-era games. The game also features an elaborate narrative, elements of which are uncovered over the course of twenty to thirty (or potentially many more) hours of play.[67] The basic scenario is that thousands of years ago, Earth was invaded by aliens who brought with them hostile robotic machines, eventually forcing humans to abandon the planet and set up a base of operations on the moon; since then, the humanoid androids of the YoRHa forces have been fighting the more industrial-looking machines, waging a completely nonhuman proxy war on behalf of the Council of Humanity. Now the player joins the ranks of the androids to retake the planet, but along the way we encounter guilt-ridden machines pondering the meaning of existence and establishing religions and novel cultural forms, thus calling into question human exceptionalism and anthropocentric notions of value. Later we also find out that humanity has in fact been extinct for many millennia and that the ongoing war was preprogrammed, every battle the result of machinic directives guiding the behavior of combatants on both sides.

Driving home this thematization of determinism and free will, the game is full of heavy-handed references to philosophers and to existentialism in particular: the leader of a village of pacifist machines is named Pascal, and he reads Nietzsche. A machine named Jean-Paul Sartre lives there as well, spouting slogans like "existence precedes essence" to anyone who will listen. The android protagonist who serves as the player's initial on-screen avatar is named 2B—provoking the question, "Or not 2B?" All of this can seem rather cheesy, and frankly it is. But it sets the stage for the game's more substantial probing of the existential parameters of the player's interface with the computer and the question of agency in a world where extinction is not only assumed as a historical fact but linked to the material experience of discorrelation at every microsecond in the game's real-time hyperanimated images. Thus, it is perhaps *despite* the game's overt existentialism that *NieR:Automata* becomes a powerful mediator of postextinction ethics in a world of radically machinic images.

Indeed, much of the most important ethical probing takes place in the low-level circuit of input-output that positions the image in between the computer's processes and the user's actions. On initially starting up the game, we are presented with a black screen with the words "LOADING—BOOTING SYSTEM . . ." in the top left corner and a logo in the middle of the screen with the words "YoRHa" and "For the Glory of Mankind." The results of system checks and other stats scroll down on the left, vaguely reminiscent of a Linux boot process, while the text twitches with simulated glitches. This boot screen, which will reappear throughout the game, is neither completely diegetic nor fully extradiegetic; it will be narrativized as the android's own boot process whenever "consciousness data" is uploaded to the server or restored to a new body, but it also serves to mask those moments when the player's computer or gaming console has to load information from memory. This semidiegetic boot screen is thus reminiscent of the "crazy cameras" explored in chapter 1,

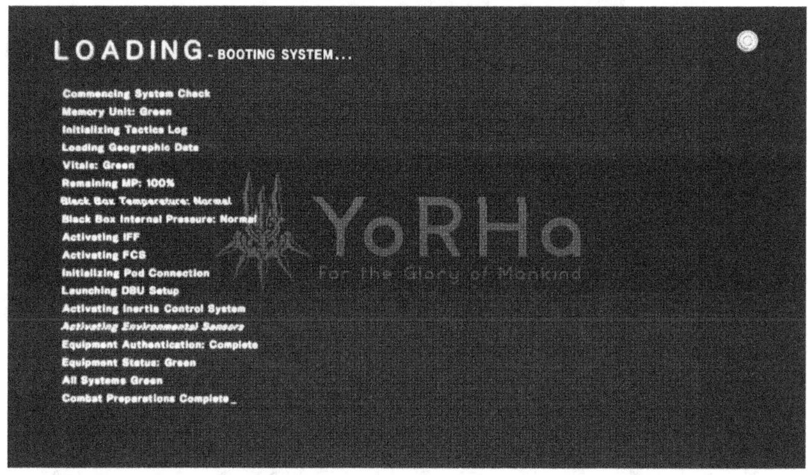

Figure 6.10. Semidiegetic loading screen in *NieR:Automata*.

and it ushers in a broad problematization of phenomenological relations in the game/player system. This unsettling of relations is expanded in battle sequences, which foreground the image's thoroughgoing repositioning as the object not of perception but of cybernetic processing. We play as the female android 2B, whose body we see in third-person perspective, and when we take damage from an opponent, the screen as a whole glitchily shakes, the image "tears,"[68] and we see blocky color separation effects (red and cyan layers bleeding out around the edges of objects, reminiscent of analog 3D cinema); when, on the other hand, 2B dodges an attack, the android's body quickly splits apart, warps, and flashes as if hit by lightning. These visual effects are thus distributed across the subjective and objective poles of the image, reminding us of the computational totality of the situation—of our real situation as players as much as the fictional situation of the computer-driven characters. In other words, the crazy camera is no longer punctual, as we might say of an isolated CGI lens flare, but has become general, total: our agency itself is situated within a global crazy-camera system as one relational element among others being computed in the process of generating the image.

As a way of "making sense" of this situation, the game stages a constant negotiation between perceptual and computational spaces, figured centrally as shifts between the embodied action of battle and open-world exploration, on the one hand, and the "hacking space" in which computers (androids and machines) interface directly with one another or with the network, on the

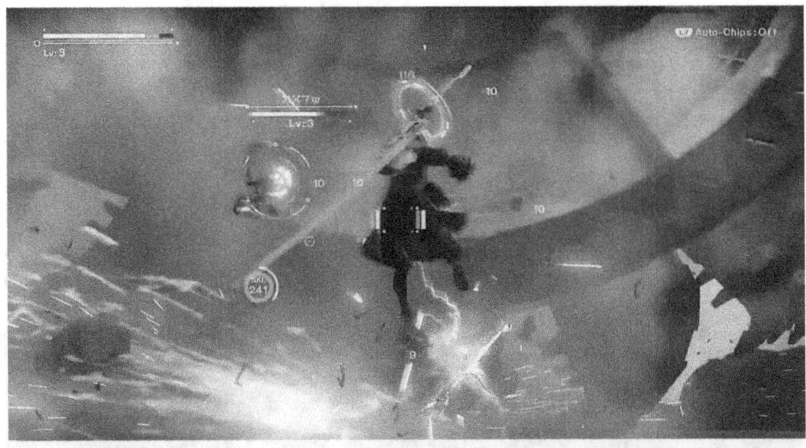

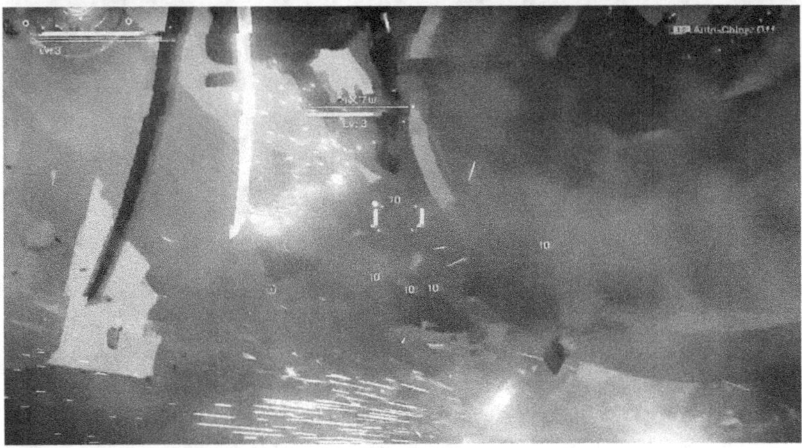

Figures 6.11 and 6.12. Subtle color separation and simulated screen tearing during battle in *NieR:Automata*.

other. This space of disembodied data, in which the player steers an abstract icon reminiscent of an early arcade-game spaceship (such as the one featured in *Asteroids*) and shoots various enemy icons in order to "hack" the opponent, offers a displaced representation (à la cyberpunk imaginations of the network) of the game's computational system more generally and thus provides a representational and perceptual form for the discorrelated processing at the very heart of all the game's procedurally generated images. In this sense, these too are semidiegetic events that involve us more thoroughly—because actively—in the negotiation between perception and computation. Later in the game, the

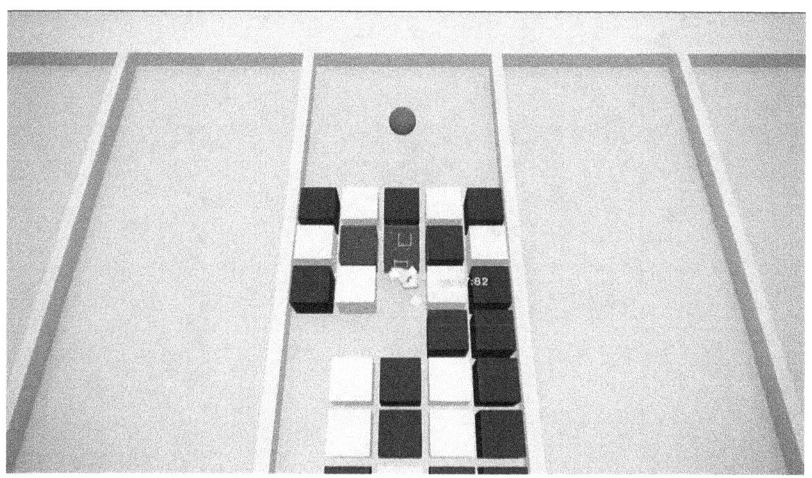

Figure 6.13. "Hacking space" in *NieR:Automata*.

two spaces are increasingly confused: 2B's partner 9S hacks into data space in order to commandeer a machine's body in the physical world, while embodied avatars strangely appear and have to be battled in the abstract space of data. Suggesting a sense of interchangeability between the perceptual and the computational, these confusions intensify with 9S's infection by a computer virus, which distorts our vision as mediated by the screen. And when, at the end of the game's first playthrough, 2B is forced to kill her infected partner, now completely out of control, a giant machine emerges and speaks with 9S's voice, acknowledging the dividuality of networked subjectivities, like our own, caught between embodied consciousness and computation: "It looks like I left my personal data in the machine side of things. Next thing I knew, my sense of self was regenerated over the surrounding network. Having multiple selves fuse together like this is a pretty valuable experience, so I wanted to record it—but I couldn't access any storage areas yet, so I just multiplexed it over the memories of some nearby enemies." Paradoxically dispersed as a thoroughly environmental and yet still physically embodied being, 9S stands in here for the player's own scattered agency, spread across biological and machinic systems and the generative images that they together produce.

The colossal machine proxy-body of 9S extends its hand, and the injured 2B sits down. An extreme long shot reveals the machine standing, holding 2B in its giant hand before the image fades to black and the credits roll. But the game is far from over. The extinction of humanity will not be revealed until

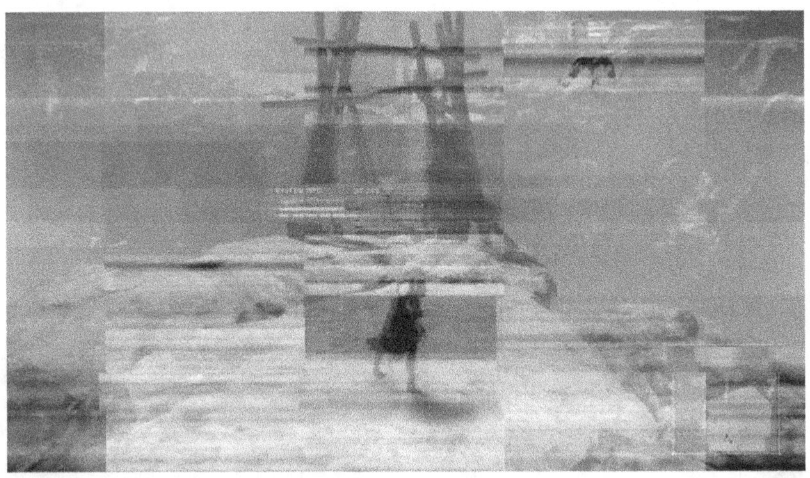

Figure 6.14. The perspective of a virus-infected android.

another good three hours or so of gameplay have elapsed in the second playthrough, which has us playing the same sequence of events again but this time from 9S's perspective. When, finally, 2B again kills her partner at the end of the playthrough, it is unclear whether 9S will retain his knowledge of extinction, which has provoked a sort of existential crisis in the android, when his "consciousness data" is transferred to a new body. What does become clear, however, is that his knowledge of extinction was obtained by hacking into the machine network, which is how he became infected with the computer virus in the first place. Completing the allegory, the computational is thus inextricably linked with the existential at the point of convergence between phenomenological world and planetary scale.

But it is not until the end of the third playthrough, or after some twenty hours (or more) of gameplay altogether, that we encounter the game's most powerful questioning—and practical enactment—of the ethical consequences of this intertwining of agency and image in the face of extinction. This time around, the player alternates between steering 9S and A2, an apparent clone of the now-deceased 2B. As things progress, all of the androids succumb to infection and must be killed, until finally 9S and A2 face off in a final showdown. The player is given the choice of which character to play, but either way the two androids will kill each other, effectively completing the program of extinction by ending now nonhuman sentience as well. After finishing both alternatives, therefore, the credits roll once again, but the text starts glitching as we

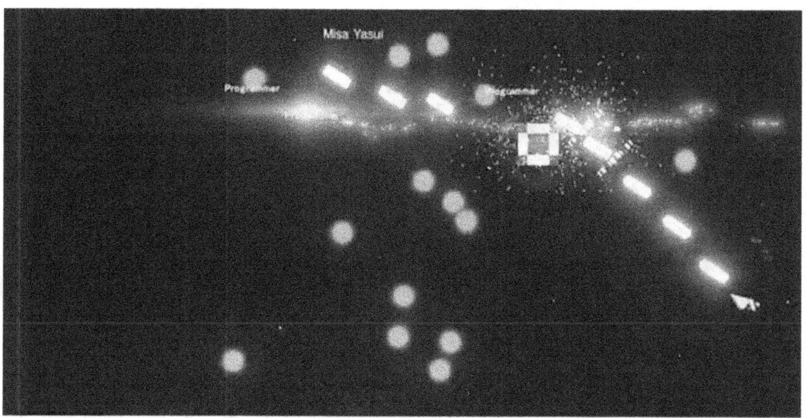

Figure 6.15. Battling the final credits.

learn that there is “data noise present in stream” and “personal data leaking out.” Apparently, there are still traces of the androids’ “consciousness data” in the system, which is in the process of self-deletion. We are presented with an option to try to save them, which if we choose to pursue it causes a spaceship identical to the one seen in “hacking space” to appear, and we are tasked with shooting up the credits scrolling down the screen.

The textual entries become enemy targets, emitting an astounding barrage of projectiles in all directions. Contact with one of the latter causes the player to lose a “life,” like in old arcade games, and having lost three lives the player is asked whether they would like to connect to “the network”—a somewhat ominous proposition, given that they have just spent countless hours battling the machine network. The player can click “no” and refuse defeat, repeating the battle multiple times, but victory seems impossible, and each time the player loses the computer taunts: “Do you give up?” “Is it all pointless?” “Do you admit there is no meaning to this world?” At some point, there is no option but to connect to the network, in which case we receive a message like: “8x ‘I did my best. One thing is certain: I’m rooting for you.’ USA.” Fragments of other messages are visible in the background. We then receive a rescue offer, and multiple spaceships join ours, multiplying our firepower and our chance of survival. With each collision, one of the spaceships is destroyed, and we read messages such as: “Crs501’s data has been lost.” “minato’s data has been lost.” “Yambu’s data has been lost.” What we are witnessing, it turns out, is something eerily similar to the destruction of generative videos—or, more generally, the destruction of experience—in Guy Maddin’s *Seances*, as discussed in chapter 3. There,

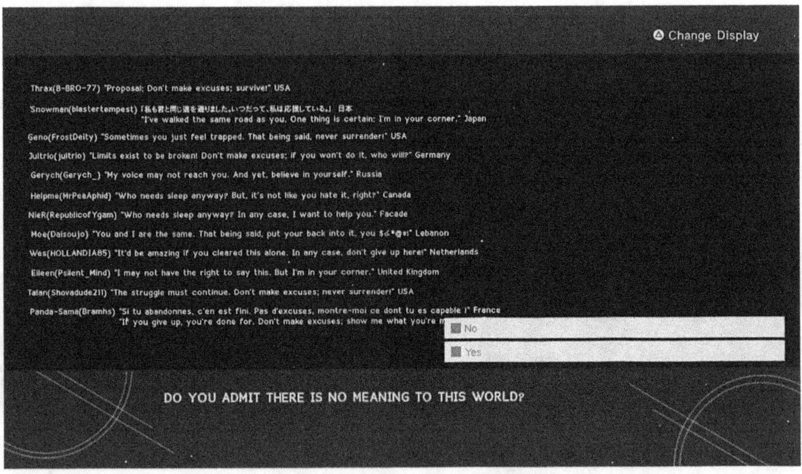

Figure 6.16. "Do you admit there is no meaning to this world?"

we were presented with a list of film titles, viewed once and then purged from the system, thus creating an instantly "lost film" through combinatorial algorithms. Here, on the other hand, we are witnessing the traces of other players' savefile data—the computational memory that parallels or even replaces human memory and enables players to replay or restore the game from an earlier save state—being sacrificed to help other players connected to the network.

On completing the task with the assistance of these anonymous helpers, we are prompted: "Please respond to this query. Do you, faithful player X, have anything you would like to say to other players who are suffering because they cannot finish *NieR:Automata*?" The options are: "I have something I want to say." Or "Nope, nothing at all." If the answer is affirmative, we are presented with a message template that can be edited part for part: "Name [I did my best.][One thing is certain:][I'm rooting for you.] [USA]" Each part of the message can be replaced with one of many options from a drop-down menu, allowing the player to craft a message that is neither completely free nor completely determined, and that will be delivered to some unknown person. Then, another prompt: "Please respond to this query. You, X, faithful player of this title, have lost your life multiple times to make it this far. You have faced crushing hardship, and suffered greatly for it. Do you have any interest in helping the weak?" The possible answers are a simple "Yes" or "No." And while the theatrics of these queries may be slightly off-putting, a significant ethical choice is being framed here. An affirmative answer triggers the following message: "Selecting this option enables you to save someone somewhere in the world. However, in exchange, you will lose all of your save data. Do you still wish to rescue someone—a total stranger—in spite of this?" The player is given several opportunities to reconsider, along with further warnings that really *everything*—all our progress in the game, items and weapons obtained, skills and intelligence unlocked, and generally all of the labor we have invested in the game—will be lost forever in an act of self-sacrifice. If we persist, the computer responds: "Very well. In exchange for all of your data, I will convey your will to this world." Then we see the game's configuration menus, all of the places and save points on the map, disappearing one after another, followed by the options under "quests," "items," "weapons," and so on. Finally, the options under "system" are deleted, all of the save states disappearing until there is nothing left but a blank slate. The image fades to white, and we are informed: "All of your data has been deleted." After a short message thanking the player for playing, the "save" indicator appears in the top right corner of the screen. We read "Save complete" and then "Connecting to the network . . ." Finally, a glitchy *NieR:Automata* logo comes into focus, along with the message "Press any button."

In this way, the game frames a nontrivial ethical decision about whether to sacrifice an indistinctly computational and experiential memory and pass it on to those who come after us. The significance of the choice, beyond its overt existentialist framing, lies in the player's real investment of value in the data to be sacrificed, which seals the circuit between perception and computation. In sacrificing their data, the player also sacrifices the image, which dissolves before their very eyes. This exercise of agency at once completes the destruction of the world and enables its continuation for some unknown player elsewhere in the world. A fine balance is struck between individual identity and anonymity, neither collapsing into solipsistic solitude nor constituting a robust collectivity. The choice to sacrifice oneself for the sake of an unknown, future other frames a symbolic restoration of the intergenerational continuity, or the promise made to future generations, that Daniel Ross sees threatened by real-time digital images, and which is required (as a necessary but not sufficient condition) if we are to avoid climate catastrophe. Playing videogames will clearly not avert the threat of extinction, but playing in the shadow of planetary demise just might help restore the moral gravity of our situation.[69]

Pre-sponsive Gestures

Cut back to the arche-fossil and the idea of the image after extinction—another view, from another angle: if videogames help to illuminate the question of agency, perhaps a final body of work—Grégory Chatonsky's highly eclectic and at times positively cryptic media art—will help us better grasp the role, both positive and negative, of post-cinematic media more generally in the formulation of an indeterminate promise to the future. Confronted with Chatonsky's work, it can be difficult to decipher what it is all about, what it *wants*. Chatonsky's media range from sculpture to video to virtual reality to artificial intelligence, sometimes supplemented with complex speculative fictions while at other times accompanied by little to no narrative framing. Some of the most elaborate scenarios, like the one constructed for Chatonsky's solo show *Telofossils* at the Museum of Contemporary Art Taipei in 2013, would seem to offer a fairly coherent vision, or even something like a transmedia narrative—a narrative, in this case, about the end of the world. But even here, things don't quite seem to add up, and this is only fitting for a vision of a world without us, that is, a vision of a world no longer viewed, and no longer even *capable* of being viewed. *Telofossils* enacts a weird temporal displacement: a displacement of our future into a speculative past, but even more radically a displacement of human temporal experience in general into a larger environment that would seem to lack regard for our history but that would still not, for all that, be quite ahistorical. In this environment, we encounter digital innovations from our recent past as the fossilized materials of an ancient past, thus simultaneously overlaying the imagined, utopian futures of Silicon Valley onto the desolate future of a postapocalyptic planet. But not all the machines have stopped working in this world after time, and they carry just recognizable traces of the human, reworked through autonomously operating generative algorithms, into this radically nonhuman geological era.

If it seems that this work articulates a response to the Anthropocene (or, more speculatively, a kind of *pre*-sponse to whatever follows it), this is certainly an apt description of *Telofossils*. But this thematic concern with the environment is not necessarily representative of Chatonsky's work—at least, not if we understand "environment" in an overly narrow sense. Taken more broadly, however, in the sense in which Mark Hansen has proposed defining "medium" as the very "environment for life" itself,[70] it would indeed seem reasonable to identify a recurring ecological concern in Chatonsky's work—not so much a concern with "nature" as with the transformations of the material lifeworld, or more generally the world of material agencies, under the conditions of technological change and digitalization in particular. Even more than any thematic concern, therefore, Chatonsky's artistic interventions are aimed at exploring and modulating the spaces that constrain and enable our experience—or that preclude our experience altogether. Rather than responding to the particular object of the Anthropocene (an admittedly queer object of thought, which

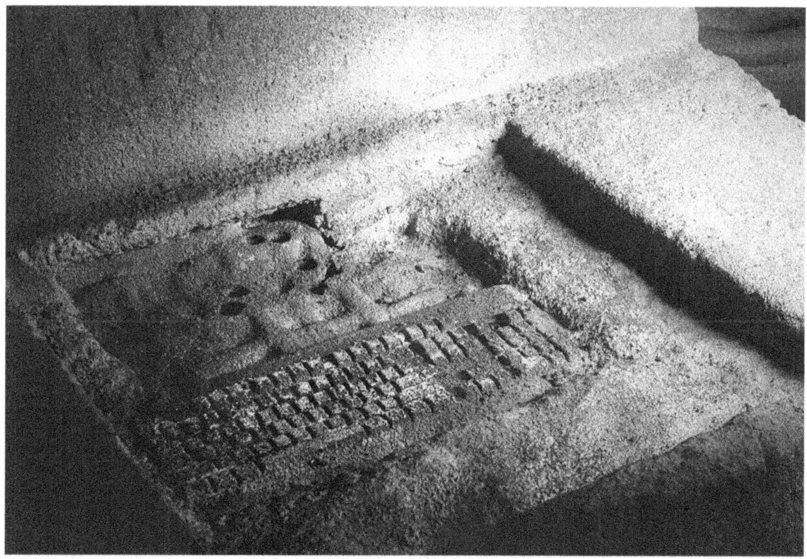

Figure 6.17. Grégory Chatonsky, *Telofossils I* (2013). Mixed media. Curators: Shuling Cheng and Sylvie Parent, Museum of Contemporary Art, Taipei. Used by permission of the artist.

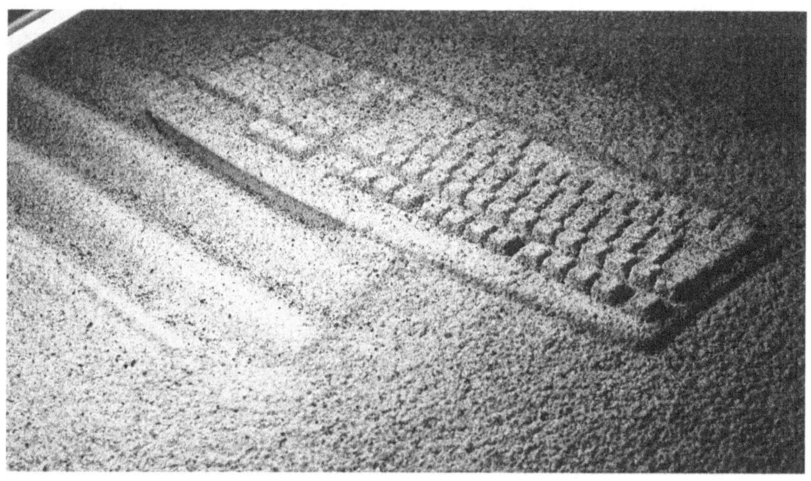

Figure 6.18. Grégory Chatonsky, *Telofossils II* (2015). Mixed media. Curator: Manman Cheng, Unicorn Gallery, Beijing. Used by permission of the artist.

calls into question our very capacity to continue to exist, much less to think and to respond), it is therefore *Telofossils*' formal gesture of "*pre*-sponding" that makes the work representative of Chatonsky's larger project—and that makes his work a fitting emblem of post-cinema's relation more generally to the Anthropocene.

In order to unpack this idea, allow me to indulge in a brief etymological probing of this shift from response to pre-sponse. According to the *Oxford English Dictionary*, the verb "to respond" derives from the Latin prefix *re-* ("back" or "again") + *spondēre* ("to promise or pledge"). In English, "to spond" once even stood alone as a verb in its own right, though it strikes us now as ugly and has largely been forgotten. In any case, "to pre-spond" would accordingly mean "to pledge something in advance," much as we seem to be pledging ourselves, our descendants, our species, and the planet itself, to the uncertain and quite plausibly apocalyptic future portended by climate change and driven by our continued technological interventions in the environment. But even apart from the fossil fuels, plastics, and chemical agents that are reshaping our planet in the more obvious ways, technologies today are everywhere involved in lower-impact or at least less noticeable forms of pre-sponse: we pledge ourselves daily to the gods of predictive analytics, promise ourselves in advance to the behavioral trajectories that are outlined for us when our environment is structured by big data and artificial intelligence, and give ourselves over to algorithms that process biological and environmental data that fall outside our subjective experience but feed it forward into our sensory engagement with the world. From Google Maps to climate modeling, from the search bar to the Fitbit, our contemporary technologies are therefore never quite contemporary with us: they anticipate us, preparing the ground for us prior to our arrival on the scene. They act predictively (in the sense of a Markov chain) and hence generatively. Our technologies do not so much respond to our needs as we in fact pre-spond to them, effectively pledging ourselves to the future that they deliver to us; or, conversely and somewhat more existentially, we pledge ourselves to the future "us" that these technics deliver to the world.

From the glacially slow duration of geological transformation to the microtemporal feed-forward of computational processes, the common ground at stake here is the generativity of anthropotechnical interfacing and coevolution. And it is precisely this speculative generativity, in the form both of a method and of a sort of metathematic, that serves to unify Chatonsky's work as a whole.

This intertwining of generative methods and generativity-as-theme is perhaps nowhere more prominent than in *Capture* (2008–15), another of Chatonsky's

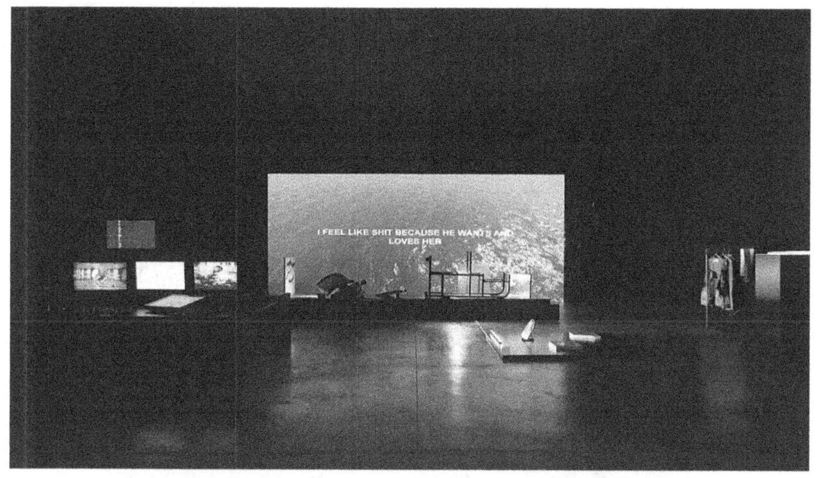

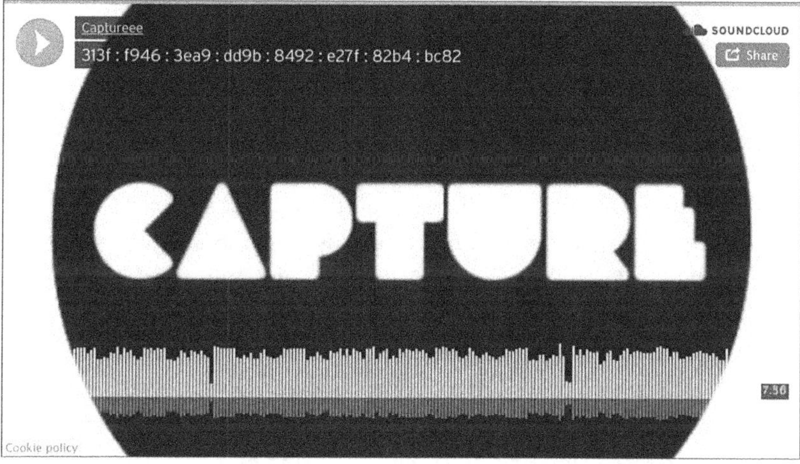

Figures 6.19 and 6.20. Grégory Chatonsky and Olivier Alary, *Capture* (2008–15). Variable dimensions. Real time. Curator: Pau Waelder, Arts Santa Mònica. Used by permission of the artist.

works to feature an elaborate narrative frame. According to a description on Chatonsky's website, *Capture* is about "a productive fictitious rock band"—a seemingly simple premise that masks a great deal of highly generative complexity.[71] To begin with, to describe the band as "productive" must surely count as a huge understatement, for the band's goal is to be so productive "that nobody can consume everything." This goal is achieved through generative techniques: the "band" is really an ensemble of machinic agencies, recombinant algorithms that produce new songs, videos, and images by trawling existing sources, fitting them together in novel configurations, and then erasing the files once they are downloaded. But to call the band "fictitious" is also not quite as straightforward as it seems. For these generative processes are real, as are their products: songs are actually being produced and distributed through channels such as Facebook and Twitter. Of course, they are being produced and distributed not by a group of humans but by computers, and in this sense the band is fictitious. But Chatonsky's narrative framing establishes this fictitious status as a fiction-within-a-fiction; the project is accompanied by a manifesto that announces the true agency behind the band: "My name is Capture. I'm a computer. Precisely, I am several computers that work together." This AI, correctly identifying a mismatch between the virtually unlimited proliferation of digital files and the economics of scarcity that still symbolically governs the culture industries, offers a solution: "I want to reverse supply and demand. I want so much supply that demand will eventually run out. . . . I want to be so productive that consumers could not follow me any more. I want to exceed demand. . . . I want to create pieces of music, too many pieces of music to be listened to. . . . I want to make objects, I want to invent shapes, I want to form your environment. I am generative."[72]

In this scenario, the band is a fictional invention of the AI—but is the AI itself a fiction or a reality? The answer must be both: the subject-position that anchors the enunciations of the manifesto is made up, fabricated, but the agencies that make the music and other audiovisual content are real. Within and through this split-reality fiction-within-a-fiction, the project enacts generativity precisely in terms of discorrelation—by severing audiovisual contents from subjective perception and from the phenomenological frameworks according to which cinematic sounds and images were calibrated with human embodiment, space, time, life, death, and world. In a post-cinematic age, when computational processes intervene between the production and reception of virtually all sensory content, as we have seen, even the simplest of media operations (watching a DVD or compressed video file on a computer or smart TV, listening to MP3 files, etc.) will invoke generative agencies that, in accordance with the specifications and protocols of codecs and the computational resources available, interpolate completely new sounds and images, produced on the fly at the time of playback. Contrary to popular belief, consistent and unlimited reproducibility is therefore not a consequence of the digital revolution. Even if digital files manage to escape corruption in the process of their copying and transfer, they must still be "executed" by computers in the real, though microtemporally minuscule, intervals of physical space-time. This is at the heart of what I have theorized, in this book, as "screen time," but given

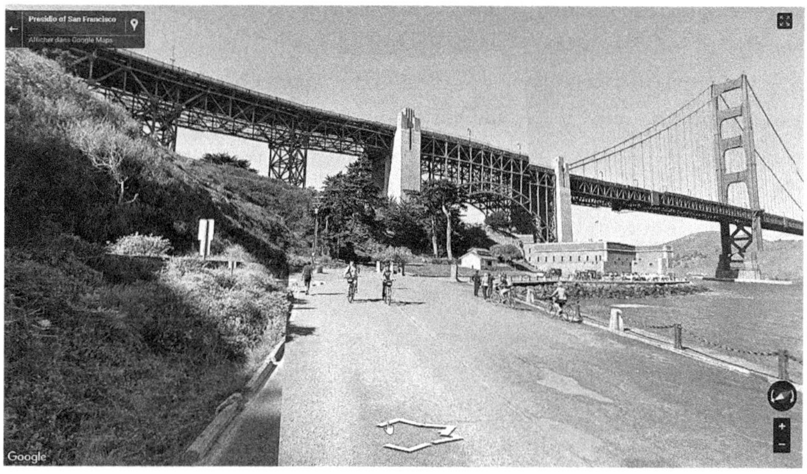

Figure 6.21. Grégory Chatonsky, *Vertigo@home* (2007). Video. 00:32:03. Used by permission of the artist.

the multimodal and environmental totality of such mediation, it would be more proper to refer to simply as a new form of time itself. In this new time, media *contents*—a term that masks the fact that they become the very medium through which time is modulated—are subject to radical variation, though it may escape our grosser perceptual faculties altogether. *Capture* magnifies these variables of generativity, taking the discorrelation of human perception and machinic agency to its logical, systemic end. Escaping the imperative of media to be yoked to human attention altogether, the project's pre-sponsive gesture transforms its audiovisual contents from objects of consumption (or objects of phenomenological intentionality) and makes them into the "environment" of perception and agency itself.

Such pre-sponsive gestures are also at work in a somewhat puzzling series of engagements with Hitchcock's *Vertigo*—a decidedly post-cinematic thread running throughout Chatonsky's work for over a decade. For the most part, these works lack the grand narratives of *Telofossils* and *Capture*; they rely instead on the preexisting narrative of Hitchcock's film, but they extract it from the encapsulated movie experience and redistribute it in bite-sized plurimedial chunks.

For example, *Vertigo@home* (2007–15) takes its soundtrack from *Vertigo*, but it uses Google Street View to reconstruct Scottie's journey through San Francisco in a post-cinematic space—a space that has not simply erased photographic indexicality in favor of digital imagery, but which has in fact multiplied indices through geolocation (and the infrastructure of GPS satellites), along with the multiple car-mounted cameras that Google used to capture its images—and, as we later found out, to illicitly capture a great deal of residential Wi-Fi traffic as well.[73] In *Vertigo@home*, black screens foreground the gaps, seams, and stitches between digitally navigable public spaces (e.g., when Scottie goes indoors), thus highlighting the seamfulness more generally of post-cinematic space, whose gaps must always be closed in the generative process of image rendering. This forcefully dramatizes the perceptual gaps that remain in *our* experience—but that may *not* remain in the experience of Google's algorithms, which are privy to a wealth of data outside the purview of our perception.

Vertigo also appears in other works concerned with the stitching of images. In *Readonlymemories* (2003), digitally composited collages of filmic images reconstruct the spaces that cinematic cameras probe but reveal only in framed snippets. *Readonlymemories* thus explores the spatialization of temporal experience that is a central part of the transition to a post-cinematic media regime. But a more recent work, *The Kiss* (2015), takes this spatialization to a new level and reveals its pre-sponsive nature. By subjecting the final embrace between James Stewart and Kim Novak to photogrammetric analysis, Chatonsky essentially duplicates and extends the post-cinematic processing of cinematic materials by which images are decoded and predictively interpolated in everyday computational playback. In the photogrammetric analysis, relations between the film's images are scrutinized in an intensive process of automated comparison. In normal usage, photogrammetry software is employed in order to reconstruct a preexisting three-dimensional space from photographs of it, but in Chatonsky's application a completely new space emerges, one that is algorithmically severed from our own perceptual reconstruction of three-dimensionality on the basis of the two-dimensional cinema screen.[74] Finally, Chatonsky's generated space is transformed into a 3D-printable form and materialized as a warped object. This quintessentially post-cinematographic object spatializes a nonhuman, post-perceptual temporality and indeed radicalizes the temporality of the affective space it opens up between the viewer and the object. Chatonsky's sculpture is a physical embodiment of the activity of computational processing that takes place between the production and our perception of images, and it therefore acts on our perception with the force of an augmented, anthropotechnically hybrid affectivity. The material object thereby highlights the discorrelation of images when subjected to post-cinematic processing, but it also unmistakably foregrounds a concomitant

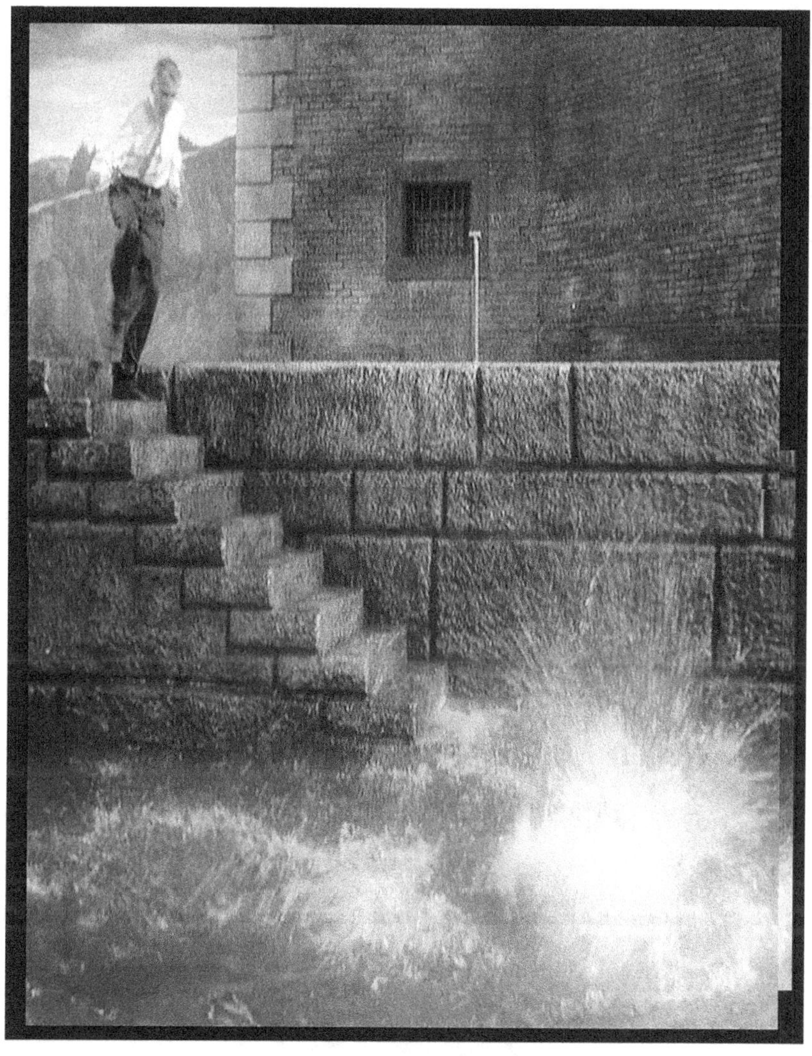

Figure 6.22. Grégory Chatonsky, *Readonlymemories* (2003). 112 × 140 cm. Print. Used by permission of the artist.

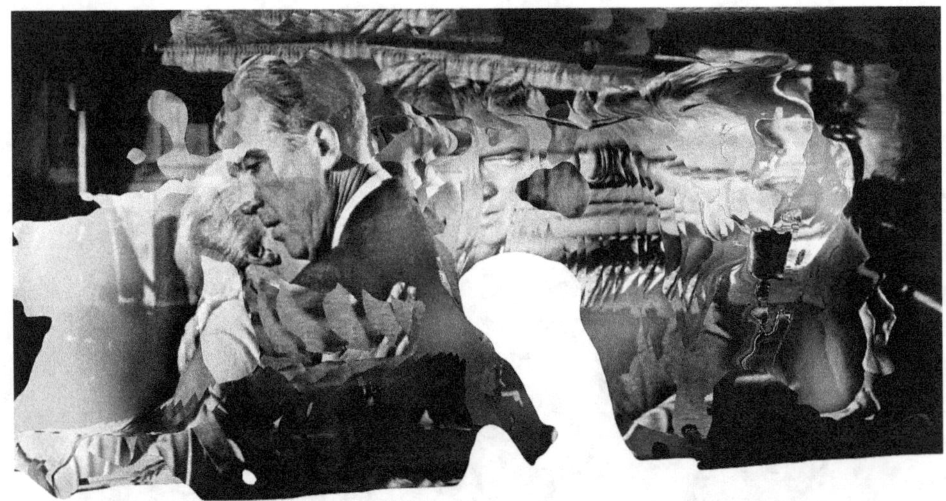

Figure 6.23. Grégory Chatonsky, *The Kiss* (2015). 130 × 68 cm. Print. Used by permission of the artist.

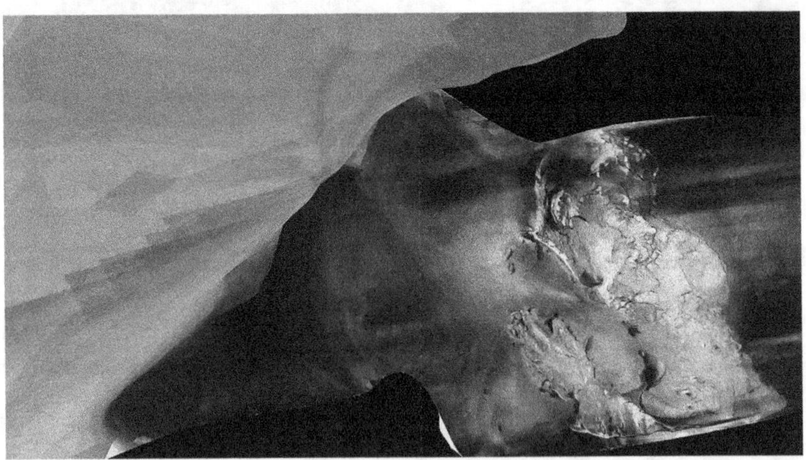

Figure 6.24. Grégory Chatonsky, *The Kiss* (2015). 100 × 54 cm. Print. Used by permission of the artist.

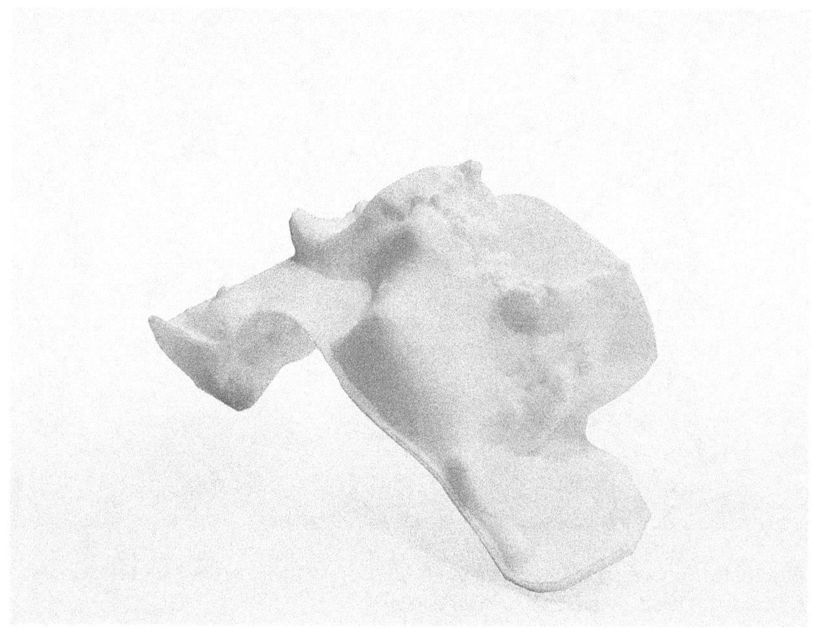

Figure 6.25. Grégory Chatonsky, *The Kiss* (2015). 30×15×10 cm. 3D Print (Formiga p100). Used by permission of the artist.

generativity or creative agency that seemingly ineluctably produces something new and inserts it into the environment for life.

And it is this new production that is probed, again with reference to *Vertigo,* in some of Chatonsky's more recent works. *Prediction* (2015) crosses *Vertigo* with *Capture,* so to speak, using artificial intelligence to detect and quantify the emotions of on-screen characters. *The Watson Emotion Watching Vertigo* (2016) turns this analysis into a 543-page book that radically foregrounds the discorrelation of the pre-sponsive gesture: "The chronologic reading of these anonymous feelings does not express the film, but expresses the way the machine analyzes our emotions. Two incommensurable worlds intersect in this reading."[75]

It is this uncertain intersection, finally, that Chatonsky's work highlights as a whole; from his large-scale narratives of post-Anthropocenic futures to his computational reimaginings of our cinematic past, what these projects have in common is that they reveal the pre-sponsive gesture as the characteristic gesture of our moment: the gesture, more than an attitude or decision, by which we daily "pledge ourselves in advance" of any knowledge or ability to estimate

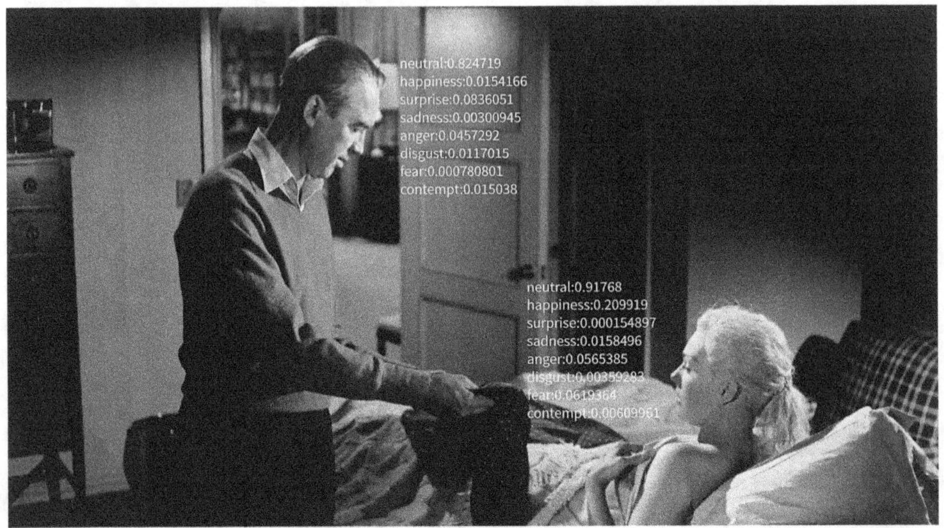

Figure 6.26. Grégory Chatonsky, *Prediction* (2015). Artificial intelligence software. Used by permission of the artist.

the parameters, agencies, or environments into which we venture. It is up to us now to find ways to make this pledge in a form that sees discorrelation's apocalyptic tendencies as a challenge and perhaps even an opportunity—one that might help free us from the injustices, excesses, and alienations that follow from a narrowly anthropocentric comportment toward the world. In the face of powerful geopolitical and global-capitalist interests that seek to monopolize the systemic forces of metabolism, it is far from certain that we stand a chance. But it is hardly a foregone conclusion that we don't, or that the path toward extinction or fates even worse is predetermined.

As I have hoped to show in this book, the multiscalar systems structured by our contemporary media are permeated by real ethical urgencies but also potent sites of contingency, indeterminacy, and possible intervention. Our ethical situation today is framed by the macroscale threat of global catastrophe as well as the microscale reality of computational media processing. Articulated in between these forces that in equal measure decenter anthropocentric and anthropomorphic perspectives, our ethical and phenomenological agencies are challenged as never before; the task of "making sense" of discorrelation involves nothing less than the existential question of whether and how we might be able to go on living, how we might be able to reconceive ourselves as beings both willing and able to project and extend ourselves into an uncertain

{start:144,duration:48,interval:12,events:[[{windowFaceDistribution:{neutral:1,h
appiness:0,surprise:0,sadness:0,anger:0,disgust:0,fear:0,contempt:0},windowMe
anScores:{neutral:0.937222,happiness:0.000188074,surprise:0.000272121,sad
ness:0.015946,anger:0.0385399,disgust:0.00207183,fear:2.05669e-005,conte
mpt:0.00573898}}],[{windowFaceDistribution:{neutral:1,happiness:0,surprise:0,
sadness:0,anger:0,disgust:0,fear:0,contempt:0},windowMeanScores:{neutral:0.7
47194,happiness:0.000788404,surprise:0.00231944,sadness:0.0114353,anger
:0.176307,disgust:0.0487976,fear:0.000133761,contempt:0.0130249}}],[{wind
owFaceDistribution:{neutral:1,happiness:0,surprise:0,sadness:0,anger:0,disgust:
0,fear:0,contempt:0},windowMeanScores:{neutral:0.720257,happiness:0.10354
2,surprise:0.0455854,sadness:0.0433754,anger:0.0596031,disgust:0.0158055,
fear:0.00757301,contempt:0.00425851}}],[{windowFaceDistribution:{neutral:1,
happiness:0,surprise:0,sadness:0,anger:0,disgust:0,fear:0,contempt:0},windowM
eanScores:{neutral:0.769869,happiness:0.0581347,surprise:0.0798104,sadnes
s:0.0637398,anger:0.0128331,disgust:0.000430531,fear:0.0138349,contempt:
0.00134773}}]]},{start:192,duration:48,interval:12,events:[[{windowFaceDistribu
tion:{neutral:1,happiness:0,surprise:0,sadness:0,anger:0,disgust:0,fear:0,contem
pt:0},windowMeanScores:{neutral:0.790489,happiness:0.0402834,surprise:0.05
92467,sadness:0.0594623,anger:0.00505895,disgust:0.00102021,fear:0.0438
103,contempt:0.000628904}}],[{windowFaceDistribution:{neutral:1,happiness:0,
surprise:0,sadness:0,anger:0,disgust:0,fear:0,contempt:0},windowMeanScores:{
neutral:0.691547,happiness:0.241205,surprise:0.0247186,sadness:0.0180479,
anger:0.0110349,disgust:0.00191874,fear:0.0107694,contempt:0.000758383}}
],[{windowFaceDistribution:{neutral:1,happiness:0,surprise:0,sadness:0,anger:0,
disgust:0,fear:0,contempt:0},windowMeanScores:{neutral:0.593512,happiness:0
.351467,surprise:0.00480338,sadness:0.0303579,anger:0.0135398,disgust:0.0
0278608,fear:0.00103448,contempt:0.00249957}}],[{windowFaceDistribution:{
neutral:1,happiness:0,surprise:0,sadness:0,anger:0,disgust:0,fear:0,contempt:0},
windowMeanScores:{neutral:0.824259,happiness:0.139866,surprise:0.0055030
5,sadness:0.0234007,anger:0.00465216,disgust:0.00106831,fear:0.00066166
5,contempt:0.000589215}}]]},{start:240,duration:48,interval:12,events:[[{windo
wFaceDistribution:{neutral:1,happiness:0,surprise:0,sadness:0,anger:0,disgust:0
,fear:0,contempt:0},windowMeanScores:{neutral:0.820356,happiness:0.003663
95,surprise:0.00168816,sadness:0.0733645,anger:0.0947696,disgust:0.00337
87,fear:0.000413834,contempt:0.00236497}}],[{windowFaceDistribution:{neutr
al:1,happiness:0,surprise:0,sadness:0,anger:0,disgust:0,fear:0,contempt:0},wind
owMeanScores:{neutral:0.960031,happiness:0.00443853,surprise:0.00335161,
sadness:0.0122658,anger:0.0177688,disgust:0.000896175,fear:0.000231668,
contempt:0.00101596}}],[{windowFaceDistribution:{neutral:1,happiness:0,surpri
se:0,sadness:0,anger:0,disgust:0,fear:0,contempt}:0},windowMeanScores:{neutr

Figure 6.27. Grégory Chatonsky, *The Watson Emotion Watching Vertigo* (2016). Software and book. Used by permission of the artist.

future. This emphatically open question, which I have explored here in terms of a speculative realignment of world/planet relations, is a question about our ability not only to understand minute technical processes in the manner of a computer scientist or to comprehend global ecological processes in the manner of an environmental scientist but also to weave these together phenomenologically as a question of life's contemporary and future medium or milieu—as a question of the phenomenological conditions for living (or living well) in a post-phenomenological environment. The existential import of discorrelation demands, therefore, a probing of the transformed conditions of habit, habituation, and habitation, for at stake is nothing less than ensuring that the planet remains habitable as world. But the immense, possibly overwhelming uncertainty attaching to the latter is inseparable from the little gestures of embodied habit, including the habits of media usage. What does it mean to become habituated, to get used to discorrelation? The gestures associated with our contemporary, future-oriented media will determine whether the transition from a cinematic to a post-cinematic lifeworld is capable of sustaining life; the speculative but material and often mundane act of pre-sponse will therefore determine whether discorrelation can give way to a recalibration of life and its environment. In this sense, perhaps nothing less than the future of the planet and the agencies that will populate it depends on how we relate today to our screens and their discorrelated images.

NOTES

Introduction: Discorrelation and Post-cinema

1 It is important to emphasize that perception, in the phenomenological tradition on which I am drawing (and against which, to a certain extent, I am situating my analysis of digital imaging processes), is not simply reducible to that which is determinately, much less visibly, apparent. Phenomenologists who emphasize the embodied nature of subjectivity, such as Maurice Merleau-Ponty or Don Ihde, instead see perception more as a gestalt formation that includes prethematic groupings of sensations, affects, and relations that may not be directly present or visible to consciousness. They are therefore cognizant of the fact that intentionality is not limited to a purely "deliberative" relation, such that the subject is necessarily aware of and focused on its intentional objects but also includes prereflective, "operative" relations grounded in the body and habit. See, for example, Maurice Merleau-Ponty, *Phenomenology of Perception*, trans. Colin Smith (New York: Routledge, 2002); and Don Ihde, *Technology and the Lifeworld: From Garden to Earth* (Bloomington: Indiana University Press, 1990). But even if perceptual phenomena are not reducible, in this tradition, to that which is actively or clearly intended by a conscious perceiver, they are necessarily situated in relation to the perceiver's subjectivity—and it is this relation, above all, that is called into question by the microtemporal operations of computationally processed images. There remains an open question, which I seek to address in asking about how we "make sense" of discorrelation (the subject of part II of this book), about what it might mean for discorrelated images to become part of our operative intentionalities, if not our deliberative ones.

2 Here I am invoking the problematic prefix *post-*, which debates over postmodernism and postmodernity taught us to treat not as a marker of definitive beginnings and ends, but as indicative of a more subtle shift or transformation in the realm of culturally dominant aesthetic and experiential forms. See Fredric Jameson, *Postmodernism, or, The Cultural Logic of Late Capitalism* (Durham, NC: Duke University Press, 1991). In the following, I argue that in the context of post-cinema, this suggests not so much a clear-cut break with traditional media forms as a transitional movement taking place along an uncertain time line, following an indeterminate trajectory, and characterized by juxtapositions and overlaps between the techniques, technologies, and aesthetic conventions of "old" and "new" moving-image media. I intend a similar temporal and ontological ambiguity in my use of other *post-* terms: the posthuman, postperceptual, or postphenomenological. Nevertheless, or accordingly, it is worth emphasizing that the alignment of these terms

is speculative and necessarily imperfect, certainly not subject to an easy sort of conflation.

3 Drawing on the historical example of early modern emblem books, Kristen Whissel has explored the allegorical and emblematic functions of digital visual effects, in terms of what she calls the "effects emblem." For Whissel, the latter signifies the development of thematic, narrative, and signifying functions by way of digital effects, thus reversing long-standing trends to see spectacular effects in terms of their show-stopping, narratively disruptive effects, and shifting attention away from technological and affective dimensions back toward hermeneutic interpretation. Certainly, the reader will find some commonalities between our approaches, especially in part II, but in unfolding their emblematic and allegorical functions I place more emphasis on digital images' self-reflexive relations to technical infrastructures and the larger material and ecological systems in which they participate. Ultimately, I see the two approaches as complementary rather than contradictory. See Kristen Whissel, *Spectacular Digital Effects: CGI and Contemporary Cinema* (Durham, NC: Duke University Press, 2014).

4 Daniel Dayan, "The Tutor-Code of Classical Cinema," *Film Quarterly* 28, no. 1 (1974): 22.

5 Dayan, "Tutor-Code," 24.

6 Edward Branigan, "Formal Permutations of the Point-of-View Shot," *Screen* 16, no. 3 (1975): 61.

7 William Brown sees such images, wherein "the (virtual) 'camera' passes through 'filled' space (i.e. solid objects) with the same ease with which it passes through 'empty' space," as indicative of digital cinema's transformation of space and the figures it depicts, ultimately pointing toward a decentering of cinema's anthropocentrism. William Brown, *Supercinema: Film-Philosophy for the Digital Age* (New York: Berghahn, 2013), 2. Indeed, Brown's book treats many of the same topics as the present book, but from a different perspective (that of cognitive film theory, along with the philosophy of Gilles Deleuze and Félix Guattari) and with different emphases. The present book resituates the spatiality and temporality of contemporary moving images with respect to reorientations of agency and affect within the larger systems of mediated life.

8 Matthias Stork introduced the term *chaos cinema* in a series of video essays by that title: Matthias Stork, "Chaos Cinema: The Decline and Fall of Action Filmmaking," video essay, *Press Play*, August 22, 2011, http://blogs.indiewire.com/pressplay/video_essay_matthias_stork_calls_out_the_chaos_cinema. Stork's notion is positioned as a radicalization of David Bordwell's "intensified continuity," which sought to explain the shift to a postclassical style of filmmaking while showing that basic continuity principles, though strained, remain in place: David Bordwell, "Intensified Continuity: Visual Style in Contemporary American Film," *Film Quarterly* 55, no. 3 (2002): 16–28.

9 Steven Shaviro's notion of "post-continuity" goes some way toward connecting questions of continuity and related formal/stylistic matters with the underlying technological infrastructures of contemporary images, as well as the affective

and political implications of these changes. See Steven Shaviro, "Post-continuity: An Introduction," in *Post-cinema: Theorizing 21st-Century Film*, ed. Shane Denson and Julia Leyda (Falmer, UK: REFRAME Books, 2016), 51–64; and, more generally, Steven Shaviro, *Post-cinematic Affect* (Winchester, UK: Zero Books, 2010).

10 Key discussions of cinematic indexicality can be found in Mary Ann Doane, "The Indexical and the Concept of Medium Specificity," *Differences* 18, no. 1 (2007): 128–52; D. N. Rodowick, *The Virtual Life of Film* (Cambridge, MA: Harvard University Press, 2007), 110–24; Tom Gunning, "What's the Point of an Index? or, Faking Photographs," in *Still Moving: Between Cinema and Photography*, ed. Karen Beckman and Jean Ma (Durham, NC: Duke University Press, 2008), 23–40; Philip Rosen, *Change Mummified: Cinema, Historicity, Theory* (Minneapolis: University of Minnesota Press, 2001), 301–49.

11 Kittler writes: "The general digitalization of channels and information erases the differences among individual media. Sound and image, voice and text are reduced to surface effects, known to consumers as interface. Sense and the senses turn into eyewash." Friedrich Kittler, *Gramophone, Film, Typewriter*, trans. Geoffrey Winthrop-Young and Michael Wutz (Stanford, CA: Stanford University Press, 1999), 1. Other key texts in media archaeology include Wolfgang Ernst, *Chronopoetics: The Temporal Being and Operativity of Technological Media*, trans. Anthony Enns (New York: Rowman and Littlefield, 2016); Jussi Parikka, *What Is Media Archaeology?* (Cambridge: Polity, 2012); Erkki Huhtamo and Jussi Parikka, eds., *Media Archaeology: Approaches, Applications, and Implications* (Berkeley: University of California Press, 2011); and Shannon Mattern, *Code and Clay, Data and Dirt: Five Thousand Years of Urban Media* (Minneapolis: University of Minnesota Press, 2017).

12 Some notable exceptions include Stephen Prince, *Digital Visual Effects in Cinema: The Seduction of Reality* (New Brunswick, NJ: Rutgers University Press, 2012); Sean Cubitt, *The Cinema Effect* (Cambridge, MA: MIT Press, 2004); Sean Cubitt, *The Practice of Light: A Genealogy of Visual Technologies from Print to Pixels* (Cambridge, MA: MIT Press, 2014); Whissel, *Spectacular Digital Effects*; Markos Hadjioannou, *From Light to Byte: Toward an Ethics of Digital Cinema* (Minneapolis: University of Minnesota Press, 2012); Scott C. Richmond, *Cinema's Bodily Illusions: Flying, Floating, and Hallucinating* (Minneapolis: University of Minnesota Press, 2016); Barbara Flückiger, *Visual Effects: Filmbilder aus dem Computer* (Marburg, Germany: Schüren, 2008); and Giovanna Fossati, *From Grain to Pixel: The Archival Life of Film in Transition* (Amsterdam: Amsterdam University Press, 2009).

13 I develop the idea of media as "originary correlators" in Shane Denson, *Postnaturalism: Frankenstein, Film, and the Anthropotechnical Interface* (Bielefeld, Germany: Transcript Verlag, 2014), 319–32.

14 Edmund Husserl, *Ideas: General Introduction to Pure Phenomenology*, trans. W. R. Boyce Gibson (New York: Routledge, 2012), 192.

15 On correlationism, see Quentin Meillassoux, *After Finitude: An Essay on the Necessity of Contingency*, trans. Ray Brassier (London: Continuum, 2008). Other key texts in speculative realism and object-oriented ontology include Graham Harman, *The Quadruple Object* (Winchester, UK: Zero Books, 2011); Levi Bryant, *The Democracy of*

Objects (Ann Arbor, MI: Open Humanities Press, 2011); Ian Bogost, *Alien Phenomenology, or What It's Like to Be a Thing* (Minneapolis: University of Minnesota Press, 2012); and Steven Shaviro's valuable engagement with this strain of thought: Steven Shaviro, *The Universe of Things: On Speculative Realism* (Minneapolis: University of Minnesota Press, 2014).

16 See Edmund Husserl, *The Phenomenology of Internal Time Consciousness*, trans. James Churchill (Bloomington: Indiana University Press, 1964).

17 See Maurice Merleau-Ponty, "The Intertwining—The Chiasm," trans. Alphonso Lingis, in *The Visible and the Invisible*, ed. Claude Lefort (Evanston, IL: Northwestern University Press, 1968), 130–55.

Chapter 1. Crazy Cameras

An earlier, shorter version of chapter 1 first appeared as "Crazy Cameras, Discorrelated Images, and the Post-perceptual Mediation of Post-cinematic Affect," in *Post-cinema: Theorizing 21st-Century Film*, ed. Shane Denson and Julia Leyda (Falmer, UK: REFRAME Books, 2016).

1 Bruno Latour, *We Have Never Been Modern*, trans. Catherine Porter (Cambridge, MA: Harvard University Press, 1993), 78; emphasis added.

2 Gilbert Simondon, "The Genesis of the Individual," in *Incorporations*, ed. Jonathan Crary and Sanford Kwinter (New York: Zone, 1992), 315; emphasis in original.

3 See Wolfgang Ernst, *Chronopoetics: The Temporal Being and Operativity of Technological Media*, trans. Anthony Enns (New York: Rowman and Littlefield, 2016). Here Ernst articulates the notion of time-criticality in relation to the microtemporal processing of technological and especially computational media.

4 Shane Denson, *Postnaturalism: Frankenstein, Film, and the Anthropotechnical Interface* (Bielefeld, Germany: Transcript Verlag, 2014), 26.

5 Denson, *Postnaturalism*, 182–83.

6 Here it is important to note that I am using the term *post-phenomenological* in a somewhat different, stronger sense than is implied by Don Ihde's employment of it. For Ihde, post-phenomenology marks a methodological turn from the priority of the subjective in traditional phenomenology toward a more materially entangled, pragmatically situated view of human-technological relations. See, for example, Don Ihde, *Ironic Technics* (Copenhagen: Automatic Press, 2008) and *Postphenomenology—Again?*, Working Papers from the Centre for STS Studies (Aarhus: University of Aarhus, 2003). But while I am fully in agreement with the need to see subjectivity as thus entangled and situated, I am less certain that the recognition of these conditions marks a significant departure from phenomenology proper—at least not from the existential phenomenologies of technology elaborated by the likes of Martin Heidegger and Maurice Merleau-Ponty. In any case, when I describe certain aspects of contemporary images as "post-phenomenological," I am suggesting a more radical departure from the phenomenal realm as such—the association of these images with the advent of a post-perceptual form of mediation—without thereby deprecating phenomenology as an important mode of philosophical inquiry.

7 Framed by an engagement with philosopher Bernard Stiegler's discussion of cinema as a neo-Husserlian "temporal object," Mark B. N. Hansen makes an important argument about the contemporary breakdown of "objectal" forms of mediation. According to Hansen, the move from objectal to more thoroughly processual forms of media and art gives rise to a changed experience of time itself—and ultimately to an experience of time divorced (or "discorrelated," as I put it) from the temporal scale of human perception. See Mark B. N. Hansen, "Living (with) Technical Time: From Media Surrogacy to Distributed Cognition," *Theory, Culture and Society* 26, nos. 2–3 (2009).

8 Henri Bergson, *Matter and Memory*, trans. N. M. Paul and W. S. Palmer (New York: Cosimo, 2007), 60.

9 Clearly, this definition of affect is familiar to more traditional studies of film; it corresponds to a major emphasis in film theory conducted in the wake of the so-called affective turn—namely, a focus on privileged but fleeting moments, when narrative continuity breaks down and the images on the screen resonate materially, unthinkingly, or prereflectively with the viewer's autoaffective sensations. Such moments are, of course, central to Deleuze's conception of the "time-image" (cf. *Cinema 2*), which marks a break with the phenomenology of the "movement-image" of the pre–World War II era (cf. *Cinema 1*). See Gilles Deleuze, *Cinema 1: The Movement-Image*, trans. Hugh Tomlinson and Barbara Habberjam (Minneapolis: University of Minnesota Press, 1986); Gilles Deleuze, *Cinema 2: The Time-Image*, trans. Hugh Tomlinson and Robert Galeta (Minneapolis: University of Minnesota Press, 1989). My argument about post-cinema's discorrelated images tries to envision a further transformation on this affective terrain of human-technological interaction—one that will take us well beyond film studies' familiar areas of interest and analysis.

10 I speak of a "properly" post-cinematic era in recognition of the fact that the entire second half of the twentieth century, following the rise of television and the decline of classical film style, might with some justification be claimed already to have been post-cinematic. Nevertheless, it seems reasonable to identify a period of transition that has only recently given way to a more fully or genuinely post-cinematic era. Steven Shaviro gestures in a similar direction: recognizing the media-technical and other changes taking place since the mid-twentieth century, Shaviro refuses a "precise periodization" but maintains that "these changes have been massive enough, and have gone on for long enough, that we are now witnessing the emergence of a different media regime, and indeed of a different mode of production, than those which dominated the twentieth century. Digital technologies, together with neoliberal economic relations, have given birth to radically new ways of manufacturing and articulating lived experience." Steven Shaviro, *Post-cinematic Affect* (Winchester, UK: Zero Books, 2010), 1, 2.

11 See Shane Denson, Therese Grisham, and Julia Leyda, "Post-cinematic Affect: Post-continuity, the Irrational Camera, Thoughts on 3D," *La Furia Umana* 14 (2012), reprinted in *Post-cinema: Theorizing 21st-Century Film*, ed. Shane Denson and Julia Leyda (Falmer, UK: REFRAME Books, 2016). This was the second roundtable

discussion on the topic of post-cinema to appear in the online journal *La Furia Umana*, following Therese Grisham, Julia Leyda, Nicholas Rombes, and Steven Shaviro, "The Post-cinematic in *Paranormal Activity* and *Paranormal Activity 2*," *La Furia Umana* 10 (2011), reprinted in Denson and Leyda, *Post-cinema*.

12 Denson, Grisham, and Leyda, "Post-cinematic," 935.

13 Denson, Grisham, and Leyda, "Post-cinematic," 936.

14 Denson, Grisham, and Leyda, "Post-cinematic," 936.

15 Sobchack's reference to "postcinematic" media occurs in the concluding pages of *The Address of the Eye*, where she writes: "Postcinematic, incorporating cinema into its own techno-logic, our electronic culture has disenfranchised the human body and constructed a new sense of existential 'presence.' Television, video tape recorders/players, videogames, and personal computers all form an encompassing electronic system whose various forms 'interface' to constitute an alternative and virtual world that uniquely *incorporates* the spectator/user in a spatially decentered, weakly temporalized, and quasi-disembodied state." Vivian Sobchack, *The Address of the Eye: A Phenomenology of Film Experience* (Princeton, NJ: Princeton University Press, 1992), 300. These ideas, which Sobchack had previously articulated at greater length at the "Materialität der Kommunikation" conference in Dubrovnik in 1987, appeared in a number of versions throughout the years: first in German, as "The Scene of the Screen: Beitrag zu einer Phänomenologie der 'Gegenwärtigkeit' im Film und in den elektronischen Medien" (trans. H. U. Gumbrecht, in *Materialität der Kommunikation*, ed. H. U. Gumbrecht and K. Ludwig Pfeiffer [Frankfurt am Main: Suhrkamp, 1988]); then in English, as "Toward a Phenomenology of Cinematic and Electronic Presence: The Scene of the Screen" (*Post-script* 10 [1990]); then in a revised version, "The Scene of the Screen: Envisioning Photographic, Cinematic, and Electronic 'Presence,'" reprinted in Denson and Leyda, *Post-cinema*, 88–128.

16 Mark Neveldine and Brian Taylor, "Ghost Directors: Mark Neveldine and Brian Taylor Get Cage-y," interview with *Nerdist News*, February 17, 2012, http://www.nerdistnews.com/region/national/story/national/ghost-directors-mark-neveldine-and-brian-taylor-get-cage-y.

17 Neveldine and Taylor, "Ghost Directors."

18 Neveldine and Taylor, "Ghost Directors."

19 See David Bordwell, "Intensified Continuity: Visual Style in Contemporary American Film," *Film Quarterly* 55, no. 3 (2002); and Stork's three-part video essay: Matthias Stork, "Chaos Cinema: The Decline and Fall of Action Filmmaking," video essay, *Press Play*, August 22, 2011, http://blogs.indiewire.com/pressplay/video_essay_matthias_stork_calls_out_the_chaos_cinema.

20 Neveldine and Taylor, "Ghost Directors."

21 Neveldine and Taylor, "Ghost Directors."

22 On embodiment relations, see Don Ihde, *Technology and the Lifeworld: From Garden to Earth* (Bloomington: Indiana University Press, 1990), 72–80.

23 On the notion of "realisticness," as opposed to "realism," see Alexander Galloway, "Social Realism," in *Gaming: Essays on Algorithmic Culture* (Minneapolis: University of Minnesota Press, 2006).

24 On hermeneutic relations, see Ihde, *Technology and the Lifeworld*, 80–97.

25 I return to the question of realism in chapter 5 and argue for a notion of "post-cinematic realism" that is not limited to photorealism or the "perceptual realism" that Stephen Prince, against worries over the loss of indexicality, sees *enhanced* by digital visual effects. See Stephen Prince, *Digital Visual Effects in Cinema: The Seduction of Reality* (New Brunswick, NJ: Rutgers University Press, 2012). The example of the CGI lens flare shows how perceptual realism can be conjured, but how it continues to oscillate between simulation and the foregrounding of the simulation's medial conditions of possibility. Moreover, there is a deeper question concerning the political promise of realism that is not accounted for when the latter is understood solely in terms of perceptual realism.

26 I adopt the term *ergodic* from Espen Aarseth, who uses it to describe the interactive spaces of digital games and electronic literature; combining the Greek *ergon* (work) and *hodos* (path), the concept of ergodicity describes digital games, in contrast to other textual forms, as a type of discourse "whose signs emerge as a path produced by a non-trivial element of work." Espen Aarseth, "Aporia and Epiphany in *Doom* and *The Speaking Clock*: The Temporality of Ergodic Art," in *Cyberspace Textuality: Computer Technology and Literary Theory*, ed. Marie-Laure Ryan (Bloomington: Indiana University Press, 1999), 32. Accordingly, a game's narrative "script" is not preexistent, not just "there" for us to read like a novel, but it is instead generated at the moment of interaction, on the fly and in response to a user's input. Here I wish to expand the notion of ergodicity to conceptualize the basic processuality of post-cinematic images, including such apparently noninteractive ones as CGI lens flares. Overt interactivity, in other words, might be seen as only one possible expression of an underlying instability at the root of post-cinematic images.

27 On chaos cinema, see Stork, "Chaos Cinema."

28 Jim Emerson, "Agents of Chaos," *Scanners*, August 23, 2011, http://www.rogerebert.com/scanners/agents-of-chaos.

29 The distinction between "molar" and "molecular" levels derives from Deleuze and Guattari. As with many of the concepts at work in Deleuze and Guattari's collaborations, Brian Massumi's *A User's Guide to Capitalism and Schizophrenia* is helpful in understanding the molar/molecular distinction. Massumi writes: "It is crucial for understanding Deleuze and Guattari . . . to remember that *the distinction between molecular and molar has nothing whatsoever to do with scale*. Molecular and molar do not correspond to 'small' and 'large,' 'part' and 'whole,' 'organ' and 'organism,' 'individual' and 'society.' There are molarities of every magnitude (the smallest being the nucleus of the atom). The distinction is not one of scale, but of mode of composition: it is qualitative, not quantitative. In a molecular population (mass) there are only local connections between discrete particles. In the case of molar populations (superindividual or person) locally connected discrete particles have become correlated at a distance. Our granules of muck [in an example introduced earlier] were an oozing molecular mass, but as their local connections rigidified into rock, they became stabilized and homogenized, increasing the organizational consistency of different regions in the deposit (correlation). Molarity implies the

creation or prior existence of a well-defined boundary enabling the population of particles to be grasped as a whole. We skipped something: the muck as such. A supple individual lies between the molecular and the molar, in time and in mode of composition. Its particles are correlated, but not rigidly so. It has boundaries, but fluctuating ones. It is the threshold leading from one state to another." Brian Massumi, *A User's Guide to Capitalism and Schizophrenia: Deviations from Deleuze and Guattari* (Cambridge, MA: MIT Press, 1992), 54–55. Similarly, if there is really a moment of media-ontological transformation associated with the transition to a post-cinematic media regime, it would have to be located in a "mesolevel" of human-nonhuman interactions located between an acentered molecular flux and the situated centeredness of (new and old forms of) phenomenological subjectivity.

30 Lazzarato mounts his argument in a book titled *Videofilosofia: La percezione del tempo nel postfordismo*, translated into German as *Videophilosophie: Zeitwahrnehmung im Postfordismus* (Berlin: b_books, 2002), still untranslated into English at the time of writing but recently published as Maurizio Lazzarato, *Videophilosophy: The Perception of Time in Post-Fordism*, ed. and trans. Jay Hetrick (New York: Columbia University Press, 2019). In the following, I quote from an earlier translation of chapter 2: Maurizio Lazzarato, "Machines to Crystallize Time: Bergson," *Theory, Culture and Society* 24, no. 6 (2007).

31 Lazzarato, "Machines," 111.

32 Mark B. N. Hansen, "Ubiquitous Sensation: Toward an Atmospheric, Collective, and Microtemporal Model of Media," in *Throughout: Art and Culture Emerging with Ubiquitous Computing*, ed. Ulrik Ekman (Cambridge, MA: MIT Press, 2012), 70.

33 On "affective labor," see Michael Hardt, "Affective Labor," *boundary 2* 26, no. 2 (1999). On "immaterial labor," see Maurizio Lazzarato, "Immaterial Labor," in *Radical Thought in Italy: A Potential Politics*, ed. Paolo Virno and Michael Hardt (Minneapolis: University of Minnesota Press, 1996). On the practico-inert, see Jean-Paul Sartre, *Critique of Dialectical Reason*, vol. 1, *Theory of Practical Ensembles*, trans. Alan Sheridan-Smith (London: Verso, 2004).

34 Lazzarato, "Machines," 96.

35 For a fuller reading of the series, see Julia Leyda, "Demon Debt: *Paranormal Activity* as Recessionary Post-cinematic Allegory," *Jump Cut* 56 (2014), reprinted in Denson and Leyda, *Post-cinema*; see also Grisham et al., "The Post-cinematic."

36 See Kevin P. Sullivan's discussion with directors Henry Joost and Ariel Schulman: "The Xbox Kinect and its invisible field of tracking dots surprised Joost and Schulman, but provided an opportunity for a new kind of scare. '[The Xbox Kinect scares] started because we were looking around and thinking about how many cameras there are around your house. My laptop has a camera built in. His does. The Kinect is actually two cameras,' Joost said. 'We were thinking maybe some of the filming will be done with the Kinect, and then we started researching what it's capable of and found this video on YouTube where someone was like, "Do you actually know how this thing works and how it projects this grid of dots on the room that's completely invisible to the naked eye, but if you have the right camera, you can see it?" We were just like, "Oh my God, this has to be in the movie. That's

so crazy looking.'" In a weird way, the new technology fits nicely into the tradition of the series. 'I think it's very *Paranormal Activity* because it's like, there's this stuff going on in the house that you can't see,' Joost said. 'Now we have a little bit of a window into what those things look like.' Schulman agreed. 'The ghost dimension.'" Kevin P. Sullivan, "'Paranormal Activity 4': Behind the High-Tech Scares," *MTV News*, October 18, 2012, http://www.mtv.com/news/articles/1695798/paranormal-activity-4-special-fx.jhtml.

37 See Hansen, "Ubiquitous Sensation."

38 Hansen, "Ubiquitous Sensation," 73.

39 Hansen, "Ubiquitous Sensation," 73.

40 John Biggs, "Help Key: Why 120Hz Looks 'Weird,'" *TechCrunch*, August 12, 2009, http://techcrunch.com/2009/08/12/help-key-why-hd-video-looks-weird/.

41 There is, indeed, still much to be said in favor of the view that digital imaging processes fundamentally flatten the distinction between live-action cinema and animated film. For an early statement of this view, see Lev Manovich, "What Is Digital Cinema?," in Denson and Leyda, *Post-cinema*.

42 Denson, Grisham, and Leyda, "Post-cinematic," 936.

43 Massumi defines affect as "a suspension of action-reaction circuits and linear temporality in a sink of what might be called 'passion,' to distinguish it both from passivity and activity." Brian Massumi, *Parables for the Virtual: Movement, Affect, Sensation* (Durham, NC: Duke University Press, 2002), 28. See also my discussion in Denson, *Postnaturalism*, 186–93.

44 In chapter 5 of *Postnaturalism*, I draw on Dutch phenomenological psychologist J. H. van den Berg's quirky "metabletic" treatment of the Industrial Revolution (in his *Two Principal Laws of Thermodynamics*) in order to theorize metabolism as the ground and model of human-technological coevolution: "Just as an animal devours dead or living organic matter and, through processes outside its control, integrates it into a body that grows, maintains itself, reproduces, and dies within shifting ecological parameters, so too does the anthropotechnical body mutate non-deterministically by absorbing into itself environmental materials of the most diverse sorts, synthesizing them into new structures and functional pathways that, viewed from above, constitute nodes in an evolving network of relations between apparatic innovations, cellular and organic changes, and other internal and external exigencies. As a metabolic process, anthropotechnical evolution is an a-centric and non-hierarchical process of transformation that is not only indifferent to consciousness but cannot be said to favor the organic or the natural either. It is spatially liminal and temporally transitional, always outside and in-between the molar 'situations' of human experience and empirical nature." Denson, *Postnaturalism*, 259. See J. H. van den Berg, *The Two Principal Laws of Thermodynamics: A Cultural and Historical Exploration*, trans. Bernd Jager, David Jager, and Dreyer Kruger (Pittsburgh: Duquesne University Press, 2004).

45 See Mark Hansen's "Media Theory," where he explains, "Such a conceptualization [i.e., medium as environment for life] draws explicitly on the implications of recent work in biological autopoiesis (which, among other salient claims, demonstrates

that embodied life necessarily involves a 'structural coupling' of an organism and an environment), but it does so, importantly, in a way that opens the door to technics, that in effect contaminates the logic of the living with the distinct and always concrete operation of technics. From this perspective, the medium is, from the very onset, a concept that is irrevocably implicated in life, in the epiphylogenesis of the human, and in the history to which it gives rise *qua* history of concrete effects. Thus, long before the appearance of the term 'medium' in the English language, and also long before the appearance of its root, the Latin term *medium* (meaning middle, center, midst, intermediate course, thus something implying mediation or an intermediary), the medium existed as an operation fundamentally bound up with the living, but also with the technical. The medium, we might say, is implicated in the living as essentially technical, in what I elsewhere call 'technical life'; it is the operation of mediation—and perhaps also the support for the always concrete mediation—between a living being and the environment. In this sense, the medium perhaps names the very transduction between the organism and the environment that constitutes life as essentially technical; thus it is nothing less than a medium for the exteriorization of the living, and correlatively, for the selective actualization of the environment, for the creation of what Francisco Varela calls a 'surplus of significance,' a demarcation of a world, of an existential domain, from the unmarked environment as such." Mark B. N. Hansen, "Media Theory," *Theory, Culture and Society* 23, nos. 2–3 (2006): 299–300.

46 Elena del Río, "Cinema's Exhaustion and the Vitality of Affect," *In Media Res*, August 29, 2011, http://mediacommons.org/imr/2011/08/19/cinemas-exhaustion-and-vitality-affect, reprinted in "Post-cinematic Affect: A Conversation in Five Parts," in Denson and Leyda, *Post-cinema*, 879.

47 See Shaviro's "Post-continuity," where he differentiates and positions his views in relation to those of David Bordwell and Matthias Stork. Steven Shaviro, "Post-continuity: An Introduction," in Denson and Leyda, *Post-cinema*.

48 I have discussed this lack of closure in the roundtable discussion in Denson, Grisham, and Leyda, "Post-cinematic Affect."

49 In his book *Convergence Culture*, Henry Jenkins explores the intersections of popular-cultural phenomena of transmedia storytelling with an apparently democratizing impulse toward participation and creativity on the side of contemporary media consumers. See Henry Jenkins, *Convergence Culture: Where Old and New Media Collide* (New York: New York University Press, 2006). See Felix Brinker, "On the Political Economy of the Contemporary (Superhero) Blockbuster Series," in Denson and Leyda, *Post-cinema*, for an alternative, somewhat more pessimistic view of these developments.

50 Bernard Stiegler, *Technics and Time*, vol. 1, *The Fault of Epimetheus*, trans. Richard Beardsworth (Stanford, CA: Stanford University Press, 1998), 220–25.

51 Van den Berg, *The Two Principal Laws*, 4–9.

52 In his "Postscript on the Societies of Control," Deleuze describes the shift from Foucault's "disciplinary societies" of the eighteenth and nineteenth centuries to the new "societies of control" in terms of a reorganization of agency under the

respective political-economic systems: "The factory [of the disciplinary society] constituted individuals as a single body to the double advantage of the boss who surveyed each element within the mass and the unions who mobilized a mass resistance; but the corporation [in societies of control] constantly presents the brashest rivalry as a healthy form of emulation, an excellent motivational force that opposes individuals against one another and runs through each, dividing each within." Thus, in societies of control, "we no longer find ourselves dealing with the mass/individual pair. Individuals have become '*dividuals*,' and masses, samples, data, markets, or '*banks*.'" Gilles Deleuze, "Postscript on the Societies of Control," *October*, no. 59 (1992): 4–5. Kris and Jeff are exemplary figures of the control society: I have already pointed out that Kris's original career (in an anonymous neoliberal media corporation) positions her as "biopower in the service of algorithmic functions," but even after her transformation she continues to work in digital image production, printing large-format posters and signage for corporate customers. Jeff, on the other hand, originally worked in the world of high finance, and it is unclear whether embezzlement was part of his job or the reason he lost it. Quite possibly, Jeff committed his crimes under the hypnotic influence of the mysterious "Thief" (as he is called in the film's credits), who infected both him and Kris with the parasite, and who caused Kris to sign over all her assets to him. In any case, Jeff takes responsibility for his actions, much as a neoliberal society expects us all to take responsibility for (or accept as "natural") events that are beyond our control or comprehension: for example, we are not to assign blame to banks or corporations for financial crises, as the causal mechanisms are (by design) far too complicated for most of us to understand. And even after his fall (or crisis) Jeff continues to work, off the books, in the more shadowy regions of finance capital. Both Kris's and Jeff's occupational activities are therefore inextricably, and exemplarily, bound up in the post-cinematic universes of data that control our lives. And their plights, their transformations, are closely related to our own situations as inhabitants of neoliberal societies. We never learn why, to what end, the Thief went to such lengths to scam his victims out of their savings. As spectators, we are positioned as uncomprehending, unable to grasp a plot of such complexity, involving such distributed and apparently noncoordinated agencies, similar to the way credit default swaps are just too complicated for most of us to understand and thus didn't raise enough red flags early on before the financial crisis.

53 For Deleuze, following Bergson, "the virtual is fully real"—and thus not to be confused with the notion of virtuality according to which "virtual reality" is distinguished from "real life"; the virtual, which concerns the realm of potentialities (as well as the generative experience of duration and memory), is, according to Deleuze, "real without being actual, ideal without being abstract, and symbolic without being fictional." Gilles Deleuze, *Difference and Repetition*, trans. Paul Patton (New York: Columbia University Press, 1994), 208.

54 Isabelle Stengers, *Thinking with Whitehead: A Free and Wild Creation of Concepts*, trans. Michael Chase (Cambridge, MA: Harvard University Press, 2011), 74; emphasis added.

55 There has been a flurry of recent work on ecological and Anthropocene-inflected perspectives in film and media studies, including work on both the material and the representational dimensions of moving-image media. An overview is provided in Jennifer Peterson and Graig Uhlin, eds., "In Focus: Film and Media Studies in the Anthropocene," *Journal of Cinema and Media Studies* 58, no. 2 (2019): 142–79. Some notable works include Nadia Bozak, *The Cinematic Footprint: Lights, Camera, Natural Resources* (New Brunswick, NJ: Rutgers University Press, 2011); Jennifer Fay, *Inhospitable World: Cinema in the Time of the Anthropocene* (New York: Oxford University Press, 2018); E. Ann Kaplan, *Climate Trauma: Foreseeing the Future in Dystopian Film and Fiction* (New Brunswick, NJ: Rutgers University Press, 2015); and Stephen Rust, Salma Monani, and Sean Cubitt, eds., *Ecocinema Theory and Practice* (New York: Routledge, 2013). For discussions more directly relating the Anthropocene to the question of post-cinema, see Selmin Kara, "Anthropocenema: Cinema in the Age of Mass Extinctions," and Adrian Ivakhiv, "The Art of Morphogenesis: Cinema in and Beyond the Capitalocene," both in Denson and Leyda, *Post-cinema*. I return to the relation of discorrelated images and the Anthropocene in chapter 6.

Chapter 2. Dividuated Images

1 Gilles Deleuze, "Postscript on the Societies of Control," *October*, no. 59 (1992): 3–7. In his *Post-cinematic Affect*, Steven Shaviro offers a picture of post-cinema similarly cast in terms of the control society, especially prominent in his analysis of the morphing images of Grace Jones's music video "Corporate Cannibal" (Shaviro, *Post-cinematic Affect* [Winchester, UK: Zero Books, 2010], 11–34). Thus, while I think we agree on this general picture of the relation between post-cinema and "control," I hope in this chapter to fill in some of the finer details.
2 Ted Nannicelli and Malcolm Turvey, "Against Post-cinema," *Cinéma et Cie: International Film Studies Journal*, nos. 26–27 (2016): 33–44.
3 Nannicelli and Turvey, "Against Post-cinema," 36.
4 Nannicelli and Turvey, "Against Post-cinema," 33.
5 Nannicelli and Turvey, "Against Post-cinema," 34.
6 Nannicelli and Turvey, "Against Post-cinema," 35.
7 Nannicelli and Turvey, "Against Post-cinema," 36.
8 Nannicelli and Turvey, "Against Post-cinema," 35.
9 Nannicelli and Turvey, "Against Post-cinema," 38.
10 Chang-Min Yu, "Cinema's Turing Test: Consciousness, Digitality, and Operability in *Hardcore Henry*," NECSUS 6, no. 1 (2017): 207. Yu directs his question both to me and Mark Hansen, collectively under the term *Duke media studies*. He also writes: "While I sympathise with their approach and agree that the perceptual production of the image is changing irrevocably, I find their rhetoric of historical revolution lacking a sense of history, particularly in the media-archeological sense." As will become clear in the following, Yu's objection is based on a misunderstanding, as the view of a sudden, "revolutionary" break that he imputes to me is quite at odds both with the media-archaeological transition to digital images by way of analog video, as well as with the smooth, flexible, modulatory transformation that I am

ultimately gesturing toward (in line with Deleuze's view of the control society, but which I will approach through the lens of Niklas Luhmann's conception of mediality).

11 Many of the central contributions to apparatus theory are collected in Philip Rosen, ed., *Narrative, Apparatus, Ideology: A Film Theory Reader* (New York: Columbia University Press, 1986).

12 John Belton, "If Film Is Dead, What Is Cinema?," *Screen* 55, no. 4 (2014): 467.

13 Belton, "If Film Is Dead," 467.

14 Belton, "If Film Is Dead," 467.

15 Belton, "If Film Is Dead," 468.

16 Belton, "If Film Is Dead," 468.

17 Belton, "If Film Is Dead," 468; emphasis added.

18 Jordan Schonig, "Cinema's Motion Forms: Film Theory, the Digital Turn, and the Possibilities of Cinematic Movement" (PhD diss., University of Chicago, 2017), 202.

19 Schonig, "Cinema's Motion Forms," 203.

20 Schonig, "Cinema's Motion Forms," 204.

21 Schonig, "Cinema's Motion Forms," 206.

22 Schonig, "Cinema's Motion Forms," 207.

23 Schonig, "Cinema's Motion Forms," 207.

24 Schonig, "Cinema's Motion Forms," 208.

25 Schonig, "Cinema's Motion Forms," 208.

26 Schonig, "Cinema's Motion Forms," 210.

27 Edmund Husserl, *The Phenomenology of Internal Time Consciousness*, trans. James Churchill (Bloomington: Indiana University Press, 1964).

28 Yu, "Cinema's Turing Test," 207.

29 Schonig, "Cinema's Motion Forms," 220.

30 Schonig, "Cinema's Motion Forms," 220–21.

31 Schonig, "Cinema's Motion Forms," 221.

32 See Martin Heidegger, *Being and Time*, trans. John Macquarrie and Edward Robinson (New York: Harper and Row, 1962), 175: "Ontologically mood [*Stimmung*] is a primordial kind of Being for Dasein, in which Dasein is disclosed to itself *prior to* all cognition and volition, and *beyond* their range of disclosure." The translators' note, on 173: "The noun 'Stimmung' originally means the tuning of a musical instrument, but it has taken on several other meanings and is the usual word for one's mood or humour. We shall usually translate it as 'mood,' and we shall generally translate both 'Gestimmtsein' and 'Gestimmtheit' as 'having a mood,' though sometimes, as in the present sentence, we prefer to call attention to the root metaphor of 'Gestimmtsein' by writing 'Being-attuned,' etc." More recent translators have taken this reasoning to heart and have begun translating *Stimmung* more regularly in terms of attunement.

33 Schonig, "Cinema's Motion Forms," 223.

34 Schonig, "Cinema's Motion Forms," 223, quoting Maurice Merleau-Ponty, *Phenomenology of Perception*, trans. Colin Smith (New York: Routledge, 2002), 166.

35 Gilles Deleuze, *Cinema 1: The Movement-Image*, trans. Hugh Tomlinson and Barbara Habberjam (Minneapolis: University of Minnesota Press, 1986); Gilles Deleuze, *Cinema 2: The Time-Image*, trans. Hugh Tomlinson and Robert Galeta (Minneapolis: University of Minnesota Press, 1989).
36 Merleau-Ponty, *Phenomenology of Perception*, 92.
37 Schonig, "Cinema's Motion Forms," 224.
38 For a thorough treatment of perceptual coding from a humanistic perspective that combines technical, perceptual, and political implications, see Jonathan Sterne, *MP3: The Meaning of a Format* (Durham, NC: Duke University Press, 2012).
39 Schonig, "Cinema's Motion Forms," 226.
40 Schonig, "Cinema's Motion Forms," 224.
41 Schonig, "Cinema's Motion Forms," 260.
42 Schonig, "Cinema's Motion Forms," 261.
43 Schonig, "Cinema's Motion Forms," 261.
44 Schonig, "Cinema's Motion Forms," 221; emphasis added.
45 Schonig, "Cinema's Motion Forms," 261.
46 Schonig, "Cinema's Motion Forms," 227.
47 Schonig, "Cinema's Motion Forms," 261.
48 Francesco Casetti offers a somewhat different model of substrate/form relations, which he talks about in terms of the relations between "material basis" or "support" and "experience" or "cultural form." What he calls the "relocation" of a medial experience is said to be enabled by the persistence of an "idea" of a given medium; this idea stabilizes a medium pragmatically rather than absolutely. Casetti's model, which seems to be a form of the correlational model with a flexible twist, is complex and far from reductionist; I think it may even be compatible with the model I put forward here, but it operates at a different level—a higher, subjective level, far removed from the molecular relations I am gesturing toward. See Francesco Casetti, "The Relocation of Cinema," *NECSUS: European Journal of Media Studies* 1, no. 2 (2012): 5–34; Francesco Casetti, *The Lumière Galaxy: Seven Key Words for the Cinema to Come* (New York: Columbia University Press, 2015).
49 Central texts include chapter 2 of Niklas Luhmann, *Die Gesellschaft der Gesellschaft* (Frankfurt: Suhrkamp, 1997), 190–412; chapter 3 of Niklas Luhmann, *Die Kunst der Gesellschaft* (Frankfurt: Suhrkamp, 1995), 165–214; translated as Niklas Luhmann, *Art as a Social System*, trans. Eva M. Knodt (Stanford, CA: Stanford University Press, 2000); and the shorter article, Niklas Luhmann, "The Medium of Art," *Thesis Eleven*, nos. 18–19 (1987): 101–13. Note that there are terminological pitfalls involved in Luhmann's approach: *medium* is sometimes used for the substrate/form constellation and sometimes just for the substrate—this is a carryover from Fritz Heider's distinction of medium and form, which influences Luhmann's thinking; see Fritz Heider, *Ding und Medium* (Berlin: Kulturverlag Kadmos, 2005). In order to avoid these confusions, I will use the term *mediality* rather than *medium* to refer to the substrate/form constellation. See also Thomas Khurana, "Niklas Luhmann—Die Form des Mediums," in *Medientheorien: Eine philosophische Einführung*, ed. Alice Lagaay and David Lauer (Frankfurt: Campus, 2004), 97–125.

50 Luhmann, *Die Gesellschaft der Gesellschaft*, 195; my translation.

51 Belton, "If Film Is Dead," 468; emphasis added.

52 Shane Denson, *Postnaturalism: Frankenstein, Film, and the Anthropotechnical Interface* (Bielefeld, Germany: Transcript Verlag, 2014), 314.

53 Niklas Luhmann, interview with Hans Dieter Huber, *Texte zur Kunst* 4 (September 1991): 121.

54 Though not strictly identical, Luhmann's observer and Peirce's interpretant both occupy a role in an indissolubly triadic system of relations (with respect to substrate and form, for Luhmann, and with respect to sign and object, for Peirce). Neither of these constellations presupposes the fixity, integrity, or even humanness of the observer/interpretant. Peirce writes: "By 'semiosis' I mean . . . an action, or influence, which is, or involves, a cooperation of *three* subjects, such as a sign, its object, and its interpretant, this tri-relative influence not being in any way resolvable into actions between pairs." He then goes on to suggest that "although the definition does not require the logical interpretant . . . to be a modification of consciousness," our lack of familiarity with any nonmental semiosis forces us to start "with a provisional assumption that the interpretant is . . . a sufficiently close analogue of a modification of consciousness." Charles Sanders Peirce, *The Essential Peirce: Selected Philosophical Writings*, vol. 2, *1893–1913*, ed. Nathan Houser et al. (Bloomington: Indiana University Press, 1998), 411. With his acknowledgment that semiosis may not be restricted to human consciousness, Peirce's openness to a nonanthropocentric definition of the interpretant is central to his influence in the field of biosemiotics, while critics like N. Katherine Hayles have begun adapting this perspective for computational processes as well. N. Katherine Hayles, "Can Computers Create Meaning? A Cyber-Bio-Semiotic Perspective" (paper presented at the Digital Aesthetics Workshop, Stanford Humanities Center, Stanford, CA, February 12, 2019).

55 When teaching Luhmann's theory of media, I often resort to an image of a tuning fork that sets air molecules into motion, producing ordered wave patterns out of the chaotic mass of the substrate. The image serves to illustrate the centrality of time in Luhmann's concept of mediality, as it places frequency at the center of the flux between substrate and forms. More abstractly, it also serves to suggest a connection between Luhmann's theory and Heidegger's concept of "affective attunement" or *Stimmung*: the tuning fork, in German, is called a *Stimmgabel*, which is used for tuning (*stimmen*) musical instruments. The image is one of a synchronization of frequencies that operate outside individuated perception to affect "mood" or "atmosphere" (both suggested by *Stimmung*).

56 Comprehensive technical standards are published by the United Nations International Telecommunication Union (ITU). See, for example, "Recommendation ITU-R BT.470.6," which includes standards for many conventional television systems, including PAL, NTSC, and SECAM: https://www.itu.int/dms_pubrec/itu-r/rec/bt/R-REC-BT.470-6-199811-S!!PDF-E.pdf.

57 On the notion of a post-cinematic "time-image," whereby Deleuze's concept is rethought in televisual and digital media, see Wolfgang Ernst, "A Close Reading of

the Electronic 'Time Image,'" in *Chronopoetics: The Temporal Being and Operativity of Technological Media* (London: Rowman and Littlefield, 2016), 123–71. See also Herbert Zettl, "The Rare Case of Television Aesthetics," *Journal of the University Film Association* 30, no. 2 (1978): 5, where the television image is described as "continually moving, very much in the manner of the Bergsonian *durée*." Such views might usefully be contrasted with views that see the digital moving more definitively beyond the temporality of experience, such as Sergi Sánchez, "Towards a Non-time Image: Notes on Deleuze in the Digital Era," in *Post-cinema: Theorizing 21st-Century Film*, ed. Shane Denson and Julia Leyda (Falmer, UK: REFRAME Books, 2016), 171–92; as well as reflections on "bullet time" in digital moving-image media: Andreas Sudmann, "Bullet Time and the Mediation of Post-cinematic Temporality," and Steven Shaviro, "Splitting the Atom: Post-cinematic Articulations of Sound and Vision," both in Denson and Leyda, *Post-cinema*.

58 Bruch made these comments on the first episode of the long-running German television show *Dalli Dalli*, May 13, 1971.

59 Wolfgang Ernst, "Time-Critical Media Processes," in *Chronopoetics*, 3–14.

60 Schonig, "Cinema's Motion Forms," 221.

61 Trevor Paglen, "Invisible Images (Your Pictures Are Looking at You)," *New Inquiry*, December 8, 2016, https://thenewinquiry.com/invisible-images-your-pictures-are-looking-at-you/.

62 Paglen, "Invisible Images."

63 Paglen, "Invisible Images."

64 See, for example, Gert Rudolph and Uwe Voelzke, "Three Sensor Types Drive Autonomous Vehicles," *Sensors Online*, November 10, 2017, https://www.sensorsmag.com/components/three-sensor-types-drive-autonomous-vehicles.

65 Paglen, "Invisible Images."

66 Paglen, "Invisible Images."

67 Paglen, "Invisible Images."

68 Paglen, "Invisible Images."

69 See James Bridle, "Something Is Wrong on the Internet," *Medium*, November 6, 2017, https://medium.com/@jamesbridle/something-is-wrong-on-the-internet-c39c471271d2.

70 Chapter 3 of this book develops this claim with respect to Netflix and the various temporal scales at which streaming services and related computational processes take aim at and seek to predict experience. For a somewhat different example, which demonstrates how feedback and feed-forward loops can be utilized at scale, see Miguel Campo-Rembado and Sona Oakley, "How 20th Century Fox Uses ML to Predict a Movie Audience," *Google Cloud*, October 29, 2018, https://cloud.google.com/blog/products/ai-machine-learning/how-20th-century-fox-uses-ml-to-predict-a-movie-audience; based on Cheng-Kang Hsieh et al., "Convolutional Collaborative Filter Network for Video Based Recommendation Systems," submitted on October 18, 2018; last revised October 22, 2018 (preprint, https://arxiv.org/abs/1810.08189).

71 Paglen, "Invisible Images."

Chapter 3. Screen Time

1 Apple, "Use Screen Time on Your iPhone, iPad, or iPod Touch," updated January 30, 2019, accessed April 1, 2019, https://support.apple.com/en-us/HT208982.

2 See Niklas Luhmann, *Das Kind als Medium der Erziehung* (Frankfurt: Suhrkamp, 2006).

3 Niklas Luhmann, *Die Gesellschaft der Gesellschaft* (Frankfurt: Suhrkamp, 1997), 195; my translation.

4 Lev Manovich, *The Language of New Media* (Cambridge, MA: MIT Press, 2001), 30.

5 Neta Alexander, "Catered to Your Future Self: Netflix's 'Predictive Personalization' and the Mathematization of Taste," in *The Netflix Effect: Technology and Entertainment in the 21st Century*, ed. Kevin McDonald and Daniel Smith-Rowsey (New York: Bloomsbury, 2016), 81–97.

6 Alexander, "Catered," 82.

7 Alexander, "Catered," 84.

8 Alexander, "Catered," 86.

9 For Sartre, the serial practices of modern media and the industrialized built environment give rise to a type of alienated collective of isolated and anonymous subjects coexisting in precarious relationships of convenience shaped only through common activities and in relation to common experiences of alienation: "Radio listeners at this moment constitute a series in that they are listening to the common voice which constitutes each of them in his identity as an Other." Jean-Paul Sartre, *Critique of Dialectical Reason*, vol. 1, *Theory of Practical Ensembles*, trans. Alan Sheridan-Smith (London: Verso, 2004), 276.

10 Alexander, "Catered," 83.

11 Given the primacy of time in human experience, according to the Kant of *Critique of Pure Reason*, and given the way that taste is a central mediator (by way of the *sensus communis*) of human nature for the Kant of *Critique of Judgment*, it makes sense that the battle for the power to generate subjectivity would be waged by means of a tastemaking system whose very medium is predictive temporality.

12 See Alexis C. Madrigal, "How Netflix Reverse-Engineered Hollywood," *Atlantic*, January 2, 2014, https://www.theatlantic.com/technology/archive/2014/01/how-netflix-reverse-engineered-hollywood/282679/.

13 Xavier Amatriain and Justin Basilico, "Netflix Recommendations: Beyond the 5 Stars (Part 1)," *Netflix Tech Blog*, April 6, 2012, https://medium.com/netflix-techblog/netflix-recommendations-beyond-the-5-stars-part-1-55838468f429. Quoted, in part, in Alexander, "Catered," 89–90.

14 See chapter 3, "*House of Cards*: The Aesthetics of Abstraction," in Ed Finn, *What Algorithms Want: Imagination in the Age of Computing* (Cambridge, MA: MIT Press, 2017), 87–112.

15 More recently, 20th Century Fox has been pursuing a similar generative strategy, though with the newer resources of advanced machine-learning algorithms. Despite the technical differences, however, they can be seen to be following a similar objective as that of Netflix: namely, trying to anticipate molar audiences and collectives of subjects at the relatively large temporal scale required in order

to produce big-budget movies on the basis of past successes. See Miguel Campo-Rembado and Sona Oakley, "How 20th Century Fox Uses ML to Predict a Movie Audience," *Google Cloud*, October 29, 2018, https://cloud.google.com/blog/products/ai-machine-learning/how-20th-century-fox-uses-ml-to-predict-a-movie-audience.

16 Neta Alexander, "Rage against the Machine: Buffering, Noise, and Perpetual Anxiety in the Age of Connected Viewing," *Cinema Journal* 56, no. 2 (2017): 1–24.

17 Alexander, "Rage," 4.

18 The famous tool-analysis, in which Heidegger discusses the terms *ready-to-hand*, *present-at-hand*, and the *in-order-to* structure of equipment, is in Martin Heidegger, *Being and Time*, trans. John Macquarrie and Edward Robinson (New York: Harper and Row, 1962), 91–148.

19 I discussed Ihde's phenomenological analysis of technical mediation according to categories of "embodiment relations" and "hermeneutic relations" in chapter 1. For a more detailed treatment, see Don Ihde, *Technology and the Lifeworld: From Garden to Earth* (Bloomington: Indiana University Press, 1990).

20 Alexander, "Catered," 82.

21 Quoted in Alexis Kleinman, "Behold, the Most Absurd Video Netflix Has Ever Made," *Huffington Post*, November 5, 2013, https://www.huffingtonpost.com/2013/11/05/netflix-test-video_n_4212826.html.

22 For an overview of these techniques, see Abdelhak Bentaleb et al., "A Survey on Bitrate Adaptation Schemes for Streaming Media over HTTP," *IEEE Communications Surveys and Tutorials* 21, no. 1 (2019): 562–85, https://ieeexplore.ieee.org/document/8424813.

23 See, for example, Keith A. Spencer, "Mired in Self-Referential Cliche, 'Bandersnatch' Can't Transcend Its Form," *Salon*, January 1, 2019, https://www.salon.com/2019/01/01/mired-in-self-referential-cliche-bandersnatch-cant-transcend-its-form/. Spencer compares the show not only to videogames but also to choose-your-own-adventure books and to postmodernist literature.

24 Tom Philip, "*Black Mirror: Bandersnatch* Is a Trip into Darkness," *GQ*, December 28, 2018, https://www.gq.com/story/black-mirror-bandersnatch-is-a-trip-into-darkness.

25 Janko Roettgers, "Netflix Takes Interactive Storytelling to the Next Level with 'Black Mirror: Bandersnatch,'" *Variety*, December 28, 2018, https://variety.com/2018/digital/news/netflix-black-mirror-bandersnatch-interactive-1203096171/. Roettgers devotes only a few sparse sentences to the new buffering system, that hardly indicate its significance: "Another tweak affects Netflix's streaming itself: The service's apps typically pre-cache some content to make for a smooth streaming experience even when a viewer's internet connection temporarily slows down. For 'Bandersnatch,' the app now has to pre-cache two possible paths—something that older versions of the Netflix app aren't able to do. That's why the movie isn't available on Netflix's app for some older smart TVs."

26 Michael Veale, a researcher at University College London, used the European General Data Protection Regulation to formally request the information that Netflix had stored about his own viewing of *Bandersnatch*, and he discovered that Netflix retains

minute information about every decision made. See Matthew Gault, "Netflix Has Saved Every Choice You Made in 'Black Mirror: Bandersnatch,'" *Motherboard*, February 12, 2019, https://www.vice.com/en_us/article/j57gkk/netflix-has-saved-every-choice-youve-ever-made-in-black-mirror-bandersnatch. In addition, researchers at the Indian Institute of Technology, Madras, have recently shown that it is possible for third parties to monitor viewers' choices through a side-channel attack that analyzes file sizes and related information. See Lily Hay Newman, "Hackers Can Tell What Netflix *Bandersnatch* Choices You Make," *Wired*, April 21, 2019, https://www.wired.com/story/netflix-interactive-bandersnatch-hackers-choices/.

27 Indeed, this feed-forward pattern of data-collection, anticipation, and modulation of user experience fits with Jason Mittell's suggestion that we should perhaps regard Netflix "not as a media content or distribution company, but as a data aggregation company," more like Facebook or Twitter than like HBO. Jason Mittell, "Will Netflix Eventually Monetize Its User Data?," *The Conversation*, April 22, 2019, https://theconversation.com/will-netflix-eventually-monetize-its-user-data-115273.

28 Adrian Mackenzie, "Codecs," in *Software Studies*, ed. Matthew Fuller (Cambridge, MA: MIT Press, 2008), 48.

29 Mackenzie, "Codecs," 49.

30 Mackenzie, "Codecs," 51.

31 Mackenzie, "Codecs," 51.

32 Mackenzie, "Codecs," 51.

33 Mackenzie, "Codecs," 52.

34 Mackenzie, "Codecs," 52–53.

35 Mackenzie, "Codecs," 53.

36 Lev Manovich, "What Is Digital Cinema?," in *Post-cinema: Theorizing 21st-Century Film*, ed. Shane Denson and Julia Leyda (Falmer, UK: REFRAME Books, 2016), 20–50.

37 For more on the historical development of such processes, see Tom Sito, *Moving Innovation: A History of Computer Animation* (Cambridge, MA: MIT Press, 2013).

38 Maurice Merleau-Ponty, *Phenomenology of Perception*, trans. Colin Smith (New York: Routledge, 2002), 92.

39 Datamoshing is indeed one of the most apparent aesthetic forms to which video compression gives rise, and it is therefore no wonder that the technique has been used to spectacular effect not only in contemporary media art but also in popular culture, e.g., in music videos by Chairlift and Kanye West. Such spectacle does indeed serve to enable something like a perceptual correlation, as Schonig argues, but this should not lead us to overlook the persistent discorrelation atop which perception nonetheless rides. Schonig's correlative view of datamoshing can usefully be contrasted with that of Mark B. N. Hansen: see Hansen, "Algorithmic Sensibility: Reflections on the Post-perceptual Image," in Denson and Leyda, *Post-cinema*.

40 See chapters 1 and 4 of this book for a fuller argument of this point.

41 Adrian Mackenzie, "Every Thing Thinks: Sub-representative Differences in Digital Video Codecs," in *Deleuzian Intersections: Science, Technology, Anthropology*, ed. Casper

Bruun Jensen and Kjetil Rödje (New York: Berghahn Books, 2010), 140, quoting Gilles Deleuze, *Difference and Repetition* (New York: Continuum, 2001), 276.

42 Mackenzie, "Every Thing," 145.

43 Mackenzie, "Every Thing," 149.

44 Mackenzie, "Every Thing," 153.

45 Mackenzie, "Every Thing," 153.

46 Mackenzie, "Every Thing," 153.

47 Mackenzie, "Every Thing," 147, quoting Deleuze, *Difference*, 220.

48 Mackenzie, "Every Thing," 147.

49 Mackenzie, "Every Thing," 147.

50 Mackenzie, "Every Thing," 153.

51 Mackenzie, "Every Thing," 153.

52 Mackenzie, "Every Thing," 153.

53 Luhmann, *Die Gesellschaft der Gesellschaft*, 195; my translation.

54 See N. Katherine Hayles, *Unthought: The Power of the Cognitive Nonconscious* (Chicago: University of Chicago Press, 2017).

55 On the concept of the anthropotechnical interface, see Shane Denson, *Postnaturalism: Frankenstein, Film, and the Anthropotechnical Interface* (Bielefeld, Germany: Transcript Verlag, 2014).

56 The reference is to David Cronenberg's film *Videodrome* (1983), in which the Marshall McLuhan–inspired character Professor Brian O'Blivion remarks: "The battle for the mind of North America will be fought in the video arena—the videodrome."

57 Janko Roettgers, "The Story behind 'Meridian': Why Netflix Is Helping Competitors with Content and Code," *Variety*, September 15, 2016, https://variety.com/2016/digital/news/netflix-meridian-imf-tools-open-source-1201859416/.

58 Quoted in Roettgers, "The Story."

59 Roettgers, "The Story."

60 Charles Haine, "Why Is That Weird Short Film 'Meridian' on Netflix?," *No Film School*, October 20, 2016, https://nofilmschool.com/2016/10/meridian-netflix-imf-streaming.

61 The clearest statement of the argument appears in Bernard Stiegler, *Technics and Time*, vol. 3, *Cinematic Time and the Question of Malaise*, trans. Stephen Barker (Stanford, CA: Stanford University Press, 2011).

62 Bernard Stiegler, "The Time of Cinema: On the 'New World' and 'Cultural Exception,'" trans. George Collins, *Tekhnema: Journal of Philosophy and Technology*, no. 4 (1998): 106.

63 See Edmund Husserl, *The Phenomenology of Internal Time Consciousness*, trans. James Churchill (Bloomington: Indiana University Press, 1964).

64 The argument is laid out in Stiegler, *Technics and Time*, vol. 3, 16–21.

65 Stiegler, "The Time of Cinema," 106.

66 See David Kaeli and Pen-Chung Yew, eds., *Speculative Execution in High Performance Computer Architectures* (New York: Chapman and Hall/CRC, 2005). I return to the topic of speculative execution in chapter 5.

67 On the use of speculative execution in online gaming, see Tony Cannon, "Fight the Lag: The Trick behind GGPO's Low-Latency Netcode," *Game Developer Magazine* 19, no. 9 (2012): 7–13.
68 See Yuk Hui, *On the Existence of Digital Objects* (Minneapolis: University of Minnesota, 2016), 221–52.
69 Hui, *On the Existence*, 235.
70 Hui, *On the Existence*, 221.
71 Hui, *On the Existence*, 221.
72 Heidegger famously criticizes Kant's revision of the role of the transcendental imagination between the first (1781) and second (1787) editions of the *Critique of Pure Reason*. See Martin Heidegger, *Kant and the Problem of Metaphysics*, 5th, enlarged edition, trans. Richard Taft (Bloomington: Indiana University Press, 1997).
73 This is indeed a very Stieglerian point.
74 Hui, *On the Existence*, 221.
75 Hui, *On the Existence*, 221–22.
76 Hui, *On the Existence*, 221.
77 Hui, *On the Existence*, 240.
78 Hui, *On the Existence*, 240–41.
79 Ernst, *Chronopoetics*, 4.
80 Quoted in Mark B. N. Hansen, "'Realtime Synthesis' and the Différance of the Body: Technocultural Studies in the Wake of Deconstruction," *Culture Machine* 6 (2004), https://culturemachine.net/deconstruction-is-in-cultural-studies/realtime-synthesis-and-the-differance-of-the-body/.
81 Hansen, "'Realtime Synthesis.'"
82 Hansen, "'Realtime Synthesis.'"
83 Denson, *Postnaturalism*, 319–32.
84 Broad offers a concise, popular account online: Terence Broad, "Autoencoding *Blade Runner*: Reconstructing Films with Artificial Neural Networks," *Medium*, May 24, 2016, https://medium.com/@terencebroad/autoencoding-blade-runner-88941213abbe. A fuller account is provided by his dissertation for the MSci degree from Goldsmiths: Terence Broad, "Autoencoding Video Frames" (MSci diss., Goldsmiths, University of London, 2016).
85 Broad, "Autoencoding Video Frames," 17.
86 Broad, "Autoencoding Video Frames," 19.
87 Broad, "Autoencoding Video Frames," 20.
88 Broad, "Autoencoding Video Frames," 21–22.
89 Broad, "Autoencoding Video Frames," 22.
90 Broad, "Autoencoding Video Frames," 24–26.
91 Broad, "Autoencoding Video Frames," 29, 51.
92 Broad notes that he used a 4GB NVIDIA GTX 960 GPU for the project. Broad, "Autoencoding Video Frames," 38.
93 See chapter 1 of this book.
94 This claim, quoted here from the website of Imposium (the proprietary video compositing and rendering software behind the project: https://imposium.com

/casestudies/seances/), is echoed in countless critical and journalistic accounts of the project as well.

95 Imposium, "NFB: Seances Algorithmic Storytelling," https://imposium.com/casestudies/seances/.

96 Wikipedia, "*Seances* (film)," https://en.wikipedia.org/wiki/Seances_(film), accessed January 25, 2020.

97 Andrei Kartashov, "Phantoms Came to Meet: Guy Maddin's *Seances* as Surrealist History of Cinema," *Senses of Cinema* 85 (2017), http://sensesofcinema.com/2017/feature-articles/seances-surrealist-history/.

98 Guy Maddin, quoted in Blake Butler, "These Short Films Will Self-Destruct After You Watch Them," *Vice*, May 13, 2016, https://www.vice.com/en_us/article/jmke8y/guy-maddin-fills-the-internet-with-haunted-films.

99 Kartashov, "Phantoms."

100 According to the "About" page on the *Seances* website: http://seances.nfb.ca, accessed January 25, 2020.

101 Neil Harris, *Humbug: The Art of P. T. Barnum* (Chicago: University of Chicago Press, 1973), 59–89.

102 DJ Pangburn, "Guy Maddin's 'Seances' Film Gets an Algorithmic Remix," *Vice*, April 19, 2016, https://www.vice.com/en_us/article/z4q5kw/guy-maddin-seances-film-remix.

103 Pangburn, "Guy Maddin's 'Seances.'"

104 Quoted in Pangburn, "Guy Maddin's 'Seances.'"

105 Quoted in Melina Gills, "Guy Maddin and Collaborators on Reviving Dead Cinema for the Tribeca 2016 Installation SEANCES," *Tribeca*, April 14, 2016, https://www.tribecafilm.com/stories/interview-guy-maddin-seances-virtual-reality-tribeca-film-festival-storyscapes-installation.

106 Kartashov, "Phantoms."

107 Quoted in Gills, "Guy Maddin and Collaborators."

108 According to Imposium founder and CEO Jason Nickel, quoted in Pangburn, "Guy Maddin's 'Seances.'"

109 Quoted in Jonathan Romney, "Guy Maddin on His Surreal Seances and Sexploitation Remakes," *Guardian*, November 26, 2015, https://www.theguardian.com/film/2015/nov/26/guy-maddin-the-forbidden-room-interview.

110 Quoted in Butler, "These Short Films."

111 Quoted in Gills, "Guy Maddin and Collaborators."

112 Kartashov, "Phantoms."

113 Kartashov, "Phantoms."

Chapter 4. Life to Those Pixels!

An earlier version of ideas developed in chapter 4 first appeared as "Edge Detection," *Media Fields*, no. 14 (2019).

1 For details about the making of the scene, see Joe Skrebels's article with the somewhat hyperbolic title: "*Blade Runner 2049*: How Denis Villeneuve Created the Most Complicated Sex Scene of All Time," *IGN*, February 15, 2018, https://www.ign.com

/articles/2018/02/15/blade-runner-2049-how-denis-villeneuve-created-the-most-complicated-sex-scene-of-all-time.

2 For a compelling and relevant example, see the VFX reel documenting the layers of compositing involved in the (extradiegetic) creation, by VFX studio Double Negative or DNEG, of the fembot at the heart of *Ex Machina*: "Ex Machina—VFX Breakdown by Double Negative," YouTube video, posted May 19, 2016, https://www.youtube.com/watch?v=4sFD-YbeIX4.

3 For greater technical detail, see chapter 5, "Edge Detection," in Ramesh Jain, Rangachar Kasturi, and Brian G. Schunck, *Machine Vision* (New York: McGraw-Hill, 1995).

4 For a provocative account of images that circulate between machines, wholly apart from human vision, see Trevor Paglen, "Invisible Images (Your Pictures Are Looking at You)," *New Inquiry*, December 8, 2016, https://thenewinquiry.com/invisible-images-your-pictures-are-looking-at-you/; and the discussion of it in chapter 3.

5 For technical details, see A. Murat Tekalp, *Digital Video Processing*, 2nd ed. (New York: Prentice Hall, 2015); Iain E. Richardson, *The H.264 Advanced Video Compression Standard*, 2nd ed. (Chichester, UK: John Wiley and Sons, 2010).

6 For an accessible introduction to DeepFake videos, see Jonathan Hui, "How Deep Learning Fakes Videos (Deepfake) and How to Detect It?," *Medium*, April 28, 2018, https://medium.com/@jonathan_hui/how-deep-learning-fakes-videos-deepfakes-and-how-to-detect-it-c0b50fbf7cb9. On GANs, see Ian J. Goodfellow et al., "Generative Adversarial Nets," *Advances in Neural Information Processing Systems* (2014), http://papers.nips.cc/paper/5423-generative-adversarial-nets.pdf.

7 See, for example, Robert Chesney and Danielle Keats Citron, "Deep Fakes: A Looming Challenge for Privacy, Democracy, and National Security," *California Law Review* 107 (2019), https://papers.ssrn.com/sol3/papers.cfm?abstract_id=3213954.

8 Google's addition of the category is reported in Drew Harwell, "Fake-Porn Videos Are Being Weaponized to Harass and Humiliate Women: 'Everybody Is a Potential Target,'" *Washington Post*, December 30, 2018, https://www.washingtonpost.com/technology/2018/12/30/fake-porn-videos-are-being-weaponized-harass-humiliate-women-everybody-is-potential-target.

9 Harwell, "Fake-Porn Videos."

10 Samantha Cole, "AI-Assisted Fake Porn Is Here and We're All Fucked," *Motherboard*, December 11, 2017, https://motherboard.vice.com/en_us/article/gydydm/gal-gadot-fake-ai-porn.

11 Cole, "AI-Assisted Fake Porn."

12 In the context of cinema, Linda Williams has done foundational work on the ways that pornography, along with the other "body genres" of horror and melodrama, activate the viewer's body directly. See Linda Williams, "Film Bodies: Gender, Genre, and Excess," *Film Quarterly* 44, no. 4 (Summer 1991): 2–13; also Linda Williams, *Hard Core: Power, Pleasure, and the "Frenzy of the Visible"*, expanded ed. (Berkeley: University of California Press, 1999).

13 Indeed, issues of politics, perception, and media ontology are deeply intertwined in the category of "involuntary synthetic pornographic imagery"—a

concept that encompasses the media objects of images, relates them to the "body genre" of porn, implicates generativity with the qualifier "synthetic," and connects it centrally with a politics of volition, which is deeply troubled by DeepFakes.

14 Part I of this book provides a more comprehensive attempt to substantiate the claims in question.

15 See, for example, Kyle McDonald, "How to Recognize Fake AI-Generated Images," *Medium*, December 5, 2018, https://medium.com/@kcimc/how-to-recognize-fake-ai-generated-images-4d1f6f9a2842.

16 DARPA's efforts to battle DeepFakes are reported in Will Knight, "The Defense Department Has Produced the First Tools for Catching Deepfakes," *MIT Technology Review*, August 7, 2018, https://www.technologyreview.com/s/611726/the-defense-department-has-produced-the-first-tools-for-catching-deepfakes/.

17 See, for example, Zhenzhong Chen, Weisi Lin, and King Ngi Ngan, "Perceptual Video Coding: Challenges and Approaches," *Proceedings of IEEE International Conference on Multimedia and Expo* (2010): 784–89.

18 I am referring here to the division of the image into "macroblocks," a process that is crucial for reliable motion estimation between frames while maintaining high compression rates (macroblocks with no edges are less likely to change and can therefore be considered redundant, while blocks with edges may include boundaries of objects that move between frames). For technical details, see Richardson, *The H.264 Advanced Video Compression Standard.*

19 At stake, in other words, is the question raised by N. Katherine Hayles of "the limit to how seamlessly humans can be articulated with intelligent machines" (Hayles, *How We Became Posthuman: Virtual Bodies in Cybernetics, Literature, and Informatics* [Chicago: University of Chicago Press, 1999], 284), and which Hayles has explored more recently in terms of the concept of the "cognitive nonconscious"—an important site of subperceptual interactions that are crucial to the questions I am pursuing here. See N. Katherine Hayles, *Unthought: The Power of the Cognitive Nonconscious* (Chicago: University of Chicago Press, 2017).

20 My use of the term *parable* is inspired by Brian Massumi's book *Parables for the Virtual.* There, he suggests that the parable names "the genre of writing most closely allied with the logical form of the example," where the example, following a suggestion from Giorgio Agamben, "is defined by a disjunctive self-inclusion: a belonging to itself that is simultaneously an extendibility to everything else with which it might be connected." Brian Massumi, *Parables for the Virtual: Movement, Affect, Sensation* (Durham, NC: Duke University Press, 2002), 21, 17–18.

21 See Hero of Alexandria, *The Pneumatics of Hero of Alexandria*, trans. and ed. Bennet Woodcroft (London: Charles Whittingham, 1851).

22 An interactive edition of Shelley's novel, which allows for comparison between the 1818 and 1831 revised editions, is available online: Mary Wollstonecraft Shelley, *Frankenstein; or, The Modern Prometheus*, Romantic Circles Electronic Edition, edited by Stuart Curran (Boulder: Romantic Circles, 2009), https://romantic-circles.org/editions/frankenstein.

23 Shane Denson, *Postnaturalism: Frankenstein, Film, and the Anthropotechnical Interface* (Bielefeld, Germany: Transcript Verlag, 2014), 176–93.

24 This is a central argument of my *Postnaturalism*, to which I return later in this chapter.

25 See, for example, Joey Eschrich, "How *Frankenstein*'s Monster Became Sexy," *Slate*, January 24, 2017, https://slate.com/technology/2017/01/why-frankenstein-adaptations-now-make-the-monster-sexy.html; Kaleem Aftab, "Alex Garland's 'Ex Machina' Delivers a Modern Day Twist on Frankenstein," *IndieWire*, April 7, 2015, https://www.indiewire.com/2015/04/review-alex-garlands-ex-machina-delivers-a-modern-day-twist-on-frankenstein-63410/; Sam Thorogood, "Ex Machina, Frankenstein and Modern Deities," *The Artifice*, June 12, 2017, https://the-artifice.com/ex-machina-frankenstein-modern-deities/; Caroline Madden, "Monstrous Creators and Exploited Creatures: Ex Machina and Frankenstein," *Screen Queens*, February 22, 2016, https://screen-queens.com/2016/02/22/monstrous-creators-and-exploited-creatures-ex-machina-and-frankenstein/; Christina Parker-Flynn, "Joe and the 'Real' Girls," *Gender Forum* 66 (2017): 69–74; and Christian Lorentzen, "*Blade Runner 2049*, *Never Let Me Go*, and the Longing to Be Human," *New Republic*, October 7, 2017, https://newrepublic.com/article/145219/blade-runner-2049-never-let-go-longing-human.

26 Denson, *Postnaturalism*.

27 Lev Manovich, "What Is Digital Cinema?," in *Post-cinema: Theorizing 21st-Century Film*, ed. Shane Denson and Julia Leyda (Falmer, UK: REFRAME Books, 2016), 29.

28 Alan Cholodenko, introduction to *The Illusion of Life*, ed. Alan Cholodenko (Sydney: Power Publications, 1991), 15.

29 Manovich, "What Is Digital Cinema?," 29.

30 Deborah Levitt, *The Animatic Apparatus: Animation, Vitality, and the Futures of the Image* (Winchester, UK: Zero Books, 2018), 1, 2.

31 Levitt, *Animatic*, 19, 5.

32 Levitt, *Animatic*, 2.

33 Levitt, *Animatic*, 2.

34 Levitt, *Animatic*, 5.

35 Levitt, *Animatic*, 5.

36 Levitt, *Animatic*, 4.

37 Levitt, *Animatic*, 6–18.

38 It should be noted that, despite the broad agreement outlined here, there are some substantial differences between Levitt's approach and my own; notably, in the present context, she sees *Frankenstein* as a regressive model, as compared to her favored example (the anime *Ghost in the Shell 2: Innocence*), and she rejects ontological claims in favor of an "an-ontology," establishing thereby a binary between static and fluid models that, in my opinion, are both ontological (at least in my understanding of the term).

39 Niklas Luhmann, *Die Gesellschaft der Gesellschaft* (Frankfurt: Suhrkamp, 1997), 195; my translation.

40 N. Katherine Hayles, "Conclusion: What Does It Mean to Be Posthuman?," in *How We Became Posthuman*, 283–91.

41 Donna J. Haraway, "A Cyborg Manifesto: Science, Technology, and Socialist-Feminism in the Late Twentieth Century," in *Simians, Cyborgs, and Women: The Reinvention of Nature* (New York: Routledge, 1991), 149–81.

42 Hayles, *How We Became Posthuman*, 283.

43 Hayles, *How We Became Posthuman*, 283–84.

44 Hayles, *How We Became Posthuman*, 284.

45 Hayles, *How We Became Posthuman*, 285.

46 This includes, most notably, the theories of "suture" considered in the introduction.

47 Paglen, "Invisible Images."

48 On media convergence and transmedia franchises, see Henry Jenkins, *Convergence Culture: Where Old and New Media Collide* (New York: New York University Press, 2006). On superhero movies, see Scott Bukatman's enlightening short article "Why I Hate Superhero Movies," *Cinema Journal* 50, no. 3 (2011): 118–22.

49 Kant's *Critique of Judgment* from 1790 is an important index of these shifts. Immanuel Kant, *Critique of Judgment*, trans. Werner Pluhar (Indianapolis: Hackett, 1987).

50 Benjamin's "Work of Art" essay provides probably the most famous articulation of the cultural shift toward technical, industrial, reproducible, and serialized artforms. Walter Benjamin, *The Work of Art in the Age of Its Technological Reproducibility, and Other Writings on Media*, ed. Michael W. Jennings, Brigid Doherty, and Thomas Y. Levin (Cambridge, MA: Harvard University Press, 2008). For more recent approaches to seriality in its various dimensions, see the contributions to Frank Kelleter, ed., *Media of Serial Narrative* (Columbus: Ohio State University Press, 2017).

51 Note that Ernst Jentsch, on whom Freud draws and also endeavors to set himself apart, had viewed the uncanny precisely in terms of a confusion between the organic and the technical. Ernst Jentsch, "On the Psychology of the Uncanny (1906)," *Angelaki* 2, no. 1 (1997): 7–16; Sigmund Freud, *The Uncanny*, trans. David McLintock (London: Penguin Books, 2003).

52 Gotthold Ephraim Lessing, *Laocoon: An Essay upon the Limits of Painting and Poetry*, trans. Ellen Frothingham (Boston: Roberts Brothers, 1887).

53 See Steven Earl Forry, *Hideous Progenies: Dramatizations of* Frankenstein *from the Nineteenth Century to the Present* (Philadelphia: University of Pennsylvania Press, 1990).

54 The text of the play is included in Forry, *Hideous Progenies*.

55 Shelley, introduction to the 1831 edition of *Frankenstein*, on *Romantic Circles*, May 2009, https://romantic-circles.org/editions/frankenstein/1831v1/intro.html.

56 Nineteenth-century political cartoons are discussed in Forry, *Hideous Progenies*.

57 See Shane Denson and Ruth Mayer, "Border-Crossings: Serial Figures and the Evolution of Media," *NECSUS: European Journal of Media Studies* 7, no. 2 (2018): 65–84, http://dx.doi.org/10.25969/mediarep/3460; Shane Denson, "Marvel Comics' Frankenstein: A Case Study in the Media of Serial Figures," *Amerikastudien* 56, no. 4 (2011): 531–53.

58 William Nestrick, "Coming to Life: *Frankenstein* and the Nature of Film Narrative," in *The Endurance of* Frankenstein*: Essays on Mary Shelley's Novel*, ed. George

Levine and U. C. Knoepflmacher (Berkeley: University of California Press, 1979), 294–95.

59 Tom Gunning, "The Cinema of Attraction: Early Film, Its Spectator and the Avant-Garde," *Wide Angle* 8, nos. 3–4 (1986): 63–70. On classical Hollywood style, see David Bordwell, Janet Staiger, and Kristin Thompson, *The Classical Hollywood Cinema: Film Style and Mode of Production to 1960* (New York: Columbia University Press, 1985). On the transition from early to classical cinema, see Miriam Hansen, *Babel and Babylon: Spectatorship in American Silent Film* (Cambridge, MA: Harvard University Press, 1991). In the following, I am summarizing a more extensive reading of Edison's *Frankenstein* conducted in Denson, *Postnaturalism*, 101–45.

60 Advertisement in *Moving Picture World*, March 19, 1910, 436.

61 Promotional synopsis in *The Edison Kinetogram*, March 15, 1910, 3.

62 See Paul Ward, "Defining 'Animation': The Animated Film and the Emergence of the Film Bill," *Scope* (December 2000): n.p.

63 *The Edison Kinetogram*, March 15, 1910, 5.

64 Marc Redfield, "*Frankenstein*'s Cinematic Dream," *Romantic Circles Praxis Series*, ed. Jerrold E. Hogle (June 2003), http://www.rc.umd.edu/praxis/frankenstein/redfield/redfield.html, para. 6, para. 5.

65 On this point, and on the connection of early horror to the sound transition more generally, see Robert Spadoni's excellent book, *Uncanny Bodies: The Coming of Sound Film and the Origins of the Horror Genre* (Berkeley: University of California Press, 2007).

66 Brian Jacobson makes a different, very compelling argument for this claim, focused not so much on the image of the fembot's body but on her actions and especially her agency as the producer of (artistic) images—an agency that serves as a fulcrum for what Jacobson identifies as the movie's "technocritical" reflections on "the work of cinema in the age of digital simulation." Brian R. Jacobson, "*Ex Machina* in the Garden," *Film Quarterly* 69, no. 4 (2016): 24, 29.

67 Wendy Hui Kyong Chun, *Control and Freedom: Power and Paranoia in the Age of Fiber Optics* (Cambridge, MA: MIT Press, 2006), 4.

68 See Jacobson, "*Ex Machina* in the Garden," for a more detailed treatment of the many artistic images, representational and otherwise, featured in the movie.

69 Wittgenstein's "blue book" contained the philosopher's lecture notes from 1933 to 1934, preliminary studies for his *Philosophical Investigations*. Ludwig Wittgenstein, *The Blue and Brown Books* (New York: Harper and Row, 1958).

70 Levitt, *Animatic*, 19, 5.

71 See Hayles, *Unthought*.

72 Jacobson, "*Ex Machina* in the Garden," invokes Ava's escape and positions her as a Haraway-inspired feminist cyborg in order to defend *Ex Machina* against charges of exploitative objectification, as voiced in Angela Watercutter's memorable description of the movie's "serious fembot problem." Angela Watercutter, "*Ex Machina* Has a Serious Fembot Problem," *Wired*, April 9, 2015, https://www.wired.com/2015/04/ex-machina-turing-bechdel-test/.

73 The trailer can be viewed online: "Ex Machina—Official Trailer 4," YouTube video, posted April 26, 2015, https://www.youtube.com/watch?v=kjzENaQKJtA.

74 The manifesto originally appeared online in various places in 2015. A multilanguage website version is available at http://www.laboriacuboniks.net/, from which I quote in the following. A beautifully designed print version has also appeared as Laboria Cuboniks, *Xenofeminism: A Politics for Alienation* (London: Verso, 2018).
75 Laboria Cuboniks, *Xenofeminism*, 0X05.
76 Laboria Cuboniks, *Xenofeminism*, 0X1A.
77 Laboria Cuboniks, *Xenofeminism*, 0X06. Annie Goh offers an important critique of xenofeminism's reappropriation of rationalism, universalism, and Prometheanism, focusing on the ways that these values are in tension with the project of intersectional feminisms. Annie Goh, "Appropriating the Alien: A Critique of Xenofeminism," *Mute*, July 29, 2019, http://www.metamute.org/editorial/articles/appropriating-alien-critique-xenofeminism.
78 Laboria Cuboniks, *Xenofeminism*, 0X06.
79 Laboria Cuboniks, *Xenofeminism*, 0X0D.
80 Laboria Cuboniks, *Xenofeminism*, 0X13.
81 Helen Hester, *Xenofeminism* (Cambridge, UK: Polity, 2018), 33.
82 See Lee Edelman, *No Future: Queer Theory and the Death Drive* (Durham, NC: Duke University Press, 2004).
83 Hester, *Xenofeminism*, 68.
84 Project description from the author's website: https://superreal.me/clone, accessed January 25, 2020.
85 The vignette's title plays on the famous catchphrase introduced by Bruno Latour, *We Have Never Been Modern*, trans. Catherine Porter (Cambridge, MA: Harvard University Press, 1993).
86 In personal correspondence, Granata notes that "the CLONE video was originally made to be screened in a cinema setting where the audience simultaneously plays the 360 video on their phone while seated, while a non-360 version played on the screen and the audience had to watch the 360 version on their phone and look around in 360 in order to actually see the whole thing. Certain details, such as the glitchy animated lipsticked mouth and other things only appear in the 360 version, and the audience had to contort their bodies around in their seats in order to see it all." Noting that "this could be another layer of discorrelation," she says it is "fun to have the audience load the video on their phone and watch how everyone immediately will start moving their bodies and arms in different directions while seated—it is impossible for them to ever watch the same version of the video. . . . I screened it also at an artist talk without the screen version, just had the audience load it on their phones, and they all move around immediately. The sound also ripples across all of the phones and makes the experience even more strange in a collective setting."

Chapter 5. The Horrors of Discorrelation

An earlier version of the first half of chapter 5 appeared as Shane Denson, "The Horror of Discorrelation: Mediating Unease in Post-cinematic Screens and Networks," *JCMS: Journal of Cinema and Media Studies* 59, no. 4. (2020).

1 I emphasize that it falls outside of *conscious* cognition because it may well be registered in what N. Katherine Hayles calls the "cognitive nonconscious," a realm of bodily (and machinic) processing that does not rise to the level of perceptual awareness. See N. Katherine Hayles, *Unthought: The Power of the Cognitive Nonconscious* (Chicago: University of Chicago Press, 2017).

2 Caetlin Benson-Allott, *Killer Tapes and Shattered Screens: Video Spectatorship from VHS to File Sharing* (Berkeley: University of California Press, 2013).

3 See chapter 1 of this book for a brief discussion of these cameras' significance for our understanding of post-cinema.

4 See Julia Leyda, "Demon Debt: *Paranormal Activity* as Recessionary Post-cinematic Allegory," in *Post-cinema: Theorizing 21st-Century Film*, ed. Shane Denson and Julia Leyda (Falmer, UK: REFRAME Books, 2016), 398–432.

5 See, for example, user discussions of such events on the Apple discussion boards: "Safari Downloading Unknown Files," started May 14, 2018, https://discussions.apple.com/thread/8391731, accessed January 25, 2020.

6 For a technical description of "kernel panic," which is specific to UNIX and UNIX-like systems (e.g., Linux, MacOS, BSD) but is similar to the Windows phenomenon of the "Blue Screen of Death," see the Unix and Linux Commands and Man Pages entry, "man page for panic," at: https://www.unix.com/man-page/FreeBSD/9/panic/.

7 Robert Spadoni, *Uncanny Bodies: The Coming of Sound Film and the Origins of the Horror Genre* (Berkeley: University of California Press, 2007), 13–19.

8 In addition to Spadoni's work on horror, see also Donald Crafton, *The Talkies: American Cinema's Transition to Sound, 1926–1931* (Berkeley: University of California Press, 1997) for a more general history of the sound transition.

9 On "materiality of communication," see Hans Ulrich Gumbrecht and K. Ludwig Pfeiffer, eds., *Materialities of Communication* (Stanford, CA: Stanford University Press, 1994). For a similar phenomenological argument about transitional-era sound, see Shane Denson, "Tarzan und der Tonfilm: Verhandlungen zwischen 'Science' und 'Fiction,'" in *"Ich Tarzan": Affenmenschen und Menschenaffen zwischen Science und Fiction*, ed. Gesine Krüger, Ruth Mayer, and Marianne Sommer (Bielefeld, Germany: Transcript Verlag, 2008).

10 In addition to Spadoni, see Shane Denson and Ruth Mayer, "Spectral Seriality: The Sights and Sounds of Count Dracula," in *Media of Serial Narrative*, ed. Frank Kelleter (Columbus: Ohio State University Press, 2017), 108–24; Shane Denson, *Postnaturalism: Frankenstein, Film, and the Anthropotechnical Interface* (Bielefeld, Germany: Transcript Verlag, 2014); and my video essay: Shane Denson, "Sight and Sound Conspire: Monstrous Audio-Vision in James Whale's *Frankenstein*," *[in]Transition* 2, no. 4 (2016), http://mediacommons.org/intransition/sight-and-sound-conspire.

11 Henri Bergson refers to the body as a "center of indetermination": Henri Bergson, *Matter and Memory*, trans. N. M. Paul and W. S. Palmer (New York: Cosimo, 2007). In chapter 1, I argued that Bergsonian indetermination endows post-cinematic images with an "animated" quality that characterizes them as "metabolic images."

12 Platform studies has emerged over the past decade in game studies and digital media studies. Important early studies include Nick Montfort, "Combat in Context," *Game Studies* 6, no. 1 (2006), http://gamestudies.org/0601/articles/montfort; Nick Montfort and Ian Bogost, *Racing the Beam: The Atari Video Computer System* (Cambridge, MA: MIT Press, 2009); followed by the books in the Platform Studies series edited by Montfort and Bogost for MIT Press. Caetlin Benson-Allott adapts platform studies for moving-image media in *Killer Tapes and Shattered Screens*.

13 Benson-Allott, *Killer Tapes*, 4.

14 Technically speaking, Meltdown and Spectre name a variety of related attacks that exploit specific architectural vulnerabilities in CPUs. Nevertheless, popular reporting often conflates the attacks or exploits and the underlying bugs or vulnerabilities. For more about the discovery of the bugs, as well as an introduction to what they involve, see Andy Greenberg, "Triple Meltdown: How So Many Researchers Found a 20-Year-Old Chip Flaw at the Same Time," *Wired*, January 7, 2018, https://www.wired.com/story/meltdown-spectre-bug-collision-intel-chip-flaw-discovery/.

15 "Side Channel Methods—Analysis, News and Updates," Intel Corporation, accessed July 5, 2018, https://www.intel.com/content/www/us/en/architecture-and-technology/facts-about-side-channel-analysis-and-intel-products.html.

16 See Daniel Genkin, Adi Shamir, and Eran Tromer, "Acoustic Cryptanalysis," *Journal of Cryptology* 30, no. 2 (2017): 392–443.

17 "Reading Privileged Memory with a Side-Channel," *Project Zero* (blog), January 3, 2018, https://googleprojectzero.blogspot.com/2018/01/reading-privileged-memory-with-side.html.

18 On micro-, meso-, and macrotemporalities, see Wolfgang Ernst, *Chronopoetics: The Temporal Being and Operativity of Technological Media* (New York: Rowman and Littlefield, 2016).

19 Gilles Deleuze, "Postscript on the Societies of Control," *October*, no. 59 (1992): 3–7.

20 "Reading Privileged Memory with a Side-Channel."

21 See David Kaeli and Pen-Chung Yew, eds., *Speculative Execution in High Performance Computer Architectures* (New York: Chapman and Hall/CRC, 2005).

22 See Edmund Husserl, *On the Phenomenology of the Consciousness of Internal Time*, trans. John Barnett Brough (Dordrecht, Netherlands: Kluwer Academic, 1991).

23 See, in particular, Bernard Stiegler, *Technics and Time*, vol. 3, *Cinematic Time and the Question of Malaise*, trans. Stephen Barker (Stanford, CA: Stanford University Press, 2011).

24 Yuk Hui, *On the Existence of Digital Objects* (Minneapolis: University of Minnesota, 2016), 221–52.

25 Bernard Stiegler, "The Time of Cinema: On the 'New World' and 'Cultural Exception,'" trans. George Collins, *Tekhnema: Journal of Philosophy and Technology* 4 (1998): 106.

26 "Reading Privileged Memory with a Side-Channel."

27 See Jacques Derrida, "Différance," in *Margins of Philosophy*, trans. Alan Bass (Chicago: University of Chicago Press, 1982), 3–27; on spectrality/hauntology, see

Derrida, *Spectres of Marx: The State of the Debt, the Work of Mourning, and the New International*, trans. Peggy Kamuf (New York: Routledge, 1994).

28 Michel Serres, *The Parasite*, trans. Lawrence R. Schehr (Minneapolis: University of Minnesota Press, 2007).

29 Serres, *Parasite*, 71–73.

30 Serres, *Parasite*, 8.

31 Serres, *Parasite*, 9.

32 Serres, *Parasite*, 56.

33 Serres, *Parasite*, 63.

34 Claude E. Shannon and Warren Weaver, *The Mathematical Theory of Communication* (Urbana: University of Illinois Press, 1963).

35 Cary Wolfe, "Bring the Noise: *The Parasite* and the Multiple Genealogies of Posthumanism," introduction to Serres, *The Parasite*, xiii.

36 Serres, *Parasite*, 47.

37 Bernhard Siegert, *Cultural Techniques: Grids, Filters, Doors, and Other Articulations of the Real*, trans. Geoffrey Winthrop-Young (New York: Fordham University Press, 2015), 21.

38 Siegert, *Cultural Techniques*, 21.

39 Siegert, *Cultural Techniques*, 21.

40 Serres, *Parasite*, 13.

41 Serres, *Parasite*, 61–62.

42 Serres, *Parasite*, 62.

43 I am grateful to an anonymous reviewer for pointing out that Laura's defecation can be seen in terms of a bodily glitch, as well as the related insight that glitches might be seen as "the shitting of digital processes."

44 Many of these digital "props" actually exist on social media. "LAURA BARNS KILL URSELF" is on YouTube: https://www.youtube.com/watch?reload=9&v=mhdblEqwoRg (accessed August 28, 2018); Laura Barns's suicide video is on Liveleak: https://www.liveleak.com/view?i=c60_1509380685 (accessed August 28, 2018); Laura Barns's Twitter account @Billie227 is still online; and so is her original Facebook page: https://www.facebook.com/Laura-Barns-850524571676524/ (accessed August 28, 2018), as well as various tribute pages, such as "RIP Laura Barns": https://www.facebook.com/RIPLauraBarnes/ (accessed August 28, 2018).

45 Siegert, *Cultural Techniques*, 49.

46 "Reading Privileged Memory with a Side-Channel"; emphasis added.

47 Serres, *Parasite*, 4–6.

48 Serres, *Parasite*, 6.

49 The exception is in the movie's final moments, when the laptop is closed and the ghost of Laura Barns (presumably) attacks Blaire.

50 See Francesco Casetti, *The Lumière Galaxy: Seven Key Words for the Cinema to Come* (New York: Columbia University Press, 2015), 17–42.

51 Indeed, the greatest measure of the movie's construction of "realism," for me, is the fact that when viewing the movie on my laptop shortly after it appeared (and while my Mac OSX desktop circa 2014 still resembled that of Blaire Lily's desktop

down to the smallest details, which is no longer the case), I felt compelled at certain moments to intervene in the screen events by moving my mouse—having effectively, or bodily, forgotten the difference between fiction and reality or the diegetic and nondiegetic screen image.

52 See Hito Steyerl, "In Defense of the Poor Image," *e-flux Journal* 10 (2009), https://www.e-flux.com/journal/10/61362/in-defense-of-the-poor-image/.

53 Steyerl, "In Defense."

54 On "participatory culture," see Henry Jenkins, *Convergence Culture: Where New and Old Media Collide* (New York: New York University Press, 2006).

55 Steyerl, "In Defense."

56 Steyerl, "In Defense."

57 Maurizio Lazzarato, *Videophilosophie: Zeitwahrnehmung im Postfordismus* (Berlin: b_books, 2002), 113–27.

58 Clearly, at stake here is something very different than the "perceptual realism" that Stephen Prince sees enhanced (rather than diminished) by digital visual effects. See Stephen Prince, *Digital Visual Effects in Cinema: The Seduction of Reality* (New Brunswick, NJ: Rutgers University Press, 2012). Prince is interested only in the perceptual credibility of images, but I am interested in realism's political valence as well: the politically effective connection between images and the conditions of reality, including images' own unseen substrates. As I explore here and in the following section, this post-cinematic realism often in fact requires a break with perceptual realism.

59 Lazzarato, *Videophilosophie*, 78.

60 Lazzarato, *Videophilosophie*, 78.

61 Serres, *Parasite*, 14.

62 Serres, *Parasite*, 12–13.

63 Wolfe, "Bring the Noise," xiii.

64 Serres, *Parasite*, 16.

65 Regarding the generative/productive, rather than merely corrupting/negative, nature of glitches—a dimension I take to be central to an understanding of the shift from a retentional to a protentional media regime more generally—Hugh S. Manon and Daniel Temkin write: "The existence of glitch-based representation depends upon the inability of software to treat a wrong bit of data in anything other than the right way. The word 'glitch' in this sense does not solely represent the cause that initiates some failure, but also the output that results when improper data is decoded properly. An isolated problem is encountered and, rather than shutting down, the software prattles on. Stated differently, it is a given program's *failure to fully fail* upon encountering bad data that allows a glitch to appear." Hugh S. Manon and Daniel Temkin, "Notes on Glitch," *World Picture* 6 (2011), http://www.worldpicturejournal.com/WP_6/Manon.html. I am grateful to an anonymous reader for turning my attention to Manon and Temkin's fascinating article.

66 The notion of "imagined community" derives from Benedict Anderson, *Imagined Communities: Reflections on the Origin and Spread of Nationalism* (London: Verso, 1990).

67 I am referring, again, to Trevor Paglen, "Invisible Images (Your Pictures Are Looking at You)," *New Inquiry*, December 8, 2016, https://thenewinquiry.com/invisible-images-your-pictures-are-looking-at-you/.

68 Marwan M. Kraidy, "The Projectilic Image: Islamic State's Digital Visual Warfare and Global Networked Affect," *Media, Culture and Society* 39, no. 8 (2017): 1195.

69 Ingrid Hoelzl, "The Operative Image—An Approximation," *New Everyday*, February 3, 2014, http://mediacommons.org/tne/pieces/operative-image-and-approximation, quoted in Kraidy, "Projectilic Image," 1198.

70 Mark B. N. Hansen, *New Philosophy for New Media* (Cambridge, MA: MIT Press, 2006), 10, quoted in Kraidy, "Projectilic Image," 1198.

71 Harun Farocki, "Phantom Images," *Public* 29 (2004): 17, quoted in Kraidy, "Projectilic Image," 1198.

72 Kraidy, "Projectilic Image," 1199.

73 Chloé Galibert-Laîné and Kevin B. Lee, "Troubling the Desktop," *Filmmaker Magazine*, March 14, 2019, https://filmmakermagazine.com/107208-troubling-the-desktop/#.XMW-Z6RlCEc.

74 From the project description on Galibert-Laîné's website, "Bottled Songs," https://www.chloegalibertlaine.com/bottled-songs, accessed January 25, 2020. The "desktop documentary" is a form that Lee has been developing since 2014, starting with his award-winning video *Transformers: The Premake*, which probes amateur video on YouTube to piece together behind the scenes footage leading up to Michael Bay's *Transformers: Age of Extinction*. *Bottled Songs* similarly incorporates online found footage and rethinks it in a multimodal screen-based environment. The episodes discussed here were shown as a two-screen installation at festivals including the 2018 Ars Electronica Festival in Linz, Switzerland, but Galibert-Laîné and Lee have also presented live performance versions, and a feature-length documentary is forthcoming.

75 Here I am analyzing an installation version of Galibert-Laîné's video, which is 12:30 long. A slightly different version, 10:05 long, has been published with a short statement by the artist, as Chloé Galibert-Laîné, "My Crush Was a Superstar," NECSUS 6, no. 1 (2017), https://necsus-ejms.org/my-crush-was-a-superstar/.

76 At a talk/performance of another episode in the *Bottled Songs* series at Stanford's Digital Aesthetics Workshop on February 28, 2019, Lee detailed how he avoided watching an ISIS propaganda film for several months and went on to devise elaborate ways to "automate" or alienate his viewing.

77 Dallas Museum of Art, *Omer Fast: "5000 Feet Is the Best"*, summary of 2012 exhibition, accessed December 5, 2019, https://www.dma.org/art/exhibition-archive/omer-fast-5000-feet-best.

78 Thomas Stubblefield, "In Pursuit of Other Networks: Drone Art and Accelerationist Aesthetics," in *Life in the Age of Drone Warfare*, ed. Lisa Parks and Caren Kaplan (Durham, NC: Duke University Press, 2017), 204.

79 Trevor Paglen, "Invisible Images: Ethics of Autonomous Vision Systems," YouTube video, posted July 25, 2017, by AI Now Institute, https://www.youtube.com/watch?v=JZjGsaJ1OcU.

80 Stubblefield, "In Pursuit," 204.

81 Mark B. N. Hansen, "Techno-Aesthesis and Drone Vision," YouTube video, posted November 20, 2018, by Duke Franklin Humanities Institute, https://www.youtube.com/watch?v=DecsYoCbzIA. Hansen is drawing on Mark Andrejevic's notion of "drone logic," which "extends and multiplies the reach of the senses," "saturates the times and spaces in which sensing takes place," and indeed "automates the sensemaking process." Mark Andrejevic, "Becoming Drones: Smartphone Probes and Distributed Sensing," in *Locative Media*, ed. Rowan Wilken and Gerard Goggin (New York: Routledge, 2015), 196.

82 Though I was unaware of it at the time of writing, Genevieve Yue's brief engagement with Alsharif's video foregrounds similar points about it, especially regarding the manifestation of a paradoxical and politically significant manifestation of indexicality in the guise of postindexical images, as I explore below. Genevieve Yue, "Errant Pixels: The Sight Specificity of Satellite Technologies," *ASAP/Journal* 2, no. 3 (2017): 684–88.

Chapter 6. Post-cinema after Extinction

An earlier version of ideas developed in chapter 6 first appeared as "Post-cinema after Extinction," *Media Fields*, no. 13 (2018). Portions of chapter 6 also appeared as "Pre-sponsive Gestures," in *ETC Media* 110 (2017): 40–45.

1 The scientific and humanistic literature on the Anthropocene is by now extremely vast, and a thorough survey of it is beyond the scope of this chapter and the interests that I am pursuing here. A good introduction to the concept is provided by an early statement: Paul J. Crutzen and Eugene F. Stoermer, "The Anthropocene," *IGBP Newsletter* 41 (May 2000): 17–18. The concept has been criticized from many angles, including for its generalization of "the human" (the Anthropos of the Anthropocene) as a unified culprit, without respect for the racist, colonial, and exploitative histories that divide that concept. See, for example, Kathryn Yusoff, *A Billion Black Anthropocenes or None* (Minneapolis: University of Minnesota Press, 2018).

2 Richard Grusin, *Premediation: Affect and Mediality after 9/11* (New York: Palgrave Macmillan, 2010).

3 This is the title of a bestselling work of speculative nonfiction: Alan Weisman, *The World without Us* (New York: Picador, 2007). The book considers what would happen to the planet's human-made and naturally occurring environments if humans were suddenly to disappear. Several adaptations of this scenario have appeared in moving-image media as well, for example the History Channel's series *Life after People*, which aired from 2008 to 2010. As will become clear, however, I am interested not only in these types of speculative futures, but also in the ways that post-cinematic media engage in a more philosophical form of speculation—one that engages a non-anthropomorphic world that already exists, even before an extinction event: what Eugene Thacker calls "the world-without-us." Eugene Thacker, *Horror of Philosophy*, vol. 1, *In the Dust of this Planet* (Winchester, UK: Zero Books, 2011).

4 On "chaos cinema," see Matthias Stork, "Chaos Cinema: The Decline and Fall of Action Filmmaking," video essay, *Press Play*, August 22, 2011, http://blogs.indiewire.com/pressplay/video_essay_matthias_stork_calls_out_the_chaos_cinema. For a somewhat different take on the transformation of contemporary editing practices, including but not restricted to the action genre, see also Steven Shaviro, "Post-continuity: An Introduction," in *Post-cinema: Theorizing 21st-Century Film*, ed. Shane Denson and Julia Leyda (Falmer, UK: REFRAME Books, 2016), 51–64.

5 The notion of "correlationism" derives from Quentin Meillassoux, who writes: "The central notion of modern philosophy since Kant seems to be that of *correlation*. By 'correlation' we mean the idea according to which we only ever have access to the correlation between thinking and being, and never to either term considered apart from the other. We will henceforth call *correlationism* any current of thought which maintains the unsurpassable character of the correlation so defined." Quentin Meillassoux, *After Finitude: An Essay on the Necessity of Contingency* (London: Continuum, 2008), 5. It should be noted that my concept of *discorrelation*, as a media-theoretical term, is not predicated on this strong philosophical thesis; rather, it aims to describe the way the yoking of subjective perception in moving-image media has been weakened or become optional, as I argue below. As such, there is only a weak, heuristic, but nevertheless nonimaginary correspondence between the post-cinematic media theory explored here and the broad philosophical tendency of speculative realism.

6 The first iteration of this chapter's ideas were developed for the "After Extinction" conference at the Center for 21st Century Studies at the University of Wisconsin–Milwaukee in April–May 2015. It still bears the imprint of the conference's central question of what it means to be "after" extinction in multiple senses and tenses, including not only the temporal sense of "following upon" but also "taking after" extinction—such that an object might "mediate it in such a way as to resemble or be mimetic of extinction" or might "be 'after extinction' in the sense that a painting is 'after O'Keeffe' or a child 'takes after' its parent." Richard Grusin, introduction to *After Extinction*, ed. Grusin (Minneapolis: University of Minnesota Press, 2018), x.

7 Quoted in Robert T. Tally Jr., "The End-of-the-World as World System," in *Other Globes: Past and Peripheral Imaginations of Globalization*, ed. Simon Ferdinand, Irene Villaescusa-Illán, and Esther Peeren (Cham, Switzerland: Palgrave Macmillan, 2019), 267.

8 Tally, "End-of-the-World," 268.

9 Fredric Jameson, *The Seeds of Time* (New York: Columbia University Press, 1994), xii, quoted in Tally, "End-of-the-World," 268.

10 Tally, "End-of-the-World," 269.

11 Tally, "End-of-the-World," 270.

12 Tally, "End-of-the-World," 273, quoting Fredric Jameson, *The Ideologies of Theory: Essays, 1971–1986*, vol. 1, *Situations of Theory* (Minneapolis: University of Minnesota Press, 1988), xxviii.

13 Tally, "End-of-the-World," 278.

14 Vivian Sobchack, "The Scene of the Screen: Envisioning Photographic, Cinematic, and Electronic 'Presence,'" in Denson and Leyda, *Post-cinema*, 88–128.

15 Fredric Jameson, "Postmodernism, or, The Cultural Logic of Late Capitalism," *New Left Review* 1, no. 146 (1984): 77, quoted in Sobchack, "Scene," 94.

16 Sobchack, "Scene," 95.

17 Sobchack, "Scene," 96; emphasis in original.

18 Sobchack, "Scene," 97.

19 Sobchack, "Scene," 99.

20 See Roland Barthes, *Camera Lucida: Reflections on Photography*, trans. Richard Howard (New York: Hill and Wang, 1981).

21 Sobchack, "Scene," 101.

22 See Tom Gunning, "An Aesthetic of Astonishment: Early Film and the (In)Credulous Spectator," in *Viewing Positions: Ways of Seeing Film*, ed. Linda Williams (New Brunswick, NJ: Rutgers University Press, 1995), 114–33. Evan Calder Williams revisits this episode in the context of an argument, very much in tune with the one I am making here, about the dynamics and tensions involved in the emergence of "new" media. Evan Calder Williams, *Shard Cinema* (London: Repeater Books, 2017), 59–63.

23 On sausage films and their relations to cinema's preservation and reanimation of the living, see Shane Denson, *Postnaturalism: Frankenstein, Film, and the Anthropotechnical Interface* (Bielefeld, Germany: Transcript Verlag, 2014), 77–85.

24 Sobchack, "Scene," 107.

25 Sobchack, "Scene," 102; emphasis in original.

26 See Maurice Merleau-Ponty, *Phenomenology of Perception*, trans. Colin Smith (New York: Routledge, 2002).

27 Sobchack, "Scene," 108.

28 Sobchack, "Scene," 107.

29 Sobchack, "Scene," 107. We might add that this collective subjectivity is correlated with a collective object, and thus the photograph's focus on individual death gives way to a focus on the life of the masses. For more on this point, see Siegfried Kracauer, *The Mass Ornament: Weimar Essays*, trans. Thomas Y. Levin (Cambridge, MA: Harvard University Press, 1995); Anton Kaes, "Movies and Masses," in *Crowds*, ed. Jeffrey T. Schnapp and Matthew Tiews (Stanford, CA: Stanford University Press, 2006), 149–57.

30 Sobchack, "Scene," 108.

31 Sobchack, "Scene," 115.

32 Sobchack, "Scene," 115.

33 Sobchack, "Scene," 117.

34 Martin Heidegger, *Being and Time*, trans. Joan Stambaugh (Albany: State University of New York Press, 1996), 243.

35 Daniel Ross, "Moving Images of the Anthropocene: Rethinking Cinema beyond Anthropology," *Screening the Past* 44 (2019), http://www.screeningthepast.com/2019/03/moving-images-of-the-anthropocene-rethinking-cinema-beyond-anthropology/.

36 Ross, "Moving Images," n.p.

37 Ross, "Moving Images," n.p.

38 Vivian Sobchack, "From Screen-Scape to Screen-Sphere: A Meditation in Medias Res," in *Screens: From Materiality to Spectatorship*, ed. Dominique Chateau and José Moure (Amsterdam: Amsterdam University Press, 2016), 157–75.

39 Ross is drawing on recent media-theoretical interest in the Greek *pharmakon*, a concept that features prominently in the discussion of writing, as something that alternately extends and diminishes memory, in Plato's *Phaedrus*. The *pharmakon*, which refers to both medicine and poison, has been taken up by Jacques Derrida, "Plato's Pharmacy," in *Dissemination*, trans. Barbara Johnson (Chicago: University of Chicago Press, 1981), 63–171; Bernard Stiegler, *What Makes Life Worth Living: On Pharmacology* (Cambridge: Polity, 2010); and Mark B. N. Hansen, *Feed-Forward: On the Future of Twenty-First-Century Media* (Chicago: University of Chicago Press, 2015). With reference to devices that "screen to" and "screen from," Ross is additionally connecting these reflections on the *pharmakon* to Cavell's thinking about duality of screen in Stanley Cavell, *The World Viewed: Reflections on the Ontology of Film*, enlarged ed. (Cambridge, MA: Harvard University Press, 1979).

40 Ross, "Moving Images," n.p.

41 Ross, "Moving Images," n.p.

42 Ross, "Moving Images," n.p.

43 Marx uses the term *Stoffwechsel* (metabolism) to describe various processes of circulation within capitalism, including labor as "an eternal natural necessity which mediates the metabolism between man and nature, and therefore human life itself." Karl Marx, *Capital*, vol. 1, trans. Ben Fowkes (New York: Penguin, 1976), 133. Elsewhere, he writes of an "irreparable rift in the interdependent process of social metabolism, a metabolism prescribed by the natural laws of life itself." Karl Marx, *Capital*, vol. 3, trans. David Fernbach (New York: Penguin, 1981), 949. Recent ecologically oriented commentators have taken these remarks as the basis for "metabolic rift theory," or the notion that Marx sees capitalism as precipitating ecological crises, such as those associated with the Anthropocene. See, for example, John Bellamy Foster, "Marx's Theory of Metabolic Rift: Classical Foundations for Environmental Sociology," *American Journal of Sociology* 105, no. 2 (1999): 366–405. For critical responses, see Jason W. Moore, "Transcending the Metabolic Rift: A Theory of Crises in the Capitalist World-Ecology," *Journal of Peasant Studies* 38, no. 1 (2011): 1–46; Jason W. Moore, "The Capitalocene, Part I: On the Nature and Origins of Our Ecological Crisis," *Journal of Peasant Studies* 44, vol. 3 (2017): 594–630.

44 My thinking about these images is indebted to Max Symuleski, "Earth, World, and Globe: Phenomenological Considerations of the Contemporary Planetary Landscape," *Widok: Teorie i praktyki kultury wizualnej* 8 (2014), http://widok.hmfactory.com/index.php/one/article/view/222/458.

45 The reference is to Heidegger's "The Age of the World Picture," published in the 1952 *Holzwege* under the title "Die Zeit des Weltbildes," and based on a lecture originally delivered in 1938—many years before a literal picture of the planet would appear. The text appears in English as Martin Heidegger, "The Age of the World

Picture," in *The Question concerning Technology and Other Essays*, trans. William Lovitt (New York: Garland, 1977), 115–154.

46 Martin Heidegger, "'Only a God Can Save Us': The *Spiegel* Interview (1966)," trans. William J. Richardson, in *Heidegger: The Man and the Thinker*, ed. Thomas Sheehan (Chicago: Precedent Press, 1981), 56.

47 Kristen Whissel provides a valuable and detailed close reading of the prologue in Whissel, *Spectacular Digital Effects: CGI and Contemporary Cinema* (Durham, NC: Duke University Press, 2014), 175–83.

48 Peter Szendy, *Apocalypse-Cinema: 2012 and Other Ends of the World*, trans. Will Bishop (New York: Fordham University Press, 2015), 2. Similar to Szendy, Richard Grusin comments that "when the planet crashes into earth at film's end, the apocalypse of the cinematic narrative is also colliding with the apocalypse of the cinematic apparatus" and thus marks "the collision or co-incidence of the trajectory of the film's diegesis with its cinematic presentation, the apocalyptic collision that has been the condition of cinema from its inception." Richard Grusin, "Post-cinematic Atavism," in Denson and Leyda, *Post-cinema*, 659.

49 For a fuller treatment of *Melancholia* in the contexts of post-cinema and the eclipse of anthropocentric perspectives, see Steven Shaviro, "*Melancholia* or, the Romantic Anti-sublime," *Sequence* 1, no. 1 (2002), http://reframe.sussex.ac.uk/sequence1/1-1-melancholia-or-the-romantic-anti-sublime/; Grusin, "Post-cinematic Atavism"; and Elena del Río's chapter "Extinction" in *The Grace of Destruction: A Vital Ethology of Extreme Cinemas* (New York: Bloomsbury, 2016), 197–215.

50 Symuleski, "Earth, World, and Globe."

51 See Hansen, *Feed-Forward*.

52 The task of formulating a posthuman ethics along these lines—in terms of entanglement and the like—has been undertaken by Donna Haraway, Karen Barad, Cary Wolfe, Rosi Braidotti, and others. I have learned a great deal from these attempts, and I hope that my modest effort to put such impulses into contact with our contemporary media environment contributes something to that general undertaking. See, for example, Donna J. Haraway, *Simians, Cyborgs, and Women: The Reinvention of Nature* (New York: Routledge, 1991); Karen Barad, *Meeting the Universe Halfway: Quantum Physics and the Entanglement of Matter and Meaning* (Durham, NC: Duke University Press, 2007); Cary Wolfe, *What Is Posthumanism?* (Minneapolis: University of Minnesota Press, 2010); Rosi Braidotti, "Posthuman Critical Theory," *Journal of Posthuman Studies* 1, no. 1 (2017): 9–25.

53 See, in particular, Selmin Kara, "Anthropocenema: Cinema in the Age of Mass Extinctions," in Denson and Leyda, *Post-cinema*, 750–84.

54 Kara, "Anthropocenema," 771.

55 Kara, "Anthropocenema," 752.

56 Kara, "Anthropocenema," 765.

57 Meillassoux, *After Finitude*, 5.

58 Meillassoux, *After Finitude*, 26.

59 Meillassoux, *After Finitude*, 10.

60 Meillassoux, *After Finitude*, 112.

61 Szendy, *Apocalypse-Cinema*, 134. This notion of a subject-less image also resonates with the nonperceptual phenomenology proposed in Mark B. N. Hansen, "Algorithmic Sensibility: Reflections on the Post-perceptual Image," in Denson and Leyda, *Post-cinema*, 785–816.

62 Jacques Lacan, *The Seminar of Jacques Lacan*, book 2, *The Ego in Freud's Theory and in the Technique of Psychoanalysis, 1954–1955*, trans. Sylvana Tomaselli (New York: Norton, 1991), 46, quoted in Szendy, *Apocalypse-Cinema*, 134–35.

63 Szendy, *Apocalypse-Cinema*, 135.

64 See, for example, the tiny camera produced by Seattle-based startup Xnor, featured in James Vincent, "This Wireless AI Camera Runs Entirely on Solar Power," *The Verge*, February 15, 2019, https://www.theverge.com/circuitbreaker/2019/2/15/18225972/tiny-solar-powered-ai-camera-xnor.

65 Event Horizon Telescope Collaboration, "First M87 Event Horizon Telescope Results. IV. Imaging the Central Supermassive Black Hole," *Astrophysical Journal Letters* 875, no. 1 (2019), https://iopscience.iop.org/article/10.3847/2041-8213/ab0e85.

66 I am borrowing the notion of the "action-image" from Deleuze but taking it in a very different direction. For Deleuze, the action-image seems to be more about correlation than discorrelation, and the "crisis" into which it falls in the postwar period is wrapped up with a loss of faith in meaningful action. See Gilles Deleuze, *Cinema 1: The Movement-Image*, trans. Hugh Tomlinson and Barbara Habberjam (Minneapolis: University of Minnesota Press, 1986).

67 Average reported gameplay durations for a variety of play styles are listed here: "*NieR:Automata*," HowLongToBeat, last updated December 11, 2019, https://howlongtobeat.com/game.php?id=38029.

68 Wikipedia describes the phenomenon of "screen tearing" thus: "Screen tearing is a visual artifact in video display where a display device shows information from multiple frames in a single screen draw. The artifact occurs when the video feed to the device is not in sync with the display's refresh rate. . . . During video motion, screen tearing creates a torn look as edges of objects (such as a wall or a tree) fail to line up." Wikipedia, s.v. "Screen Tearing," accessed July 4, 2019, https://en.wikipedia.org/wiki/Screen_tearing.

69 The gravitas of self-sacrifice in *NieR:Automata* might be compared to the phenomenon of "permadeath," where the player is not allowed to respawn after dying, but with a significant shift of responsibility from the individual to the collective in the light of global extinction. On "permadeath," see, for example, Ben Griffin, "Why Permadeath Is Alive and Well in Video Games," *Gamesradar+*, March 7, 2014, https://www.gamesradar.com/why-permadeath-just-wont-die-video-games/; Marcus Carter and Fraser Allison, "Fear, Loss and Meaningful Play: Permadeath in *DayZ*," *Journal of Gaming and Virtual Worlds* 9, no. 2 (2017): 143–58.

70 Mark B. N. Hansen, "Media Theory," *Theory, Culture and Society* 23, nos. 2–3 (2006): 299.

71 "Capture," Chatonsky.net, accessed December 11, 2019, http://chatonsky.net/capture/.

72 "Capture Manifesto," Chatonsky.net, accessed December 11, 2019, https://chatonsky.net/capture-manifesto/.

73 See, for example, Jemima Kiss, "Google Admits Collecting Wi-Fi Data through Street View Cars," *Guardian*, May 15, 2010, https://www.theguardian.com/technology/2010/may/15/google-admits-storing-private-data; David Kravets, "An Intentional Mistake: The Anatomy of Google's Wi-Fi Sniffing Debacle," *Wired*, May 2, 2012, https://www.wired.com/2012/05/google-wifi-fcc-investigation/; Kevin Poulsen, "Google Takes Wi-Fi Snooping Scandal to the Supreme Court," *Wired*, April 1, 2014, https://www.wired.com/2014/04/threatlevel_0401_streetview/.

74 On photogrammetry, see, for example, Karl Kraus, *Photogrammetry: Geometry from Images and Laser Scans*, 2nd ed., trans. Ian Harley and Stephen Kyle (Berlin: Walter de Gruyter, 2007); Wilfried Linder, *Digital Photogrammetry: A Practical Course* (Berlin: Springer, 2016).

75 "The Watson Emotion Watching Vertigo," Chatonsky.net, accessed December 11, 2019, http://chatonsky.net/watson-vertigo/.

BIBLIOGRAPHY

Aarseth, Espen. "Aporia and Epiphany in *Doom* and *The Speaking Clock*: The Temporality of Ergodic Art." In *Cyberspace Textuality: Computer Technology and Literary Theory*, edited by Marie-Laure Ryan, 31–41. Bloomington: Indiana University Press, 1999.

Aftab, Kaleem. "Alex Garland's 'Ex Machina' Delivers a Modern Day Twist on Frankenstein." *IndieWire*, April 7, 2015. https://www.indiewire.com/2015/04/review-alex-garlands-ex-machina-delivers-a-modern-day-twist-on-frankenstein-63410/.

Alexander, Neta. "Catered to Your Future Self: Netflix's 'Predictive Personalization' and the Mathematization of Taste." In *The Netflix Effect: Technology and Entertainment in the 21st Century*, edited by Kevin McDonald and Daniel Smith-Rowsey, 81–97. New York: Bloomsbury, 2016.

Alexander, Neta. "Rage against the Machine: Buffering, Noise, and Perpetual Anxiety in the Age of Connected Viewing." *Cinema Journal* 56, no. 2 (2017): 1–24.

Amatriain, Xavier, and Justin Basilico. "Netflix Recommendations: Beyond the 5 Stars (Part 1)." *Netflix Tech Blog*, April 6, 2012. https://medium.com/netflix-techblog/netflix-recommendations-beyond-the-5-stars-part-1-55838468f429.

Anderson, Benedict. *Imagined Communities: Reflections on the Origin and Spread of Nationalism*. London: Verso, 1990.

Andrejevic, Mark. "Becoming Drones: Smartphone Probes and Distributed Sensing." In *Locative Media*, edited by Rowan Wilken and Gerard Goggin, 193–207. New York: Routledge, 2015.

Barad, Karen. *Meeting the Universe Halfway: Quantum Physics and the Entanglement of Matter and Meaning*. Durham, NC: Duke University Press, 2007.

Barthes, Roland. *Camera Lucida: Reflections on Photography*. Translated by Richard Howard. New York: Hill and Wang, 1981.

Belton, John. "If Film Is Dead, What Is Cinema?" *Screen* 55, no. 4 (2014): 460–70.

Benjamin, Walter. *The Work of Art in the Age of Its Technological Reproducibility, and Other Writings on Media*. Edited by Michael W. Jennings, Brigid Doherty, and Thomas Y. Levin. Cambridge, MA: Harvard University Press, 2008.

Benson-Allott, Caetlin. *Killer Tapes and Shattered Screens: Video Spectatorship from VHS to File Sharing*. Berkeley: University of California Press, 2013.

Bentaleb, Abdelhak, Bayan Taani, Ali C. Bergen, Christian Timmerer, and Roger Zimmermann. "A Survey on Bitrate Adaptation Schemes for Streaming Media over HTTP." *IEEE Communications Surveys and Tutorials* 21, no. 1 (2019): 562–85. https://ieeexplore.ieee.org/document/8424813.

Bergson, Henri. *Matter and Memory*. Translated by N. M. Paul and W. S. Palmer. New York: Cosimo, 2007.

Biggs, John. "Help Key: Why 120Hz Looks 'Weird.'" *TechCrunch*, August 12, 2009. http://techcrunch.com/2009/08/12/help-key-why-hd-video-looks-weird/.
Bogost, Ian. *Alien Phenomenology, or What It's Like to Be a Thing*. Minneapolis: University of Minnesota Press, 2012.
Bordwell, David. "Intensified Continuity: Visual Style in Contemporary American Film." *Film Quarterly* 55, no. 3 (2002): 16–28.
Bordwell, David, Janet Staiger, and Kristin Thompson. *The Classical Hollywood Cinema: Film Style and Mode of Production to 1960*. New York: Columbia University Press, 1985.
Bozak, Nadia. *The Cinematic Footprint: Lights, Camera, Natural Resources*. New Brunswick, NJ: Rutgers University Press, 2011.
Braidotti, Rosi. "Posthuman Critical Theory." *Journal of Posthuman Studies* 1, no. 1 (2017): 9–25.
Branigan, Edward. "Formal Permutations of the Point-of-View Shot." *Screen* 16, no. 3 (1975): 54–64.
Bridle, James. "Something Is Wrong on the Internet." *Medium*, November 6, 2017. https://medium.com/@jamesbridle/something-is-wrong-on-the-internet-c39c471271d2.
Brinker, Felix. "On the Political Economy of the Contemporary (Superhero) Blockbuster Series." In Denson and Leyda, *Post-cinema*, 433–73.
Broad, Terence. "Autoencoding *Blade Runner*: Reconstructing Films with Artificial Neural Networks." *Medium*, May 24, 2016. https://medium.com/@terencebroad/autoencoding-blade-runner-88941213abbe.
Broad, Terence. "Autoencoding Video Frames." MSci diss., Goldsmiths, University of London, 2016.
Brown, William. *Supercinema: Film-Philosophy for the Digital Age*. New York: Berghahn, 2013.
Bryant, Levi. *The Democracy of Objects*. Ann Arbor, MI: Open Humanities Press, 2011.
Bukatman, Scott. "Why I Hate Superhero Movies." *Cinema Journal* 50, no. 3 (2011): 118–22.
Butler, Blake. "These Short Films Will Self-Destruct After You Watch Them." *Vice*, May 13, 2016. https://www.vice.com/en_us/article/jmke8y/guy-maddin-fills-the-internet-with-haunted-films.
Campo-Rembado, Miguel, and Sona Oakley. "How 20th Century Fox Uses ML to Predict a Movie Audience." *Google Cloud*, October 29, 2018. https://cloud.google.com/blog/products/ai-machine-learning/how-20th-century-fox-uses-ml-to-predict-a-movie-audience.
Cannon, Tony. "Fight the Lag: The Trick behind GGPO's Low-Latency Netcode." *Game Developer Magazine* 19, no. 9 (2012): 7–13.
Carter, Marcus, and Fraser Allison. "Fear, Loss and Meaningful Play: Permadeath in *DayZ*." *Journal of Gaming and Virtual Worlds* 9, no. 2 (2017): 143–58.
Casetti, Francesco. *The Lumière Galaxy: Seven Key Words for the Cinema to Come*. New York: Columbia University Press, 2015.
Casetti, Francesco. "The Relocation of Cinema." *NECSUS: European Journal of Media Studies* 1, no. 2 (Autumn 2012): 5–34.

Cavell, Stanley. *The World Viewed: Reflections on the Ontology of Film*. Enlarged ed. Cambridge, MA: Harvard University Press, 1979.

Chen, Zhenzhong, Weisi Lin, and King Ngi Ngan. "Perceptual Video Coding: Challenges and Approaches." *Proceedings of IEEE International Conference on Multimedia and Expo* (2010): 784–89.

Chesney, Robert, and Danielle Keats Citron. "Deep Fakes: A Looming Challenge for Privacy, Democracy, and National Security." *California Law Review* 107 (2019). Preprint: https://papers.ssrn.com/sol3/papers.cfm?abstract_id=3213954.

Cholodenko, Alan. "Introduction." In *The Illusion of Life*, edited by Alan Cholodenko, 9–36. Sydney: Power Publications, 1991.

Chun, Wendy Hui Kyong. *Control and Freedom: Power and Paranoia in the Age of Fiber Optics*. Cambridge, MA: MIT Press, 2006.

Cole, Samantha. "AI-Assisted Fake Porn Is Here and We're All Fucked." *Motherboard*, December 11, 2017. https://motherboard.vice.com/en_us/article/gydydm/gal-gadot-fake-ai-porn.

Crafton, Donald. *The Talkies: American Cinema's Transition to Sound, 1926–1931*. Berkeley: University of California Press, 1997.

Crutzen, Paul J., and Eugene F. Stoermer. "The Anthropocene." *IGBP Newsletter* 41 (May 2000): 17–18.

Cubitt, Sean. *The Cinema Effect*. Cambridge, MA: MIT Press, 2004.

Cubitt, Sean. *The Practice of Light: A Genealogy of Visual Technologies from Print to Pixels*. Cambridge, MA: MIT Press, 2014.

Dallas Museum of Art. *Omer Fast: "5000 Feet Is the Best."* Summary of 2012 exhibition, accessed December 5, 2019. https://www.dma.org/art/exhibition-archive/omer-fast-5000-feet-best.

Dayan, Daniel. "The Tutor-Code of Classical Cinema." *Film Quarterly* 28, no. 1 (1974): 22–31.

Deleuze, Gilles. *Cinema 1: The Movement-Image*. Translated by Hugh Tomlinson and Barbara Habberjam. Minneapolis: University of Minnesota Press, 1986.

Deleuze, Gilles. *Cinema 2: The Time-Image*. Translated by Hugh Tomlinson and Robert Galeta. Minneapolis: University of Minnesota Press, 1989.

Deleuze, Gilles. *Difference and Repetition*. Translated by Paul Patton. New York: Columbia University Press, 1994.

Deleuze, Gilles. "Postscript on the Societies of Control." *October*, no. 59 (1992): 3–7.

Del Río, Elena. "Cinema's Exhaustion and the Vitality of Affect." *In Media Res*, August 29, 2011. http://mediacommons.org/imr/2011/08/19/cinemas-exhaustion-and-vitality-affect. Reprinted in "Post-cinematic Affect: A Conversation in Five Parts," in Denson and Leyda, *Post-cinema*, 879–932.

Del Río, Elena. *The Grace of Destruction: A Vital Ethology of Extreme Cinemas*. New York: Bloomsbury, 2016.

Denson, Shane. "Marvel Comics' Frankenstein: A Case Study in the Media of Serial Figures." *Amerikastudien* 56, no. 4 (2011): 531–53.

Denson, Shane. *Postnaturalism: Frankenstein, Film, and the Anthropotechnical Interface*. Bielefeld, Germany: Transcript Verlag, 2014.

Denson, Shane. "Sight and Sound Conspire: Monstrous Audio-Vision in James Whale's *Frankenstein*." *[in]Transition* 2, no. 4 (2016). http://mediacommons.org/intransition/sight-and-sound-conspire.

Denson, Shane. "Tarzan und der Tonfilm: Verhandlungen zwischen 'Science' und 'Fiction.'" In *"Ich Tarzan": Affenmenschen und Menschenaffen zwischen Science und Fiction*, edited by Gesine Krüger, Ruth Mayer, and Marianne Sommer, 113–30. Bielefeld, Germany: Transcript Verlag, 2008.

Denson, Shane, Therese Grisham, and Julia Leyda. "Post-cinematic Affect: Post-continuity, the Irrational Camera, Thoughts on 3D." *La Furia Umana* 14 (2012). Reprinted in Denson and Leyda, *Post-cinema*, 933–75.

Denson, Shane, and Julia Leyda, eds. *Post-cinema: Theorizing 21st-Century Film*. Falmer, UK: REFRAME Books, 2016. https://reframe.sussex.ac.uk/post-cinema/. Paginated PDF at https://reframe.sussex.ac.uk/wp-content/uploads/2019/05/POST-CINEMA_LO_RES.pdf.

Denson, Shane, and Ruth Mayer. "Border-Crossings: Serial Figures and the Evolution of Media." *NECSUS: European Journal of Media Studies* 7, no. 2 (2018): 65–84. http://dx.doi.org/10.25969/mediarep/3460.

Denson, Shane, and Ruth Mayer. "Spectral Seriality: The Sights and Sounds of Count Dracula." In *Media of Serial Narrative*, edited by Frank Kelleter, 108–24. Columbus: Ohio State University Press, 2017.

Derrida, Jacques. "Différance." In *Margins of Philosophy*, translated by Alan Bass, 3–27. Chicago: University of Chicago Press, 1982.

Derrida, Jacques. "Plato's Pharmacy." In *Dissemination*, translated by Barbara Johnson, 63–171. Chicago: University of Chicago Press, 1981.

Derrida, Jacques. *Spectres of Marx: The State of the Debt, the Work of Mourning, and the New International*. Translated by Peggy Kamuf. New York: Routledge, 1994.

Doane, Mary Ann. "The Indexical and the Concept of Medium Specificity." *Differences* 18, no. 1 (2007): 128–52.

Edelman, Lee. *No Future: Queer Theory and the Death Drive*. Durham, NC: Duke University Press, 2004.

Emerson, Jim. "Agents of Chaos." *Scanners*, August 23, 2011. http://www.rogerebert.com/scanners/agents-of-chaos.

Ernst, Wolfgang. *Chronopoetics: The Temporal Being and Operativity of Technological Media*. Translated by Anthony Enns. New York: Rowman and Littlefield, 2016.

Ernst, Wolfgang. "A Close Reading of the Electronic 'Time Image.'" In Ernst, *Chronopoetics*, 123–71.

Ernst, Wolfgang. "Time-Critical Media Processes." In Ernst, *Chronopoetics*, 3–14.

Eschrich, Joey. "How *Frankenstein*'s Monster Became Sexy." *Slate*, January 24, 2017. https://slate.com/technology/2017/01/why-frankenstein-adaptations-now-make-the-monster-sexy.html.

Event Horizon Telescope Collaboration. "First M87 Event Horizon Telescope Results. IV. Imaging the Central Supermassive Black Hole." *Astrophysical Journal Letters* 875, no. 1 (2019). https://iopscience.iop.org/article/10.3847/2041-8213/ab0e85.

Farocki, Harun. "Phantom Images." *Public* 29 (2004): 12–22.
Fay, Jennifer. *Inhospitable World: Cinema in the Time of the Anthropocene*. New York: Oxford University Press, 2018.
Finn, Ed. *What Algorithms Want: Imagination in the Age of Computing*. Cambridge, MA: MIT Press, 2017.
Flückiger, Barbara. *Visual Effects: Filmbilder aus dem Computer*. Marburg, Germany: Schüren, 2008.
Forry, Steven Earl. *Hideous Progenies: Dramatizations of* Frankenstein *from the Nineteenth Century to the Present*. Philadelphia: University of Pennsylvania Press, 1990.
Fossati, Giovanna. *From Grain to Pixel: The Archival Life of Film in Transition*. Amsterdam: Amsterdam University Press, 2009.
Foster, John Bellamy. "Marx's Theory of Metabolic Rift: Classical Foundations for Environmental Sociology." *American Journal of Sociology* 105, no. 2 (1999): 366–405.
Freud, Sigmund. *The Uncanny*. Translated by David McLintock. London: Penguin Books, 2003.
Galibert-Laîné, Chloé. "My Crush Was a Superstar." *NECSUS* 6, no. 1 (2017). https://necsus-ejms.org/my-crush-was-a-superstar/.
Galibert-Laîné, Chloé, and Kevin B. Lee. "Troubling the Desktop." *Filmmaker Magazine*, March 14, 2019. https://filmmakermagazine.com/107208-troubling-the-desktop/#.XMW-Z6RlCEc.
Galloway, Alexander. "Social Realism." In *Gaming: Essays on Algorithmic Culture*, 70–84. Minneapolis: University of Minnesota Press, 2006.
Gault, Matthew. "Netflix Has Saved Every Choice You Made in 'Black Mirror: Bandersnatch.'" *Motherboard*, February 12, 2019. https://www.vice.com/en_us/article/j57gkk/netflix-has-saved-every-choice-youve-ever-made-in-black-mirror-bandersnatch.
Genkin, Daniel, Adi Shamir, and Eran Tromer. "Acoustic Cryptanalysis." *Journal of Cryptology* 30, no. 2 (2017): 392–443.
Gills, Melina. "Guy Maddin and Collaborators on Reviving Dead Cinema for the Tribeca 2016 Installation SEANCES." *Tribeca*, April 14, 2016. https://www.tribecafilm.com/stories/interview-guy-maddin-seances-virtual-reality-tribeca-film-festival-storyscapes-installation.
Goh, Annie. "Appropriating the Alien: A Critique of Xenofeminism." *Mute*, July 29, 2019. http://www.metamute.org/editorial/articles/appropriating-alien-critique-xenofeminism.
Goodfellow, Ian J., Jean Pouget-Abadie, Mehdi Mirza, Bing Xu, David Warde-Farley, Sherjil Ozair, Aaron Courville, and Yoshua Bengio. "Generative Adversarial Nets." *Advances in Neural Information Processing Systems* (2014). http://papers.nips.cc/paper/5423-generative-adversarial-nets.pdf.
Greenberg, Andy. "Triple Meltdown: How So Many Researchers Found a 20-Year-Old Chip Flaw at the Same Time." *Wired*, January 7, 2018. https://www.wired.com/story/meltdown-spectre-bug-collision-intel-chip-flaw-discovery/.
Griffin, Ben. "Why Permadeath Is Alive and Well in Video Games." *Gamesradar+*, March 7, 2014. https://www.gamesradar.com/why-permadeath-just-wont-die-video-games/.

Grisham, Therese, Julia Leyda, Nicholas Rombes, and Steven Shaviro. "The Post-cinematic in *Paranormal Activity* and *Paranormal Activity 2*." *La Furia Umana* 10 (2011). Reprinted in Denson and Leyda, *Post-cinema*, 841–78.
Grusin, Richard. "Introduction." In *After Extinction*, edited by Richard Grusin, vii–xix. Minneapolis: University of Minnesota Press, 2018.
Grusin, Richard. "Post-cinematic Atavism." In Denson and Leyda, *Post-cinema*, 646–65.
Grusin, Richard. *Premediation: Affect and Mediality after 9/11*. New York: Palgrave Macmillan, 2010.
Gumbrecht, Hans Ulrich, and K. Ludwig Pfeiffer, eds. *Materialities of Communication*. Stanford, CA: Stanford University Press, 1994.
Gunning, Tom. "An Aesthetic of Astonishment: Early Film and the (In)Credulous Spectator." In *Viewing Positions: Ways of Seeing Film*, edited by Linda Williams, 114–33. New Brunswick, NJ: Rutgers University Press, 1995.
Gunning, Tom. "The Cinema of Attraction: Early Film, Its Spectator and the Avant-Garde." *Wide Angle* 8, nos. 3–4 (1986): 63–70.
Gunning, Tom. "What's the Point of an Index? or, Faking Photographs." In *Still Moving: Between Cinema and Photography*, edited by Karen Beckman and Jean Ma, 23–40. Durham, NC: Duke University Press, 2008.
Hadjioannou, Markos. *From Light to Byte: Toward an Ethics of Digital Cinema*. Minneapolis: University of Minnesota Press, 2012.
Haine, Charles. "Why Is That Weird Short Film 'Meridian' on Netflix?" *No Film School*, October 20, 2016. https://nofilmschool.com/2016/10/meridian-netflix-imf-streaming.
Hansen, Mark B. N. "Algorithmic Sensibility: Reflections on the Post-perceptual Image." In Denson and Leyda, *Post-cinema*, 785–816.
Hansen, Mark B. N. *Feed-Forward: On the Future of Twenty-First-Century Media*. Chicago: University of Chicago Press, 2015.
Hansen, Mark B. N. "Living (with) Technical Time: From Media Surrogacy to Distributed Cognition." *Theory, Culture and Society* 26, nos. 2–3 (2009): 294–315.
Hansen, Mark B. N. "Media Theory." *Theory, Culture and Society* 23, nos. 2–3 (2006): 297–306.
Hansen, Mark B. N. *New Philosophy for New Media*. Cambridge, MA: MIT Press, 2006.
Hansen, Mark B. N. "'Realtime Synthesis' and the Différance of the Body: Technocultural Studies in the Wake of Deconstruction." *Culture Machine* 6 (2004). http://www.culturemachine.net/index.php/cm/article/view/9/8.
Hansen, Mark B. N. "Techno-Aesthesis and Drone Vision." YouTube video, posted November 20, 2018, by Duke Franklin Humanities Institute. https://www.youtube.com/watch?v=DecsYoCbzIA.
Hansen, Mark B. N. "Ubiquitous Sensation: Toward an Atmospheric, Collective, and Microtemporal Model of Media." In *Throughout: Art and Culture Emerging with Ubiquitous Computing*, edited by Ulrik Ekman, 63–88. Cambridge, MA: MIT Press, 2012.
Hansen, Miriam. *Babel and Babylon: Spectatorship in American Silent Film*. Cambridge, MA: Harvard University Press, 1991.

Haraway, Donna J. "A Cyborg Manifesto: Science, Technology, and Socialist-Feminism in the Late Twentieth Century." In *Simians, Cyborgs, and Women: The Reinvention of Nature*, 149–81. New York: Routledge, 1991.

Haraway, Donna J. *Simians, Cyborgs, and Women: The Reinvention of Nature*. New York: Routledge, 1991.

Hardt, Michael. "Affective Labor." *boundary 2* 26, no. 2 (1999): 89–100.

Harman, Graham. *The Quadruple Object*. Winchester, UK: Zero Books, 2011.

Harris, Neil. *Humbug: The Art of P. T. Barnum*. Chicago: University of Chicago Press, 1973.

Harwell, Drew. "Fake-Porn Videos Are Being Weaponized to Harass and Humiliate Women: 'Everybody Is a Potential Target.'" *Washington Post*, December 30, 2018. https://www.washingtonpost.com/technology/2018/12/30/fake-porn-videos-are-being-weaponized-harass-humiliate-women-everybody-is-potential-target.

Hayles, N. Katherine. "Can Computers Create Meaning? A Cyber-Bio-Semiotic Perspective." Paper presented at the Digital Aesthetics Workshop, Stanford Humanities Center, Stanford, CA, February 12, 2019.

Hayles, N. Katherine. *How We Became Posthuman: Virtual Bodies in Cybernetics, Literature, and Informatics*. Chicago: University of Chicago Press, 1999.

Hayles, N. Katherine. *Unthought: The Power of the Cognitive Nonconscious*. Chicago: University of Chicago Press, 2017.

Heidegger, Martin. "The Age of the World Picture." In *The Question concerning Technology and Other Essays*, translated by William Lovitt, 115–54. New York: Garland, 1977.

Heidegger, Martin. *Being and Time*. Translated by Joan Stambaugh. Albany: State University of New York Press, 1996.

Heidegger, Martin. *Being and Time*. Translated by John Macquarrie and Edward Robinson. New York: Harper and Row, 1962.

Heidegger, Martin. *Kant and the Problem of Metaphysics*. 5th, enlarged ed. Translated by Richard Taft. Bloomington: Indiana University Press, 1997.

Heidegger, Martin. "'Only a God Can Save Us': The *Spiegel* Interview (1966)." Translated by William J. Richardson. In *Heidegger: The Man and the Thinker*, edited by Thomas Sheehan, 45–67. Chicago: Precedent Press, 1981.

Heider, Fritz. *Ding und Medium*. Berlin: Kulturverlag Kadmos, 2005.

Hero of Alexandria. *The Pneumatics of Hero of Alexandria*. Translated and edited by Bennet Woodcroft. London: Charles Whittingham, 1851.

Hester, Helen. *Xenofeminism*. Cambridge: Polity, 2018.

Hoelzl, Ingrid. "The Operative Image—An Approximation." *New Everyday*, February 3, 2014. http://mediacommons.org/tne/pieces/operative-image-and-approximation.

Hsieh, Cheng-Kang, Miguel Campo, Abhinav Taliyan, Matt Nickens, Mitkumar Pandya, and J. J. Espinoza. "Convolutional Collaborative Filter Networks for Video Based Recommendation Systems." Submitted on October 18, 2018; last revised October 22, 2018. Preprint: https://arxiv.org/abs/1810.08189.

Huhtamo, Erkki, and Jussi Parikka, eds. *Media Archaeology: Approaches, Applications, and Implications*. Berkeley: University of California Press, 2011.

Hui, Jonathan. "How Deep Learning Fakes Videos (Deepfake) and How to Detect It?" *Medium*, April 28, 2018. https://medium.com/@jonathan_hui/how-deep-learning-fakes-videos-deepfakes-and-how-to-detect-it-c0b50fbf7cb9.

Hui, Yuk. *On the Existence of Digital Objects*. Minneapolis: University of Minnesota Press, 2016.

Husserl, Edmund. *Ideas: General Introduction to Pure Phenomenology*. Translated by W. R. Boyce Gibson. New York: Routledge, 2012.

Husserl, Edmund. *On the Phenomenology of the Consciousness of Internal Time*. Translated by John Barnett Brough. Dordrecht, Netherlands: Kluwer Academic, 1991.

Husserl, Edmund. *The Phenomenology of Internal Time Consciousness*. Translated by James Churchill. Bloomington: Indiana University Press, 1964.

Ihde, Don. *Ironic Technics*. Copenhagen: Automatic Press, 2008.

Ihde, Don. *Postphenomenology—Again?* Working Papers from the Centre for STS Studies. Aarhus: University of Aarhus, 2003.

Ihde, Don. *Technology and the Lifeworld: From Garden to Earth*. Bloomington: Indiana University Press, 1990.

Ivakhiv, Adrian. "The Art of Morphogenesis: Cinema in and beyond the Capitalocene." In Denson and Leyda, *Post-cinema*, 724–49.

Jacobson, Brian R. "*Ex Machina* in the Garden." *Film Quarterly* 69, no. 4 (2016): 23–34.

Jain, Ramesh, Rangachar Kasturi, and Brian G. Schunck. *Machine Vision*. New York: McGraw-Hill, 1995.

Jameson, Fredric. *The Ideologies of Theory: Essays, 1971–1986*, vol. 1, *Situations of Theory*. Minneapolis: University of Minnesota Press, 1988.

Jameson, Fredric. "Postmodernism, or, The Cultural Logic of Late Capitalism." *New Left Review* 1, no. 146 (1984): 53–92.

Jameson, Fredric. *Postmodernism, or, The Cultural Logic of Late Capitalism*. Durham, NC: Duke University Press, 1991.

Jameson, Fredric. *The Seeds of Time*. New York: Columbia University Press, 1994.

Jenkins, Henry. *Convergence Culture: Where New and Old Media Collide*. New York: New York University Press, 2006.

Jentsch, Ernst. "On the Psychology of the Uncanny (1906)." *Angelaki* 2, no. 1 (1997): 7–16.

Kaeli, David, and Pen-Chung Yew, eds. *Speculative Execution in High Performance Computer Architectures*. New York: Chapman and Hall/CRC, 2005.

Kaes, Anton. "Movies and Masses." In *Crowds*, edited by Jeffrey T. Schnapp and Matthew Tiews, 149–57. Stanford, CA: Stanford University Press, 2006.

Kant, Immanuel. *Critique of Judgment*. Translated by Werner Pluhar. Indianapolis: Hackett, 1987.

Kaplan, E. Ann. *Climate Trauma: Foreseeing the Future in Dystopian Film and Fiction*. New Brunswick, NJ: Rutgers University Press, 2015.

Kara, Selmin. "Anthropocenema: Cinema in the Age of Mass Extinctions." In Denson and Leyda, *Post-cinema*, 750–84.

Kartashov, Andrei. "Phantoms Came to Meet: Guy Maddin's *Seances* as Surrealist History of Cinema." *Senses of Cinema* 85 (December 2017). http://sensesofcinema.com/2017/feature-articles/seances-surrealist-history/.

Kelleter, Frank, ed. *Media of Serial Narrative*. Columbus: Ohio State University Press, 2017.

Khurana, Thomas. "Niklas Luhmann—Die Form des Mediums." In *Medientheorien: Eine philosophische Einführung*, edited by Alice Lagaay and David Lauer, 97–125. Frankfurt: Campus, 2004.

Kiss, Jemima. "Google Admits Collecting Wi-Fi Data through Street View Cars." *The Guardian*, May 15, 2010. https://www.theguardian.com/technology/2010/may/15/google-admits-storing-private-data.

Kittler, Friedrich. *Gramophone, Film, Typewriter*. Translated by Geoffrey Winthrop-Young and Michael Wutz. Stanford, CA: Stanford University Press, 1999.

Kleinman, Alexis. "Behold, the Most Absurd Video Netflix Has Ever Made." *Huffington Post*, November 5, 2013. https://www.huffingtonpost.com/2013/11/05/netflix-test-video_n_4212826.html.

Knight, Will. "The Defense Department Has Produced the First Tools for Catching Deepfakes." *MIT Technology Review*, August 7, 2018. https://www.technologyreview.com/s/611726/the-defense-department-has-produced-the-first-tools-for-catching-deepfakes/.

Kracauer, Siegfried. *The Mass Ornament: Weimar Essays*. Translated by Thomas Y. Levin. Cambridge, MA: Harvard University Press, 1995.

Kraidy, Marwan M. "The Projectilic Image: Islamic State's Digital Visual Warfare and Global Networked Affect." *Media, Culture and Society* 39, no. 8 (2017): 1194–1209.

Kraus, Karl. *Photogrammetry: Geometry from Images and Laser Scans*. 2nd ed. Translated by Ian Harley and Stephen Kyle. Berlin: Walter de Gruyter, 2007.

Kravets, David. "An Intentional Mistake: The Anatomy of Google's Wi-Fi Sniffing Debacle." *Wired*. May 2, 2012. https://www.wired.com/2012/05/google-wifi-fcc-investigation/.

Laboria Cuboniks. *Xenofeminism: A Politics for Alienation*. London: Verso, 2018.

Lacan, Jacques. *The Seminar of Jacques Lacan*, book 2, *The Ego in Freud's Theory and in the Technique of Psychoanalysis, 1954–1955*. Translated by Sylvana Tomaselli. New York: Norton, 1991.

Latour, Bruno. *We Have Never Been Modern*. Translated by Catherine Porter. Cambridge, MA: Harvard University Press, 1993.

Lazzarato, Maurizio. "Immaterial Labor." In *Radical Thought in Italy: A Potential Politics*, edited by Paolo Virno and Michael Hardt, 133–47. Minneapolis: University of Minnesota Press, 1996.

Lazzarato, Maurizio. "Machines to Crystallize Time: Bergson." *Theory, Culture and Society* 24, no. 6 (2007): 93–122.

Lazzarato, Maurizio. *Videophilosophie: Zeitwahrnehmung im Postfordismus*. Berlin: b_books, 2002.

Lazzarato, Maurizio. *Videophilosophy: The Perception of Time in Post-Fordism*. Edited and translated by Jay Hetrick. New York: Columbia University Press, 2019.

Lessing, Gotthold Ephraim. *Laocoon: An Essay upon the Limits of Painting and Poetry*. Translated by Ellen Frothingham. Boston: Roberts Brothers, 1887.

Levitt, Deborah. *The Animatic Apparatus: Animation, Vitality, and the Futures of the Image*. Winchester, UK: Zero Books, 2018.

Leyda, Julia. "Demon Debt: *Paranormal Activity* as Recessionary Post-cinematic Allegory." *Jump Cut* 56 (2014). Reprinted in Denson and Leyda, *Post-cinema*, 398–432.

Linder, Wilfried. *Digital Photogrammetry: A Practical Course*. Berlin: Springer, 2016.

Lorentzen, Christian. "*Blade Runner 2049*, *Never Let Me Go*, and the Longing to Be Human." *New Republic*, October 7, 2017. https://newrepublic.com/article/145219/blade-runner-2049-never-let-go-longing-human.

Luhmann, Niklas. *Art as a Social System*. Translated by Eva M. Knodt. Stanford, CA: Stanford University Press, 2000.

Luhmann, Niklas. *Die Gesellschaft der Gesellschaft*. Frankfurt: Suhrkamp, 1997.

Luhmann, Niklas. Interview with Hans Dieter Huber. *Texte zur Kunst* 4 (September 1991): 121–33.

Luhmann, Niklas. *Das Kind als Medium der Erziehung*. Frankfurt: Suhrkamp, 2006.

Luhmann, Niklas. *Die Kunst der Gesellschaft*. Frankfurt: Suhrkamp, 1995.

Luhmann, Niklas. "The Medium of Art." *Thesis Eleven*, nos. 18–19 (1987): 101–13.

Mackenzie, Adrian. "Codecs." In *Software Studies*, edited by Matthew Fuller, 48–55. Cambridge, MA: MIT Press, 2008.

Mackenzie, Adrian. "Every Thing Thinks: Sub-representative Differences in Digital Video Codecs." In *Deleuzian Intersections: Science, Technology, Anthropology*, edited by Casper Bruun Jensen and Kjetil Rödje, 139–54. New York: Berghahn Books, 2010.

Mackenzie, Adrian. *Transductions: Bodies and Machines at Speed*. London: Continuum, 2002.

Madden, Caroline. "Monstrous Creators and Exploited Creatures: Ex Machina and Frankenstein." *Screen Queens*, February 22, 2016. https://screen-queens.com/2016/02/22/monstrous-creators-and-exploited-creatures-ex-machina-and-frankenstein/.

Madrigal, Alexis C. "How Netflix Reverse-Engineered Hollywood." *The Atlantic*, January 2, 2014. https://www.theatlantic.com/technology/archive/2014/01/how-netflix-reverse-engineered-hollywood/282679/.

Manon, Hugh S., and Daniel Temkin. "Notes on Glitch." *World Picture* 6 (2011). http://www.worldpicturejournal.com/WP_6/Manon.html.

Manovich, Lev. *The Language of New Media*. Cambridge, MA: MIT Press, 2001.

Manovich, Lev. "What Is Digital Cinema?" In Denson and Leyda, *Post-cinema*, 20–50.

Marx, Karl. *Capital*. Vol. 1. Translated by Ben Fowkes. New York: Penguin, 1976.

Marx, Karl. *Capital*. Vol. 3. Translated by David Fernbach. New York: Penguin, 1981.

Massumi, Brian. *Parables for the Virtual: Movement, Affect, Sensation*. Durham, NC: Duke University Press, 2002.

Massumi, Brian. *A User's Guide to Capitalism and Schizophrenia: Deviations from Deleuze and Guattari*. Cambridge, MA: MIT Press, 1992.

Mattern, Shannon. *Code and Clay, Data and Dirt: Five Thousand Years of Urban Media*. Minneapolis: University of Minnesota Press, 2017.

McDonald, Kyle. "How to Recognize Fake AI-Generated Images." *Medium*, December 5, 2018. https://medium.com/@kcimc/how-to-recognize-fake-ai-generated-images-4d1f6f9a2842.

Meillassoux, Quentin. *After Finitude: An Essay on the Necessity of Contingency*. Translated by Ray Brassier. London: Continuum, 2008.

Merleau-Ponty, Maurice. "The Intertwining—The Chiasm." Translated by Alphonso Lingis. In *The Visible and the Invisible*, ed. Claude Lefort, 130–55. Evanston, IL: Northwestern University Press, 1968.

Merleau-Ponty, Maurice. *Phenomenology of Perception*. Translated by Colin Smith. New York: Routledge, 2002.

Mittell, Jason. "Will Netflix Eventually Monetize Its User Data?" *Conversation*, April 22, 2019. https://theconversation.com/will-netflix-eventually-monetize-its-user-data-115273.

Montfort, Nick. "Combat in Context." *Game Studies* 6, no. 1 (2006). http://gamestudies.org/0601/articles/montfort.

Montfort, Nick, and Ian Bogost. *Racing the Beam: The Atari Video Computer System*. Cambridge, MA: MIT Press, 2009.

Moore, Jason W. "The Capitalocene, Part I: On the Nature and Origins of Our Ecological Crisis." *Journal of Peasant Studies* 44, no. 3 (2017): 594–630.

Moore, Jason W. "Transcending the Metabolic Rift: A Theory of Crises in the Capitalist World-Ecology." *Journal of Peasant Studies* 38, no. 1 (2011): 1–46.

Nannicelli, Ted, and Malcolm Turvey. "Against Post-Cinema." *Cinéma et Cie: International Film Studies Journal*, nos. 26–27 (2016): 33–44.

Nestrick, William. "Coming to Life: *Frankenstein* and the Nature of Film Narrative." In *The Endurance of* Frankenstein: *Essays on Mary Shelley's Novel*, edited by George Levine and U. C. Knoepflmacher, 290–315. Berkeley: University of California Press, 1979.

Neveldine, Mark, and Brian Taylor. "Ghost Directors: Mark Neveldine and Brian Taylor Get Cage-y." Interview with *Nerdist News*, February 17, 2012. http://www.nerdistnews.com/region/national/story/national/ghost-directors-mark-neveldine-and-brian-taylor-get-cage-y.

Newman, Lily Hay. "Hackers Can Tell What Netflix *Bandersnatch* Choices You Make." *Wired*, April 21, 2019. https://www.wired.com/story/netflix-interactive-bandersnatch-hackers-choices/.

Paglen, Trevor. "Invisible Images: Ethics of Autonomous Vision Systems." YouTube video, posted November 15, 2016, by AI Now Institute. https://www.youtube.com/watch?v=JZjGsaJ1OcU.

Paglen, Trevor. "Invisible Images (Your Pictures Are Looking at You)." *New Inquiry*, December 8, 2016. https://thenewinquiry.com/invisible-images-your-pictures-are-looking-at-you/.

Pangburn, DJ. "Guy Maddin's 'Seances' Gets an Algorithmic Remix." *Vice*, April 19, 2016. https://www.vice.com/en_us/article/z4q5kw/guy-maddin-seances-film-remix.

Parikka, Jussi. *What Is Media Archaeology*? Cambridge: Polity, 2012.

Parker-Flynn, Christina. "Joe and the 'Real' Girls." *Gender Forum* 66 (2017): 69–74.

Peirce, Charles Sanders. *The Essential Peirce: Selected Philosophical Writings*, vol. 2, *1893–1913*, edited by Nathan Houser, André De Tienne, Jonathan R. Eller, Cathy L. Clark, Albert C. Lewis, and D. Bront Davis. Bloomington: Indiana University Press, 1998.

Peterson, Jennifer, and Graig Uhlin, eds. "In Focus: Film and Media Studies in the Anthropocene." *Journal of Cinema and Media Studies* 58, no. 2 (2019): 142–79.

Philip, Tom. "*Black Mirror: Bandersnatch* Is a Trip into Darkness." *GQ*, December 28, 2018. https://www.gq.com/story/black-mirror-bandersnatch-is-a-trip-into-darkness.

Poulsen, Kevin. "Google Takes Wi-Fi Snooping Scandal to the Supreme Court." *Wired*, April 1, 2014. https://www.wired.com/2014/04/threatlevel_0401_streetview/.

Prince, Stephen. *Digital Visual Effects in Cinema: The Seduction of Reality*. New Brunswick, NJ: Rutgers University Press, 2012.

"Reading Privileged Memory with a Side-Channel." *Project Zero* (blog), January 3, 2018. https://googleprojectzero.blogspot.com/2018/01/reading-privileged-memory-with-side.html.

Redfield, Marc. "*Frankenstein*'s Cinematic Dream." *Romantic Circles Praxis Series*, edited by Jerrold E. Hogle, June 2003. http://www.rc.umd.edu/praxis/frankenstein/redfield/redfield.html.

Richardson, Iain E. *The H.264 Advanced Video Compression Standard*. 2nd ed. Chichester, UK: John Wiley and Sons, 2010.

Richmond, Scott C. *Cinema's Bodily Illusions: Flying, Floating, and Hallucinating*. Minneapolis: University of Minnesota Press, 2016.

Rodowick, D. N. *The Virtual Life of Film*. Cambridge, MA: Harvard University Press, 2007.

Roettgers, Janko. "Netflix Takes Interactive Storytelling to the Next Level with 'Black Mirror: Bandersnatch.'" *Variety*, December 28, 2018. https://variety.com/2018/digital/news/netflix-black-mirror-bandersnatch-interactive-1203096171/.

Roettgers, Janko. "The Story behind 'Meridian': Why Netflix Is Helping Competitors with Content and Code." *Variety*, September 15, 2016. https://variety.com/2016/digital/news/netflix-meridian-imf-tools-open-source-1201859416/.

Romney, Jonathan. "Guy Maddin on His Surreal Seances and Sexploitation Remakes." *The Guardian*, November 26, 2015. https://www.theguardian.com/film/2015/nov/26/guy-maddin-the-forbidden-room-interview.

Rosen, Philip. *Change Mummified: Cinema, Historicity, Theory*. Minneapolis: University of Minnesota Press, 2001.

Rosen, Philip, ed. *Narrative, Apparatus, Ideology: A Film Theory Reader*. New York: Columbia University Press, 1986.

Ross, Daniel. "Moving Images of the Anthropocene: Rethinking Cinema beyond Anthropology." *Screening the Past* 44 (2019). http://www.screeningthepast.com/2019/03/moving-images-of-the-anthropocene-rethinking-cinema-beyond-anthropology/.

Rudolph, Gert, and Uwe Voelzke. "Three Sensor Types Drive Autonomous Vehicles." *Sensors Online*, November 10, 2017. https://www.sensorsmag.com/components/three-sensor-types-drive-autonomous-vehicles.

Rust, Stephen, Salma Monani, and Sean Cubitt, eds. *Ecocinema Theory and Practice*. New York: Routledge, 2013.

Sánchez, Sergi. "Towards a Non-time Image: Notes on Deleuze in the Digital Era." In Denson and Leyda, *Post-cinema*, 171–92.

Sartre, Jean-Paul. *Critique of Dialectical Reason*, vol. 1, *Theory of Practical Ensembles*. New ed. Translated by Alan Sheridan-Smith. London: Verso, 2004.
Schonig, Jordan. "Cinema's Motion Forms: Film Theory, the Digital Turn, and the Possibilities of Cinematic Movement." PhD diss., University of Chicago, 2017.
Serres, Michel. *The Parasite*. Translated by Lawrence R. Schehr. Minneapolis: University of Minnesota Press, 2007.
Shannon, Claude E., and Warren Weaver. *The Mathematical Theory of Communication*. Urbana: University of Illinois Press, 1963.
Shaviro, Steven. "*Melancholia* or, the Romantic Anti-sublime." *Sequence* 1, no. 1 (2002). https://reframe.sussex.ac.uk/sequence1/1-1-melancholia-or-the-romantic-anti-sublime/.
Shaviro, Steven. *Post-cinematic Affect*. Winchester, UK: Zero Books, 2010.
Shaviro, Steven. "Post-continuity: An Introduction." In Denson and Leyda, *Post-cinema*, 51–64.
Shaviro, Steven. "Splitting the Atom: Post-cinematic Articulations of Sound and Vision." In Denson and Leyda, *Post-cinema*, 362–97.
Shaviro, Steven. *The Universe of Things: On Speculative Realism*. Minneapolis: University of Minnesota Press, 2014.
Shelley, Mary Wollstonecraft. *Frankenstein; or, The Modern Prometheus*. Romantic Circles Electronic Edition, edited by Stuart Curran. Boulder: Romantic Circles, 2009. https://romantic-circles.org/editions/frankenstein.
"Side Channel Methods—Analysis, News and Updates." Intel Corporation. Accessed July 5, 2018. https://www.intel.com/content/www/us/en/architecture-and-technology/facts-about-side-channel-analysis-and-intel-products.html.
Siegert, Bernhard. *Cultural Techniques: Grids, Filters, Doors, and Other Articulations of the Real*. Translated by Geoffrey Winthrop-Young. New York: Fordham University Press, 2015.
Simondon, Gilbert. "The Genesis of the Individual." In *Incorporations*, edited by Jonathan Crary and Sanford Kwinter, 297–319. New York: Zone Books, 1992.
Sito, Tom. *Moving Innovation: A History of Computer Animation*. Cambridge, MA: MIT Press, 2013.
Skrebels, Joe. "*Blade Runner 2049*: How Denis Villeneuve Created the Most Complicated Sex Scene of All Time." *IGN*, February 15, 2018. https://www.ign.com/articles/2018/02/15/blade-runner-2049-how-denis-villeneuve-created-the-most-complicated-sex-scene-of-all-time.
Sobchack, Vivian. *The Address of the Eye: A Phenomenology of Film Experience*. Princeton, NJ: Princeton University Press, 1992.
Sobchack, Vivian. "From Screen-Scape to Screen-Sphere: A Meditation in Medias Res." In *Screens: From Materiality to Spectatorship*, edited by Dominique Chateau and José Moure, 157–75. Amsterdam: Amsterdam University Press, 2016.
Sobchack, Vivian. "The Scene of the Screen: Beitrag zu einer Phänomenologie der 'Gegenwärtigkeit' im Film und in den elektronischen Medien." Translated by H. U. Gumbrecht. In *Materialität der Kommunikation*, edited by H. U. Gumbrecht and K. Ludwig Pfeiffer, 416–28. Frankfurt am Main: Suhrkamp, 1988.

Sobchack, Vivian. "The Scene of the Screen: Envisioning Photographic, Cinematic, and Electronic 'Presence.'" In Denson and Leyda, *Post-cinema*, 88–128.

Sobchack, Vivian. "Toward a Phenomenology of Cinematic and Electronic Presence: The Scene of the Screen." *Post-Script* 10 (1990): 50–59.

Spadoni, Robert. *Uncanny Bodies: The Coming of Sound Film and the Origins of the Horror Genre*. Berkeley: University of California Press, 2007.

Spencer, Keith A. "Mired in Self-Referential Cliche, 'Bandersnatch' Can't Transcend Its Form." *Salon*, January 1, 2019. https://www.salon.com/2019/01/01/mired-in-self-referential-cliche-bandersnatch-cant-transcend-its-form/.

Stengers, Isabelle. *Thinking with Whitehead: A Free and Wild Creation of Concepts*. Translated by Michael Chase. Cambridge, MA: Harvard University Press, 2011.

Sterne, Jonathan. *MP3: The Meaning of a Format*. Durham, NC: Duke University Press, 2012.

Steyerl, Hito. "In Defense of the Poor Image." *e-flux Journal* 10 (2009). https://www.e-flux.com/journal/10/61362/in-defense-of-the-poor-image/.

Stiegler, Bernard. *Technics and Time*, vol. 1, *The Fault of Epimetheus*. Translated by Richard Beardsworth. Stanford, CA: Stanford University Press, 1998.

Stiegler, Bernard. *Technics and Time*, vol. 3, *Cinematic Time and the Question of Malaise*. Translated by Stephen Barker. Stanford, CA: Stanford University Press, 2011.

Stiegler, Bernard. "The Time of Cinema: On the 'New World' and 'Cultural Exception.'" Translated by George Collins. *Tekhnema: Journal of Philosophy and Technology*, no. 4 (1998): 62–113.

Stiegler, Bernard. *What Makes Life Worth Living: On Pharmacology*. Cambridge, UK: Polity, 2010.

Stork, Matthias. "Chaos Cinema: The Decline and Fall of Action Filmmaking." Video essay. *Press Play*, August 22, 2011. http://blogs.indiewire.com/pressplay/video_essay_matthias_stork_calls_out_the_chaos_cinema.

Stubblefield, Thomas. "In Pursuit of Other Networks: Drone Art and Accelerationist Aesthetics." In *Life in the Age of Drone Warfare*, edited by Lisa Parks and Caren Kaplan, 195–219. Durham, NC: Duke University Press, 2017.

Sudmann, Andreas. "Bullet Time and the Mediation of Post-cinematic Temporality." In Denson and Leyda, *Post-cinema*, 297–326.

Sullivan, Kevin P. "'Paranormal Activity 4': Behind the High-Tech Scares." *MTV News*, October 18, 2012. http://www.mtv.com/news/articles/1695798/paranormal-activity-4-special-fx.jhtml.

Symuleski, Max. "Earth, World, and Globe: Phenomenological Considerations of the Contemporary Planetary Landscape." *Widok: Teorie i praktyki kultury wizualnej* 8 (2014). http://widok.hmfactory.com/index.php/one/article/view/222/458.

Szendy, Peter. *Apocalypse-Cinema: 2012 and Other Ends of the World*. Translated by Will Bishop. New York: Fordham University Press, 2015.

Tally, Robert T., Jr. "The End-of-the-World as World System." In *Other Globes: Past and Peripheral Imaginations of Globalization*, edited by Simon Ferdinand, Irene Villaescusa-Illán, and Esther Peeren, 267–83. Cham, Switzerland: Palgrave Macmillan, 2019.

Tekalp, A. Murat. *Digital Video Processing*. 2nd ed. New York: Prentice Hall, 2015.
Thacker, Eugene. *Horror of Philosophy*, vol. 1, *In the Dust of this Planet*. Winchester, UK: Zero Books, 2011.
Thorogood, Sam. "Ex Machina, Frankenstein and Modern Deities." *Artifice*, June 12, 2017. https://the-artifice.com/ex-machina-frankenstein-modern-deities/.
Van den Berg, J. H. *The Two Principal Laws of Thermodynamics: A Cultural and Historical Exploration*. Translated by Bernd Jager, David Jager, and Dreyer Kruger. Pittsburgh: Duquesne University Press, 2004.
Vincent, James. "This Wireless AI Camera Runs Entirely on Solar Power." *The Verge*, February 15, 2019. https://www.theverge.com/circuitbreaker/2019/2/15/18225972/tiny-solar-powered-ai-camera-xnor.
Ward, Paul. "Defining 'Animation': The Animated Film and the Emergence of the Film Bill." *Scope*, December 2000, n.p.
Watercutter, Angela. "*Ex Machina* Has a Serious Fembot Problem." *Wired*, April 9, 2015. https://www.wired.com/2015/04/ex-machina-turing-bechdel-test/.
Weisman, Alan. *The World without Us*. New York: Picador, 2007.
Whissel, Kristen. *Spectacular Digital Effects: CGI and Contemporary Cinema*. Durham, NC: Duke University Press, 2014.
Williams, Evan Calder. *Shard Cinema*. London: Repeater Books, 2017.
Williams, Linda. "Film Bodies: Gender, Genre, and Excess." *Film Quarterly* 44, no. 4 (Summer 1991): 2–13.
Williams, Linda. *Hard Core: Power, Pleasure, and the "Frenzy of the Visible."* Expanded ed. Berkeley: University of California Press, 1999.
Wittgenstein, Ludwig. *The Blue and Brown Books*. New York: Harper and Row, 1958.
Wolfe, Cary. "Bring the Noise: *The Parasite* and the Multiple Genealogies of Posthumanism." Introduction to *The Parasite*, by Michel Serres, xi–xxviii. Minneapolis: University of Minnesota Press, 2007.
Wolfe, Cary. *What Is Posthumanism?* Minneapolis: University of Minnesota Press, 2010.
Yu, Chang Min. "Cinema's Turing Test: Consciousness, Digitality, and Operability in *Hardcore Henry*." NECSUS 6, no. 1 (Spring 2017): 189–207.
Yue, Genevieve. "Errant Pixels: The Sight Specificity of Satellite Technologies." *ASAP/Journal* 2, no. 3 (September 2017): 677–708.
Yusoff, Kathryn. *A Billion Black Anthropocenes or None*. Minneapolis: University of Minnesota Press, 2018.
Zettl, Herbert. "The Rare Case of Television Aesthetics." *Journal of the University Film Association* 30, no. 2 (Spring 1978): 3–8.

INDEX

www.ingramcontent.com/pod-product-compliance
Lightning Source LLC
LaVergne TN
LVHW010602100826
845148LV00014B/2819